GROLIER'S
MASTERPLOTS
1981 ANNUAL

GROLIER'S MASTERPLOTS

1981 ANNUAL

GROLIER'S LITERARY ANNUAL
Essay-Reviews of 100 Outstanding Books Published in the United States During 1980

GROLIER ENTERPRISES INC.
Danbury, Connecticut

Grolier Enterprises Inc.

Robert B. Clarke, Publisher

ISSN 0194-0503
ISBN 0-7172-8161-2

Prepared by
Sachem Publishing Associates, Inc.
Guilford, Connecticut

Printed in the United States of America

LIST OF TITLES

vii

CONTRIBUTING REVIEWERS FOR 1981 ANNUAL

DAVID ALVAREZ
RICHARD BIENVENU
JOHN CARLIN
ROBERT B. COSTELLO
PAMELA KYLE CROSSLEY
JOHN MACK FARAGHER
D. W. FAULKNER
GREGORY FEELEY
STEVEN P. FLOMAN
SUSAN FLOMAN
ESTHER M. FRIESNER
ILONA FUCCI
LISA HALTTUNEN
MICHELE HOFFNUNG
MARILYNN MALIN HUFCUT
JULIE V. IOVINE
RICHARD LACHMANN
DAVID M. LUBIN
ELIZABETH LUBIN
THOMAS MCCUE
A. S. MAULUCCI

ARLYN MILLER
PAMELA MURFIN
MARTHA PADDICK
THOMAS PALMER
ALICE C. PARKER
R. A. PARKER II
CYRUS QUINN, JR.
D. S. RUBENSTEIN
PATRICIA J. RUSSELL
JUDITH SANDSTROM
LOUIS SASSO
NEIL ASHER SILBERMAN
ADRIENNE SUDDARD
WALLY SWIST
ANNIE TALBOT
VIVIAN WERNER
ROBERT B. WESTBROOK
S. N. WHITE
JAY WICKERSHAM
JOAN BARRETT WICKERSHAM

PREFACE

The literature of 1980 was characterized, not by the bold spirit of innovation that might seem appropriate at the dawn of a new decade, but rather by a renewed interest in traditional values and issues and in influential figures of the past. Like the nation itself in the first year of the 1980's, many of the books published in the United States reflected a sober concern for the problems of today. This edition of Grolier's *Masterplots* reviews 100 of the most outstanding of these works.

Several writers took a close look at the world economic condition. Milton and Rose Friedman defended a laissez-faire approach to the nation's economy in *Free to Choose*. Peter F. Drucker offered practical advice for survival in a changing world economy in *Managing in Turbulent Times*, and Alvin Toffler predicted the future of society in *The Third Wave*, in which economic reality forecasts a revolution in government and social institutions.

The family under stress, particularly the pain involved in its dissolution, was another popular theme. Margaret Atwood's *Life Before Man*, Herbert Gold's *He/She*, Erich Segal's *Man, Woman and Child*, Gilbert Rogin's *Preparations for the Ascent*, Ann Beattie's *Falling in Place*, and Avery Corman's *The Old Neighborhood*, are six novels that examined marriages coming apart.

The individual's quest for identity continued to be an important theme. Truman Capote published his reminiscences in *Music for Chameleons*, in which a number of disparate people were described, both with and without their protective coloring. Two women sought contact with their heritage in P. D. James's *Innocent Blood* and Cynthia Freeman's *Come Pour the Wine*, while several generations of women in one family were the central focus of *A Woman's Age* by Rachel Billington. A man facing middle age was the subject of *The Second Coming* by Walker Percy, *Morgan's Passing* by Anne Tyler, and *Joshua Then and Now* by Mordecai Richler.

Larger-than-life historical figures were the subjects of several biographies, including *Catherine the Great* by Henri Troyat and *Peter the Great* by Robert K. Massie. Chosen from the more recent past were Helen Keller in Joseph P. Lash's *Helen and Teacher*, Lyndon Johnson in *Lyndon* by Merle Miller, Walter Lippman in *Walter Lippmann and the American Century* by Ronald Steel, and Marshal Tito in *Tito: The Story from Inside* by Milovan Djilas. Prominent figures from the arts who were featured include Somerset Maugham, in *Maugham* by Ted Morgan, and Arthur Rubinstein, who issued a second volume of memoirs in *My Many Years.* Irving Stone, veteran author of biographical novels, produced *The Origin,* about the life and work of Charles Darwin. In *The Return of Eva Perón,* V. S. Naipaul focused on more controversial figures, including Argentina's Eva Perón and Zaire's Mobutu. In *The Court Years* the late William O. Douglas recalled his thirty-six years on the Supreme Court. Michael R. Beschloss examined the relationship between Joseph Kennedy and Franklin D. Roosevelt in *Kennedy and Roosevelt.* Eleanor Roosevelt was the subject of a biography by her close friend Lorena Hickok. Events that took place during the 1930's were the focus of several works. The liberal idealism of that period captured the attention of Malcolm Cowley in *The Dream of the Golden Mountains.* E. L. Doctorow's rags-to-riches story, *Loon Lake,* was set in the 1930's, as were much of Lillian Hellman's fourth volume of memoirs, *Maybe,* and Barbara Goldsmith's biography of Gloria Vanderbilt, *Little Gloria . . . Happy at Last.*

Fantasy novels in 1980 also looked back into history. Erica Jong told the imaginative tale of an 18th century liberated woman in *Fanny.* Jean M. Auel portrayed the life of a Neanderthal tribe in *The Clan of the Cave Bear,* while Joyce Carol Oates described an unusual and eccentric family in *Bellefleur.*

Novels of international intrigue and espionage abounded in 1980. Such veteran writers of the genre as John Le Carré and Frederick Forsythe published new novels. Le Carré's *Smiley's People* detailed another episode in the career of the British master of counterespionage, George Smiley. Forsythe's *The Devil's Alternative* depicted the United States and the U.S.S.R. on the verge of global war. Jack Higgins' novel *Solo* dealt with an international assassin, as did Robert Ludlum's *The Bourne Identity.* Other suspense novels included *Who's on First* by William F. Buckley, *The Key to Rebecca* by Ken Follett, *The Spike* by Armand de Borchgrave and Robert Moss, and *The Fifth Horseman* by Larry Collins and Dominique Lapierre.

These are just a few of the excellent works represented in the 1980 edition of Grolier's *Masterplots.* There are 52 novels; 12 biographies and autobiographies; 8 volumes of memoirs, diaries, and letters; 6 of essays; 5 of short stories; 1 of poetry; 2 travel works, 8 of social sciences, and 6 dealing with history or current affairs.

Susan Carter Elliott

AMERICAN DREAMS: LOST & FOUND

Author: Studs Terkel (1912–   )
Publisher: Pantheon Books (New York). 470 pp. $14.95
Type of work: Social criticism
Time: Late 19th century to the present
Locale: The United States

Interviews that reveal how Americans from various walks of life perceive the American Dream and how they achieved or fell short of their dream in the course of their own lives

> *Principal personages:*
> EMMA KNIGHT, Miss U.S.A. of 1973
> LEONEL CASTILLO, former director of the U.S. Immigration and Naturalization Service
> GAYLORD FREEMAN, retiring chairman of the First National Bank of Chicago
> S. B. FULLER, seventy-three-year-old black businessman
> C. P. ELLIS, former member of the Ku Klux Klan, now a union organizer
> MRS. GEORGE UPHAM BAYLIES, president of the Daughters of the American Revolution
> JAMES ABOUREZK, former U. S. Senator from South Dakota
> JANN WENNER, publisher of *Rolling Stone*

American Dreams: Lost & Found begins with a question. "Is that all there is to the American Dream, as celebrated in thousands of sixty-second, thirty-second, and ten-second spots each day on all channels? A mercantile language, debased, and nothing else? Is there no other language, no other dream?" Studs Terkel, in his interviews with hundreds of Americans, has found many different voices, many visions of what his country has to offer, of what can be accomplished in a lifetime. Terkel captures the voices of 100 Americans in this book. Each interview is introduced with only a few lines, detailing the location of the interview and sometimes the age and occupation of the speaker. Very few of Terkel's questions are included in the edited transcripts of the interviews. The author does not draw conclusions for the reader. The interviews are grouped in several sections: bosses, immigrants at the turn of the century, immigrants today, farmers, inhabitants of urban neighborhoods, social activists, politicians, editors, young delinquents who have found useful work, and men turning thirty.

The first interview presented is with Emma Knight, who became Miss U.S.A. at age twenty-two. Emma entered the contest as a way of furthering her career as a model. Once she had won, Emma discovered that she was an employee of Miss Universe, Inc., a subsidiary of

Kaiser-Roth, Inc. Paid a salary of $15,000 for a year, the Miss U.S.A. made hundreds of appearances before corporate and charitable groups, each of whom paid a fee to Miss Universe, Inc. Emma resented being forced to live an invented version of the American Dream, to conform to a stereotype of the Miss U.S.A., even more than the financial exploitation. On the night when the new Miss U.S.A. was crowned, Emma stood on stage and rubbed her nose, in a gesture borrowed from the movie *The Sting*. Her gesture meant, "the con is on."

The bosses, successful businessmen and managers of large corporations, interviewed by Terkel, see the American Dream as real. They are proud of their life's work. Gaylord Freeman tells that he gave up all hobbies and entertainment in his years as chairman of the board of a bank. Freeman is satisfied that he had been a responsible businessman and had developed true friendships with his business colleagues. However, once retired, Freeman sees his old friends lose interest in him and worries that the corporate world has become too competitive, that too many people have no dream beyond financial success. S. B. Fuller was one of the first blacks who managed to make a fortune in the North. He had been reduced to bankruptcy in 1968 and had begun an effort to rebuild his fortune. At age seventy-three, Fuller believes he has fulfilled his dream, not by becoming rich, but by teaching other blacks how to become successful capitalists.

Immigrants have always been drawn to America by the dream of freedom and material success. Some of the most eloquent voices in *American Dreams* are of recent arrivals in the United States. Arnold Schwarzenegger, born in Austria, tells how he turned his dream of being the best body builder in the world into reality. He sees no obstacles to business success and physical achievement in America. Jessie de la Cruz, a Mexican immigrant, began as a migrant farm laborer. She achieved her goal of owning her own farm, yet sees most farm land in America being bought by large landowners and agricorporations. For her, America has created obstacles to the independence and achievement of new immigrants from Mexico. She still has hope that struggle can change the chances for migrant farm laborers, that they can win a chance to achieve the American Dream.

One of the outstanding persons presented by Terkel is C. P. Ellis, of Durham, North Carolina. He found that despite hard work he could not rise above poverty. "I really began to get bitter . . . Hatin' America is hard to do because you can't see it to hate it. You gotta have somethin' to look at to hate." Ellis joined the Ku Klux Klan. The more deeply he became involved in political activity, the more clearly Ellis saw that he and the Klan were being used by the rich whites of Durham to divide the races and to preserve the power of the rich. Later, Ellis was elected co-chairman of the school committee, serving with a black woman. He began to moderate his racism as he saw that the daily problems faced by poor blacks and whites were similar. Ellis's willingness to see blacks as fellow humans allowed him to organize the workers at his place of employment, most of whom were black, into a union. He is now a union business manager, working to organize badly paid employees of both races in North Carolina.

Terkel presents the vision of America held by the rich and powerful, as well as the deprived and recent immigrants. Mrs. George Upham Baylies, president of the Daughters of the American Revolution, defines the American Dream as love of country. She is concerned about "the Soviet threat," the Panama Canal Treaty, and the Equal Rights Amendment. Dr. Whitney Addington comes from a background similar to that of Baylies. During his medical training, Addington saw that the principles of profit and loss were used in deciding on treatments for rich and poor patients. As a way of continuing his dream of curing the truly sick, he now works at a Chicago public hospital.

James Abourezk was interviewed by Terkel toward the end of his term as U.S. Senator from South Dakota. Abourezk had come to doubt that the American Dream of equality had any reality within a government dominated "by the establishment, for the establishment." Abourezk, like Dennis Kucinich, the former mayor of Cleveland, hopes that the American people can be awakened to the true nature of their government and can take hold of their right to determine their own lives.

Another section of *American Dreams* presents interviews with younger Americans who have just turned thirty. One is Jann Wenner, a founder, and now publisher, of *Rolling Stone* magazine. Wenner attributes his success to the traditional American ingredients: hard work, talent, and willingness "to make certain compromises." At *Rolling Stone* those compromises have involved softening the political edge on the magazine's articles about music and culture. Nevertheless, Wenner doubts that young people are losing interest in political issues. "People are just taking their lives more seriously in a different way." Wenner has just recently moved his office from San Francisco to midtown Manhattan. He feels self-confident and powerful, "dealing with . . . bigger amounts of money," at the center of the communications world.

Linda Haas, age 16, is in a technical high school in Chicago. She hopes for an interesting job, a good marriage, and the opportunity to travel. Her present happiness and security come from her life at home with her parents and in her familiar neighborhood. Sam Lovejoy studied physics as a college student and then moved to a commune in

Montague, Massachusetts. In 1973 plans were announced to build a nuclear power plant in the town. Lovejoy reviewed the physics he had learned and spoke at town meetings to oppose the plant. As he saw the power company circumvent town decisions that delayed construction, Lovejoy began to worry that the popular New England democracy he had learned about as a child no longer could survive in the United States. On George Washington's birthday, 1974, Lovejoy knocked down an experimental tower erected by the utility. At his trial, Lovejoy convinced the judge and jury that nuclear power was a public danger, justifying his destruction of property. After the trial, the Montague plant was delayed for four years. At present, Lovejoy is involved in trying to prevent construction of other nuclear power plants in New England. The Montague plant remains unbuilt.

Studs Terkel's own voice and interpretation are absent from the interviews in *American Dreams*. His talent lies in drawing out the life stories and beliefs of the 100 individuals presented to the reader. Most interviews are only three or four pages, none is longer than a dozen. Yet, every personality presented is convincing. The subjects all convey a full and meaningful picture of themselves, of their beliefs and lives.

Terkel's ability to get people to speak in their own voices is extraordinary. If there is a lesson the reader learns after reading the words of 100 very different Americans, it is that Terkel's initial question has an answer. The voice of mass advertising and mass politics is not the only voice of the American people. Terkel has found other, more sincere voices. Most of those interviewed have other dreams than material success and glamour. The reader finishes *American Dreams* knowing that other values also create dreams, dreams of an America of equality and justice, of city neighborhoods and countrysides preserved for future generations, dreams of useful work that open new futures for the next generation of American dreamers.

Arlyn Miller

THE AMERICAN ESTABLISHMENT

Author: Leonard and Mark Silk
Publisher: Basic Books (New York). 351 pp. $13.95
Type of work: Current affairs
Time: 20th century
Locale: The United States

An examination of the institutions, including Harvard, The New York Times, *the Ford Foundation, the Brookings Institution, and the Council on Foreign Relations, that influence national public policy and constitute the American Establishment*

In recent years, Harvard University, the Brookings Institution in Washington, D.C., and the Ford Foundation, caught in a financial crunch, have been reassessing their roles in social action projects. *The New York Times* has been showing a new sensitivity to the financial bottom line. The Council on Foreign Relations has been rethinking its philosophical positions. Authors Leonard Silk and Mark Silk assess the current dilemma facing organizations that they have termed the American public policy establishment.

The term "establishment" has inspired interesting, if not unusual, definitions and, over the years, has acquired something of a mythology. The term came into fashionable use in the 1950's when a British journalist, describing the English aristocracy, likened them to members of a state church. In the United States, "the concept of the Establishment seemed to have lost something; it was a metaphor without clear referent."

The authors see the American Establishment as clearly "democratic"—it is not an economic class but an idea of public morality passed down from the Unitarian church of the Massachusetts colony. The organizations that constitute the establishment follow rules remarkably similar to those set down by the 18th-century theologian William Paley, who defined an established church as needing a professional clergy to spread the word, "tolerance" to listen to the views of dissenters, and most of all, "flexibility"—the ability to change. According to the authors, establishment organizations are changing, acquiring a new conservatism for the 1980's.

Harvard is a good case in point. The 1960's brought Harvard to national leadership, with Harvard graduates occupying many top policy positions in the Kennedy and Johnson administrations. The failures of Vietnam, urban violence, and the broken promises of the Great Society programs caused many to see Harvard as having failed not only at national political leadership but also at public moral leadership. The convalescence has been long and painful, but Harvard is now assuming a new role as the model for professional training and leadership in government. Hopes are riding on the new John F. Kennedy School of Government to correct mistakes in policy leadership during the Kennedy and Johnson administrations. But this faith in good management ignores a sticky internal issue. Harvard University derives financial support from investments in the apartheid regime in South Africa, and despite student protests, the administration refuses to divest.

The adjustments of *The New York Times* and the Ford Foundation to the right are equally contradictory. Leonard Silk, economic affairs columnist for *The New York Times,* focuses on publisher Arthur Ochs Sulzberger and his efforts to turn the paper into a highly profitable business. Silk traces the paper's history from its purchase by Sulzberger's grandfather through publication of the Pentagon Papers to the final internal disagreements over editorial policy, leading to heavy use of feature material over news analysis.

The third organization, the Ford Foundation, grew out of corporate philanthropy inspired as much by tax breaks as altruistic fervor. The Ford Foundation was created by Ford Motor Company creator Henry Ford, who passed ninety percent of the company's stock to the foundation, reducing inheritance taxes from 300 million to only a few million, the cost of which was picked up by the foundation. The immense wealth of the foundation grew and so did the range of its charities. During the late 1950's and early 1960's the foundation pioneered programs in black and hispanic education, neighborhood renovation, and community development corporations. These programs were models for Lyndon Johnson's Great Society and brought the gradual acceptance of minorities into the establishment network. In 1979 the Ford Foundation appointed its first black president, Franklin Thomas.

In recent years, however, the trend at Ford has been away from grants toward "assured results" in the form of loans, direct investment, and recoverable grants. Ironically, Ford supports a public interest law firm in South Africa to represent blacks against the regime while Ford itself receives support from investments in corporations that practice apartheid in South Africa.

Perhaps nowhere does the amorphous establishment begin to assume shape more clearly than through its network of contacts, the "old-boy network." Since their founding in the early 20th century both Brookings in Washington, D.C., and the Council on Foreign Relations in New York City have been revolving doors for their members to and from high-level government service.

Brookings, dubbed a liberal think-tank by its conservative competitor, the American Enterprise Institute, has become a government in exile for former members of the Democratic administrations, as the AEI employs former members of the Republican administrations. Critics claim that the "disinterested" research and evaluation of government programs for which Brookings was founded have all but disappeared. The organization, according to some, is dominated by partisan politics and self-promotion. But the institution is changing. Herbert Stein, a former fellow at Brookings and currently senior fellow at the AEI, notes that "both are moving to the middle, but the middle is moving toward the right."

The Council on Foreign Relations in New York City has been called "an incubator of men and ideas." Its membership at one time included David and Nelson Rockefeller, William and McGeorge Bundy, George Bush, Cyrus Vance, and Henry Kissinger. Despite the council's influence on every administration, it is a private, nongovernmental organization, founded in 1914 to provide a forum for discussion and debate. But like the other organizations of the establishment, the power and sense of public purpose that the council once had seemed to have eroded. Much of the erosion can be traced back to the Vietnam era. Another reason for the current lack of consensus is the nation itself, which lacks consensus and direction. In recent years, the council has started serious reevaluation of its role and its future. Former council president Bayless Manning summed up the council's position, "We're moving into a period when we don't have any idea of what we're doing in foreign relations. Vietnam was the last spasm of one way of looking at the world. The council's role, as I envision it, will be to help the country evolve a new consensus."

While the establishment has always existed comfortably within these organizations, it has never coexisted easily with big business interests. During the past decades, business interests formed an uneasy alliance with public interest groups. But the economic considerations of recent years have spurred many business interests to combat government regulations, consumer demands, pricing, and profits. William Simon, former secretary of the Treasury, says, "this absurd financing of one's philosophical enemies must not be tolerated in new foundations."

As organizations enter the next decade—some struggling for new leadership, others dropping back—a number of issues surface. Will public morality have a place in the decision-making of the future? To what degree will decisions regarding social and human rights be governed by financial considerations? Will schools such as Harvard's Kennedy School of Government provide effective national leadership or produce a national elite of power brokers?

The authors see the establishment as surviving. They are concerned, however, that organizations and individuals of the establishment will be overruled on critical issues of public morality by economic considerations. They also think that public morality may in future years take on more of a regional character, being subject to splits between North and South, East and West, as competition for available resources increases.

Despite these concerns, the authors conclude that the establishment should and will remain "more than a collection of worthy and visible institutions: it is a spirit, a ghost, a force that draws others to it, especially in times of national crisis." They believe it is imperative that it remain "a secret organization, a secret from its own membership." And that it remain "a spirit, a ghost, borne on the wind, an American thing, a myth."

The American Establishment is an informative, although somewhat tedious tour through the backrooms and private clubs of prestigious American institutions in search of where and what is the establishment. The authors, having determined that the establishment is an idea of moral behavior, devote considerable effort to weaving their opinions throughout the book. One gets the impression that the establishment is a catch-all term to recall the ghosts of political liberalism and that this book is their epitaph. The book reads more like a group of essays than reporting and analysis.

Nevertheless, the authors Leonard Silk and his son, Mark Silk, approach their subject with ambition, enthusiasm, and research. The profiles of the institutions are relieved by anecdotes that probably only an "insider" would know. Forewarned of editorial pitfalls, readers will find *The American Establishment* a compact social history and commentary on the institutions that influence national policy.

Martha Paddick

BEING HERE

Poetry 1977–1980

Author: Robert Penn Warren (1905–   )
Publisher: Random House (New York). 108 pp. $8.95
Type of work: Poetry
Time: Primarily the 20th century
Locale: Southern and Western United States, New York City

One of the most respected and successful American poets deals with the themes of aging, identity, and time in what is his strongest collection of poetry to date

At the age of 75, when most poets and writers look back upon their lives and their work, Robert Penn Warren, author of thirty-two books, is not only adding to his already impressive literary works, but he is writing stronger, more exacting, and much more gripping poetry than ever before. He is one of the few poets writing today who is able to write a truly moving narrative poem. It is a feat in itself to write a successful shorter poem—to crystallize experience and language into the diamond of vision—but to keep a longer poem buoyant with this discipline and hold the reader's attention to the very end, enthralled, is Warren's remarkable genius.

Being Here, his latest book of poetry, is not just an achievement of technical excellence. It is a mature work of the heart. Warren writes about childhood memories, the quest for truth and substance in adulthood, and the questions that plague everyone. He wrestles with the problems of aging, identity, and time from the position of one who has weathered inclemencies and has "borne the outrageous," but not without coming away with a flash of insight about the cosmos. Warren is one of the great metaphysical poets of today—always plunging into the cold water of the commonplace in search of truth or beauty and surfacing with reason and uncommon clarity.

Often with a touch of the luminous, Warren concentrates on childhood memories in the book's first section. "October Picnic Long Ago," a poem in italics that casts a sepia light to introduce the work as a whole, is a ballad about a family picnic that takes place in the South, where Warren was born and raised, in the days of horse and buggy. The poem is italicized because it serves as the first of two brackets for the book. "Passers-By on Snowy Night," the last poem of the book, also in italics, is the other bracket, giving the book its shape. The first poem deals with reminiscence and the last deals with a life's journey through the dark forest of the years. The lyric closes on a note not only of understanding of this arduous trip, but one of compassion:

We hear the distant friction,
Then crack of bough burdened with snow,
And each takes the owl's benediction,
And each goes the way he will go.

The poems in between reverberate against each other thematically like bells in a carillon. As in "Speleology," a poem about his discovery of a cave when he was a child, Warren continually probes into himself, into the different identities that a life embraces, and returns to daylight having found the lodestone, the inner man, the "heart beating as though to a pulse of darkness and earth." "When Life Begins" recalls his grandfather, a Civil War veteran, whose "curl-tangled" beard was "like skill-carved stone/ with chisel-grooved shadow accenting the white." While sitting at the old man's feet, Warren listened in silent awe to stories of battles and recollections of a long life. He "wondered when life would begin,/ nor knew that, beyond the horizon's heave,/ time crouched, like a great cat, motionless." Again like carillon bells, the thematic reverberations of the poems become more life-affirming, joyous, and musical—aging, identity, and time.

"Filling Night with the Name: Funeral as Local Color" unearths the rich fragrance of rural life as Warren remembers it to have been. A farmer, Mr. Clinch, returns from his wife's funeral with the outlook of "when a thing's gonna be" you better "git used to it fast." Promptly, with his good clothes on, he proceeds to milk his cows at sundown. But upon finishing his chores, he is unable to sleep and sits down to write his son about what has happened, only to find that "no word would come, and sorrow and joy/ all seemed one." At his desk he hears one sound outside his window that pierces the night and his grief: "whip-o-will," the bird plaintively cries, "whip-o-will."

In "Recollection in Upper Ontario, from Long Before," one of the many stunning narrative poems in the book, Warren explores human fallibility and weakness and the inability ever really to come to terms with truth. While camping far north "on the Hudson Bay slope" he asks himself "Why do I still wake up and not know?" He is "lost in forests and lakes," but still disturbed by a recurring dream of an accident he witnessed as a child. The question is whether Old Zack, "pore ole white-trash," did or did not push his club-footed wife in front of a train's path while they were scrounging coal near the tracks. Warren remembers seeing Old Mag getting her foot stuck in the switch-V, and of Zack's hands out to grab her. Lying in bed, after her pauper's funeral and after running into Zack, who is drunk, he imagines a beautiful scene of the old scoundrel loving his crippled wife with tenderness. But years later he can only think the exact opposite—Zack's murderous rancor directed at the cripple he married. A loon's high-pitched laughter wakes Warren, who wonders what he really did see and what he did not see. But Warren possesses the wisdom to understand that in order to see clearly one must know what clouded vision is and in order to know truth one must know what illusion is.

The next section of *Being Here* deals with the passions, the unraveling of questions, the complicated answers, and strivings of adulthood. Running down a beach, south of San Francisco, as a youth, he is filled with the awesomeness of life. He believes that "you dream that somewhere, somehow, you may embrace/ the world in its fullness and threat." In "Snowshoeing Back to Camp in Gloaming," his past flows backward on a numbing hike through bare trees that are "as though of all deeds unleafed, and/ dead leaves lost are only/ old words forgotten in snowdrifts." Warren experiences the stripping away of the old and the exhilarating flush of the new warming him in the snow. He is warmed by the human, and, through the evolution of the human in himself, he is able to warm and to be warmed. As in most of his poems, when he probes for the source, the fires of revelation flame.

In the astuteness of his probing, Warren explores life's reverse aspect also. The result is as sobering as the other can be warming. "Black ruins of arson in the Bronx are whitely/ redeemed" in "Function of Blizzard." The snow piling down on city streets is covering up, if only for a while. It is a forgetting of "three infants locked in a tenement in Harlem," and a remembering, paradoxically, that "God's bosom is broad"—soon snow will completely cover the ruins. He hopes that the snow will fall without melting. "Sky," another poem in the middle section of the book, exudes this same quiet human desperation. "We all, have much endured, buckling/ belts, hearts," he writes. But we have survived despite our losses and our fear of losing even more. "What we most fear," Warren concludes, is what "advances on/ tiptoe, breath aromatic." And not only does it sneak up on us, but "its true name is what we never know."

As true a poet as Warren is, he is also prophet. In a poem entitled "Truth," tackling the concept straight-on, he states that it is precisely "what you cannot tell." It is something that is shapeless and unclear in strong light or devouring darkness. Truth is history's trick, and "the serpent's joke." He believes truth is what the dead could tell if they were able to converse with the living, for their "accumulated wisdom must be immense." In another poem, "Trips to California," that exhibits the strength of the last two parts of *Being Here*, Warren follows the savage path of the western movement in U.S. history. Now California waits like a dream, but Warren does not forget the bloody injustices that made the dream a reality. Rifles cracked night and day into herds of buffalo. Skinners worked off the hide and left the flesh to

waste. California dreams, now the diseased facsimile of eastern cities'
urban sprawl, are now what they are because they were nurtured by
our predecessors with the "dark humus of history or our/ own fate,
which blindly blooms, like a flower."

The poetry of Robert Penn Warren transcends the personal and res-
onates in the particular. He is a poet in complete control of the subtle
nuances of language and is receptive to the sublime and tortuous
depths of humanity. Through a half century of practicing his craft,
Warren has achieved clarity and vision.

Wally Swist

BELLEFLEUR

Author: Joyce Carol Oates (1938–   )
Publisher: E. P. Dutton (New York). 558 pp. $13.95
Type of work: Novel
Time: Mid - 18th mid - 20th century
Locale: Adirondack Mountains of New York State

A work of fantasy about the rich and powerful Bellefleur family from the time of their arrival in America to the early 20th century

> *Principal characters:*
> GIDEON BELLEFLEUR, son of old Noel Bellefleur and father of Germaine
> LEAH PYM BELLEFLEUR, Gideon's wife
> GERMAINE, their daughter
> BROMWELL, their son
> VERNON BELLEFLEUR, a poet, son of Noel's brother Hiram
> JEDEDIAH BELLEFLEUR, son of the first Bellefleur in America
> RAPHAEL BELLEFLEUR, son of Gideon's brother Ewan

Bellefleur is a curious synthesis, a family saga told in broad Gothic terms. All the elements are here: a spooky old house with weird inhabitants, psychic phenomena, ghosts, trolls, enchanted animals, and vampires. These set the tone and provide a vehicle for Oates's vision of an inexplicable and brutal world.

The book follows the Bellefleur family through six or seven generations, but there is no straight chronology or plot line. Bellefleurs have a "lofty contempt" for chronology, and by centering on character instead of plot the novel imitates their own paramount concern for themselves. A continual loose jumble of facts about each character is presented and only gradually made clear, although certain characters do return at regular intervals. Chronology is entirely abandoned halfway through the family tree Oates provides; dates are given for the patriarch Jean-Pierre, his offspring and grandchildren, but thereafter only the names appear.

The action centers on Gideon Bellefleur, his wife Leah, and the other Bellefleur relatives who live in the strange castle built by Raphael Bellefleur in the 19th century. In this time frame dates are not mentioned, although plot details suggest the 1920's and 1930's. In Bellefleur country "time is clocks, not a clock," as Samuel Bellefleur once told his family. Several characters experience disorientation of time: Young Raphael, who spends his days seeking the mysteries of life in Mink Pond; Jedediah, who renounces his wordly existence to seek God in the mountains; and Samuel, who makes the mistake of entering the castle's haunted "Turquoise Room" and is lost to an obscene black ghost who keeps him occupied for days when he imagines himself only gone for hours. The more mystical Bellefleurs not only understand the fluidity of time but use it to escape an unacceptable world. Raphael eventually escapes into his pond, to the dismay of his psychic baby cousin Germaine, who sees his face floating beneath her feet. Samuel disappears into the Turquoise Room forever (although with typical Bellefleur genius for missing the point, his father is upset not by his eerie disappearance but by the fact that Samuel has "gone over to the blacks").

Not only are there different times, but different worlds as well. Gideon's and Leah's genius son Bromwell speculates on the existence of simultaneous universes where there are exact replicas of ourselves. Some Bellefleurs actually see such replicas; for example there is a belief that the Bellefleur dead are assembled beneath the waters of Lake Noir, and shortly before his death Hiram Bellefleur sees their mirrorlike images hanging upside down beneath the ice. Characters supposedly dead also have a mysterious way of popping up again, like Vernon Bellefleur, who somehow manages to publish a book of poetry after being drowned by a drunken mob.

Nothing, not even death, is certain for the Bellefleurs. Everything in the novel is in flux, and the family is unsure of the most basic facts. Mountains change in height; Raphael's pond grows and then entirely disappears; family stories are notoriously unreliable. The story of Jean-Pierre, "the Innisfail Butcher" who was convicted of murdering 11 people, changes each time it is retold. Even the boundaries between human and animal are uncertain. Some people who threaten the Bellefleur children turn into whining yellow dogs, and Hepatica Bellefleur has the misfortune of marrying a young man who gradually turns into a bear and must be shot.

The world of *Bellefleur* is a brutal one, and there is no "God" as He is sentimentalized. Some of the family believe in God, but they are rapidly disillusioned. Leah's mother, Della Pym, rejects her belief upon the death of her young husband, Stanton, while the sweet-natured Vernon Bellefleur is converted from his cheerful philosophy when Gideon's illegitimate daughter Cassandra is killed by the Noir Vulture. It is in the character of Jedediah that this drama is most fully worked out. Jedediah abandons his family to seek God in the mountains, where he waits year after year for God to show Himself. When he finally goes out onto a ledge and asks God, for the last time, to show His face, his only answer is a nightlong bout of diarrhea that leaves him agonized with pain and humiliation. "So God showed His face to His servant Jedediah, and forever afterward kept His distance."

Throughout the book Bellefleurs discuss the "curse" that is supposed to be upon them, and many explanations are suggested as to what it might be. But to Hiram Bellefleur, the most pessimistic member of the family, "the 'curse' was just chance: and 'chance' is just what happens." The curse of the Bellefleurs is no more than the curse of all living things, that they are governed by the whims of an unpredictable and often brutal universe. Those who refuse to accept their lack of control are destroyed. In spite of his recognition of chance, Hiram aspires to a high degree of control himself, maintaining a rigid hold over his actions and emotions. During the night, however, he becomes a sleepwalker whose nocturnal ramblings put him in constant danger of death. Like several other Bellefleurs, Hiram has a disdain for accidental death because it suggests that the victim has been "bested" by chance; this is the attitude of old Raphael Bellefleur toward the 1825 mass murder of his ancestors. Hiram's is the most ridiculous death of all, as he succumbs to an infected scratch inflicted by a cat who refused to get off Hiram's bed.

This need for power and control is evidence of a sort of spiritual sickness. Young Raphael and Bromwell understand the world and their relation to it, recognizing that all things are bound together by a common life force, but without this understanding a character like Leah must fill the emptiness of her life with constant activity and a striving for power. At the beginning of the novel Leah and Gideon are wildly in love, but this fades when Leah becomes pregnant and concentrates solely on her daughter Germaine. Germaine has psychic powers that Leah uses to guide her monomania of recovering the vast Bellefleur empire. Leah flies into rages when her control is threatened, or worse, sinks into one of the famous Bellefleur "moods," a euphemism for black despair. Near the end of the novel she wakes up one day in a depression so deep she can scarcely move, with the words "the jaws devour, the jaws are devoured" going through her head. Jedediah is to find it a peaceful thought, but Leah cannot endure the bowing to necessity that it implies.

Gideon is also spiritually empty by the end of the novel. Rejected by his wife, he tries to fill the void with a frenzy of sexual activity but gradually shrinks in size until he is known locally as "Old Skin and Bones." Eventually even the activity of sex palls, and the only time Gideon really feels alive is when he is flying his airplane. In a stunning climax he becomes a force of destruction not only for himself but for most of his family as well, as he deliberately crashes a plane loaded with explosives directly into Bellefleur Castle.

Leah and Gideon are destroyed by their blind self-centeredness, but this is not where the novel ends. Although Jedediah actually lived several generations before Leah and Gideon, the story of the Bellefleurs ends with his decision to return to the outside world. A young Indian seeks out Jedediah and tells him that he must return and continue the Bellefleur line, as his family has been wiped out by mass murderers. The book ends with Jedediah's cry "I don't know what I believe," but the reader knows from previous chapters that he does return to marry his sister-in-law and save the family from extinction. He becomes a kind of secular saint, dying with the words "the jaws devour, the jaws are devoured" on his lips.

Bellefleur is a triumph of the novelist's art on several levels. The Gothic genre is ideal for Oates's purposes, enabling her to show the world in all its baffling complexity without need for explanation. Men disappear into mirrors, young women become vampires, and trolls are found bowling in meadows, but the Bellefleurs take little note. Such occurrences can hardly be amazing to a family who know that they themselves are "haunted things." The supernatural mysteries are part and parcel with the mysteries of everyday life, in which the Bellefleurs are always asking questions but never receiving answers. At one point Gideon cruelly injures his mistress Garnet Hecht by asking if he really is the father of her child; the question seems to come out of nowhere and is as much a surprise to himself as it is to her. As Garnet flees the room, Gideon sobs, ". . . why am I plagued as I am, who is playing this vile trick, whom should I murder. . . ." The sad truth is that there are no answers to Gideon's questions and no one to murder.

More important, *Bellefleur* is superbly written. The Gothic style is particularly suited to Oates's lurid imagination, and she captures the reader from the first chapter, with its description of a wild storm and the strange creature Leah rescues from it. Many of Oates's supernatural episodes have been used time and time again, but she revives them with just the right mixture of chilling detail and humor. Asked by her mother if anything is amiss, Hepatica Bellefleur (whose husband has turned into a bear) answers tearfully, "I don't *know*, Mamma— I've never been married before." Poor Hepatica is not likely to find an answer to her dilemma. *Bellefleur* is a brilliant evocation of a world in which all the signposts of normal life have disappeared.

Lisa Halttunen

THE BLEEDING HEART

Author: Marilyn French
Publisher: Summit Books (New York). 377 pp. $12.95
Type of work: Novel
Time: 1970's
Locale: London and Oxford, with flashbacks in the United States

*Two Americans in England who meet and fall in love, recount to each other
how stereotyped sexual roles have shaped their lives*

> *Principal characters:*
> DOLORES DURER, a professor of English
> VICTOR MORRISSEY, a successful businessman
> ANTHONY DURER, Dolores's ex-husband, who committed suicide
> ELSPETH DURER, their eldest child, also a suicide
> EDITH MORRISSEY, Victor's wife
> VICKIE MORRISSEY, their daughter
> JACK NAPOLI, Dolores's former lover
> MARY JENKINS, Dolores's friend, a divorced Englishwoman now studying medicine
> MACH, the chairman of Blanchard Oil, a wealthy and powerful industrialist

Marilyn French's novel *The Bleeding Heart* has a plot so simple it is almost nonexistent. Dolores Durer is an American professor of English, a specialist in the Renaissance, who is in England for a year on a federal grant, researching and writing a book. On a train between London and Oxford she meets Victor Morrissey, an American businessman who is also in the country for a year. They fall instantly in love and almost as quickly into bed. Their affair lasts as long as they are abroad together. Victor visits Dolores in Oxford, and she visits him in his London apartment. At Christmas Victor's daughter Vickie arrives unannounced to visit her father and after her initial surprise finds the situation agreeable. Sometimes Dolores accompanies Victor on business trips, only to end up angry and drunk when Victor leaves her alone in their hotel room while he is out dining with clients. In the end, Dolores's book is finished, and she is ready to return home and resume her career, as Victor will resume his. Life goes on.

There is more to the story than that, of course. Dolores and Victor are not two people chosen randomly by fate. They are exemplars of female and male roles in society. Through the book, as they explore each other's pasts, we learn how they became the people they are now.

Victor has been a winner all his life. Starting in high school, and continuing through college and graduate school, he has always been the best. His jobs have been a succession of profitable deals, big bonuses, and lightning-fast promotions. "I was going to be the next Mach," he tells Dolores. Mach is the chairman of Blanchard Oil, a legendary business leader. "He's power incarnate, the mover and shaker . . . Well, I wanted that."

But Victor has paid for his success. Just as his career was beginning he married Edith, the daughter of a well-to-do New York executive. It seemed to be a perfect match; he was handsome and aggressive, she pretty and deferential. But as Victor devoted more and more time to his job, Edith began to feel neglected and jealous. On the surface she still smiled, but her feelings atrophied. Victor started having affairs. Finally, Edith saw him in a New York restaurant, dining with his mistress. That night, after a raging argument, she left the house and drove her car into an embankment. Now she is paralyzed, confined to a wheelchair, holding Victor captive through her passivity and his feelings of guilt.

Dolores is a woman of sorrows, a bleeding heart. "I specialize in grief," she thinks. "I was apprenticed to it early by my mother who was apprenticed to it by hers. You might call it the family business." It was not her mother who hurt her the most deeply, though, but her husband, Anthony. Anthony's father had been a wealthy invalid, a man who either abused his son or ignored him. Anthony acted in exactly the same way toward his and Dolores's children. He picked on them, he yelled at them, and he punished them. He even tried to hit them or kick them when Dolores was not looking. With Dolores he suffered fits of insane jealousy and went into hour-long bouts of screaming accusations and obscenities at her. She had first fallen in love with him largely because of the stories he had told her of his childhood, because of the shy, unloved boy she sensed in him. "It took me years to discover that the real Anthony . . . wasn't ever going to come out and play."

Finally, Dolores went to Mexico to get a divorce from Anthony. The night after her return he went into the garage, closed the door, and left the car engine running. Their twelve-year-old daughter Elspeth found him dead the next morning.

Elspeth had been Anthony's favorite. She blamed her mother for her father's death. Dolores and the children moved to Cambridge, Massachusetts. While she devoted herself to teaching and writing, Elspeth made friends with a group of sophisticated, amoral teenagers in her school. She began shoplifting and using drugs. She skipped school constantly and was eventually expelled. Dolores found herself powerless to control her daughter. She tried talking to her, tried sending her to a psychiatrist. Nohing worked. She says to Victor, "She wanted to lose herself in something. She wanted oblivion."

She found it. When Elspeth was sixteen Dolores threw her out of the house, telling her that she would have to take responsibility for herself. Elspeth disappeared for four days. Then Dolores and her boyfriend Jack came home one night to find the garage doors closed and the car engine running once again. Elspeth, like her father, was dead.

After hearing these life stories, Dolores and Victor know the worst about each other and attain in the end a kind of peace. This is due largely to Dolores's knowledge of her impending return to America. Victor wants to accompany her, to leave Edith and live with her. But Dolores refuses; there remain too many differences between them. "After all," she says to herself, "if it had not been doomed to end, would you have been able to savor it so?"

For all its ideological prejudices, *The Bleeding Heart* is a very traditional novel. In almost every way it follows the traditions of romantic fiction. The heroine and hero fall in love at first sight, are separated by the hint of dark mysteries in each other's pasts, and then overcome their fears and declare their love for one another. All the revelations of plot and character are handled as mechanically as in any other piece of escapism. And the final separation of the protagonists is just another formula, the bittersweet ending common in modern fiction.

Even the traditional stereotypes of sexual roles remain intact. Man is rational and cerebral, woman intuitive and emotional. All evil in the world can be attributed to men and their aggressive behavior. "Men declared women invalid, and built that illegitimacy into the laws, into the very dreams of the human race."

The structure of *The Bleeding Heart* is schematic and predictable. The narration is flat, and when the book rouses itself and frolics through a few pages of "good" writing, words and phrases succeed one another in a breathless fashion, with only a slight condescension toward intelligible meaning or grammatical sense.

The Bleeding Heart is a flawed book. But it is not a deceitful book, nor a cynical one, nor an evil one. Marilyn French may be criticized for her clumsy plotting or inelegant prose but not for the sincerity of her feelings. She has passionate beliefs and a coherent set of ideas to support them. It is this very coherence that dooms her novel. Any writer who can so easily divide the human race into two autonomous halves will have great difficulty in entering imaginatively the world of anyone outside herself. Yet, in isolated passages, especially during the story of Elspeth, the reader reacts to the tangled feelings of real people, sensing the beginnings of a real story starting to force its way out of the confines of Marilyn French's ideology.

Jay Wickersham

THE BOURNE IDENTITY

Author: Robert Ludlum
Publisher: Richard Marek (New York). 523 pp. $12.95
Type of work: Novel
Time: August 24, 1974 to the spring of 1975
Locale: Ile de Port Noir, Marseilles, Zurich, Paris, New York

An amnesia victim searches for his identity and with the help of a lovely, intelligent woman attempts to trap an international assassin

Principal characters:
JASON BOURNE, an amnesia victim
MARIE ST. JACQUES, a beautiful Canadian economist
CARLOS, an international assassin and terrorist
GENERAL ANDRÉ VILLIERS, a French statesman

A man with gunshot wounds in his body and head is found unconscious clinging to a piece of flotsam in the ocean by a fishing boat. He is taken to the isolated island of Ile de Port Noir, where he is nursed back to health by the island's doctor. When the man regains consciousness, Dr. Geoffrey Washburn asks "Who are you?" and the answer is an anguished "I don't know." There are many clues to the stranger's identity: physical strength, knowledge of several languages (including one the doctor cannot identify), a face altered by plastic surgery, evidence that contact lenses have been worn in eyes with perfect vision, and a surgically implanted microfilm containing a Swiss bank account number.

Once the man has recovered his health, Dr. Washburn makes arrangements for him to enter France secretly. There the man obtains money, a car, and documents illegally. He makes his way to Zurich and checks into a hotel that seems familiar, where he is greeted by the desk clerk as "Mr. Bourne." In Zurich he also learns that he works for an American company called Treadstone Seventy-One, but he is unable to find a telephone listing for any such firm. When he goes to the Swiss bank, his file lists his full name as Jason Charles Bourne and his assets at $5,000,000. He transfers some money to Dr. Washburn, some to a bank in Paris, and keeps some cash. When he leaves the bank, however, three men try to kill him. He returns to his hotel, and the same men stalk him there. He escapes by taking as hostage Marie St. Jacques, a lovely Canadian economist. The physical effort of the escape damages his recently healed wounds, and Bourne must force her to drive him from the hotel.

A book of matches triggers the memory of a Zurich restaurant and, with Marie as an unwilling chauffeur, Bourne goes there. He is seen by a fat, frightened man who implies that Bourne is a hired killer and directs Bourne to a legless war veteran whom Bourne kills in self defense. Marie runs away in terror. She finds several men and, in the belief that they are plainclothes policemen, directs them to Bourne. Too late she realizes that they are actually killers, and because she can identify them, Marie is to be killed. Bourne manages to escape the killers and rescues Marie, but he is seriously wounded in the effort.

Marie, grateful that Bourne has saved her life, takes him to a small country hotel for medical treatment. She becomes intrigued by his story and decides to stay with him for a few days to piece together the information he has. In the course of their efforts to discover his past, they fall in love. Marie goes with Jason to Paris to look for more clues.

There, Marie's financial expertise enables Jason to withdraw his funds from the Paris bank without being traced. She uses her connections to get information on Treadstone Seventy-One. Her boss institutes a covert investigation into the company and is subsequently found dead. Jason recognizes the style of killing as that of an international assassin, Carlos, and fears that he is either one of Carlos's soldiers or a rival.

He follows a clue to a leading fashion house, Les Classiques, where he is convinced that he is, indeed, the assassin known as "Cain." While he is there, Jason is seen by Philippe d'Anjou, a man who worked with him in Vietnam in a secret operation called Medusa and who is now working for Carlos. Since Cain is a threat to Carlos's position as premier assassin, Bourne's situation is precarious. To protect Marie he decides to leave her, but, before he can do so, he sees a newspaper headline naming her as a murderer and thief. The lovers are forced to run together, isolated from any help by Carlos and by their lack of knowledge.

Meanwhile, Treadstone Seventy-One, which is Washington's most carefully controlled secret operation, has had its strategy exposed. Jason Bourne was planted by the United States government to pose as a competitor to Carlos. Treadstone hoped that Carlos would be drawn out by the temptation to kill Bourne and then could himself be killed. Now, with no evidence that Jason is alive other than the fact that the money has been withdrawn from his Swiss account, Treadstone sends out coded instructions for him to get in touch, instructions that his amnesia prevents him from understanding. Carlos, meanwhile, capitalizes on their confusion, killing the chief and several members of Treadstone, including Jason's brother. Carlos leaves two fingerprints belonging to Jason Bourne that had been lifted off a water glass in the Swiss bank. Washington is thus led to believe that Jason has turned traitor and returned to destroy Treadstone.

Jason and Marie have continued working and have discovered a connection between Les Classiques and General André Villiers, a respected elder statesman of France. Jason confronts him with the charge that he has ties to Carlos, but his denial is both vehement and convincing. General Villiers's son, a young member of parliament, was murdered by Carlos. Together, Jason and Villiers discover that the connection to Carlos is Villiers's young wife, Angelique. She is Carlos's cousin and lover, who has regularly relayed state secrets to him.

Jason makes contact with Philippe d'Anjou, who realizes that he was planted by Carlos to attract Bourne and is in line for a quick death. He tells Jason that "Cain" was a deceit set up by American intelligence. Immensely relieved, Jason hurries back to tell Marie and to get in touch with Treadstone Seventy-One. Carlos's ploy of killing the chief members of Treadstone and leaving Bourne's fingerprints was convincing, however, and Alexander Conklin, one of the remaining Treadstone officers, tries to kill Jason. With no other option available, Jason goes to Villiers with the intention of using the general's wife. He plans to draw Carlos out, kill him, and thereby clear himself.

He is too late. Villiers, unable to tolerate the humiliation any longer, has killed Angelique. Jason claims the killing as his own, sends a message to Carlos, and after leaving Marie in General Villiers's care, flies to New York to meet Carlos for a final confrontation at the Treadstone headquarters, a discreet brownstone on a quiet street. Too late to stop him, Marie realizes Jason's intention and tells his whole story to Villiers, who then repeats it to the American secretary of state.

Conklin has meanwhile discovered Jason's arrival in New York and planted agents around Treadstone to kill him. The head of consular operations, on the instructions of the secretary of state, tries unsuccessfully to stop Conklin and finally reaches General I. A. Crawford, also an officer of Treadstone. Crawford meets Marie, who has flown over from Paris, and situates her in a bullet-proof car in front of the Treadstone headquarters in the hope that she will be able to identify Jason, a master of disguises. Crawford himself walks the streets and is spotted by Conklin. They both perceive the trap Carlos has set for Jason but not in time to prevent the latter from entering the house, unrecognized by Marie.

Once inside Jason goes to an upstairs room that brings back incomplete memories. This time, however, only Carlos is there and, in a desperate struggle, two master assassins fight for their lives. Before either is killed, however, Crawford and Conklin break into the house and the resulting confusion allows Carlos, wounded but mobile, to slip away. Jason is critically wounded yet, in a panic, fights even his deliverers, those who had once tried to kill him. Only Marie can calm him.

Weeks later Jason is healed physically, and Marie knows his painful story. David Webb, a talented foreign service officer whose wife and two children had been killed by an unidentified plane that had bombed and strafed their home in Phnom Penh, Cambodia, had offered his deadly skills to Medusa and become the most effective operative in the secret search-and-destroy outfit. The North Vietnamese had kidnapped his brother to use as bait for a trap for Webb. Webb had rescued his brother and executed the mission's traitor, Jason Bourne, whose identity he assumed when he agreed to pose as Cain.

Now he has time and peace, with Marie, to discover his true self. He is promised government protection until the day comes when enough of his memory has returned for him to identify Carlos. He is the only man alive who has seen Carlos in his role as a killer. Jason knows the identity, for Carlos is a public figure, but it is locked away in his mind. At the close of the book he is beginning to find himself for he comes running to Marie to say "My name is David . . ."

Robert Ludlum's *The Bourne Identity* is the latest of the author's nine novels. It has the complex plot of the previous thrillers but boasts characters that are more developed. Jason Bourne is reminiscent of Brandon Scofield, the protagonist of *The Matarese Circle,* but Marie St. Jacques is unique in Ludlum's works, for she is a woman who plays an important, active role throughout the novel.

Putting a new twist on the classic "man searching for his identity" plot, Ludlum places his protagonist in the midst of countless unknown antagonists. Jason Bourne's fear of what he might discover and the pain of incomplete memories at times dangerously paralyze his will to act. Bourne operates in a vacuum, fighting against men he does not know for reasons he cannot understand. He is a principled man who is disgusted by what he perceives in himself. Fortunately, he picks as a hostage a woman who recognizes his good qualities.

Bourne's search for himself is complicated by his mixed identities: he is an amnesiac who had assumed a new role in life, that of a hired assassin. His search for either of his two old identities is interrupted by the tantalizing possibility of a third, for he is presented with the option of running away to a quiet life with Marie and abandoning his search for his lost selves. It is in his inability to run away from himself that Bourne discovers his own character.

Ludlum tells his story in a transparent, unself-conscious style. The story is all. And that is sufficient, for the plot of *The Bourne Identity* holds the reader hostage until its exciting, rewarding conclusion.

Pamela Murfin

CATHERINE THE GREAT

Author: Henri Troyat (1911–   )
Publisher: E. P. Dutton (New York). 377 pp. $15.95
Type of work: Biography
Time: 1729–1796
Locale: Czarist Russia, specifically the royal court at St. Petersburg

A heroic biography that fully describes Catherine II of Russia—her ambitions, loves, and beliefs—her thirty-four-year reign, and the overall atmosphere of Russia during the Enlightenment

> *Principal personage:*
> CZARINA CATHERINE II, Empress of Russia for thirty-four years, called "the Great"

In 1729 a Lutheran princess was born in northern Germany and christened Sophie. She was destined to become Catherine the Great of Russia. Her parents belonged to Germany's large population of poor aristocracy with distant relatives and connections in several royal courts of Europe, including Frederick II of Prussia. When young Peter Ulrich was chosen to become czar of Russia, all of Europe began wondering to whom he should be married. For both political and personal reasons, Sophie turned out to be eminently eligible. The Prussian king himself, who was a close friend of her mother, was anxious for stronger ties to St. Petersburg and initiated negotiations to present Sophie to the imperial court. In 1744 mother and daughter were summoned for an interview with the Russian Empress Elizabeth II. Sophie's noble lineage of minor note was an added advantage because it implied that here was a girl with no claims or personal ambitions for power.

Quite the opposite was true. Sophie was all ambition. She had met Peter Ulrich when she was 13 and began at a very early age to imagine herself queen, or rather czarina. In St. Petersburg, she was closely examined and auditioned for the part of the next czar's wife and, even more important since Peter was clearly feeble-minded, for the role of mother of many czars-to-be. Knowing exactly what she wanted, Sophie abandoned her Lutheran heritage, converted to the Greek Orthodox faith, and took a new name—Catherine. She even renounced her mother, who proved to be too meddlesome and possibly a spy for Frederick II of Prussia. Catherine also studied Russian, a language that Prince Peter never really bothered to learn. Bored by the shallow dazzle of the imperial court, Catherine read an immense amount and was influenced particularly by the major thinkers of the Enlightenment: Montesquieu, Voltaire, and Rousseau.

After Peter and Catherine were married, Empress Elizabeth became suddenly aware that she was sharing the palace with her successors. Afraid that they might usurp the throne from her, Elizabeth ordered the prince and princess into isolated quarters where no one could help them plan a *coup d'état*. Confined to her quarters, Catherine was condemned to live with an immature husband incapable of consummating their marriage. Catherine's early extramarital affairs were condoned, if not encouraged, by an aging Elizabeth, who realized that otherwise there might be no heir.

After Elizabeth's death, Peter III ruled for only six months in a reign characterized by manic militarism and wild disregard for Russian traditions. At the czarina's funeral he practically danced a jig while Catherine impressed the masses with her pious mourning for the dead. As Peter III became more reckless, the royal court began to consider a palace revolution. Catherine discreetly encouraged all dissenters and took Gregory Orlov, an officer of the royal guard, as her lover. He and his four brothers, all officers, convinced regiment after regiment to swear loyalty to Catherine.

The palace rebellion was set in motion by the Orlov brothers on June 28, 1762. In St. Petersburg, the printing press faked the outrageous announcement that Peter III had already abdicated and that Catherine was empress. The people, in total confusion, were ready to defend the czar if so ordered, but all they heard was the swelling exaltation "Long Live Our Little Mother Catherine!" Oblivious to events, Peter found that he had lost his crown in a *fait accompli*. Seven days later he was secretly killed by Orlov and his men.

Without hesitation, Catherine took command and began to practice all the theories of leadership she had dreamed of while reading French philosophers. Her strategems to modernize Russia and prove her glory to all Europe were pragmatic, radical, audacious, and often successful. When she found no money in the royal coffers, she had it printed. She prepared a code of laws, invited the French philosopher Denis Diderot to finish his encyclopedia in her palace, arranged for an ex-lover to become king of Poland, and was one of the first in Europe to receive a smallpox vaccination. She also began to extend the Russian borders, far into Turkey and Poland.

Catherine did not always get her way without opposition. Peter III was not the only one to die that she might thrive. All rebellions were quelled ruthlessly and disloyal subjects executed. Ivan VI, previously locked up by Elizabeth, was murdered, as was a madwoman who called herself Elizabeth II. It was more difficult to put an end to Pugachev, a populist hero and legendary rebel, who believed he was Peter III and gathered an army of Cossacks, mystics, peasants, and robbers. They roamed the countryside denouncing Catherine and massacring the noblemen. Pugachev's immense success in stirring up a peasant revolt worried Catherine all the more because its force was so spontaneous. In the future, she would have to be merciless. Regardless of Enlightenment tolerance, Catherine followed the practical rule that anything that might augment her power (and thereby Russia's) was justifiable. Catherine also began to develop a creeping paranoia about her own son and his wife, and, just as Elizabeth had before her, she kept them cut off from all potential supporters. The moment her daughter-in-law gave birth to a son, Catherine snatched up the child to bring up herself.

Not since Peter the Great had a ruler of Russia been so involved in running the country. Catherine loved Russia passionately. She delighted in attending personally to every detail of governing. She worked twelve to fourteen hours a day, rarely attended balls, and frustrated court ladies by forbidding Parisian fashions.

Catherine II had an enormous appetite not only for fame and power, but also for men. Her lovers were many, usually young and almost never her intellectual equals. Catherine ruled for twelve years before she met the love of her life, Potemkin. A soldier and a statesman, he embodied all that was passionately Russian with the refined sophistication and the intellect of a French diplomat. It is said, and believed by most scholars, that they were secretly married. The physical side of their attraction did not last very long, but Potemkin always remained her closest, most trusted adviser and friend. Appreciatively, Catherine presented him with the newly annexed territories and dubbed him "Prince of Taurida."

In 1787, Catherine decided to visit Potemkin in Taurida thousands of miles away on the Caspian Sea. She embarked in winter from St. Petersburg with 178 sledges and 600 fresh horses waiting at every stop. Her entourage included diplomats, courtiers, and at least two kings. More than just a journey, it was a campaign to prove Catherine's magnificence to her subjects and to the world. When they reached the Dnieper River, barges with orchestras carried the entire court on its way. If Catherine became bored, she ran a red flag up the masthead, and the wittiest diplomats and acrobats would hasten to entertain her. All along the banks of the river, village houses were decked with garlands and painted brightly. There was not a slum in sight, and in every town brilliantly outfitted soldiers suddenly appeared in cavalcade to salute the queen. Potemkin had arranged the entire show, and these were the famous "Potemkin villages" built overnight to add even more glory to Catherine's legend.

The culmination of her rule, Catherine's journey through the Crimea, only postponed the moment when she would have to face the growing disturbances at home and abroad. France was on the brink of a revolution that Catherine considered an outrage, having long ago outgrown her notions of democracy. She was now more interested in acquiring Persia. By 1791, Russia was just entering into or negotiating out of wars with Sweden, Prussia, Turkey, and Poland.

Catherine at 62, with Potemkin dead, was exhausted and frightened by popular threats against monarchies throughout Europe. Her son Paul was weak-willed, fanatically Prussian, arrogant, and stupid. Paul also hated his mother, having never forgiven her for the death of Peter III. All of the czarina's hopes were pinned on her grandson Alexander. She had educated him herself, and she had seen him develop into a well-bred and intelligent adult dedicated to the cause of justice. The great tragedy of Catherine's final years was that Alexander learned too much of what she taught. When she tried to make him her heir, he declined, preferring a quiet life in the country.

Catherine was not to be thwarted by any human being and planned to name Alexander her successor anyway, but fate defied the czarina. On November 6, 1796, two weeks before the announcement of her heir-to-be, Catherine II died of a massive stroke.

Henri Troyat writes that "Catherine was not a 'tyrant,' but she expected to be obeyed blindly. With good humor if possible, and with French manners." Troyat has found the ideal tone for his biography of Catherine the Great. His account of the czarina's career is full of body and verve, and *Catherine the Great* should take a first place in the long tradition of heroic biographies that have been published in the last decade about the czarina of Russia. Troyat has read, and wherever possible quoted from, the letters, diaries, and diplomatic correspondences written by members of the Russian court. He writes with precise detail of court life and gives the reader the feeling of learning something about history rather than merely reading a historical romance. Troyat does not dwell overlong on international politics or on the social structure of 18th-century Russia. Specific reforms, laws, and administrative policies are referred to only in passing. Occasionally, Troyat gives too much credence to gossip and hearsay. According to modern scholars, the stories about Potemkin picking Catherine's lovers for her are unfounded. For a more complete account of Catherine's reign, it would be better to consult works of scholarship. For a lively biography, perfectly true to the spirit of the times, Henri Troyat's *Catherine the Great* is the best possible choice.

Julie V. Iovine

CHINA MEN

Author: Maxine Hong Kingston
Publisher: Alfred A. Knopf (New York). 308 pp. $10.95
Type of work: Novel
Time: Mid-19th century to the present
Locale: South China, western United States, and New York City

A novelistic recreation of the experiences of a Chinese family traveling to, working in, and immigrating to the United States

Principal characters:
BAK GOONG, great-grandfather of the narrator
AH GOONG, grandfather of the narrator
BABA ("ED"), father of the narrator
THE BROTHER, brother of the narrator, American born

China Men is the second work in which Maxine Hong Kingston, an English teacher, has written about the experience of Chinese becoming Americans. Her 1976 *The Woman Warrior,* lavishly praised for both its style and content, concentrated on the female aspect of that experience; now, in *China Men,* the male is the object of imaginative recreation. Both of these books are novels, although the first has been described as "autobiography" and the second as "biography." This is not a negligible point. Works about American minorities with an explicitly "minority" orientation apparently have difficulty being accepted as mainstream American literature. Yet Kingston's novels are not only literature, but are also intensely American.

China Men is a collection of episodes, some of which have been published previously in *Hawaii Review, The New York Times, The New Yorker,* and other periodicals. The theme coordinating them is the experience of four generations of the men of a Chinese family (although never named, they are an imaginative representation of the Hong family) in China and America. As in *The Woman Warrior,* Kingston borders her episodes with folktale and fact. As in the earlier novel, this work, despite its almost exclusive preoccupation with the lives of men, is ultimately about women—their rejection by the old Chinese society, by the new China men, and, in many ways, by themselves.

The Ch'ing China of fact, the old China of legend, is the beginning of the story. In their village in south China, the family members work their land, educate their youngest son, and begin to dream of making a fortune in the Gold Mountain, a land where fish fall from the sky and gold lies on the ground. The great-grandfather is eventually recruited for a plantation gang in Hawaii, where he learns to disguise his contempt for—and fear of—the white "demons." His son, the grandfather, becomes a railroad man in the Sierra Nevada mountains, joining the early labor movement, but he is later driven out by angry white workers. Both men return to their village; both men are the "sojourners" of Chinese-American history. The father, "born in a year of the Rabbit, 1891 or 1905 or 1915," is the privileged son of the family, a personification of the educated man in old China: delicate, elitist, favored at the expense of his brothers, and effete. He is also the means by which the family becomes American. Stifled and futureless in his village, he determines to go to America. In New York, he is a laundryman, instantly ignorant and uncultured. He has expensive tastes but no business sense, and after working in the city for fifteen years and finally sending back to the village for his wife, he has accumulated nothing and in fact is on the verge of being cheated out of his investment by his business partners. The book ends with his son, a California high school teacher who joins the Navy to avoid being sent to Vietnam. Refusing to attend language school in Chinese because he fears being assigned as an interrogator, he passes the war years in Taiwan as a communications specialist with secret clearance. Ultimately he is welcomed back home to Stockton.

Rather than let the legendary themes in her work undermine the historical realities with which she is dealing, Kingston uses her hovering imagination to intensify them. The father, for instance, in his immigration to America makes not one journey but two: one strictly illegal, smuggled in a small crate through Cuba to New York, making friends on the underground alien network and dodging white immigration officials; the other a slow, degrading process through Angel Island, the San Francisco immigration courts, and finally eastward to New York, where he becomes "Ed." Thus, Ed has his story, and Chinese immigrants as a group have theirs. Similarly Ed, in his Chinese life, is given the education and upbringing of a young man of the late Ch'ing, before the Republican revolution of 1911 destroyed the old Chinese world; it is in this way that Kingston suggests the progress of Chinese Americans not only from one land and one culture to another, but literally from one time to another, for the ancestral home of Chinese Americans is in many ways a world that no longer exists. The means of conveyance here, the time machine, is the body of American immigration law, and in her chapter "The Laws" Kingston points out that contemporary, relatively free immigration statutes, which seem to embody ancient and basic American ideals, are themselves only tender young things. During the 19th century, Chinese men were limited in their immigration to minuscule quotas (during periods in which they were not absolutely forbidden to enter the country), and once admitted were forbidden to marry, request entry for their family, or ever apply for citizenship. Only after 1898 were persons born to Chinese parents in the United States considered Americans. Only after 1946 could Chinese immigrants apply for citizenship. Only after 1952 could Chinese women apply for independent admission to the country, and only after 1959 could the parents and children of immigrants apply for entrance. These stipulations were all directed exclusively against the Chinese, who have perhaps been the object of more peculiar immigration legislation than any other single people. Kingston's China men are not flowing with the tide but fighting against it, in a fierce, arduous, and wholly unconscious struggle to become American.

The American transformation is undoubtedly lonely for everyone, but for these village Chinese whose obligations toward parents and attachment to the closeness of children are so strong, the loneliness is often unbearable. They are frequently visited by ghosts. A grandfather settled in California is visited by his dead younger brother on several occasions, and only rids himself of the specter by shouting, "Go home. Go back to China. Go now. To China." An uncle is haunted more persistently by the ghost of his mother, who harangued him for years from China with letters describing her poverty and begging for money and his return, pleas he never satisfied, using the money for the establishment of himself and his family in America. Before he receives the news of his mother's death she has already begun to haunt him. He throws food and money at the ghost, all to no avail. His desperate final solution is to accompany his mother back to China (by ocean liner), back to her village, and back to her grave. "You're home, Mother. I'm home too. I brought you home." He returns to America on the same ship, "where he acted normal again, continuing his American life, and nothing like that ever happened to him again."

To a certain degree, history mandates that the story of Chinese immigration to America will be a story of men, yet Kingston's personal consciousness, enveloping the narrative, is the meaning of the male experience for women. The book begins with a short fable in which a Chinese explorer is captured and tortured by a group of mysterious women—their tortures being an imitation of the ear-piercing and foot-binding practices to which women were subjected for centuries in China. Near the beginning of the book is a small meditation on the father's verbal degradation of women. "What I want from you is for you to tell me that those curses are only common Chinese sayings. That you did not mean to make me sicken at being female." No such assurances are forthcoming. For these men, coming from the old China, where female babies were killed in lean times, raised to be sold in better times, and raised to be married off profitably in the best of times, the American "Women's Land" is both a curse and a release. For the grandfather who suffered the abuse of his wife and ridicule of his village for arranging to exchange his fourth son for a daughter, America, where all men can wish for daughters without being ashamed, is a land in which legal strictures still frustrate his hopes. He comes near to his dream only in a moment of holding a blond baby whose sex he cannot determine. "I wish you were my baby. My daughter. My son." The young uncle later haunted by his mother only sharpens her anger by raising daughters in America. "I order you to come back. It's all those daughters, isn't it? They've turned your head. Leave them. Come back alone. You don't need to save enough money to bring back a litter of females. What a waste to bring girls all the way back here to sell anyway."

Kingston's motifs, like this shadow of women behind men, lead, as they did in *The Woman Warrior,* back to her own observing consciousness, creating the distinctive structure and style of the two novels. Yet these are two very different books. The lesser self-absorption of *China Men* has served to make a more readable, less stylistically precious, more compassionate, more successful book. The language of *The Woman Warrior* was too often overworked. Behind that language lay an obtrusive personal interest, a resentment that seemed to prevent her from presenting her characters as credible human beings; rather they often appeared only near-human in their prejudices and petty brutalities. *China Men* seems the product of a more mature, more charitable vision. In many ways, the men may have been intended to answer the questions raised in *The Woman Warrior* about women, their condition, and their attitudes toward themselves. Instead, *China Men* has only revealed, in its patient, deliberate way, that men are not the answer to the women's question but part of the puzzle itself. In this final way, as in its general treatment of the American process, *China Men* is distinctively American.

Pamela Kyle Crossley

THE CLAN OF THE CAVE BEAR

Author: Jean M. Auel
Publisher: Crown Publishers (New York). 468 pp. $12.95
Type of work: Novel
Time: The Ice Age, about 35,000 years ago
Locale: Central Europe

An orphaned girl, appearing by chance in the midst of a Neanderthal clan, becomes the link between their tribe and the Cro-Magnon peoples

Principal characters:
AYLA, a child of the Others, the Cro-Magnons
IZA, Medicine Woman of the Clan
BRUN, leader of the Clan
CREB, the Mog-ur, or magician, of the Clan
BROUD, son of Brun
OGA, Broud's mate
BRAC, child of Broud and Oga
VORN, a male of the tribe
UBA, Iza's daughter
DURC, Ayla's son

When a cataclysmic earthquake devastates a section of Central Europe during the Ice Age, only one member of a Cro-Magnon tribe, a five-year-old girl, survives. As she wanders about the countryside, she stumbles into the cave of a lion and is attacked. Although she escapes, she bears four deep gashes on her thigh, the mark of the lion's claws.

The child is near death when she is found by another group of earthquake survivors, members of the "Clan," now seeking shelter. The Medicine Woman Iza, widowed by the quake and pregnant for the first time, insists that the child join them, despite the protests of Brun, their leader. Not only is the totem of the cave lion scratched on her thigh, but her survival itself is an omen that she will bring the Clan good fortune, Iza assures them.

That prophecy appears to be fulfilled when the child discovers a cave suitable to the needs of the Clan after all others have given up hope. As the Clan settles into its new dwelling, Ayla, the little girl, is taken under the wing of Iza, and of Iza's own protector, Creb, the Mog-ur or magician.

The crippled, one-eyed Creb is so hideously deformed, the result both of birth defects and a savage mauling by a wild animal, that he has never mated. Yet Ayla has no fear of him. Instead, she develops great affection for the Mog-ur. He returns it and rears the child at his own fireside, teaching her the Clan's customs as well as the gestures used in place of speech by those who have not yet learned to verbalize.

Ayla also learns from Iza, who soon imparts to the child all her knowledge concerning healing herbs and potions. When Iza's daughter, Uba, is born, the two girls are brought up together and become almost inseparable.

Ayla is soon accepted by all the Clan, despite the fact that she is so different from them. They are dark, their bowed legs covered with hair. They have no chins; their jaws seem to be muzzles. And their foreheads slope sharply back. They are typical Neanderthals. Ayla, however, is taller and walks erect. Her legs are straight and slender. Her hair is blonde, her forehead high. And she can laugh and cry as well as speak. The greatest difference between her and the others, though, is that she can reason while they can only remember.

Accepted by the Clan, Ayla is adopted by it as well, as part of a ceremony at which Broud, the son of the leader, is initiated into manhood. When Ayla's totem is revealed as that of the Cave Lion, a male totem never before given to a female, all are amazed. The attention focused on the girl infuriates Broud, who feels ignored. From that moment, he is Ayla's implacable enemy.

Broud finds Ayla's manner, less submissive than is required by custom of females, especially galling. He constantly torments her, frequently beating her because of this. To escape him, Ayla often wanders away, on the pretext of gathering herbs for healing potions.

On one such excursion, she watches as Vorn is taught the use of a slingshot. Although she is forbidden even to look at a weapon, let alone use one, she fashions a slingshot for herself and with practice becomes an expert shot. She hides her skill from the others, just as she hides her slingshot in a small cave she has discovered and where she spends much time.

Ayla's secret is revealed, however, when she kills a hyena that has snatched Brac, the son of her persecutor, Broud. Although she saves the child's life and tends his wounds so skillfully that they heal almost without a trace, she has broken the most sacred of the tribal taboos and must be punished. Because of the circumstances, though, she is not put to death as tradition demands, but banished for one month, which in effect is a death sentence since no one has ever survived such an experience.

Ayla, however, able both to hunt and to defend herself, proves to be the exception. When she returns, in a blizzard, to the cave that had been her home, the others are incredulous. They soon see her survival, though, as one more sign that she is favored by the spirits who guide all their lives.

Only Broud is displeased by Ayla's return. More jealous than ever, he becomes increasingly more abusive. In a final effort to humiliate and subjugate the young woman, he brutally rapes her. Broud's assaults continue. Ayla becomes pregnant and gives birth to a son, Durc. The child in many ways resembles the mother: he, too, has the high forehead of the Cro-Magnon, and the long, thin neck that makes it impossible for him, in infancy, to hold his head up. He is therefore judged to be deformed and Ayla, again in keeping with tradition, is ordered to kill the boy. His life is spared after an impassioned plea from his mother, and like her, he is brought up by Creb and Iza.

Iza now suffers from tuberculosis; Creb is old and becoming feeble. Still, he is able to attend the festive, periodic Clan Gathering, although it is held at a distant site. Iza remains behind because of her failing health, and Ayla replaces her as Medicine Woman. Her presence at the Gathering is resented by members of other clans—she is different and therefore ugly—and threatens to cost her Clan its position of leadership in the larger group.

At the Gathering, however, Ayla meets a woman who also has borne a child of mixed heritage, one who therefore closely resembles her own son. The two agree that their offspring will eventually mate, thus relieving each of fears that have long haunted them. And once again Ayla proves her courage by rescuing a wounded warrior and by helping to heal him. Before the Clan returns to its own cave, she has won the admiration of all.

Soon after Creb and Ayla have returned to their own hearth, Iza dies. Ayla is overcome with grief and guilt for having left the old woman. Once more she retreats to her small, private cave.

She returns, but is no longer able to nurse Durc. He must from this time be suckled by other women. No longer Ayla's child, he becomes the "child of the Clan." Yet she and Durc remain at Creb's fireside until the ceremony at which Creb relinquishes his post to Goov and Brun abdicates in favor of his son, Broud.

Broud at once announces that he will take Ayla as his second mate; she must live thereafter at his hearth. His intention is to torment her further. As a final turn of the screw, he decrees that her son can no longer live with her but must be brought up by others. Ayla, ignoring strict tribal rules against disobedience to a male, hotly disputes his order. Broud, who has hoped for just such a reaction, is able to banish her to the spirits forever as punishment, fulfilling his most devout wish.

The entire Clan is shocked by the harsh sentence, and there is a general outcry against Broud. It is just at that moment that the earth trembles again in a quake similar to the one that opened the book. Creb rushes to the cave, where Iza's body still lies, and is killed. Ayla, heeding Iza's last admonition to her, sets off to find her own people, leaving the Clan—and Durc—behind forever.

The Clan of the Cave Bear is based on a highly imaginative idea. In the hands of a more skillful writer, it might have succeeded as a novel. Unfortunately the book fails. It fails largely, and surprisingly, because of the author's lack of imagination in the development both of character and action.

The Ice Age setting Jean M. Auel has chosen is described by her publisher as "a world that truly might have been." But Auel's problem, and that of her book, is that that world truly *is,* and that it is *now.* It is the familiar world of the women's magazines and the confessions, the world of any lower middle-class area of any modern American city.

Although Auel's characters supposedly communicate only through gestures, she has given them speech. They talk interminably and almost exclusively in clichés. Their activities are equally banal and trite. Women gossip over cups of tea; they pack lunches or the Ice Age equivalent of their bags before going on a fishing or hunting expedition. Even such major events as the mammoth hunt or the Clan Gathering are stereotypes—a football game, the Olympic Games—barely disguised as ancient rituals.

At times, Auel is unintentionally funny, as when she describes a meal in terms worthy of a food writer: "A mountain of wild lettuce . . . freshly washed, was waiting to be served raw with a dressing of hot bear grease, seasonings, and salt, added at the last moment."

Auel is serious about her work, though, and that may be the novel's saving grace. Her sincerity, her genuine belief in what she writes overcome her leaden prose, her frequently misused words, and her platitudes. The reader forgives her and reads on, to take a certain pleasure in the tale of *The Clan of the Cave Bear.*

Vivian Werner

THE COLLECTED STORIES OF EUDORA WELTY

Author: Eudora Welty (1909–)
Publisher: Harcourt Brace Jovanovich (New York). 622 pp. $17.50
Type of work: Short stories
Time: 20th century
Locale: Primarily Mississippi; some European settings

The published short stories by Eudora Welty, a writer whose vivid presentation of characters—their language, personalities, and environment—has made her one of the most elegant and enjoyable of contemporary American writers

Eudora Welty published her first short story in 1936. From then until 1966, when she published her most recent story, she produced four collections of shorter fiction: *A Curtain of Green* (1941), *The Wide Net* (1943), *The Golden Apples* (1949), and *The Bride of Innisfallen* (1955). She has also written a number of novellas, novels, and essays. In short, she has led an active and productive literary life. The publication of her collected short stories allows the reader to examine and appreciate the art of that literary life and to enjoy the range of Welty's styles and themes.

Most of the stories in this collection are set in and around Morgana, Mississippi, Welty's fictionalized version of her own native city, Jackson. As with many other great writers of America's Deep South, Welty successfully allows setting and locale to be at once all-pervasive and unobtrusive. Against this backdrop the dimensions of her characters are shown in strong relief. In her preface to the collection, Welty notes; "I have been told, both in approval and accusation, that I seem to love all my characters. What I do in writing of any character is to try to enter the mind, heart, and skin of a human being who is not myself. Whether this happens to be a man or a woman, old or young, with skin black or white, the primary challenge lies in making the jump itself. It is the act of a writer's imagination that I set most high."

It only takes a handful of the stories in the collection to demonstrate how ably Welty uses her own imaginative powers. In "Lily Daw and the Three Ladies" a feeble-minded girl is about to be sent from her small town to a home for the retarded by her guardians, the three ladies of the title, a trio of skittish and meddling Baptist churchwomen. They are worried that as she becomes more "mature" she might fall easy prey to men without honorable intentions. As the ladies plan her train trip for her, Lily quietly packs her trunk and announces that she is not planning to go to the home at all, but is, rather, about to go off to marry a musician she met at a tent show the previous night. The women, hysterical over the fact that Lily's honor may have already been compromised, try to hurry her to the train. En route Lily and the ladies meet the musician who has, indeed, come for Lily's hand. It suddenly appears that Lily is not feeble-minded at all and that she has found a man of honorable intentions. The man, a xylophone player, affirms that he wants to marry her, and the three ladies shift gears and head off to find a preacher who can wed the two on the spot. In this light-hearted story, Welty is able to present poor Lily by contrasting her shyness with the bickering of the matrons.

Some of Welty's stories have a deep, moody quality. "June Recital" unfolds slowly and, at times, is almost dreamlike. It concerns a piano teacher, Miss Eckhart, whose progressive disorientation and mad obsession become the story's subject. She is a woman of quiet, yet fierce, passion who falls in love with a shoe salesman in her town of Morgana. The salesman drowns, and Miss Eckhart, distraught in her grief, tries to follow him to the grave. Confused, she returns to her piano teaching and conducts a yearly recital, all lace and lemonade, for her students' parents. Eventually she loses many of her students and finally moves away from the town. One day she reappears at the now empty and faded house in which she conducted her recitals. As before, she goes through the motions of slowly decorating the house for another recital, this time with newspapers, and then sets fire to them. The town marshal comes in time to put out the fire and lead the deranged Miss Eckhart away. As they leave, she sees one of her old pupils on the sidewalk. The unfolding of the story, its meandering narrative, its tone of lingering remorse, and its slow pace create the desired dreamlike effect.

As a storyteller Welty has many faces. "Powerhouse," the most dynamic story in the collection, shows Welty experimenting with an almost impressionistic prose style. That the story succeeds wonderfully again demonstrates her virtuosity as a writer. Powerhouse, a black jazz piano player modeled, it is said, on Fats Waller, is everything his name denotes. He exudes energy, and his unrelenting musical power drives his band and the audience to a frenzy. Powerhouse can get low and mournful. He plays sad, rolling blues. Throughout the story it is never clear whether he has just gotten news that his wife has died or if he has just made the whole thing up. The story ends just as it began, with a high-pitched wheeling force. Powerhouse is singing "Somebody loves me."

Eudora Welty also uses her sense of spoken language for comic effect. Her story "Why I Live at the P.O." is a pure farce. In the story the narrator, a girl at odds with her family, tells of a hilarious argument with her relatives at a Fourth of July gathering. The tale, replete with a drunken uncle, a quibbling mother, and a spiteful sister, ends with the narrator, who also happens to be postmaster of China Grove, the hamlet where the story is set, grabbing a few belongings and moving into the Post Office for some peace and quiet. As Welty's character recounts it with a sense of self-righteousness: "I just picked up the kitchen clock and marched off, without saying 'Kiss my foot' or anything."

One of the previously uncollected stories in this book, "Where is the Voice Coming From?", is much more serious in tone. Welty wrote it in 1963, after Medgar Evers was shot outside of Jackson. In the story she imagines the character of Evers's assassin and through first-person narrative has the murderer explain his motives. It is a chilling profile of a hypothetical bigot who plans a murder with malice. The story's effect, an impassioned denunciation of racism and violence, is fully achieved through the seemingly objective presentation of the murderer's tale.

Eudora Welty's stories are distinguished by linguistic virtuosity and clever plotting. She has a remarkable ear for the spoken language and an ability to convey its richness. Her stories, although sometimes dreamlike or brooding, are more frequently bubbling with wit and irony. They demonstrate an understanding of the complexity of people's motives and affirm Welty's care for the humanity of her fellows.

In all, this book is a fine collection of stories. Almost all are compelling and fully believable. Welty has a style that allows her to achieve a sincerity and candor in her writing that other writers simply envy. That she is able to convey these qualities with apparent ease is a testament to her virtue as a writer.

D. W. Faulkner

COME POUR THE WINE

Author: Cynthia Freeman
Publisher: Arbor House (New York). 390 pp. $12.95
Type of work: Novel
Time: 1953 to the present
Locale: The United States, specifically New York City's Manhattan; Westchester County, New York; and Wichita, Kansas

A beautiful woman who seems to have everything comes to understand the emptiness of her life, and to find fulfillment through embracing the religion of her forebears

Principal characters:
JANET STEVENS, a beautiful young model
KIT BARSTOW, Janet's best friend, also a model
FAYGE KOWALSKI, owner of a yard goods shop on New York's Lower East Side
MENDEL KOWALSKI, Fayge's husband
NAT WEISS, a stockbroker, Kit's lover
BILL MCNEIL, a young and brilliant engineer
NICOLE, Janet's and Bill's daughter
JASON, Janet's and Bill's son
MARK, son of Kit and Nat
ALLAN BLUM, a wealthy businessman, Janet's admirer

At the age of nineteen, Janet Stevens leaves her home in Wichita, Kansas, and heads for New York City, filled with an ambition to become a top fashion model. A year later she has realized that hope and is considered one of the most successful of those in her profession. Janet finds New York cold and lonely, however, and makes almost no friends. One dreary Sunday, when she is especially bored and depressed, she forsakes her usual midtown haunts and wanders to the Lower East Side. There she meets Fayge Kowalski, the proprietor of a small yard goods shop. Fayge pities Janet and invites her into her home. From then on, the girl makes a practice of visiting Fayge and her family each weekend.

She spends Sundays with the Kowalskis—Fayge and her husband, Mendel, as well as Fayge's mother, Rivke. But she takes a very special pleasure in sharing their Friday evenings and the Sabbath Eve service that is their weekly ritual. When the Kowalskis learn that Janet's great-grandfather was Jewish, their interest in their guest increases. At the same time, Janet's own sudden introduction to Jewish customs, through the Kowalskis, arouses her curiosity about her background. And on a visit home she learns the story of her father's grandfather, Yankel Stevensky.

Born in Russia, Yankel had emigrated to America, making his way

to Wichita, en route to California. Attracted by the town, he had for-
saken his goal and settled there, marrying an Irish—and Protestant—
boardinghouse owner, Pegeen. The happy marriage, one in which each
guarded his religion and religious customs, produced one child, a boy.

But the marriage was brief; Yankel had died at the age of forty-two.
His last wish was that his son, Sean, honor him annually with the
Jewish prayers for the dead. When Sean, his surname now changed to
Stevens, had died fifteen years later, he had made the same request of
his son, James, like Sean a doctor. James, telling the family saga to his
daughter Janet, acknowledges the faith of his fathers by asking to be
buried in a Jewish ceremony. As a result, when Janet returns to New
York, it is with "a far deeper sense of her own self."

Inevitably, one of Janet's first acts thereafter is to journey to Or-
chard Street to see her friends the Kowalskis. There she finds them on
the point of departure; Mendel, who suffers from tuberculosis, has
taken a turn for the worse and must go to Florida. Once again, Janet is
alone. Within the next year, however, she has become the great and
good friend of an equally sought-after model, Kit Barstow. Kit, who is
a few years older than Janet, is the mistress of a Jewish stockbroker,
Nat Weiss. Scion of a wealthy and respected family, the youngest-ever
graduate of the Harvard Business School, Nat has made a reputation
as "the boy wonder of Wall Street." It will be Kit's function to serve
as *shadkyn*—matchmaker—as well as confidante to Janet from then
on.

In the first role, she invites her friend to a party to which she has
also invited her own former lover, Bill McNeil. An engineer still in his
early twenties, he is as wealthy and successful as the others. Considering him the handsomest man she has ever seen, Janet immediately falls
madly in love with him.

Bill finds Janet immensely attractive, more so than any woman he
has known. But he has just recently freed himself from his mother's
apron strings, and he has no desire to become involved with any
woman. He therefore ignores Janet, both at this meeting and at a
second, also arranged by Kit. At last, Janet, desperate, takes matters
into her own hands and corners Bill in the lobby of his office building.
The two have dinner together; a few days later, they become lovers.

The affair continues. Bill is happy with the relationship, but Janet
longs for marriage. When Kit, after converting to Judaism, marries
Nat, Janet becomes more determined than ever. Through subterfuge,
she maneuvers him into a position from which he cannot escape. The
two are subsequently wed, in a formal ceremony at Janet's Kansas
home. Janet is soon bored with marriage. She has given up her career
and finds nothing to occupy her. When Kit is delivered of twins, Mark

and Deborah, Janet decides that her own happiness depends on her having children. Bill would prefer to postpone having a family, but gives in to Janet after a quarrel. Within a few months she is pregnant.

After the birth of the child, a girl they name Nicole for Janet's French grandmother, Bill's bachelor apartment proves too small for the family. When Janet presses a home in Westchester on him—one discovered by Kit and within a few miles of her own home—he reluctantly agrees to buy it. It is there that a son, Jason, is born, a child no more wanted than Nicole. Yet, Bill adores his two offspring. He and Janet, with the children, live the lives of typical suburbanites; aside from minor accidents to the children, nothing ruffles them for eighteen years.

Then, without apparent warning, everything changes. Bill, still longing for freedom, looks at his life and decides that his responsibilities are suffocating him. Consequently, he asks Janet for a divorce. She agrees. To pick up the pieces of her life, Janet goes off on a cruise where she meets Allan Blum, a wealthy Jewish businessman who is very much attracted to her. Still bitter as a result of her divorce, Janet discourages his attentions. To forget her troubles, she opens a small shop.

The children remain with Janet, and side with her. Nicole turns to Mark, Kit's and Nat's son, for consolation and lives with him. After she converts to Judaism they are married. Jason goes off to M.I.T., his father's school, to become an engineer like Bill. Nicole, deeply wounded at first by her father's abrupt departure, eventually forgives him and actively promotes a reconciliation between her parents.

Nicole's efforts to reunite her parents have almost succeeded when Allan Blum again appears, now asking Janet to spend two years with him, cruising the world on a small freighter. She spends the night with him, sleeping with a man for the first time since she has left Bill, the second man with whom she has slept in her life and agrees to go with him.

During the time they are together, Janet is able to reassess her life, to redefine her goals. She finds her hopes fulfilled by Allan, her aspirations realized by her own conversion to his religion, Judaism, the religion of her own forefathers. With this knowledge, she marries Allan; as a telegram to her good friend, Kit, explains, there is a rabbi on board the ship who performs the ceremony for the couple.

Cynthia Freeman has been preoccupied with the question of Jewish heritage in her other books, notably in her first, *A World Full of Strangers*. In that, a Jewish woman marries a Jew who, in order to advance himself in the business world, denies his religion. She is forced to hide

her own beliefs, but she never discards them: ultimately, that turns out
to be her salvation. In much the same way Janet Stevens, the heroine
of *Come Pour the Wine*, recognizes her roots and finds meaning to her
life as a result.

The idea is valid; in *A World Full of Strangers* it is realized. *Come
Pour the Wine*, however, fails to convince. One reason is that the
question of identity—of Janet's Jewishness—is so nebulous. It is difficult to believe that a woman with no knowledge of her background
should find that background so comforting. It is difficult, as well, to
care deeply about Cynthia Freeman's characters. They are shallow
and superficial; because they are dull, they lead dull lives. Very little
happens to Janet that is more momentous than her preparations for a
dinner party when she must "stop at Godiva's for chocolates, then
race over to a Madison Avenue gourmet shop to pick up some fancy
frilled toothpicks for hors d'oeuvres."

"Godiva" is the shorthand Mrs. Freeman uses as a substitute for
character delineation. Little more is known about these people than
that they take suites at the Waldorf, the Pierre, or the Plaza; that they
dine at Maxwell's Plum or the Italian Pavilion. From the names
dropped, Janet and her friends are recognizable as wealthy, as "beautiful people." The reader never learns much more.

Finally, Freeman is curiously blind to the effect of her writing. She
clearly sympathizes with Janet and expects the reader to feel the same
way. Janet is basically spoiled and childish, though, and only those
who share her values would find her appealing.

Vivian Werner

CONFEDERATES

Author: Thomas Keneally
Publisher: Harper & Row (New York). 427 pp. $12.95
Type of work: Novel
Time: March to September 1862
Locale: Virginia, Maryland

An impressionistic story of the Civil War centering on the experiences of
Stonewall Jackson's Shenandoah Volunteers

Principal characters:
> USAPH BUMPASS, a Virginia farmer and member of the Shen-
> andoah Volunteers
> EPHEPHTHA, his wife
> DECATUR CATE, a conscript in Bumpass's regiment
> LAFCADIO WHEAT, their colonel
> GUS RAMSEUR
> ASHABEL JUDD
> DANNY BLALOCK } friends of Bumpass
> BOLLY QUINTARD
> GENERAL STONEWALL JACKSON, head of the Shenandoah Val-
> ley forces
> HORACE SEARCY, a foreign correspondent for the London
> *Times*
> DORA WHIPPLE, a widow and hospital matron
> GENERAL ROBERT E. LEE, Commander, Army of Northern Vir-
> ginia

Confederates is composed of four separate but converging plot lines.
The main story centers on Usaph Bumpass and the Shenandoah Volunteers, a division of Stonewall Jackson's army. Bumpass and his
friends are largely farmers, men who believe in the Confederate cause
but are more concerned with getting enough to eat and eventually
arriving home alive. Usaph, Ash Judd, Danny Blalock, Gus Ramseur,
and Bolly Quintard make pacts with one another to that purpose, sharing food and utensils and promising to save each other from the hands
of the surgeons, whose sole remedy for battle wounds is amputation.

Usaph Bumpass's most consuming worry is his beautiful wife Ephe-
phtha, whose faithfulness he reluctantly but constantly doubts. The
arrival of Decatur Cate heightens his fears to fever pitch. Cate is a
conscript and a professed "Lincoln man," but as far as Usaph is concerned Cate's greatest crime lies in handing him a letter from Ephie.
Cate tells him that he is a traveling portraitist and only knew Ephie
through his work, but Usaph conceives an instant suspicion that Cate
has made love to his wife.

Cate's and Ephie's story is told in short sections throughout the book. Cate is the son of a wealthy Pennsylvanian but had shown no aptitude for college, becoming an itinerant painter instead. When he arrives at Usaph's Aunt Sarrie's to paint Ephie's portrait, he falls instantly in love. Awed by his superior education and in need of a man, Ephie does sleep with him, but the next day the Confederate army arrives to conscript him; Aunt Sarrie had begged a favor from an army friend. Ephie becomes pregnant but eventually miscarries.

Usaph continually struggles with hatred for Cate, swinging from one extreme to the other. At one point he tries to castrate Cate with a knife; at another, he helps carry Cate's equipment when the man is too sick to do it himself. Usaph's struggles are all part of the larger theme of men's basic decency. The war is cruel, but it seems a force apart from the men in it, who help each other when they are sick and search for friends' bodies to give them proper burial.

Another story line concerns the affair between Horace Searcy, a British correspondent for the London *Times,* and Dora Whipple, war widow of a Confederate major. Both are spies. Searcy, a veteran correspondent of many European wars, despises all Southern institutions, particularly slavery. Dora simply believes that the South cannot win, and passes information to the Union in the hope of ending the conflict as soon as possible. Through their spying activities the two meet and fall in love. Searcy asks Dora to marry him, but she refuses to leave the South before the war has ended. Soon, however, she is arrested when her name is found among a known spy's belongings. When Searcy learns of her arrest, he arrives with a minister and begs her to marry him, reasoning that the Confederacy would not dare execute the wife of a British nobleman. Dora not only refuses his offer of protection but finds herself unable to lie to the court in her own defense. Her calm recital of treason leaves them no alternative but to hang her.

The unifying force of the book is Stonewall Jackson, the legendary general who inspired awe not only from his own men but from the enemy as well. Keneally's portrait of the man is compelling. Before the war, Jackson had lived quietly as a professor at the Virginia Military Institute. Once it had begun, however, his career was meteoric. Deeply religious, he truly believed that God was behind the Southern cause, telling his men that battles had been won "by the grace of God."

With an ability to change almost instantly from kindly Southern gentleman to blazing visionary, Jackson has a magnetic effect on his men. It is Jackson's charisma and military genius that makes him one of the moving forces of the southern war machine. His function during this period is to distract Union troops in Virginia, forcing them to remain in defense of Washington instead of joining the fight against the rest of the Confederate army. But the real story of *Confederates* lies in Jackson's inexorable push northward against considerable odds. It begins in response to the Union General Pope's move south in defense of Washington, since in the process Pope threatens a major Confederate railroad link, the Virginia Central. In skirting Pope to reach the vital town of Manassas, Jackson breaks all tactical rules by splitting an already small army and passing along Pope's flank. Jackson's tactics worry the other generals, since they are predicated on his own lightning speed and the caution of the Union generals, but in the end he is vindicated. By the time Pope discovers his mistake, Jackson is well out of reach and heading northward.

General Lee's plan is to open up the Shenandoah Valley as his line of supply, but the Union-occupied Harper's Ferry stands directly in his way. In a top secret order called Special Order #191, he details his plan to split his now consolidated army once again, sending Jackson to take Harper's Ferry. Copies are sent to each general, but General Hill's copy is lost along the way and later found by a Union soldier, who passes it along to the Union General McClellan. McClellan's knowledge of Lee's plans nearly brings about a complete defeat for the South.

In Keneally's narrative it is Horace Searcy who is responsible for the loss of General Hill's orders. Searcy becomes friendly with a young officer named Angus, who tells him of the general's plans for Harper's Ferry. When Angus is ordered to deliver Hill's orders, Searcy rides along with him and surreptitiously steals the orders after causing Angus to fall from his horse. He hides them where the Union is most likely to find them. Angus has no suspicion, since by a quirk of fate Hill has received a copy of Special Order #191 from General Jackson. Only after McClellan has read the stolen orders do the Confederates realize what has happened. As a respected foreign correspondent Searcy is not arrested but only ordered to leave the country. He makes his last attempt to save Dora Whipple, then sails for England.

The Battle of Antietam, the culmination of the invasion of Maryland and perhaps the bloodiest battle of the war, brings together all of Keneally's themes concerning war and history. The educated and fatalistic Cate is one of the few who understand that individual lives mean nothing in wartime, seeing himself as flowing into a great river of history. Cate has been gradually losing his will to live throughout their trek northward and during the battle simply stands up to the gunfire. Ironically, although badly wounded, he does not die. Usaph's friend Ash Judd is certain of his own invulnerability, having met a witch who cast a spell on him. Ash is caught by a rain of bullets and dies with the phrase "Prince of Lies" ringing quietly in his ears. The thoughtful Gus

Ramseur, who has kept himself sane by composing a "war symphony" in his head, is found dead by his friend Usaph in the most prosaic of postures. Battle reduces all men to a common denominator.

Usaph's view of the battle is almost surrealistic, as human limbs fly through the air and friends bleed to death, while a neighboring farmer haggles with Union officers concerning damage to his property. Usaph too is wounded, but manages to leave the scene without being butchered by surgeons or shot as a deserter. He makes his way home to Ephie and is given six months to recuperate. In the spring he is sent back to the front, but soon returns home with a bad lung condition, a condition that is responsible for his death in 1873.

Confederates is an affecting portrait of the Civil War as experienced by those who fought it and those who stayed at home. Keneally captures well the excitement felt by generals like Stonewall Jackson, whose quiet lives were suddenly filled with drama and adventure. Keneally's Jackson goes about in a sort of ecstasy, secure in his faith that Confederate victories demonstrate divine support for the Southern cause. For common soldiers like Usaph there is no such sustaining grace, only lice and diarrhea and sudden death. For these men, the author insists, the difference between courage and cowardice is only a hair's breadth; the same men who run from battle one day may fight like devils the next. Keneally's long account of the slaughter at Antietam is one of the finest sections in the book. His love scenes can be a bit forced, but his battle scenes are superb, filled with all the ambiguity and complexity of the war itself.

Lisa Halttunen

CONGO

Author: Michael Crichton
Publisher: Alfred A. Knopf (New York). 348 pp. $10.95
Type of work: Novel
Time: June 1979
Locale: Zaire, Africa

Two men, a woman, and a sign-language speaking gorilla search the Congo River basin for diamonds in the lost city of Zinj

> *Principal characters:*
> PETER ELLIOT, a young primatologist who specializes in communication with apes
> KAREN ROSS, an ambitious and chilly woman determined to find the industrially-valuable diamonds
> MUNRO, a "white hunter" whose savvy about the jungle is derived from his background as a Congo mercenary
> AMY, the sensitive and intelligent "talking" gorilla who, through Elliot's instruction, has mastered 620 words

Michael Crichton's *Congo* opens with the swift and mysterious destruction of an expedition in the Virunga region of Zaire. This party has been sent to a virtually unexplored area by Earth Resources Technology Services (ERTS), a Houston-based consortium with worldwide, covert interests, to locate the lost city of Zinj and its cache of blue, industrial-grade diamonds. Despite impressive technological detection and weaponry systems, the party is wiped out. In order to determine why, ERTS and Karen Ross, the Congo Project Supervisor, check all available information and come to the startling conclusion that the party was destroyed by a unique form of gorilla. It is decided that Karen Ross will lead another expedition into the Congo to search for the diamonds. These diamonds, because of their peculiar physical properties, threaten to transform overnight the process by which information is gathered and disseminated. Since other consortia are also interested in the diamonds, time is of the essence. Hurriedly, Ross recruits Peter Elliot, an expert on gorillas and head of the Project Amy program in California, as well as a famous white hunter named Munro. Munro has an unsavory past, but he is the acknowledged expert on jungle exploration and without him the mission would be impossible. Aided by a dazzling array of electronic gadgetry, as well as Peter Elliot's "talking" ape, the team sets out into the heart of the jungle. Ross is constantly preoccupied with her computer's projected time-factors, and Elliot is absorbed with gathering data concerning the mysterious enemy gorillas. Munro, with his porters, is concerned only with getting them all to their destination safely.

This proves to be no easy task. Assailed by cannibals, tribal warfare, killer hippos, and an unyielding rain forest, their progress is slow. Additionally, their communications with Houston are hampered by sunspot activity. Amy, fascinated at being returned to the jungle, proves as useful as the computers as she is intuitively able to understand the ways of the wilderness. Still, it appears that their rivals will beat them to the site. It is only after they discover the wrecked remains of their competitor's aircraft that they realize their way is clear.

Soon after establishing a camp near the lost city of Zinj, the party is attacked by the killer gorillas. These gorillas attack by night, intelligently evading and confounding an impressive array of laser guns, tear gas, machine guns, and electrical barriers. Elliot insist that this is not the behavior of gorillas, suspecting, rightly as it turns out, that they must have been trained by men many years ago. When he discovers that the gorillas employ man-made tools, he begins to understand what a tremendous breakthrough has been accomplished in human-animal relations. Further, he is convinced that he has discovered a new variety of gorilla and, possibly, a new species.

Karen Ross, meanwhile, cares only about locating the diamonds. During the day the team searches the lost city, while at night it struggles desperately to protect itself. Finally, the defenses begin to crumble. Just as it seems certain that they will all die, Elliot, with Amy's help, devises a means of communication. Isolating certain key words, he broadcasts them through a speaker at the height of an attack, miraculously stopping the gorillas in mid-charge. Desperately, the team returns its attention to the locating of the diamonds. They finally find them near the base of the volcano Mukenko and are astonished at their abundance. As they rejoice and make plans for their transport, the volcano, which has been smoking ominously for days, begins to erupt. Amy signals that they should leave right away, but Karen Ross is reluctant. Elliot, concerned with gathering evidence for his discoveries, also tarries. Only Munro realizes the danger they are in, and it is he who finally succeeds in getting them to flee. But the flight is late, and the volcano erupts with a vengeance, generating massive electrical storms in its wake. Ash and gases rain down, burying the lost city of Zinj and the diamonds as well. Racing through the jungle, Munro knows that they must reach the crashed plane of their competitors; there, they would find a semblance of shelter and supplies. Once inside the plane, they are immediately attacked by Kigani cannibals. "If they get you, they eat you," Munro warns, wielding his machine gun. Once more, the situation looks hopeless. At the last second, Ross locates a number of propane cylinders, realizes how they can be used, and within minutes the jungle party escapes in their rival consortium's air balloon, headed toward Kenya and civilization.

As a straight thriller, *Congo* follows all the clichés and most of the rules. Crichton provides all the elements essential to any successful thriller—an exotic locale, sophisticated gadgetry, and the quest for a valuable object. The plotting itself, however, is generally thin and predictable, and the characterization is confined to stereotypes.

What is of interest in this book is the array of questions asked and ideas raised. In discussing possible communicative abilities in primates, Crichton has done his homework. For those who may disagree with some of his more pointed observations, there is an extensive bibliography at the end of the book for reference. As most readers of Crichton's work by now know, the author is highly educated. The real questions raised in regard to animal intelligence and its potential for cognitive language demonstrate this, as does his hard look at computers. Again, the issues that arise concerning machinery that thinks quicker and better than humans are equally thought-provoking. When is a machine a tool, and when does it become a tool-user in its relationship with people? Confronted in the future not only with thinking animals but with thinking machines as well, can people afford to be as thoughtless as they have been in the past?

Although Michael Crichton may not be the most gifted writer of fiction today, he is a competent storyteller. In addition, Crichton has raised some questions that are not only interesting but vital to the future of man as a thinking entity.

David Alvarez

CONSENTING ADULTS
Or the Duchess Will Be Furious

Author: Peter De Vries
Publisher: Little, Brown & Company (Boston). 221 pp. $10.95
Type of work: Novel
Time: The present
Locale: Pocock, Illinois, and New York City

The comical first-person narration of a young man whose sexual appetite is exceeded only by his craving for pyrotechnic prose

Principal characters:
> TED PEACHUM, a furniture mover turned soap opera actor
> MRS. D'AMBOISE (THE "DUCHESS"), the cultural leader and arbiter of taste in Pocock, Illinois
> COLUMBINE D'AMBOISE, the duchess's daughter
> AMBROSE D'AMBOISE, Columbine's older brother and companion to Ted
> SNOOKY VON SICKLE, young heiress to a brewery fortune
> FRANK CANDLESTICKMAKER, a Broadway producer

Ted Peachum, the audacious narrator of *Consenting Adults*, recounts the adventures of his youth with an almost embarrassing candor. "A self-disparaging egomaniac," he calls himself, delighting both in paradoxes and highbrow language that leave his companions, and often his readers, in awe of his intellect yet baffled by his meaning. Ted's penchant for fancy language stems from his desire to rise above the circumstances of his birth. His family runs a furniture moving business in Pocock, Illinois, where Mr. Peachum·hibernates—quite literally—every winter, causing Ted ceaseless embarrassment. Thus, Ted's youth turns into a struggle to overcome the Neanderthal inclinations latent in his breeding. He decides that "The society of people who did not ask for ketchup in public restaurants would be cultivated on a broad front."

Ted, cast in a high school play, is spotted by Mrs. d'Amboise, the Duchess: "A woman of quality who chewed her gum with her front teeth." Mrs. d'Amboise selects Ted to model for a statue of Shelley she plans to sculpt. Ted proves a successful model and, having completed Shelley, Mrs. d'Amboise has him posing as various classical figures. Ted discusses classical literature and becomes prime candidate for the hand of Columbine, Mrs. d'Amboise's ten-year-old "bijou."

Despite his remarkable knowledge of language and literature, Ted is rejected by Harvard and goes instead to Burwash College, where he studies nihilist philosophy and the theory of entropy. Says Ted, "In early youth we wear our nihilism with a certain bravado. It's part of our panache." But when Ted's roommate is drowned, he begins to believe all the rhetoric he has mouthed and consequently lapses into a deep depression. His breakdown is not, however, a total loss; he writes it up as a paper for credit in both English and psychology.

Having regained his mental equilibrium, Ted takes up with Snooky von Sickle, a girl "built like a Clydesdale," an appropriate description as she is the heiress to a brewery fortune. Ted is attracted both to her copious breasts and her trust fund. Yet he fears being engulfed in the von Sickle "Hun hordes." At a von Sickle reunion he observes, "Ten thousand Germans . . . pitching horseshoes and blowing horns . . . and eating ham and potato salad and drinking beer."

Immediately following this von Sickle orgy, Ted attends the opening of Mrs. d'Amboise's sculpture show. At this gathering Ted is introduced to Kathy Arpeggio d'Amboise, a policewoman who is married to Columbine's brother Vim but currently obtaining an amicable divorce. But having examined the several nude figures of Ted on display, her interest is piqued by this well-muscled furniture mover.

Ted finds himself torn between the voluptuous Snooky, the lusty Kathy Arpeggio, and the innocent little d'Amboise bijou. Ted remarks one day to a group of disciples (he is the Socrates of Pocock, offering peripatetic lectures as he carries armchairs) that, "if America can be thought of as polarized between two sets of James brothers, Jesse and Frank at one end and you know who at the other, why, we dramatize to ourselves in this one configuration its infinite cultural variety." And indeed, Ted's present dilemma, his amorous attachments, reflects this same expansive America. There is something illicit about Kathy and Snooky while Columbine definitely excites the philosophically effete side in Ted, the William and Henry James.

Ted shows up at the Pocock Country Club the night of the Pumpkin Ball in order to peer through the window at his lovely young and innocent Columbine. His attempt to play the patient older man waiting at the window is undermined by the appearance of Kathy Arpeggio who is patrolling the grounds. Ted soon finds himself tussling with Kathy in the backseat of her patrol car. Making love to a policewoman presents a new set of problems: "Deploying my right hand slowly downward along her waist, I tried to unzip her trousers, but first had to contend with her cartridge belt, after which in a maneuver with my left hand I bruised my knuckle against the butt of her revolver."

His inability to choose one of his three loves ultimately leaves him with none. Snooky marries Ambrose d'Amboise, Kathy becomes engaged to Phooey Haverstock, another Pocock bachelor, and Columbine has promised to wait for Chuck Larsen. What then is left for Ted in Pocock? He sets off to make his fortune in New York.

His first night in Greenwich Village, Ted flicks a cigarette that accidentally hits a passerby, Frank Candlestickmaker, who turns out to be a Broadway producer in search of just such an actor as Ted with that "smoldering intensity" that is so popular. Together with a small band of actors he performs at various Upper East Side addresses.

One night the company performs at the apartment of a midwestern brewery heiress and her husband: Snooky and Ambrose have moved East. The spark between Ted and Snooky rekindled, they spend torrid afternoons together until Snooky confesses to her husband. Ambrose considers it a perfectly legitimate relationship, but feels it his right to join in. The ensuing sex can only be described as gymnastic.

If three in bed is fun, what about four? Ted finds out after meeting the identical Peppermint Triplets. Acting in soap operas during the week and weekending with the triplets, Ted is sinking into the depths of depravity. One can only guess how low he would have sunk had he not received a phone call from the Duchess.

Columbine, he learns, has been hospitalized with anorexia nervosa. After putting Chuck Larsen through medical school, she had been dumped by him. Ted rushes back to Pocock where he nurses Columbine back to health, marries her, and returns to New York where he and "Colly" happily live out their old age.

The storyline of *Consenting Adults* is unquestionably thin, with the resolution of character abandoned for the sake of the one-liner. In fact De Vries introduces characters merely for a single good laugh; Dr. d'Amboise is a chiropractor who has thrown out his back while examining a patient. Columbine's oldest brother, Islip, it is learned, is "so laconic you couldn't tell whether he was speaking to you or not." Yet despite this looseness of plot, *Consenting Adults* is, paradoxically, a page-turner. Rather than plot, it is the richness of the humor and originality of the writing that compel the reader.

Although moving through a universe peopled with stick figures and caricatures, Ted as narrator becomes a true character, consistently inconsistent, irreverent, idealistic, idiosyncratic, in short, complexly human. While caught up in his studies, Ted confesses to underlining in library books passages that are of no interest whatsoever, a pastime that guarantees "no end of people scratching their heads in bewilderment . . ." Ted is a character to whom it is easy to relate, and Ted relates back, accusing the reader of his own foibles. While these accusations are certainly unfounded, the reader gladly forgives his occasional outbursts, for Ted Peachum is an entertaining narrator.

Elizabeth Lubin

COSMOS

Author: Carl Sagan (1934–   )
Publisher: Random House (New York). 345 pp. $19.95
Type of work: Essays

A collection of essays on the universe and man's observations of it, written in conjunction with a television series of the same name

Sagan introduces the reader to *Cosmos* with the essay *The Shores of the Cosmic Ocean,* which explains that the cosmos is all there is, or was, or will be. In an obscure corner of one of billions of galaxies is our planet, where all our perceptions of the universe originate. Scholars have speculated about the nature of the universe for centuries. Today it is known that the universe is far bigger and far older than any of the ancients ever dreamed. The universe has undergone innumerable transformations, not the least of which is the human race.

One Voice in the Cosmic Fugue is a study of life on Earth, an essential start to any search for life elsewhere. All life forms on Earth are more or less similar, having a common chemical makeup and evolutionary heritage. The mechanism of evolution is natural selection, the process by which random mutations succeed and reproduce, or fail and die out. One line of current scientific thought holds that complex organic compounds were formed from elements in primitive Earth's atmosphere, when charged by lightning. These compounds began to replicate, combining with others to form one-celled animals. The key to the cell is contained within the DNA molecule, which controls the way the cell grows and functions. On another planet, life would be radically different, having a different biochemical origin.

Sagan's third essay, *The Harmony of Worlds,* is concerned with the beginnings of astronomy. Ancient observers saw patterns in the stars and saw in them a connection with their own lives. Heavenly bodies were seen to have predictable motions, corresponding to seasonal changes. The moon and stars were thought to influence, rather than coincide with, earthly events and individual lives. Astrology, as codified by Ptolemy, is a combination of Babylonian mysticism and 2nd-century astronomy. Ptolemy's Earth-centered Cosmos was unchallenged for a millennium, until Reformation-era telescopes allowed Copernicus, Kepler, and Tycho Brahe to observe for themselves phenomena that could only be the result of the Earth orbiting the Sun. Noting the orbits of the planets, Kepler proposed that the same laws of nature apply to heavenly bodies as well as on Earth. "Astronomy," said Kepler, "is part of physics." Starting with Kepler's principles, Newton was able to discover the laws on which Kepler's principles were based.

Heaven and Hell begins with an account of the Tunguska Event, a titanic explosion in 1908 in Siberia, probably caused by a comet, which have been observed and associated with disaster for centuries. Velikovsky theorized that Venus was a comet, pulled into orbit around the sun only a few thousand years ago. Other disproved theories saw Venus as a steaming jungle, or a vast sea of petroleum. Venus, as shown by U.S. and Soviet unmanned probes, is more like the traditional image of Hell—sulfuric acid clouds, crushing atmospheric pressure, and searing heat. Similar in size and mass, Earth has a climate that contrasts sharply, with liquid water and an atmosphere of nitrogen and oxygen. Venus's grim climate is largely due to a greenhouse effect, the trapping of the sun's heat within impenetrable clouds. Industrial pollution on Earth causes similar acid clouds, perhaps contributing to a worldwide greenhouse effect. Venus serves as an example of a planetary disaster.

Is there life on Mars? *Blues for a Red Planet* explores this question and man's search for life on Earth's nearest neighbor. H. G. Wells' *War of the Worlds,* written in 1897, captured the imagination of young Robert Goddard, who designed a rocket to be flown as a means to travel to Mars. The U.S. Viking probe has now landed on Mars. Viking's testing equipment has not detected any life, or any liquid water, but this is hardly conclusive. A thorough, manned exploration of Mars remains in the future. If no life is found, Earth colonists may be able to make Mars more habitable, by introducing oxygen-releasing lichens, or by melting Mars icecaps. If Mars ever has canals, they will be built by humans living on Mars. They will be the Martians.

Deeper in the sea of space are the massive planets Jupiter and Saturn, the subjects of *Traveler's Tales*. The two Voyager space probes, powered by tiny nuclear reactors, are designed to traverse the solar system, ultimately headed for interstellar space. The Voyagers have sent back photographs of exceptional clarity of Jupiter and its satellites. Io, an inner satellite, is shrouded in incandescent clouds of sulfur, generated by volcanic activity. Europa, in contrast, is icebound. Ganymede and Callisto, the outer satellites, are seen against the background of Jupiter, larger than a thousand Earths. Covered by multicolored atmospheric disturbances, Jupiter presents Earth scientists with ongoing mysteries, such as the Great Red Spot. Some months later, Voyager I radioed back breathtaking pictures of Saturn, including unprecedented details of Saturn's rings.

The Backbone of Night is the name given the Milky Way by the tribesmen of Botswana. To them, the Milky Way holds up the night sky, keeping the darkness from crashing down on them. Mankind has always used metaphor to explain the Cosmos. Each culture has its own myths and gods. Ionia, the ancient Greek island-state, was located in a geographical crossroads, adjacent to Greece, Egypt, and Mesopotamia. Ionian scientists, from Thales to Democritus, saw the universe as understandable through direct experimentation. Scientific thought fell out of favor for a thousand years, until Copernicus. Modern-day scientists carry on the Ionian approach to science.

The nature of time is the theme of *Travels in Space and Time*. In dealing with enormous distances common to astronomy, the exact speed of light holds a special significance. Light from certain stars reaches Earth thousands of years after it was emitted, blurring the distinction between space and time. According to Einstein's Special Theory of Relativity, space and time are interdependent. Light travels at a constant rate of speed, regardless of the velocity of the source of the light. Nothing can exceed the speed of light, although the speed of light can be approached. Since all motion is relative, a ship traveling at nearly the speed of light would not experience the same passage of time that, say, the Earth would. Trips of ten years ship-time would be 30,000 years Earth-time, with no backward travel in time. By the time such relativistic spacecraft are constructed, scientists will know which stars to visit, and today's speculation will be tomorrow's fact.

"To make an apple pie from scratch you must first invent the universe." Thus begins *The Lives of the Stars*. Hydrogen and helium, the most common elements, are transformed within a star's interior into heavier elements, by nuclear fusion. When the star's nuclear fuel is expended, these elements are released into space in a nova or, in massive stars, a supernova. Neutron stars are the remains of such stars, atomic nuclei a few miles across, with more mass than the Sun. If the star is even larger, the collapse of the star's interior will be so great that the star will contract into a black hole, whose extreme gravity traps its own light. Variously called a warp, hole, or wrinkle in the fabric of space, perhaps leading to other dimensions, black holes are directly connected to the lives of the stars.

The limits of the universe is the theme of *The Edge of Forever*. By measuring the red shift of light from distant galaxies, scientists infer that the universe is expanding. If there is sufficient mass in the universe to slow down and reverse the universe's expansion, the force of gravity will draw it all back together, starting another cycle. If not, the universe will dissipate into a thin cold haze. Sagan speculates that the universe may be a single elementary particle in another universe, and that every particle in our universe is a microcosm of its own.

The Persistence of Memory, Sagan's 11th essay, considers the nature of intelligence. One measure of intelligence is the amount of information an organism can store. If an organism needs amounts of information greater than the amount stored in the genetic DNA code, a brain is required. Human brains carry information from books and, more recently, from radio and television broadcasts. Any technical civilization within a few tens of light-years would notice Earth's transmissions, the largest source of radio waves in the solar system. Voyagers I and II both carry a recording of Earth languages, along with playing equipment and instructions. The first steps toward membership in the cosmic community have been taken.

Could such messages be deciphered? *Encyclopedia Galactica* begins with the story of one man who decoded an alien language—the hieroglyphics of Egypt. By translating the Rosetta Stone, Champollion was the first person in 2,000 years to understand the cryptic messages from another time. Radio astronomy allows man to send and perhaps receive information across interstellar distances. If technical civilizations do not routinely destroy themselves, the number of civilized worlds scattered throughout the universe may be in the millions.

Who Speaks for Earth? Sagan asks in his final essay. If humankind is not committed to its own survival as a species, who will be? As hard as it tries to learn the secrets of the cosmos, mankind seeks means by which to destroy itself. In all the cosmos, mankind lives on but a single world. That alone makes humanity worth preserving.

Cosmos is a comprehensive, understandable view of the universe, complementing the television series and making science accessible to the non-specialist. Always informative and often captivating, Sagan's cosmos is rich in evocative images, from the birth of a galaxy to the destruction of the Library of Alexandria, with special emphasis on the human enterprise of seeking knowledge. The underlying theme of the book is that mankind is as much a part of the cosmos as are the stars. Avoiding mystical implications, Sagan reveals to his readers what the scientist has always known—that the universe is a place to live and a place that can be understood.

Thomas McCue

THE COURT YEARS

Author: William O. Douglas (1898–1980)
Publisher: Random House (New York). 434 pp. $16.95
Type of work: Autobiography
Time: 1939–1975
Locale: United States Supreme Court

An autobiographical work emphasizing legal and personal reflections on America since World War II by Supreme Court Justice William O. Douglas, a man known for his outspoken championship of the Bill of Rights

When William O. Douglas was appointed to the Supreme Court in 1939 at the age of 40, he joined an impressive bench, including Hugo Black, Felix Frankfurter, and Charles Evans Hughes. Never one to let his genuine respect for his colleagues prevent him from enjoying their foibles, Douglas soon became acquainted with their working personalities and ideological commitments. With the issues being brought before the court so directly linked to basic philosophical principles, the justices could not help but have strong feelings about their work. Even at the highest level of constitutional law, Chief Justice Hughes told Douglas, "ninety percent of any decision is emotional." Still Douglas felt the court remained basically a friendly place despite the legal disagreements.

A few key legal issues would follow Douglas throughout his career. A case involving a Jehovah's Witness who had been forced to salute the flag in a public school confronted Douglas with the principle of due process early on and led to a major misstep. Not yet clear on his interpretation of the Fourteenth Amendment, Douglas followed Frankfurter, who argued that states did have the right to regulate areas of freedom protected by the Bill of Rights as long as they followed reasonable standards. Thus, a public school could insist on a salute. It was a view Douglas came to oppose bitterly. For him, due process meant that the states were bound absolutely by the Bill of Rights and could not modify them. Government at any level, Douglas felt, must yield before individual rights. During his long tenure, Douglas saw his view prevail in such key cases as *Gideon* v. *Wainwright* and *Miranda* v. *Arizona,* landmarks that led to the application of due process to state law enforcement.

Douglas's views, however, were not always as in tune with the court. At the end of his first decade of service, he faced a bleak period when America experienced one of the gravest attacks on the Constitution ever attempted, and the court failed to respond. It began when Harry Truman instituted a loyalty program that ushered in the vicious search for Communists under Senator Joseph McCarthy. When the House Un-American Activities Committee took over judicial functions without following such basic tenets as the assumption of innocence, double jeopardy, or the right to face one's accuser, Douglas was ashamed of the court's avoidance of a direct confrontation with the executive and legislative branches of government. After Douglas spoke out against the restriction of ideas, lecturing on the subject outside of the court, he opened himself to attack. Then a Special Term of Court rejected the stay of execution that Douglas ordered for Julius and Ethel Rosenberg, who had been sentenced to death for espionage. Douglas was briefly threatened with impeachment and found himself a social outcast. For solace he took to hiking the Appalachian Trail, becoming in the process a staunch champion of its preservation from the encroachments of industry. Not until Earl Warren, Abe Fortas, and Arthur Goldberg joined the court did Douglas feel comfortable with its record on cases that pitted the cause of civil rights against the fear of subversion.

The advent of Chief Justice Warren set the stage for *Brown* v. *Board of Education,* one of the most important civil rights cases ever argued. Warren handled the case superbly. He made it clear from the first that he could not accept segregated schools, but he did not pressure those justices who disagreed with him. Using his diplomatic skills, he was able to announce a unanimous decision in favor of desegregation in 1954. While Douglas was pleased, he was disappointed that Frankfurter had been able to persuade Warren to include the phrase "with all deliberate speed" in his opinion. States successfully used this loophole to maintain their dual school systems. For what progress toward integration there was in the South in this period Douglas gave credit to two judicial heroes: Judges J. Skelly Wright and Frank M. Johnson.

Two other legal questions repeatedly stirred Douglas. First, he was wary of refusing judicial recourse to those whom the political system had failed. Douglas felt that the citizenship rights granted by the Constitution carried with them the protection of the courts and that the Supreme Court occasionally refused significant cases because they were political in order to avoid controversial questions that required court action. For example, in 1903 the court had ruled that blacks could not use federal courts to ensure their voting privileges because the remedy was properly a matter of politics. Douglas disagreed, asserting that the court's passive attitude in such matters helped to fuse the explosions of the 1960's. He also found himself in a dissenting position when the court turned away cases brought by young men drafted to fight in the Vietnam War. Douglas thought the constitutional authority for a war that was never declared by Congress a legitimate legal issue.

Finally, while Douglas fought hard to see that all citizens received due process, he opposed extending the Fourteenth Amendment to corporations. The Amendment had clearly been passed to grant full rights to blacks following the Civil War and was not intended to apply to businesses. Further, two sections of the amendment dealt with representation and service in Congress, rights that could in no way be granted to corporate entities. Corporations were already well served by their money and their prestige, Douglas argued. To construe the Constitution as additional ballast for them seemed to him to set the stage for corporate control of the democratic process. Once again, Douglas often found himself in the minority.

Legal principles were only one aspect of Douglas's experience on the court. He also had the opportunity to deal with a large number of people, many of them lawyers and legal personalities who were a constant source of pleasure as well as exasperation. Each year, for instance, he worked closely with law clerks fresh out of school. While Douglas liked many of his clerks as individuals—his first seemed almost a son—he had hesitations about letting clerks take over too much of the work from the justices. He used his own clerks mainly to check the accuracy of the facts and precedents that he used in the opinions he wrote. Innovative in his selections, Douglas appointed clerks in his Ninth Circuit from schools in the western states rather than from Harvard. He was the first justice to choose a woman for his clerk, and when he acquired a fourth clerk he often looked for someone with training in one of the social sciences rather than law. From his years on the bench Douglas concluded that the best way to argue an appeal was to present the facts of the case in a manner that clarified why a particular case followed one of two possible precedents. Too often, he found, lawyers gave lectures on principle. After all, the justices already understood the law. Of course a stylish flair was always welcome, especially if it helped the justices see the case in a new way. Mere flourish, however, was not welcome. Equally unwelcome but much more frequent was incompetence, which Douglas observed in 40% of the lawyers he heard.

If Douglas was often disappointed in his fellow advocates, he was even less impressed with most journalists. Still, he felt that any tampering with the freedom of the press would only lead to even less accuracy and the airing of even fewer viewpoints. In particular, Douglas feared that the press was losing its independence. By accepting leaks without fully checking them out or indicating their sources, journalists were playing into the hands of special interest groups, becoming propagandists rather than trustees of the public's right to know. Doug-

las blamed the Vietnam War at least in part on the government's use of
the news media in this way. Nor did Douglas look to the future with
much hope. The rich, he believed, were increasingly in control of the
news.

Douglas served under five chief justices. He respected all of them to
some degree, but he singled out two as truly outstanding, Charles
Evans Hughes and Warren. Douglas ranked them with John Marshall
as America's greatest chief justices. Although not a liberal, Hughes
was a staunch defender of the individual and had a formidable ability
to sense the important facts in any case. Warren's hallmarks were
absolute devotion to justice, a profound personal integrity, and a genuine empathy for the common man. Of the five, Douglas was least able
to accept the views of Warren Burger. He was appalled when Burger
ordered Vietnam veterans arrested for their peaceful protest on the
front steps of the court. Even so, Douglas appreciated Burger's gesture
when the chief justice arranged for Warren's body to lie in state in the
court's Great Hall.

Appointed by Franklin D. Roosevelt, Douglas had strong views on
all of the presidents during his years on the court. Of them all, he
called Roosevelt the best loved and the most principled. Truman
brought common sense to the job and started out with a good understanding of domestic issues. His defensiveness on foreign affairs, however, soon led to grave errors, including a security program that turned
against the American people. Douglas liked Eisenhower when he met
him but was never really impressed by him. The Kennedy family became close friends and never swerved in their loyalty to Douglas,
although he disagreed with them about President Kennedy's handling
of the Vietnam War. He felt that Johnson's need to be loved and his
inability to trust led him to create a credibility gap that undermined the
nation. As for Nixon, his unethical attacks on the Constitution put the
entire democratic system of government in jeopardy. By attempting to
undermine the First Amendment, which Douglas always held made the
United States a unique country by making possible the diversity of
expression necessary for a multiethnic, multiracial society, Nixon almost destroyed America.

Nixon also tried to destroy Douglas. In 1970, after two of Nixon's
court nominees failed to be confirmed, he assisted Gerald Ford in
leading an impeachment effort against Douglas. Using Douglas's defense of pornography under free speech, his extension of due process
to Communists, and a multitude of alleged improprieties, they succeeded in having Douglas investigated, but he was subsequently ex-
onerated from all of the charges. The Nixon years, however, left
Douglas with a renewed faith in the importance of "constitutional law

and order,'' and an increasing fear that the executive and legislative branches were moving away from this commitment.

William O. Douglas was an outspoken man with strong opinions about the most important issues and events of recent times, and *The Court Years* offers a fascinating compilation of his views. It is not, however, an autobiography in the full sense, since Douglas's personal life is almost entirely missing from its pages. Rather, one finds a series of topical discussions of major legal principles and public personalities. The book is full of behind-the-scenes glimpses of important cases and famous individuals. The first half consists of clear, concise analyses of the legal reasoning behind the actions of the Supreme Court; the second half offers truly eloquent capsule portraits of the personalities that have shaped recent history. While Douglas can be scathing at times, he is, on the whole, generous with his praise. Regardless of his opinion, he shows a powerful ability to select the telling anecdote that will both bring a person to life and summarize an entire career in a few lines.

While the book is in part a justification of and argument for Douglas's positions, it is in no way a piece of propaganda. Douglas is rarely defensive, and he never lets a sense of personal injury become overpowering. On the other hand, he is not afraid to make his interpretations clear, and by the end of the book it is obvious where he stands on the major issues. What remains elusive is Douglas the man as opposed to Douglas the Supreme Court justice. This is especially a loss because his reflections on the law reveal him to be a man of great passion and energy. Still, if one wants to understand the fundamental ideological questions that confront America today, *The Court Years* is an excellent place to start.

S. N. White

THE COVENANT

Author: James A. Michener (1907–   )
Publisher: Random House (New York). 881 pp. $15.95
Type of work: Novel
Time: 1453 to the present
Locale: South Africa, Java, Holland, England

A narrative of the settlement of South Africa and its subsequent history, told through the lives of three families over the generations they inhabited South Africa

Principal characters:
>WILLEM VAN DOORN, first Dutchman to farm South Africa
>LODEVICUS VAN DOORN, Boer farmer who fought the Xhosa for land
>PAULUS DE GROOT, great Boer general in the war against the British
>DETLEEF VAN DOORN, author of the laws of apartheid
>RICHARD SALTWOOD, English soldier and settler in South Africa
>HILARY SALTWOOD, Richard's brother, a missionary
>FRANK SALTWOOD, grandson of Richard and assistant to Cecil Rhodes
>LAURA OGILVY SALTWOOD, opponent of apartheid
>PHILIP SALTWOOD, American cousin who comes to South Africa to mine diamonds
>DANIEL NXUMALO, professor imprisoned for teaching Black Consciousness

The Covenant presents the events of five hundred years of South African history from the perspective of three very different families—the van Doorn, Saltwood, and Nxumalo families—whose destinies were part of that history. Each generation of the families plays a leading role in the events of its time. James Michener, thus, juxtaposes real events and personages with the fictional characters of the three families. The experiences and beliefs of the Dutch in South Africa are embodied in the archetypal van Doorn family, those of the English in the Saltwoods, and the black South Africans in the Nxumalos.

The first Nxumalo arrived in the great city of Zimbabwe as a boy. He rose to become a trader and government official. When the city was abandoned in 1459, Nxumalo joined the migration to the largely uninhabited lands in the south. There he and his descendants became herdsmen and farmers. Farther west, in the area around what was to become Cape Town, Bushmen had lived for centuries as hunters. The Bushmen were the first blacks encountered by the Dutch who stopped at the Cape for provisions on the journey from Holland to the spice ports in India and Java.

The establishment of permanent colonies on Java increased the number of ships traveling between Europe and Asia. The high death rate among sailors making the journey was a matter of concern to the Dutch East India Company, if only because it added to the expense of the voyages. In 1647 a ship carrying spices to Holland foundered at the Cape. The ship's crew and passengers were stranded for over a year. Willem and Karel van Doorn, sons of a prominent Dutch family on Java, were among those passengers. By the time they were finally rescued, the East India Company had decided to establish a colony to provision its ships on voyages to and from Asia. Willem van Doorn, enchanted with the natural beauty and limitless possibilities of Africa, became the first European to spend his life in South Africa, to found his own farm, to marry, and to have children there.

Van Doorn's children and grandchildren were joined by an increasing number of other Dutchmen, as well as French Huguenots eager to find a refuge where they could live as Calvinists without persecution. All the white settlers shared the Calvinism of Hendrik van Doorn, grandson of Willem. Hendrik read the Old Testament for practical guidance. He saw Africa as the promised land, given to his people, the new Israelites, in a covenant from God. The blacks were Canaanites, sons of Ham to be enslaved or exterminated if they did not surrender the promised land to the chosen people.

Blacks were migrating in greater numbers to the rich farm and grazing lands of South Africa. Their attempts to trade, on a fair basis, with the white settlers were rejected. Skirmishes over land rights led to large battles, involving hundreds of men, in the 1760's. Lodevicus, grandson of Hendrik, earned the name "the Hammer" for the brutality with which he killed black herdsmen who opposed the expansion of Dutch farms. Lodevicus was among the first "Trekboers," settlers who traveled beyond the established areas of white settlement to find more land and slaves for their farming.

War in Europe between Britain and Holland resulted in the transfer of control of South Africa to England in 1806. Englishmen began to settle in South Africa, among them Richard and Hilary Saltwood. These two brothers were typical of the kind of Englishmen attracted to Africa. Both boys were younger sons of a prominent English family, forced to go abroad for wealth and success. Richard arrived as a soldier, charged with enforcing Dutch allegiance to English rule. During his lifetime, Richard established the basis of a family fortune in finance and trade. Hilary came to South Africa as a missionary, hoping to convert the blacks to Christianity. His activities aroused the anger of the van Doorns, who saw the blacks as less than human and therefore unworthy of Christian salvation.

Despite the treks of farmers like the van Doorns, most of northern South Africa along the Indian Ocean was inhabited only by small groups of hunters and farmers. In 1816, Shaka became king of the Zulu, the tribe to which Nxumalo's descendants belonged. A Nxumalo became an aide to Shaka in his campaigns to defeat rival armies. Shaka's ability to unite diverse tribes into a growing Zulu army and empire was a result of the policy, which Nxumalo helped to administer, of allowing defeated peoples full membership in the Zulu nation. Shaka's policy was cut short when Nxumalo, with two co-conspirators, killed Shaka in 1828. The empire was weakened and fell to the army of Mzilikazi. Mzilikazi's campaign became known as the Mfecane, a plan that involved the slaughter of enemy soldiers and the destruction of opposing tribes' farmlands. The Mfecane united most Zulu under Mzilikazi, but weakened blacks' ability to resist the further encroachments of the Boers.

Shortly after the Mfecane, Tjaart van Doorn, son of Lodevicus, learned that Britain had ordered the freeing of all black slaves. The policy, as planned by Richard Saltwood, meant that Tjaart would receive no compensation for the lost slaves. Tjaart, along with his neighbor, considered Saltwood's actions to be an attack on his freedom. The van Doorns, together with the other Calvinist immigrants to South Africa, had come to see themselves as separate from those Europeans, primarily the British, who retained the values of their home countries, returning to Europe for vacations or retirement. Tjaart van Doorn called himself an Afrikaner. He was prepared to push farther into Africa, abandoning his established farm, to found a new Boer republic. Thus, after the British order to free the slaves, van Doorn embarked upon the Voortrek. The Zulus and Xhosa, weakened by the Mfecane, were defeated, and new Afrikaner farms and a republic were established.

Conflicts over the proper methods for subduing free blacks and over trade and the autonomy of the Boer republic, continued throughout the 19th century. The Anglo-Boer War erupted in 1899. The British victory came in 1902. During the war the English had pursued a policy of confining Boer women and children to concentration camps and burning Boer farms to starve the soldiers. Richard Saltwood's grandson, Frank, played a central role in the new Union of South Africa. In an attempt to mollify the Afrikaners, Frank excluded blacks from the national sports teams and passed laws restricting the vote to whites.

Frank's racist laws were codified after the Afrikaners' National Party won the election in 1948. Detleef van Doorn was especially anxious to exclude the coloureds, those of mixed race, from white society. For Detleef, the coloureds were a living reminder of the sins of early

Dutch settlers. Blacks and coloureds were confined to poor black "homelands," allowed to work for whites in the cities but forced to live in all-black townships, slums far from the downtowns where they worked.

The laws of apartheid were protested by Laura Saltwood, Frank's daughter. The government silenced her with "banning," an order forbidding her to see more than one person at a time, or to be quoted in print. The victims of apartheid included two Nxumalo brothers, Jonathan and Daniel. Daniel was educated at all-black schools and the integrated Witwatersrand University. As a professor, Daniel taught his students pride in their race and the knowledge that they could someday control the life of their country. Despite his suggestions that compromise with the white residents of South Africa was still possible, Daniel was arrested by BOSS (Bureau of State Security), tried, and sentenced to ten years in prison for "endangering the security of the state." Daniel's brother, Jonathan, having had his hopes for peaceful change dashed, is training for armed conflict. The novel concludes with Marius van Doorn musing on the possibilities for compromise, while his daughter Sannie marries Frikkie Troxel, an Afrikaner border guard who is ready to die to preserve white rule and racial separation.

The Covenant is a well-written story of several generations of three families in South Africa. Each fictional character is vividly described, imparting a reality that matches the historical events in which he or she participates. The characters interact with actual historical figures. Michener intends to give the reader an understanding of the beliefs and motivations of the three main groups that have inhabited South Africa —the Dutch, the English, and the blacks. The actions and perceptions of each group are embodied in the members of the representative family. Michener's novel, thus, presents South African history on an immediate personal level. The reader views history along with the intimate events of the characters' lives.

Although the novel generally succeeds in its purpose, at some points the history seems unreal as it is mixed with Michener's invented characters. It becomes impossible to know which events actually took place and which ones Michener invented along with the van Doorns, Saltwoods, and Nxumalos. *The Covenant* is an absorbing story that should leave the reader eager for a nonfictional account of South Africa's tragic history and current reality.

Arlyn Miller

CRACKERS

Author: Roy Blount, Jr.
Publisher: Alfred A. Knopf (New York). 291 pp. $10.95
Type of work: Essays
Time: The present
Locale: Georgia and other parts of the South; Washington, D.C.; New York
City; New England

*A humorous examination of the author's Southern heritage, often prompted
by or centered on the presidency of Jimmy Carter*

> *Principal personages:*
> JIMMY CARTER, 39th President of the United States
> BILLY CARTER, the President's brother
> ROY BLOUNT, JR., the author, a native of Georgia who relo-
> cated in New York and New England

In this salty and witty book Roy Blount, Jr., pokes fun at Jimmy
Carter, his brother Billy, and a host of other Carters, most of them
figments of Blount's wide-ranging imagination. Blount also gives an
insider's humorous view, replete with absurd scenarios and comical
country-western song lyrics, of life in the South.

Crackers is full of a Southern pride symbolized by the howling response of one of Blount's friends to the nomination of Jimmy Carter:
"We ain't trash no more!" With equanimity Blount recounts the typical responses to his Georgian background he has encountered all his
life: being called "grit," "cracker," "redneck," and the like (or
worse); having people at cocktail parties constantly say to him, "I just
love the way you talk;" feeling forced, in every situation from eleva-
tors to dime stores, to assume the guilt for racial problems in America,
problems that are in no way limited to the South. But Blount's feelings
do not bruise that easily. He makes his experiences and his heritage
material for his work, albeit with, at times, a stingingly spiteful tone.
Like Mark Twain's, Blount's humor is cheery and unthreatening at
one moment and acerbic the next.

For instance, in one section of the book—*Crackers* is basically a
series of loosely connected essays—Blount reviews one of Jimmy
Carter's famed "town meetings," held during a visit to Yazoo City,
Mississippi. Telling the story, mixing the qualities of a reporting Norman Mailer and a mocking Mark Twain, Blount tells of trying to meet
the new President on one of his first post-election visits to Blount's
old "backyard." Blount visits the house where the President is to stay
the night and sacrifices his desire for recognition in favor of a noble but
unheralded gesture on the President's behalf; he fixes the leaky toilet
tank in the bathroom of the overnight "Presidential suite." As Blount

puts it, "Here I had been trying to squeeze some personal recognition out of the President's visit to the people. Yet in playing a constructive role, I had secured my anonymity. I was representative of millions. Selflessly, I replaced the gleaming porcelain slab that masked my contribution."

The town meeting, Blount realizes, is a White House publicity stunt, an effort to show to the rest of the nation a Jimmy Carter enjoying the praise and adoration of his own people. Blount recognizes this, yet remains enthusiastic, the involved reporter. He writes about Yazoo City the way Mailer had written about Chicago in 1968. Blount writes: "I enjoyed being in that crowd, all of us flapping our cardboard fans with the funeral parlor ads on them. Jimmy was a sign of the obsolescence of the old lurid Southland, which was stark enough to provide the nation with grounds whereon anyone with gumption could fight for or against the rights of man. Now maybe we could all, all God's children, black and white, North and South, get back to scratching, scuffling, ingloriously adjusting our float arms, and fighting for the right-of-way."

In two other essays, Blount casts his mocking eye upon the President's notorious brother, Billy. The essays, entitled "Early Billy" and "Later Billy," reflect the vastly different climates of opinion that developed about the President's brother during the four years of the Carter incumbency. The early Billy is the beer-guzzling, wise-cracking wild man of Plains, whose antics were a novelty to a curious nation. Blount shows a Billy Carter who quickly fulfilled everyone's stereotyped expectations of what a Southern "good ol' boy" was like: a man willing to look like a fool in the public eye for the sake of a dollar; a man willing to cash in on a relative's new-found fame. He presents Billy's views on every aspect of the national political scene from women's liberation to states' rights. For example, Billy on capital punishment: "I think everybody who deserves it ought to get it." On former Alabama governor George Wallace: "George Wallace is not a racist. He stands for the common man. He stands for the common man a hell of a lot more than Jimmy Carter." On women's rights: "I've got a brother that's in favor of it, a sister-in-law that's behind it, and four daughters that I don't want drafted." The early Billy, as Blount shows him, is a phenomenon, a circus sideshow clown in the public eye, but one who is a lot more intelligent and quick than he appears.

In "Later Billy" Blount remarks about Billy Carter, "He let the media use him. The media use people like stripminers use land." In what becomes a more sympathetic and reflective view of Billy, especially in the light of Billy's controversial involvement in foreign policy, Blount notes a need to respond to the caricatured "good ol' boy mentality'' that had sprung up as an estimation of Southerners in general. One of the most stingingly irrational views on this front was put forward by Norman Podhoretz, the editor and social critic. Podhoretz' wife apparently remarked that the first "good ol' boy" who could manage without a beer in his hand might just become president. Such remarks incur Blount's wrath. He seems to indicate that if forced to make a choice, he would prefer the straightforward crudeness of a Billy Carter to the haughty remarks of intellectuals.

This reaction is indicative of a pattern in Blount's writing. When he is secure in his own regard of the South, he feels free to poke and jab at the Southern mentality with no holds barred. He feels comfortable in a self-effacement that indicates "it takes one to know one." The cold eye of Northern opinion, however, polarizes the issues for him instantaneously. At these points he becomes circumspect and humorless. Remarkably, the quality of Blount's writing never suffers from this shift of voice; his criticism is as compelling as his humor.

Nevertheless, it is as the Twain-like humorist that Blount is most effective. Musing that perhaps Jimmy Carter would have been a better president if he were more like an old Southern boy, Blount launches into one of his frequent country-western song lyric interludes:

> I got the redneck White House blues.
> I thought he'd give a lift to us Yahoos.
> He's got 98 advisers
>   and none of them chews.
> I got the redneck White House blues.

Also interspersed throughout the book are brief profiles of the various fictitious members of the extended Carter clan. Among them are Sister Muriel Oriola Carter, who speaks in tongues; A. Don and E. Don Carter, gospel-singing twins who argue with each other like Tweedledee and Tweedledum; a topless go-go dancer named "Limber Kimber Lee" Carter who's developed a new "Lust in her Art" routine in honor of her presidential relative; and L. Harwood Carter, a rather blueblood-sounding Northerner from Grosse Pointe, Michigan. Each of the twenty or so profiles is a word-cartoon, and although some are rather coy and others less than tasteful, all have humorous effect.

The most rollickingly funny pieces in *Crackers,* however, have nothing to do with the Carters at all. In two of them, "Things in the Wrong Hands," and "Smack Dab in the Media," Blount shows a virtuosity that is pure comic genius. The first of the two (both pieces have a run-on conversational style that reads like a stand-up comedian's routines) extols the virtues of the new "miracle" glues and recounts the adventures of a woman who accidentally gets stuck to a clothes conveyer belt at a drycleaner's when she comes to pick up her laundry and spills a tube of this glue. She is stuck there for days, and while she spins back and forth in the drycleaner's, her lawyers argue with the incorrigible proprietor. The story itself has an interlude about robbers who break into a house and, when they are unable to find anything of real value to steal, tie up the owners. They become fascinated with an assortment of household appliances, especially the food processor and super hair dryer. They run amuck and alternately curl and purée virtually everything in the house, including schefflera bushes and tennis shoes.

"Smack Dab in the Media" is another Blountian tour-de-force. The essay offers proposals for the various banes of city life. For instance, for those who frequent concerts yet hate the effort that must be put forth to get across town to the concert hall, a service has been developed whereby messengers will come to your home and chloroform you, drag you to the concert hall, and revive you just in time for the concert. A major problem with the idea, Blount concedes, is that the streets become clogged with all the drugged individuals being dragged around town.

Another idea, designed to combat the insensitivity of the media to the affairs of the common man, is the personalized newspaper. Blount offers the example of the "Phil DiLiberto Times." There it would be, on your doorstep each morning, chock-full of news items related to your own views on international affairs, with extensive quotes of your statements. The entertainment sections of the paper would contain reviews of recent meals you have cooked and would allow for advance publicity on, for example, your plants as they approach their blooming stages. You could even have instant morning-after analysis of arguments with your spouse that defends your point of view. Blount wonders what would happen when an individual starts getting mixed reviews or pans in his or her own newspaper. All this could be had for a mere $2,400,000 a year.

It is too bad for Blount that Jimmy Carter was not reelected. Although he is fairly ambivalent about Carter and often uses discussion of him as an occasion to speak more generally about the South, the former President is a continual focal point of *Crackers*. A month after *Crackers* appeared—its publication date was October 1980—its primary figure began to fade from the American scene, threatening to leave this book in an unattended heap of Carter-related humor. This is unfortunate, for besides being good fun, the book is an important contribution to the tradition of American humor. It is also, in spite of, or perhaps because of, its tongue-in-cheek qualities, a good documentary of the contemporary South, the last true "region" in the increasingly homogenized American culture.

Given the hilariousness of several pieces and the insightfulness of many of the others in *Crackers,* one can fairly safely assume that Blount's abilities are not exhausted by plying his comic talent to the Carter years. He will be heard from in the future, the more frequently, the better.

D. W. Faulkner

CREEK MARY'S BLOOD

Author: Dee Brown
Publisher: Holt, Rinehart & Winston (New York). 401 pp. $12.95
Type of work: Novel
Time: 1770 to 1905
Locale: the westward-moving frontier of the United States, including the lands
of the Creek and Cherokee in the Old Southwest, the Western Nation
of the Cherokee in Indian Territory (Oklahoma), and the Great Plains
from Independence to Pikes Peak, Sante Fe to the Little Bighorn

The saga of an American Indian family—Creek Mary's "blood"—who
range over the 19th-century American West, taking part in the great events
that produced Anglo-America and destroyed a whole civilization

>   *Principal characters:*
>   CREEK MARY (AMAYI), daughter of a Creek chief
>   OPOTHLE KINGSLEY, half-breed son of Amayi and John King-
>   sley
>   THE LONG WARRIOR, Cherokee chief, second husband of
>   Amayi
>   TALASI THE RUNNER, full-blood son of Amayi and Long War-
>   rior
>   DANE, the narrator, full-blood grandson of Amayi, son of Talasi
>   JOTHAM KINGSLEY, half-breed grandson of Amayi, son of
>   Opothle, and close cousin and companion of Dane
>   YOUNG OPOTHLE KINGSLEY, son of Jotham, Christian mis-
>   sionary to Sioux Indians at the Pine Ridge Reservation,
>   South Dakota
>   JERUSHA MCALPIN, mother of Dane's first son
>   PLEASANT MCALPIN, half-breed son of Dane and Jerusha
>   SWEET MEDICINE WOMAN, Dane's Cheyenne wife
>   SWIFT EAGLE, full-blood son of Dane and Sweet Medicine
>   Woman
>   AMAYI, full-blood daughter of Dane, Creek Mary's namesake
>   MARY AMAYI, Dane's full-blood granddaughter, daughter of
>   Amayi and inheritor of Creek Mary's proud tradition
>   FLATTERY JACK BELCOURT, greedy and cruel white trader,
>   later militia colonel and Colorado congressman
>   RED CLOUD, Sioux war leader

A young reporter, driven by curiosity, journeys to Montana to interview an ancient Indian, descendant of Akusa Amayi—Creek Mary—a
legendary matriarch of the Five Civilized Tribes. Dane's recollections
of his family stretch back years before his own birth, to a decisive
journey of his famous grandmother. Betrayed to the British by her
Anglo husband, John Kingsley, in 1770, Mary flees to the back country
with her son Opothle. Captured by Long Warrior, Mary soon won a
place among the Cherokee and position as Long Warrior's wife
through her indomitable spirit and beauty. Together they raise another

son, Talasi.

The Indian wars surrounding the American Revolution convince Mary that the enemy of her peoples are the land-grabbing *unegas*—the Anglo-Americans. Yet, the Cherokee fight against the rebels only results in the loss of land, and Long Warrior concludes that he must ally with the United States. Mary's implacable opposition to the whites is also ignored by her half-breed son. In the new century Mary follows the lead of pan-Indian leader Tecumseh, while Long Warrior dies fighting against Creek rebels with Andrew Jackson, whose life the young Talasi saves—an act he lives to regret. Mary's full-blood grandson, Dane, born in 1814 as his grandfather dies, is raised to a pledge never to marry a *unegas*.

Through the 1820's the Cherokee advance toward assimilation. Missionaries like the McAlpin family live among the people and teach them the ways of "civilization." With Jackson's election in 1828, however, the advocates of "Indian Removal" take power, and the family is racked by the attacks of frontiersmen intent upon stealing Cherokee lands. In a smaller, yet significant version of the conflict, Dane falls in love with Jerusha McAlpin and she bears a son, Pleasant, but Dane refuses to marry her. In the mid-1830's, the Cherokee are rounded up and exiled to Indian territory, along the infamous "Trail of Tears." Talasi dies in indignity along the way.

Book Two opens with this terrible journey to Indian Territory. The conflict between full-blood and half-blood, nourished by the bitterness of the removal, results in the murder of Opothle. In despair Dane leaves the Cherokee Nation for a journey that takes him to the far West as a driver on the Santa Fe Trail. There he encounters the proud Indian peoples of the Plains. He rescues a beautiful Cheyenne, Red Bird Woman, from frontiersman Jack Belcourt, and the two traverse the Plains searching for her people. Dane is attracted to the life of the Cheyenne, who seem to him to have escaped the ravages of the *vehoes* —their word for white men. He makes a final pilgrimage to the Cherokee Nation where Amayi, on her death bed, blesses him and passes to him her amulet—a Danish coin given to her by a long-dead white lover.

Dane returns to the Cheyenne, where he falls in love with Sweet Medicine Woman, successfully woos her, wins himself a place among the warriors, and becomes a full member of the band that camps at Ghost Timbers on the Platte River. In what Dane describes as the happiest years of his life, he and Sweet Medicine Woman have two sons and two daughters, including Amayi, named for his grandmother. On a trading trip to Missouri in 1846 he bumps into his cousin Jotham and his own half-breed son Pleasant, who later move to take over operation of a trading post not far from Ghost Timbers. The two branches of the family are now reunited as traders and buffalo hunters in the glory-days of the 1840's.

The emigrant traffic on the Overland Trail, the Gold Rush, the land rushes of the 1850's, bring thousands of *vehoes* to this world. Dane's son Pleasant agonizes over his identity, Indian or white, and finally, but unhappily, settles for life as a Cheyenne warrior. The 1850's are a time of escalating violence, the Indians fighting a losing battle for existence. Dane, through his relationship with the Sioux chief Red Cloud, becomes convinced that the end of Indian America is in sight and that the only hope is in retreat to the hunting grounds of the north.

The Civil War years are a paroxysm of violence for the family. Jotham, Swift Eagle, and Young Opothle fight for the Confederacy, while Pleasant dons a blue coat. The family emerges from these battles only to be engulfed by even greater tragedy on the Plains. Unrestrained by federal troops, frontier militia led by Jack Belcourt attack and massacre Plains Indians. In separate battles many kith and kin are murdered or fall fighting. Pleasant's Cheyenne wife and two of Dane's children are among the murdered. Ghost Timbers falls to the bluecoats. Finally, Dane and his remaining family flee to the north.

Book Three, then, opens with yet another journey. The family joins the Sioux people. Even here, though, the *wasicus*—Siouan for "white men"—follow, trying to open the Bozeman Trail to the Montana gold fields. Through 1865 and 1866, Dane fights with the Sioux and acts as Red Cloud's interpreter at the treaty signed at Ft. Laramie to guarantee the Powder River country to the Plains Indians "forever." In 1870, Dane accompanies Red Cloud to Washington, where the next move of the *wasicus* into the sacred Black Hills is announced by Dane's old enemy, Belcourt, now a congressman. The indignity shown to Red Cloud, and the leader's own debasement through liquor are emblematic of the final humiliation and destruction of the native people.

Back in the north country, the climactic struggle for the Black Hills begins. Dane's camp is overrun by bluecoats, and many die in a forced winter retreat to the camp of Crazy Horse. In 1876, Dane is present for the annihilation of Custer's men at Little Bighorn. Dane knows this is the end, however, and in the military apocalypse that follows he and Sweet Medicine Woman are driven into Canada with Sitting Bull, while his surviving children and their families are separated from him. Crazy Horse surrenders and is murdered, and in final desperation the half-breed Pleasant martyrs himself by forcing a suicidal confrontation with bluecoats.

Dane loses his wife during the hard exile in Canada, but he returns with Sitting Bull in 1881 and after a long search is reunited with his daughter and new granddaughter, Mary Amayi. His final tragedy is the massacre of his daughter, son-in-law, and two grandsons at Wounded Knee Creek in 1890. The dying daughter passes Creek Mary's amulet to Mary Amayi. Young Mary learns the arts of healing, and after setting the broken leg of a friend of Teddy Roosevelt's she is invited to attend medical school in the East. The novel ends with Mary's triumphal return to Montana with her dream of building a hospital for her people. She is clearly the inheritor of Creek Mary's vision and spirit.

Dee Brown knows his Western history well. The characters move in and out of places and events with a precision that will please historians. Great Native American figures—Menewa, Tecumseh, Sequoya, John Ross, Red Cloud, Sitting Bull, Crazy Horse—are woven into the story with convincing ease. Jackson is a natural in the novel, and although the appearance of Roosevelt seems less probable it works as a bit of fun. By focusing on the family of Creek Mary, Brown encourages the reader to see the events of U.S. history from the human eyes of the victims, not the conquerors. In this sense *Creek Mary's Blood* is the novelistic counterpart to Brown's earlier *Bury My Heart at Wounded Knee*. Brown's purposes are political: to force a reconsideration of a national legacy, to urge the attempt at different perceptions.

As a creator of characters Brown is less effective. The considerable opportunities for irony in the theme of "blood" are alternately ignored or harped upon. Moreover, with few exceptions the white characters are simply embodiments of treachery and greed. Brown chronicles a distressing and yet true story and urges the reader to consider the costs. Yet nowhere does he provide insight into why this happened. Certainly racism runs deep in this nation's history, but one suspects that its wellsprings are more complicated than Brown's red and white characters suggest. Nonetheless, this book is an interesting beginning at a new historical attitude.

John Mack Faragher

DESTINATIONS

Author: Jan Morris
Publisher: Oxford University Press/Rolling Stone (New York). 242 pp. $12.95
Type of work: Travel
Time: 1974–1979
Locale: United States, Central America, Europe, Asia

Ten essays on cities and nations, from Los Angeles westward to Delhi

In 1974 the editors of *Rolling Stone* magazine asked the British journalist Jan Morris to undertake a series of travel pieces for them. This was an unusual request for this rather hip and aggressive journal, since Morris, first as James Morris, writing for the *Times* of London and *The Guardian,* and then, after a surgical change of sex documented in the autobiographical *Conundrum,* as Jan Morris, had established an international reputation for reportage and historical writing especially notable for its thoughtfulness, analytical precision, and elegance. Probably what attracted the editors of *Rolling Stone,* along with Morris's many virtues as a reporter, was her far-ranging familiarity with places and peoples all over the globe and her deeply original interpretation of what she sees, hears, smells. The new association was obviously a provocative one for Morris. The essays are uniformly zestful. It is as though she had been assigned the agreeable task of introducing old, cherished friends to bright new acquaintances that she knew in advance were going to get on fine together. This sense of emotional involvement with places is characteristic of Morris. She has written elsewhere that she could not come to love a city or a country unless she had first owned a house there or written a book about the place. This was clearly too restrictive. One has only to be on board the plane with her as she appreciatively examines the insouciant sprawl of Los Angeles as it looms glittering by the Pacific or in the car beside her as she travels gleefully and breathlessly over the spectacular freeways, reflecting on the combination of supertechnology, expertise, historical richness, and awful, hard-edge glitz that energizes Los Angeles to realize that what she is describing is a profoundly visceral response to the *being* of the place. Unlike many gifted travel writers who describe skillfully what the reader may expect to see when visiting a place, or who, in effect, see it as a surrogate, Morris makes one *feel,* through vision and a kind of spiritual affinity that senses what is beyond sight, the experience of the place. An American reader might reasonably expect her essays on the unfamiliar, like Trieste or Delhi or Istanbul, to be of chief interest in the book. But a reader long familiar with Manhattan may have been numb to the subtle, distinctive vibrations of aliveness of that granitic, noisy island. What many take for a grinding dynamo of a town Morris convincingly argues is a gracefully mellowing dowager. Washington, D.C., with its symmetrical patterns, its museumlike collection of monuments and mausoleums, and its pervasive sense of grandeur and self-importance, begins to assert its *genius loci* as Morris mingles with the people who inhabit its august halls and chambers and the townhouses of Georgetown, introducing embassy wives, members of the immense black community, history-stunned tourists and pilgrims. Suddenly one is immersed in a population dedicated to belief in the historical significance and power of their world, and at the same time touchingly uncertain either of its reality or its permanence.

Each of the portraits captured in these essays is a moment frozen in time. With some, like South Africa and Rhodesia (1977), the moment trembles with historical imminence: Rhodesia on the verge of birth as Zimbabwe, South Africa in its plunge toward the seemingly inevitable terminal confrontation between black and white. Others, like those of Delhi and Istanbul, are penetrating glimpses into places now immutable and nearly impervious to the existence or passing of dynasty, revolution, poverty, wealth, corruption, or social improvement. London ("the Stage-City") leans heavily on its theatrical character, on pageantry and tradition quaint and arthritic with age, and deals uneasily and resentfully with a feeble economy, a tilting racial imbalance, and an invasion by preposterously rich Arabs arrogant with petrodollars. But, behind the appearances, Morris finds London as it has always been—tough, resilient, and ruled at its center, as ever, by The City, the financial center, which remains unchangeably ruthless, cunning, knowledgeable, and suave.

In some places, like Cairo, Morris makes one conscious of life existing on several levels at once. Morris's acquaintance with Cairo and the Egyptians goes back to the late 1940's, when she served a postwar stint with the Arab News Agency. At the time this essay was written in 1978, Cairo is long past the years of Farouk and Nasser and is on the eve of Sadat's pact with Israel. It is not the political moment, however, that preoccupies Morris, but the city's spirit. Cairo "has a dazzle to it now: a fairground dazzle, perhaps, with hustlers and red lights. Like it or not, this creates fizz. I have never known Cairo to be so alive. . . . I swear this is a more cheerful population than any in Europe or America." Coexisting with this fizz is the somber pull of Islam and the presence of its scholar-priests; the sinister subworld of subversion and secret watchers; the salons of rich women who consult oracles and ignore their prophecies; the lurking pyramids of Giza, for which Morris feels such deep antipathy. And overall, a frenetic air presaging sudden, meaningless explosion that Morris finds frightening and, at the same time, exhilarating. It is hard not to read this essay without experiencing a powerful urge to catch the next flight to Egypt's capital.

Indeed, so adroit and penetrating is Morris's evocation of the time and character of a place and its people, so rounded her characterization and historical perspective, that the piece on the Panama Canal, written in 1975, at the time a new Canal Treaty was under debate in the United States, was, at the request of Senator George McGovern, read in its entirety into the Congressional Record. One would hope that her sympathetic and humane study of South Africa and its grievously conflicting internal strivings had a similarly appreciative response in high places.

Perhaps the most estimable of Morris's virtues as a writer is the persuasiveness of her human involvement. She cares deeply that the best attributes and instincts in each of her subjects prevail in the shaping of its destiny. (It is interesting that in earlier writings, as James Morris, she rebuked herself for reportage that, for all its finesse, was marred by an unbreachable attitude of uninvolvement.) Morris now so successfully captures the spirit of place and time that the reader emerges with the strange illusion of having actually, for a moment, been there. Traveling with her, the globe seems at once smaller, more accessible, and, at the same moment, wonderfully various and new.

Each essay, unlike the usual newspaper dispatch, was written in reflection, at a leisure measured out to obtain the right balance, the adjusted perspective that balances the real and the illusory, the immediate and the protracted, the factual and the legendary or the fabricated. Great landscapes are perceived, but it is often her observation of the modest, humble, or mundane that illuminates and humanizes the terrain. Much of the pleasure in the reading lies in the sheer suppleness and originality of her style. The leisurely pace and frequent breeziness of its flow are deceptive, drawing attention from its density of mood and detail. An unexpected adjectival sequence, an idiosyncratic turn of phrase, summarizes the atmosphere in a Washington drawing room or makes heroes out of two retiring but crack sound engineers on a Hollywood set full of stars and technicolor egos.

In many ways, the most moving essay is about the most modest of her ports of call: Trieste, the faded but still elegant and knowing *entrepôt* on the northern Adriatic Sea, caught between the past and the present, the worlds of Western and Eastern Europe. Titled "What Became of Waring," in reference to a figure in a Robert Browning poem who vanished from Trieste, the piece is an affectionate, humorous testimonial to a favorite place. Trieste becomes irresistible under loving scrutiny, an aristocrat among cities, caught in the backwash of time, beautiful, slightly shopworn, snobbish, and content. For of all the places in which Morris finds herself at home, this is the most congenial. In a valedictory that might suit the book as a whole, she writes, "If ever you hear them saying 'What's become of Morris?', tell them to come to Trieste, and look for me loitering with my adjectives along the waterfront, where the trains go by, or laughing in the stern-sheets of one of the . . . tugs." One would like to join her among those stern-sheets and listen as she placed those adjectives in their special, perfect order.

Robert B. Costello

THE DEVIL'S ALTERNATIVE

Author: Frederick Forsyth
Publisher: Viking Press (New York). 403 pp. $12.95
Type of work: Novel
Time: 1982–83
Locale: Moscow; Washington, D.C.; London; Berlin; Rotterdam Harbor

The story of the struggles between two opposing factions within the Soviet Politburo and the efforts of the United States to influence the outcome of that struggle and prevent war in Europe

> *Principal characters:*
> WILLIAM MATTHEWS, President of the United States
> MAXIM RUDIN, Chairman of the Soviet Communist Party
> YEFREM VISHNAYEV, Rudin's rival for the Soviet leadership
> ADAM MUNRO, British spy in the Soviet Union
> ANDREW DRAKE, son of a Ukrainian exile who is determined to strike a blow against the Soviet Union
> VALENTINA (NIGHTINGALE), Politburo secretary and former girlfriend of Adam Munro

The Soviet Politburo meets on June 10, 1982, to learn that disaster has hit the Soviet grain crop. Less than half the normal crop will be harvested in the fall. To avert famine, 55,000,000 tons of grain will have to be bought from the United States. All eleven members of the Politburo realize that the enormous size of Soviet purchases will make it impossible to buy the grain secretly on international markets. The United States, no doubt, will demand military concessions in return for the needed grain. Yefrem Vishnayev, the party theoretician and the Politburo member with the greatest hatred of the United States, proposes an alternative solution to the grain shortage. The Red Army could plunge through Germany and France, seizing Western grain reserves. Vishnayev argues that war would yield the needed grain and extend Soviet dominance over Western Europe while averting the domestic unrest that would result from famine. Maxim Rudin, the Communist Party chairman, counters with the observation that while America and its Western allies would be defeated in a land war in Europe, nuclear war would be inevitable. Rudin is given the authority to negotiate for the needed grain in a 6 to 5 vote. Nevertheless, Rudin realizes that he is one vote away from being forced out of power by Vishnayev. Favorable terms from the United States become imperative for Rudin and for peace in Europe.

Two months before the Politburo meeting, the KGB, the Soviet secret police, had arrested a group of Ukrainian nationalists. One member of the group, Miroslav Kaminsky, escaped by sea to Turkey.

He is befriended by Andrew Drake, the son of a Ukrainian exile. Drake, although born in England, identifies with the Ukrainian people and longs to avenge them by striking a blow at the KGB. With Kaminsky's help, Drake plans to purchase weapons and smuggle them into the Soviet Union, enabling two Jewish dissidents known to Kaminsky to assassinate the director of the KGB, Ivanenko.

Several days after the Politburo meeting, Adam Munro, a British spy assigned to the embassy in Moscow under the cover of First Secretary in the Commercial Section, receives a note from Valentina. More than twenty years earlier, when Munro was a journalist in Berlin, he had fallen in love with a beautiful Russian girl named Valentina. She had refused to exile herself from Russia in order to marry him. After several months he returned to England and she to the Soviet Union. Now, two decades later, Valentina has discovered that Munro is assigned to Moscow and has sent him a note arranging a meeting. Valentina tells Munro that she is a secretary with the job of transcribing Politburo meetings. Disturbed that her country's leaders are planning a war with the Western allies, she presents Munro with a transcript of the June 10 discussion in the hope that he can alert his government, allowing them to counter the move toward war.

Munro delivers Valentina's information to his superiors in London. Returning to Moscow, he is torn between his eagerness to continue to "run" the West's first informant with access to the Politburo and his concern that if Valentina continues to deliver transcripts to him she could be caught and killed. At the same time, only by providing useful information to his superiors from his contact, code-named Nightingale, can Munro hope to prevail upon his superiors to bring Nightingale out of the Soviet Union to safety and marriage with him in England.

Munro is faced with the devil's alternatives: expose Valentina to danger or lose her again; provide valuable information to English and American intelligence and risk the consequences of the discovery by Soviet leaders that their secrets are known to their enemies. All the characters in this novel are faced with devil's alternatives. William Matthews, the President of the United States, can withhold the needed grain from the Soviet Union, risking the possibility of war in Europe. Yet, if he sells the grain without any concessions, he strengthens the enemy for possible future attacks. Further, Matthews knows from the transcripts of Politburo meetings, secured through Nightingale, just what concessions Soviet leader Rudin can make without losing control to Vishnayev, who would just use the grain crisis to move his country toward war.

Nightingale helps Matthews and his advisers to choose the least dangerous alternatives. Matthews and Rudin agree to a conference, held in Ireland, at which the two countries are to negotiate double treaties. The first treaty would contain agreements by the two countries to control nuclear arms and to reduce troop levels in Europe and the rest of the world. The second treaty, granting the needed grain to the Soviet Union at low prices, would be the reward for the first. Nightingale provides the information that allows the American negotiators to know the limits to which they can push for concessions.

The progress of the negotiations, the resolution of the potential Soviet famine, and the prevention of war are thrown into jeopardy when Drake's Ukrainian friends succeed in assassinating Ivanenko, the head of the KGB. Ivanenko's murder removes one of Rudin's key allies on the Politburo, improving the chances that the warmonger Vishnayev will prevail. News of Ivanenko's murder is kept from the Soviet population and the world. The Soviet leaders fear that knowledge of the assassination will undermine the KGB's aura of absolute power. Rudin is able to keep knowledge of Ivanenko's fate from spreading beyond the Politburo. For the rest of the world, the story that Ivanenko has suffered a heart attack is convincing.

Drake's friends know that they must escape from the Soviet Union if the world is to learn of their deed. They hijack a Soviet plane to West Berlin. Once in the West, they are tried for hijacking and imprisoned without revealing their true crime. Drake then seizes the world's largest supertanker in the North Sea just outside of Rotterdam harbor. He threatens to destroy the ship, releasing 1,000,000 tons of oil into the sea, unless his two friends, imprisoned in Berlin, are allowed to fly to Israel. As Europe faces ecological disaster, West Germany agrees to Drake's demands.

While Drake is holding the ship hostage, negotiations between the United States and the Soviet Union are successfully completed. Military concessions, acceptable to the Politburo, are made in return for the needed American grain. However, the KGB has learned that the two hijackers are, in fact, Ivanenko's assassins. The Politburo hardliners refuse to go along with the treaty if the assassins are allowed to escape and publicize their deed. Rudin, with no alternative open to him, delivers an ultimatum to President Matthews: if the two prisoners are released the treaty will be rejected in favor of war. Matthews is at a loss to explain the reasons for Rudin's strange demand. He prevails upon Adam Munro to contact Nightingale on a few hours' notice to see if she can shed light upon the situation.

Munro is reluctant to contact Valentina. Her escape to the West is scheduled for only two weeks later. He is fearful that if she checks Politburo minutes her cover will be exposed. Finally placing patriotism above love, Munro learns the secret of Ivanenko's death. President

Matthews now faces the ultimate devil's alternative. Either he allows the release of the prisoners, which will cancel the treaty and lead to war, or he must allow the destruction of the supertanker and its crew. Munro devises a plan that can avoid both possibilities.

The final chapters of *The Devil's Alternative* present the unfolding drama of the final hours of Drake's occupation of the supertanker. The two prisoners are flown to Israel after Munro has had the chance to give them a poison that will act hours later. Drake, assured by an accomplice that the two have arrived safely in Israel, releases the tanker crew and departs in a small boat. The boat is found and blown up; the two assassins die from the poison hours later, without revealing the secret of Ivanenko's assassination.

With the peace treaty between the two superpowers signed, Munro is only concerned with saving Valentina. In a meeting with Rudin, now secure after his triumph over Vishnayev, Munro pleads for Valentina's freedom. As the novel concludes, Rudin tells Munro that Valentina had been his agent. Through Munro, Rudin had been able to tell the American President of his situation, enlisting President Matthews in Rudin's own power struggle with Vishnayev.

The Devil's Alternative is a fast-paced novel that carries the reader to the final conclusion through the excitement and plausibility of the plot. Forsyth is a knowledgeable guide to the inner councils of the American and Soviet governments and the various spy agencies that are central to the novel's action. The reader is allowed to see the motives of each of the novel's main characters: Matthews, Rudin, Vishnayev, Drake, and Munro. These key characters have well-developed personalities, and their passions and weaknesses, their abilities and ambitions, are presented in the course of the novel. With the basis for each character's actions established, the plot moves forward with its own momentum. The reader is cheered when Rudin and Matthews are able to maneuver their countries toward peace and dismayed when the actions of Vishnayev or Drake and his band of terrorists threaten to force the two countries toward war.

Forsyth manages to convey the environment in which the spy or terrorist works in the modern world. Munro and Drake emerge as the two great opponents in *The Devil's Alternative*. Although they never meet, they are working at cross purposes. Drake is driven by hatred to strike a blow against the Soviet Union. Munro comes to see that he must aid the Soviets if peace is to be kept. Yet even Munro does not know the whole truth, as the final revelation about Valentina demonstrates. Forsyth keeps his best secrets for the very end.

Richard Lachmann

THE DRAGON'S VILLAGE

Author: Yuan-tsung Chen (1932–   )
Publisher: Pantheon Books (New York). 285 pp. $10.00
Type of work: Novel
Time: 1949–1951
Locale: The People's Republic of China, mainly Longxiang (literally "the dragon's village") in Gansu province

An autobiographical novel recounting the experiences of a wealthy Shanghai girl who becomes a cadre on a land reform team in the desolate village of Longxiang in northwestern China

Principal characters:
    LING-LING, the narrator and central figure
    MA LI, her school friend and fellow cadre
    WANG SHA, a senior cadre, official of the theater troupe in
        Shanghai, coordinator of a group of work teams
    MALVOLIO CHENG, a senior cadre and former actor
    SHEN, village cadre
    TU, village cadre
    CHI, the most powerful landlord in Longxiang
    DA NIANG, an old widow

Marveling in retrospect at the apparent calm of her family and friends as Communist and Nationalist (Guomindang) forces gathered for battle in 1949 on the outskirts of Shanghai, Ling-ling describes a dinner party expeditiously arranged by her aunt and uncle, a prosperous mill owner, at their villa in the former French Concession. The ostensible occasion was her uncle's latest poem, which feigned enthusiasm for the Communist revolution, but everyone present was soon anxiously exchanging political gossip, trying to decide whether to stay in China or flee. Ling-ling, orphaned at an early age, had been brought up by her aunt and uncle, sent to the fashionable St. Ursula's missionary school, and now moved with polished grace in this elite social world of wealthy Chinese entrepreneurs.

Most of the guests, like Ling-ling's aunt and uncle, eventually fled to Hong Kong or other refuges. Ling-ling, only seventeen at the time, decided to remain in China and by the following year, 1950, had become a cadre working hard to dispossess the landlord class. *The Dragon's Village* is the perceptive story of her motivations, experiences, and reactions during these two years.

In a quick sequence of events, beginning with her inadvert ent complicity in the radical activities of her school friend Ma Li, Ling-ling, a very believable girl mildly rebellious over the dull predictability of life in the traditional society, does a turnaround and becomes an eager cadre obedient to the revolutionary doctrines. Ling-ling absorbed much of her zeal for the revolution from Ma Li, seeing the poverty and filth of the Shanghai slums for the first time, for example, on a visit to the rickety house where Ma Li was defiantly sharing a room with a factory girl. Ma Li also helped her get a job in the library of the revolutionary theater troupe in Shanghai. Through a brilliant reconstruction of a discussion meeting held there and attended by many of the most famous revolutionary playwrights (all actual people) Ling-ling conveys the intoxicating atmosphere that involved her in helping to write playlets about social evils for the troupe. When the call went out for volunteers to carry out the land reform in faraway Gansu province, the young lady from St. Ursula's could hardly contain her excitement at being among those accepted.

Under the Land Reform Law of 1950 all landlords (as distinguished from rich peasants, middle peasants, or farm laborers and poor peasants) were divested of their land, draft animals, farm implements, surplus grain, and any surplus housing. The work team of cadre assigned to a village had first to identify the landlords and persuade the peasants of the desirability of the land reform. Then came the formation of peasants' associations to help the cadre with the searches and classification of the landlords' holdings, their confiscation, and finally the redistribution. Ling-ling, being young and inexperienced, was sent to the village of Longxiang with two veteran cadres, Malvolio Cheng (so nicknamed after his superb performance once in Shanghai of the role in Shakespeare's *Twelfth Night*) and Wang Sha, an official of the theater troupe who led the group of volunteers to Gansu province and was coordinator of the work teams into which the group was divided.

As the only female cadre on the Longxiang team, Ling-ling was given the task of rallying the women and children. It was a tortuous process with only one real success: a young girl with some education who turned activist and was elected a member of the peasants' association. The other peasant women, withered by the brutal conditions of their lives and totally submissive to their husbands, could only bring themselves to share a few of their tragic personal sorrows—like the wife in her fourth pregnancy at age twenty who explained that her three earlier babies, all girls, had been taken from her at birth by her husband as "useless" and left exposed to die. Ling-ling recalled her youthful desire to act out in real life the grand passions of the heroines of Western fiction and noted: "But in the past year I had moved into a very different world, one filled with living women of creative achievement, and women of the slums. Here in Longxiang I had gone even further into a whole new environment. The sufferings of Anna [Karenina] and Madame Bovary seemed like luxuries in which only ladies of leisure could indulge."

The local cadre Shen and Tu helped interest the villagers in attending meetings as the cadre from Shanghai struggled to unravel the situation in Longxiang and the silence of the peasants. But Ling-ling had become suspicious of the true loyalty of Tu and began a little detective work. Why did Tu, in charge the day the search of the powerful landlord Chi's house was to take place, lead the peasants in a search of another house? Why did Da Niang, a widow who had become blind in one eye from crying over the losses of her husband and eleven of her children because of the indifference to their survival by landlord Chi, keep silent and sometimes seem to be on his side? The pieces of the puzzle refused to come together.

Ling-ling, somewhat prepared for the frustrations of political activism, was jolted time and again in her contact with the miserable existence of the peasants. Even before reaching Longxiang, Ling-ling had spent a sleepless night huddled with the other cadres in a cold hovel in the cleft of a cliff watching in horror as ugly black bugs and spiders crawled along the beams just above her head. She vomited her first meal with a poor peasant family. Lice infested her clothes. Water was too precious to use for bathing—the peasants got only three baths in a lifetime: at birth, at marriage, at death. As winter cold gripped the unheated peasant cottages, her body began to ache and grow numb. And always there was the hunger, especially the traditional "spring hunger" as the meager winter food supply ran out before the new harvest was ready. One day Ling-ling found herself desperately searching the floor of her room with a twig for a piece of pancake missing from its hiding place under her pillow.

All of the cadre Wang Sha had led to Gansu province seemed to have had moments of disillusionment, wavering, and doubt. And one lost his life. Word reached Longxiang one day that a Shanghai cadre working in another village had had his head twisted around "as if somebody wanted to wrench it off." Wang Sha himself confessed to Ling-ling during a long talk that his twenty years as an activist had meant the sacrifice of his dream of becoming a writer and that "sometimes I've felt as if I were on a treadmill exerting a lot of energy but going nowhere."

The clue to the mysterious silence of the Longxiang villagers finally came to light. After the arrest of landlord Chi (for attacking the militia headquarters) and of local cadre Tu (for cavorting with the village prostitute), Ling-ling managed to trick Tu's wife into hinting at the connection between the two men. Tu had raped his wife's daughter from an earlier marriage and when the girl became pregnant murdered her and buried her corpse in the earthen floor of their cottage. Chi, for whom Tu was then working as a farmhand, had found out about the crime and used the knowledge to blackmail Tu into acting as his agent in the guise of a cadre. The villagers believed that any cooperation with the cadres would bring retaliation of terrible proportions from landlord Chi.

On the day of the redistribution, when the new deeds were at last in plain sight, Da Niang called Ling-ling to her side and with her old yellow teeth picked away the thread holding a tightly rolled piece of paper in the hem of her jacket. It was a worthless "grant" of a few acres of land that landlord Chi had given her to bribe her into silence. Da Niang, like the other villagers that day, tearfully welcomed release from a lifetime of landlord oppression.

The Dragon's Village is an unfinished story. The peasants of China, like those of Russia earlier in the century, soon found themselves "landless" again as the Communist rulers pressed on to the socialization of agriculture. Within three years, collectives were being formed in which the peasants jointly owned the land, and by 1958 the first communes, in which all land belongs to "the people," had been established. The promulgation and implementation of the Land Reform Law of 1950 constitutes a key chapter in the political history of modern China and has been the focus of numerous academic studies as well as a torrent of popular Chinese literature. *The Dragon's Village* is, however, the first account to deal with this harsh interval from so completely candid and personal a perspective free of the constraints of socialist realism. More than the progress of history is therefore implied in saying this is an unfinished story. Chen spent another twenty years in the People's Republic of China before coming to the United States in 1972 with her husband, also a writer and a former staffer at the Foreign Languages Press in Beijing. The story of Ling-ling is her own story in semifictional guise, and the skill and integrity Chen has brought to the telling prompt the hope that *The Dragon's Village* is part of a larger design.

A new liberalization of the policies governing art and literature in the People's Republic of China has recently been proclaimed and augurs a new realism among writers from the first generations of revolutionaries. In the race to put in enduring literary form the people's story of the revolution Yuan-tsung Chen, now an American, may turn out to be the winner.

Adrienne Suddard

THE DREAM OF THE GOLDEN MOUNTAINS

Author: Malcolm Cowley (1898–)
Publisher: Viking Press (New York). 328 pp. $14.95
Type of work: Memoirs
Time: 1929–1939
Locale: The United States, primarily New York City and Washington, D.C.

> *One of the most discerning literary historians describes the crisis and strug-*
> *gle of the Depression years, a time when the literary world reflected the prob-*
> *lems of American society*

> *Principal personages:*
> MALCOLM COWLEY, literary critic and staff writer for *The New*
>   *Republic* during the 1930's
> PEGGY BAIRD COWLEY, his first wife
> MURIEL COWLEY, his second wife
> EDMUND WILSON, literary editor and roving correspondent for
>   *The New Republic* during the same time as Cowley
> HART CRANE, poet and close friend of Cowley's

Three weeks before the Wall Street crash of 1929, Malcolm Cowley started work as a copy editor and proofreader for *The New Republic,* a magazine founded in 1914 as "a weekly journal of opinion." At a time when Hollywood films avoided controversial issues; when radio concerned itself with Amos 'n' Andy, the big band sound, and brand-name advertising; and when most newspapers printed negligible news on their front pages while the glossed-over reports of strikes and the closing of banks were tucked away on their inside pages, *The New Republic* was one of the few sources of in-depth coverage of important topics. From this vantage point, Cowley came face to face with an America in despair. Cowley's position at *The New Republic,* later that of book review editor and reporter, brought him into the whirlwind of social changes sweeping the depression-riddled nation.

Cowley's *The Dream of the Golden Mountains* chronicles the decade of American history when writers marched among the 15,000,000 workers that were out of jobs, striking with the dream "that a City of Man would rise on the other side of disaster." Never before had writers so assiduously and passionately followed the unfolding of historical events. And never before has this turbulent period of literature and history been portrayed with such poignance and clarity.

Densely packed with both fact and personal anecdotes, Cowley's memoir depicts an era fraught with disillusion and dismay. Workers did not know where to turn for help, and the administration of President Herbert Hoover offered little. The Smoot-Hawley Tariff, for instance, designed to balance the economy by increasing tariffs on certain imported goods while decreasing tariffs on others, proved an embarrassing failure. Everything seemed to be falling to pieces. There was the sense that something was ending in American society. Poverty-stricken Midwestern farmers found it was cheaper to burn the wheat that they could not sell than to buy coal shipped in from the eastern states. Hoovervilles, small cities of unemployed workers living in tarpaper shacks with roofs of flattened tin cans, sprang up in vacant lots.

Americans were in want of an economic and political alternative to a system that had failed them, and for many that answer was communism. Writers, like Edmund Wilson, began expressing this belief, demanding that "communism be taken away from the communists." The more capitalism was scrutinized, the more it seemed illogical. There was a desperate need for a movement in which workers could at least unite spiritually. Communism filled that need.

Organizations such as the John Reed Club were formed. Named after the author of *Ten Days that Shook the World,* a book describing the Russian Revolution of 1917, these clubs served as centers for the formulation of American proletarian thought. Platforms were raised, speeches delivered, and publications produced in the hope of winning the struggle of the workers.

Under the aegis of Theodore Dreiser, an organization called the National Committee for the Defense of Political Prisoners (NCDPP) took shape. Dreiser, author of the classic novels *Sister Carrie* and *An American Tragedy,* drew together a large group of writers, artists, scientists, teachers, and professional people to join ranks with the workers and to "aid its work."

Cowley, active in the NCDPP as well as in other communist-oriented groups, was among the contingent of writers, including Edmund Wilson, Waldo Frank, Quincy Howe, and Mary Heaton Vorse, who became involved in the Harlan County coal strike in Kentucky. Their intention was to distribute food, hear grievances, and consult with the miners. The miners were paid for each ton of coal produced with scrip that was worth about sixty cents on the dollar and could only be redeemed at the company store. For their situation to be termed unfair would be understatement. The strike had been a bloodbath, and their families were starving.

At Pineville, Harlan's county seat, the writers' contingent was greeted by machine guns, aimed at them from the courthouse. Arrested and intimidated, they were finally driven out of town, but not before they had handed out some food and spoken with the striking miners. Their presence did not win the strike, but they were able to raise funds for the miners.

Actions such as these taken by writers were not uncommon during the Depression years. Books produced during those years, such as *The Big Money* by John Dos Passos, *Tender is the Night* by F. Scott Fitzgerald, and *To Have and Have Not* by Ernest Hemingway, dealt with social collapse. There were novels about the coal, cotton, and lumber strikes including *Marching! Marching!* by Clea Weatherwax, *To Make My Bread* by Grace Lumpkin, *Gathering Storm* by Myra Page, and *The Land of Plenty* by Robert Cantwell. The poetry of Kenneth Fearing, Alfred Hayes, and Muriel Rukeyser portrayed the cause of the jobless, the oppressed, and the needy.

In 1935 a young playwright, Clifford Odets, read of Hitler's Germany in a report in *The New Masses*. He was so moved that in one evening he wrote a play that was to be produced in over thirty American cities, *Till the Day I Die*. It almost always appeared with another short play by Odets entitled *Waiting for Lefty,* inspired by a report of the New York taxi drivers' strike of 1934.

Protests and protest writing were common to the 1930's. The Bonus Expeditionary Force, a group of angry World War I veterans, marched on Washington, for example, in one of many related incidents. The government had promised them "adjusted compensation certificates," and these certificates were to be redeemed in dollars in 1945. Living on the very edge of starvation, the BEF demanded that they be paid immediately, arguing that help was needed now, that they might not live to see 1945. The Hoover administration reacted harshly. Led by Gen. Douglas MacArthur, a column of infantry routed the BEF, burning their camp on Anacostia Flats near the Capitol and scattering thousands of ex-servicemen and their families across the countryside.

Such government shows of power did not inspire confidence in Americans already doubting the political system and discontented and confused by it. It was obvious in the election of 1932 that voters wanted a government that would work for them and not against them. In addition to the two major parties, there were candidates representing 23 minor parties. Of these minor parties, the Socialists' candidate for president, Norman Thomas, received the highest number of votes with 885,458. This put the Communist candidates, William Z. Foster and John W. Ford, behind them in second place with 103,152 votes. These minor parties were not so much disgraced on election day as abandoned by supporters, for Americans, however disillusioned, do not like to waste their votes. They like to choose a winner, and the winner was Franklin Delano Roosevelt, a Democrat.

The communist loss in the election of 1932 had little or no effect on organizers and sympathizers, who remained active in the provocation of strikes, hunger marches, and other protests on behalf of common people. The party actually accomplished a good deal, in spite of political infighting such as that described by Cowley, for instance, among the League of Professional Groups. The league consisted of various factions, each of which wanted to save the world, each believing emphatically that its ideology was the only way to do it.

Cowley also became critical of the principle underlying proletarian literature that writing should deal only with the struggle of the workers. He often wondered if communists had any interest in the changing of seasons, making love, or the flight of birds. Cowley thought that a sense of the humane was lacking in communist ideology.

Despite several programs sponsored by Roosevelt's New Deal administration, such as the National Industrial Recovery Act (NIRA), cutting excessive hours on the job for workers and encouraging collective bargaining, and the Civilian Conservation Corps (CCC), creating jobs for the unemployed, many Americans still doubted the capitalist system of government. These people maintained the view that capitalism would eventually die even if improvements in the system were made. Although Cowley continued to remain unflagging in his political activism, he held little respect for this concept, and his preference for communism waned, primarily because of the news of Stalin's bloody tyranny in the Soviet Union.

The Dream of the Golden Mountains is not without moments of personal happiness and tragedy for Cowley. Personal items include the poet Hart Crane's suicide; Cowley's divorce from his first wife, Peggy; the sound marriage with his second wife, Muriel; and the purchase in 1936 of a barn (later remodeled) in Sherman, Connecticut, in which Cowley still lives. These occurrences play just as large a part for Cowley in the unfolding drama of the 1930's as the political speeches he delivered to the League of Professional Groups in smoky rooms packed with folding chairs.

Malcolm Cowley's memoir of the era of the Great Depression—an era in which literature and politics were hand in hand—is a highly accomplished and informative work, ambitious in scope. It is written with humility, insight, and a compassionate understanding of what transpired. Cowley has written an important book, one that portrays the dream of the common man in turbulent times, a dream that shone, lighting up the surrounding darkness.

Wally Swist

ELEANOR ROOSEVELT

Author: Lorena A. Hickok
Publisher: Dodd, Mead & Company (New York). 176 pp. $8.95
Type of work: Biography
Time: 1928–1934
Locale: New York; Washington, D.C.; Canada; Maine; the West Coast

Her friend Lorena Hickok gives a personal view of Eleanor Roosevelt's reactions to being First Lady

> *Principal personages:*
> LORENA A. HICKOK, reporter and friend of Mrs. Roosevelt
> ELEANOR ROOSEVELT, First Lady, wife of Franklin D. Roosevelt
> FRANKLIN D. ROOSEVELT, President of the United States

The full title of Lorena Hickok's work is *Eleanor Roosevelt: Reluctant First Lady,* and the subtitle is necessary if the reader is to understand the scope and purpose of this work. Unlike most biography, Hickok has not detailed the entire life of Eleanor Roosevelt, but has limited the book to a relatively small, though highly interesting, slice of her life.

After a brief backward glance to 1930, when Franklin Roosevelt was governor of New York State, Hickok's real participation in the action begins when she is assigned to cover Eleanor Roosevelt for the media. This professional assignment soon evolves into a deep personal friendship, and Lorena Hickok—"Hick" to her friends—finds herself in an excellent position for a truly intimate view of the First Family.

One of the first things she notes is Mrs. Roosevelt's reaction to her husband's public life. Far from being thrilled at the idea of being First Lady, Eleanor Roosevelt fears that her own personality, her likes and dislikes, will have to take second place to the responsibilities of her office. For example, she will have to give up the jobs she loves—teaching at New York's Todhunter School for Girls and editing the magazine *Babies—Just Babies.* However, as time passes, she manages to maintain her own identity, sometimes to the despair of the more etiquette-bound people surrounding her.

Although the real story of this book begins in 1932, Hickok also describes for the reader her very first impressions of Eleanor Roosevelt during the 1928 campaign. These recollections provide insight into the evolution of Mrs. Roosevelt's style and character in the years that follow, but also introduce a very important figure out of the past who looms large in her story, yet is never seen. This is former President Theodore Roosevelt, to whom Eleanor was related before her marriage to Franklin. Teddy is no longer a person, but an image to live up to, as are the ladies who shared his time in the White House.

Mrs. Roosevelt, reticent during this first meeting with Hick, seems to be the model of acquiescence to the fate that has made her husband governor. As the years pass and FDR wins the presidential election, her relationship with Hick becomes more frank and open, she allows her reporter friend to see the misgivings she harbors concerning public life.

Perhaps influenced by her husband's philosophy, "The only thing we have to fear is fear itself," Eleanor Roosevelt conquers her uncertainties and plunges into life at the White House with true Roosevelt spirit. With Hick trailing after as frequent White House guest and witness, Eleanor makes changes in everything from the placement of furniture to White House etiquette. Rather than consigning her guests to tedious waiting in a reception room until the First Lady's presence is announced, she takes to greeting them at the door. If she and her family must live there, she will make the White House into a real home.

The Depression is severe when FDR takes office. He is not alone in urging and creating new programs for the relief of the nation. Eleanor shares her husband's concern for the poor and acts as his eyes and ears during several expeditions to review conditions in the more seriously depressed areas. Having left the Associated Press to work for the Federal Emergency Relief Administration (FERA), Hick too learns the personal tragedies behind the cold statistics of the relief rolls.

Chief among Mrs. Roosevelt's works for the poor is the establishment of Arthurdale. During the Depression, the mining towns of West Virginia are very hard hit. People are living in shacks that modern farmers would consider unfit for pigs. Overwhelming squalor and hunger are everywhere, affecting the children most severely. The government buys an old family estate, provides seed, equipment, and limited livestock, and settles many families there. "Arthurdale," as it is called, becomes Eleanor Roosevelt's personal concern, and with the help of a Quaker charity, it becomes a success. Given a chance, the disadvantaged families are for the most part able to achieve self-sufficiency and eventually even to pay the government back for the homes and land it provided.

Like the king in the fairy tale who disguised himself to walk among his subjects, Mrs. Roosevelt enjoys taking trips with Hick like a couple of ordinary tourists. Her insistence on privacy and inconspicuousness throws the Secret Service into a panic, but she remains firm. As Hick remarks, it is impossible to guard the First Lady because she usually sets a pace too fast for the agents.

Some of Hick's fondest recollections center upon these trips. Together they motor up to Canada to tour the Gaspé Peninsula, returning through Maine. The undercover fairytale king had an easier time maintaining his anonymity in the days before photography. Sometimes it becomes simply impossible for Mrs. Roosevelt's well-known face to escape detection. A vacation on the West Coast suffers several unwelcome interruptions by the press. In San Francisco, despite their staying at a decent though modest hotel, Eleanor and Hick are found by reporters.

Toward the end of that Western trip, while staying in Oregon, Mrs. Roosevelt is compelled to submit to the kind of formal reception that she hates and has been trying to avoid. Returning to her room, she admits defeat. There is no way, without incredible effort and subterfuge, that the First Lady of the land can ever go back to being just plain Mrs. Roosevelt. Hick herself, White House intimate, has noted the attitude of awe she has developed towards FDR, although she is almost a member of the family. The mantle of the presidency covers the First Lady too. She can not go back to being an ordinary woman.

Lorena Hickok's biography of Eleanor Roosevelt is enhanced by her first-hand knowledge of the subject, enabling her to give the reader much insight and many anecdotes to help reveal the person, Eleanor Roosevelt, rather than the image. Yet, even as one appreciates the charming and personal tribute contained in this book there is speculation that the merits of the book itself are not the sole reason for its publication. This year Eleanor Roosevelt's voluminous correspondence with Lorena Hickok was released. They sometimes wrote to each other more than once a day, and the nature of these letters has given the public cause to infer a sexual element in the passionate friendship of these women. But it is to be hoped that the promise of sensationalism will not distract the reader from the inherent value of this book.

Esther M. Friesner

EMMELINE

Author: Judith Rossner
Publisher: Simon & Schuster (New York). 331 pp. $12.95
Type of work: Novel
Time: 1839–1899
Locale: Fayette, Maine; Lowell and Lynn, Massachusetts

The story of a young girl who, before her fourteenth birthday, is sent to work in the mills to earn money for her destitute family living on a farm in Maine

> *Principal characters:*
> EMMELINE MOSHER, the oldest child of Henry and Sarah Mosher
> HENRY MOSHER, an impoverished farmer in Fayette, Maine
> SARAH MOSHER, Henry's wife and the mother of nine children
> HANNAH WATKINS, Sarah's sister who lives in Lynn, Massachusetts
> ABNER WATKINS, a Lynn shoemaker and the husband of Hannah
> MRS. BASS, the woman who owns the boardinghouse in Lowell where Emmeline lives
> STEPHEN MCGUIRE, a supervisor at the mill who befriends then seduces Emmeline
> IVORY MCGUIRE, Stephen's wife and heiress to a milling fortune
> SIMON FENTON, one of Emmeline's suitors in Lowell, and Henry's employer at a sawmill
> MATTHEW GURNEY, a migrant worker who courts and finally marries Emmeline

Henry and Sarah Mosher's dairy farm in Fayette, Maine, provides enough food during a good year for the Moshers and their nine children, but during a bad year, all are hungry. The past three years have been bad ones, and with no jobs available in Fayette, the Moshers are resigned to taking drastic measures.

In late November 1839, before Emmeline turned fourteen, Sarah's sister Hannah and her husband, Abner Watkins, come from Lynn for a visit. Hannah suggests that Emmeline be sent to Lowell where she can work in the mills and keep her family from starvation. She leaves Fayette the next day in an open wagon with her aunt and uncle.

While journeying to Lowell, Emmeline meets a young woman, Florina, who is traveling with three children. She too hopes to find work in the mills. Five years earlier, when she was only fifteen, Florina married an older man named Walter, who fathered three children and then had the urge to travel west, leaving his young family to make out on their own. Emmeline is shocked by this story since at home even pregnancy was an unmentionable topic. Florina hopes to find work at Lowell but is turned away because of her children. She is frantic but Hannah tells her "We can't help you, Miss. . . . You've gotten yourself into this and you'll have to get yourself out."

Hannah's intolerant response expresses society's attitude toward young women victimized by their sex. This pathetic interval in the wagon, rather than serving as a warning for Emmeline, foreshadows her own dismal fate at Lowell. The paradox central to the entire novel is presented here: how are women raised in a totally repressive society where sex is an unspeakable word to be blamed for their sexual blunders?

Emmeline is placed in Mrs. Bass's boardinghouse and given work with one of the major cotton mills in Lowell. The work day is from five in the morning until seven at night with only two breaks, one for breakfast and another for lunch. Emmeline, younger than the rest of the girls, feels miserable and out of place. Soon, however, she is moved to the weaving room where she is under the supervision of Mr. McGuire, the first person to show Emmeline any kindness.

Stephen McGuire had come to Lowell years ago as a migrant worker. He courted Ivory Stone whose father, Elijah Stone, owned the mill. Elijah disapproved but allowed the two to marry and move into the lavish Stone house. Stephen was, accordingly, given a major post in the mill.

Stephen invites Emmeline to a Christmas tea that Ivory gives annually for family and homesick young mill workers. Mrs. Bass warns Emmeline that McGuire is evil, but Emmeline sees in him only the caring father figure that she so desperately lacks. At the tea, a sumptuous affair, Ivory, the town philanthropist, gives Emmeline a beautiful shawl. The shawl becomes a symbol to the rest of the factory girls of McGuire's affection for Emmeline, causing her to feel even more rejected by them. As a result, she turns more and more to McGuire, who eagerly comforts her.

One Sunday afternoon, Emmeline leaves the boardinghouse and heads down the road that leads to the falls and the forest, hoping to find some "country." She meets McGuire, who has gone for a ride. He hoists her onto his saddle and promises to show her the country she longs for. They kiss in the forest and then ride back to his deserted house—the rest of the family is in Boston. He drinks coffee and whisky, encouraging Emmeline to join him. Soon they are together in Ivory's bedroom. Stephen makes love to Emmeline, who knows only that she is giving him pleasure, never having learned the meaning of sex or adultery.

Stephen and Emmeline continue to meet regularly while Ivory is in Boston. She becomes a sort of doll for Stephen, naively playing his

little games and enacting his fantasies. Then at Easter time Stephen
tells Emmeline that she has been transferred to the dressing room,
where she will be under a new supervisor, Mr. Whitehead. The money
is better there, but Emmeline feels rejected. And Stephen loses interest. Whitehead detects her loneliness and asks her home for dinner one
night. While sitting around the dinner table, they are interrupted by a
visit from Mrs. Bass, who makes a scene about Emmeline's absence
that ends with her pointing at Emmeline's dress, which had recently
become tight across the stomach.

Emmeline is with child. She writes to her aunt to make plans for
leaving Lowell immediately. McGuire, whom she never again sees,
gives her more than a year's wages, money she can mail home monthly
so that her family will never suspect she has lost her job.

The Watkinses take Emmeline to Lynn, where she helps Abner with
his shoes. Abner, embarrassed by the arrangement, refuses to set eyes
on Emmeline until she has delivered. Thus, she spends her pregnancy
in hiding. When the baby is born, before Emmeline has even seen it,
Hannah gives it to a couple traveling west.

Emmeline returns to Fayette. Thanks to the money she has sent,
conditions have improved for the Mosher family. Henry has found an
outside job working at Simon Fenton's lumber mill, and the other
children are old enough to help out with farm work. Emmeline is unable to tell anyone—not the pastor, not her mother—just what she had
done to earn her wages.

Twenty years pass, and all the Mosher children have married except
Emmeline, now thirty-four, who has resigned herself to a life of celi-
bacy. Simon Fenton, who insists on paying Henry his wages even
though he has broken his leg and is unable to work at the mill, courts
Emmeline. He offers financial security to the Moshers, and Emmeline,
responding to her sense of duty, would certainly have married this man
for whom she felt no love had not Matthew Gurney come along.

Matthew, a migrant worker hired by Fenton as part of a road crew,
moves in as a boarder at the Moshers'. He and Emmeline are immediately drawn to one another despite his being considerably younger. His
worldliness, his good humor, and his warmth bring to life again that
part of Emmeline that seemed to have died back in Lynn when her
baby was sent away. Henry grudgingly consents to their marriage and
gives them a piece of land on which to build a home. They are blissfully
devoted to one another.

Not long after the marriage, Sarah Mosher becomes very ill. The
entire family is sent for, including the Watkinses. Hannah is delighted
to learn that Emmeline has married at last, but her delight turns to
horror when she hears the young man's name, for she had given

Emmeline's child to a family named Gurney. Matthew, who had tried to keep his age a secret, discloses his birthday. He is Emmeline's lost child.

Horrified, Emmeline tries to drown herself in their pond but is rescued. Matthew leaves Fayette, but Emmeline stays, deciding it is better to live openly with one's sins than to try and hide them among strangers. Rejected by her family, she spends the rest of her life in the cabin that Matthew built, receiving from time to time not a letter, since Matthew never learned to write, but newspapers from various towns throughout the country. In the winter of 1899, a particularly cold one, Emmeline dies of starvation.

Judith Rossner's novel is based on a historical incident told her by a ninety-four-year-old resident of Fayette. It matters little whether the facts are entirely accurate. Her depiction of a sexually repressed and biased society presents a startling view of life in 19th-century New England. Florina and Emmeline are not unique in their predicaments; they are not "bad women." Emmeline had learned the Ten Commandments by heart but when she asked the meaning of "adultery," she was told she would learn when it was time. Clearly she did not learn soon enough. Thoughts about sexuality were considered, like Emmeline during her pregnancy, dangerous, and hidden in the back room or the attic.

Rossner's narration of the novel, which is almost entirely from Emmeline's point of view, is elliptical when dealing with sex. The reader is informed that Stephen has carried Emmeline to the chaise lounge and then she is waking from a sleep. The sleep could be metaphoric, since Emmeline does not possess the vocabulary to confront what she has experienced. Thus, what is an almost Victorian approach to sex becomes appropriate in a novel dealing with sexual repression and avoidance.

While Gothic in some of its conventions, *Emmeline* is a story well told. Rossner's recreation of life in a mill town is romanticized at times, yet the story is compelling and the problems faced by the heroine only too authentic.

Elizabeth Lubin

FALLING IN PLACE

Author: Ann Beattie
Publisher: Random House (New York). 342 pp. $10.95
Type of work: Novel
Time: Summer 1979
Locale: New York City; New Haven; suburban Connecticut

*A human comedy of young adults of the sixties grown up, of the nihilistic
confusion of those who have come of age in the seventies, and of the insensitivity and boredom of their children*

Principal characters:
> JOHN KNAPP, an anxiety-ridden man, about forty years old
> LOUISE, John's wife
> MARY, John's fifteen-year-old daughter
> JOHN JOEL, John's ten-year-old son
> BRANDT, John's youngest son, about seven years old
> NINA, John's twenty-five-year-old mistress
> NICK, John's co-worker and confidant
> CYNTHIA FORREST, a graduate student at Yale who lives in
> New Haven
> PETER SPANGLE, Cynthia's boyfriend and an old friend of
> Nina's
> PARKER, an overweight and sadistic contemporary of John
> Joel's

Falling in Place opens with two of John's children, the ten-year-old
overweight John Joel and his sister, Mary, having an argument, exchanging typically adolescent jibes and innuendos. Mary, who is in
summer school for having failed English, is intelligent enough, but she
is distracted and bored and would rather be thinking of her heartthrob,
the rock star Peter Frampton. Cynthia Forrest, Mary's summer school
teacher, lives in New Haven, hates her summer school job, and is
awaiting the return of her boyfriend, Peter Spangle, who has gone off
to Spain to fetch his brother from an overextended vacation. Spangle's
mother calls Cynthia with unnerving regularity, and Cynthia has no
choice but to entertain the older woman's babbling. As if her present
circumstance were not depressing enough, she encounters in a laun-
dromat a magician who develops an instant crush on her and tries to
entertain her with inane magic tricks.

John Knapp, the protagonist of the novel, is terribly depressed and
guilt-ridden. He is entertaining thoughts of leaving his family and moving in with Nina, his twenty-five-year-old mistress, but these very
thoughts leave him fitful and anxious. Nina lives in New York City and
works at the Lord and Taylor department store. John's affair with her
is conveniently removed from his home life in suburban Connecticut,

and yet he cannot refrain from speaking continuously to Nina of his family.

Threads of the story begin to weave together as John takes John Joel into New York one day. The two stop at John's mother's house in Rye, just outside of the city. Like Mrs. Spangle, John's mother is a petulant and querulous woman. John Joel, whose greatest interest in coming to New York lies in getting as many free candy bars as possible, is taken by Nick, John's office friend, to see a show of Segal's sculptures at the Whitney Museum. Segal's frozen, white sculptures of people in seeming boredom or despair become a motif of the novel. John, meanwhile, suffers from moments of increasing anxiety over seemingly trivial matters. He constantly seeks out Nina in the midst of these anxiety attacks. John believes that only she and Nick can understand the depth of his anxieties, that they are the only ones who could reasonably reassure him.

Mary and her "cool" friend Angela exchange intimacies, makeup, and fan-magazine talk as they prepare to go to a party, while John consults with Cynthia over his daughter's lack of progress in summer school. Cynthia has been having the students read Thackeray's *Vanity Fair,* and Mary is not the only student unmotivated by the material. John, trying to impress Cynthia with his understanding of Mary's intellectual perspicacity, tells her of Mary's epigrammatic sketch of the entire work: "Things just fall into place," she says. This, obviously, has more meaning for John than for Mary, or, even, Cynthia.

John takes Cynthia out to lunch and has a great deal of difficulty interacting with her. Cynthia reminds him of Nina. Both women are intelligent and attractive. Both are working at jobs beneath their capacities. Conversation between the two shifts to a personal level. They become extremely self-conscious and end their meeting awkwardly.

Another setting shift focuses attention on John Joel and his friend Parker. Like John Joel, Parker is almost obese. Both are cynical, cruel, and oblivious to the value of money or their parents' possessions. Their relationship seems to be based on their mutual regard for junk food and on Parker's continual baiting of John Joel. Gradually Parker's irrational nature is revealed. Among other things, he is sure that his family is spying on him, and so will allow no one in his room. He keeps a collection of perverse and pornographic comic books under his mattress. He regularly rummages through his parents' keepsake boxes, has put a pinhole in his mother's diaphragm, and has found and hidden a gun that was his grandfather's. John Joel is his regular audience for these revelations.

In the meantime John has separated from Louise, has taken his youngest son, Brandt, with him, and is living with his mother in Rye.

His relationship with Nina has intensified, and he has become increasingly dependent upon her. Louise, who remains in Connecticut, stoically shoulders the burden of caring for Mary and John Joel. She tries, without much success, to cajole them into a more lively attitude. Cynthia continues to keep her vigil for Spangle, entertaining the increasingly predictable calls from his mother.

When John receives a call at the office from Louise asking him to come home for dinner that night, John is sure she is going to ask for a divorce and does not know how to react to the potential situation. When he arrives he finds the house deserted, and the police waiting to ask him questions. John Joel has shot Mary with Parker's gun. Both children have been taken to the hospital, Mary to have her wound attended to, and John Joel to be put in psychiatric confinement. John and Louise return from the hospital in shock. There John finds a note on the kitchen table headed, "Petition for a Vacation at Nantucket." He realizes that Louise was not planning to ask for a divorce but for a family vacation.

John gets in his car and begins to drive aimlessly. As dawn approaches he arrives at Nina's apartment, anticipating her comfort and understanding, but finding Nina with Peter Spangle, who has just returned from Spain and has decided to stay the night in New York. The two have stayed up most of the night smoking pot, and their disarray compounds John's sense of shock. Spangle asserts that he and Nina did not sleep together and promply leaves. It takes John some time to tell Nina what, exactly, has happened.

The ensuing days are a torment for everyone. Cynthia, in New Haven, has not heard from Spangle. Louise accuses John of irresponsibility for leaving as he did. The two visit the hospital, seeing each of their children separately. Nina feels a guilty responsibility for having broken up John's family. Spangle continues to wander around New York, unsure of whether he wants to return to Cynthia.

John sees a family therapist who claims that John Joel has acted out John's desire to destroy his family. Distraught and depressed, he continues to make frequent calls to Nick and Nina. Under examination John Joel claims he did not believe the gun was loaded. Parker, whose gun John Joel used, remains blasé about the whole affair. Mary has reacted to the shooting with a strange equanimity. It seems somehow to have resolved much of the tension between her and John Joel. Although John Joel has similar feelings, he remains confused.

Nina, meanwhile, has begun to feel the burden of the many visits from both Spangle and John. When John and Spangle arrive simultaneously and commence to ruminate with each other, Nina decides she has had enough and kicks them both out. She then departs for the country to gain some perspective on the situation. John and Louise go to the coast for a vacation and a last-ditch attempt to repair their failing marriage. As it becomes clear that their marriage has failed, Louise indicates that she is contemplating moving into a New York apartment with a friend who has also separated from her husband.

John's friend Nick visits and tells him that he has seen Nina back in New York and that she wants to talk with him. John, desperately afraid that Nina wants to put an end to the whole affair, calls her and finds, happily, that she wants to marry him. In the closing scene of the book, Cynthia, in New Haven, receives proposals from both a friend of Spangle and the magician. As she throws her hands up in frustration at the absurdity of the situation, she turns and sees Spangle, sitting on her doorstep, waving, smiling, returned. Things have, in their way, fallen in place.

Critics have acclaimed *Falling in Place,* comparing it to the work of Gustave Flaubert. It would not be difficult to argue that Beattie shares similar powers of observation and comic wit. One must question, however, whether the book will have the same immediacy or impact in ten years. One would almost expect, because of its remarkable attention to the mood and factual detail of the 1970's, that there would be an annotated version of *Falling in Place* published in 1990.

It has become a hallmark of Beattie's style that she presents little or no physical description of her characters. The reader has no idea, for example, of even the color of John's or Nina's hair. By working against the accepted convention of attending to the physical description of characters in novels, Beattie is able to focus attention on the forces and events to which the characters react. In so doing, she creates a both believable and compelling portrait of the passivity and interiority of our times.

D. W. Faulkner

FANNY

Author: Erica Jong (1942–   )
Publisher: New American Library (New York). 505 pp. $12.95
Type of work: Novel
Time: Circa 1724
Locale: Country England, London, and the high seas

The trials and travels of a high-spirited 18th-century woman

Principal characters:
>   FANNY, or Frances Bellars, also known as Fanny Hackabout-
>   Jones
>   LORD BELLARS OF LYMEWORTH, Fanny's stepfather
>   ISOBEL WHITE, a Wise Woman of the woods and suspected
>   witch
>   LANCELOT ROBINSON, leader of the Merry Men
>   MOTHER COXTART, Madam of Fanny's brothel
>   SUSANNAH, Fanny's servant and trusted friend
>   HORATIO, Lancelot's learned and heroic companion
>   BELINDA, Fanny's daughter
>   ANNE BONNY, the notorious and beautiful female pirate

Set in 1724 and written entirely in imitation of 18th-century English,
Fanny opens with Frances Bellars' idyllic young girlhood at Lymeworth, in the English countryside. The stepchild of a wealthy but
blighted marriage (Lord Bellars' devotion to gaming and whoring causing him to live away in London much of the time), young Fanny secretly aspires to become a great poetess and spends much of her time
poring over the classics in her stepfather's library. The impending visit
of the great poet Alexander Pope briefly reunites the family and fills
the still-naive Fanny with great anticipation. When Pope arrives, she
is disappointed to encounter an old, deformed, and lecherous relic of a
man. Having met her first "Great Man," she learns immediately that it
is "easier to be a Great Man in one's work than in one's life."

A series of remarkable events transpires during Pope's visit. Having
retired from the guest of honor's dinner, Fanny is visited first in her
chamber by Pope, whose advances she repels, then by her stepbrother
Daniel, whom she also thwarts, and, finally, by Lord Bellars himself,
whom she has considerably more difficulty keeping at bay. It is only
when he dazzles her with a great oratorical and physical performance
(threatening, at one point, to run himself through with his sword
"rather than dishonour you") that Fanny succumbs to her first sexual
encounter. Starry-eyed and love-struck, she is shattered the next day
to discover a letter from Lord Bellars to his lover in London in which
he delightedly relates the conquest of his stepdaughter and the clever
strategies employed, calling the encounter "Capital Sport!" Crest-

fallen, 17-year-old Fanny decides to leave Lymeworth forever and seek her fortunes in London, a decision that leads her into a series of trying and edifying adventures.

Disguised as a young man, she travels the country roads astride her beloved horse, Lustre, and at a small-town fair is quickly robbed of her steed and much of her earlier confidence. On foot in the woods, she encounters Isobel, a Wise Woman of the Woods, and Isobel's friend Joan. She is taken in and cared for, and instructed in a few of the ways of witchcraft. After accepting the challenge of initiation, as well as a red garter for luck, she is a horrified witness to the sudden and brutal massacre of her new friends by attackers on Stonehenge Downs. Forced to flee, she boards a stage for London. On her way, she and her fellow passengers are waylaid by Lancelot Robinson and his Merry Men. Allowed to join their band, along with Paul (a highly educated black man who is immediately dubbed Horatio by Lancelot, and who becomes his most trusted companion), she takes sick soon after and is nursed back to health by Lancelot himself, who tells her of his adventurous life, his dreams for a utopia, and his aversion to women. Fanny quickly falls in love with Lancelot, who fancies himself a modern-day Robin Hood, and journeys with him by river to London, barely escaping with her life as Lancelot and his Merry Men are captured on the Thames.

Alone, friendless, and penniless in London, a desperate Fanny is taken in by a seemingly kind baker who turns out to be Madam Coxtart, the wily and exacting mistress of a well-known brothel. Fanny finds herself a captive of necessity and begins a life of whoredom. Quickly stripped of the last vestiges of her naivety, she learns she is pregnant from her earlier encounter with Lord Bellars and determines that she must somehow lose the babe or risk being thrown out into the streets of London. After painfully and unsuccessfully attempting an abortion, she learns that Lancelot is a captive in Newgate Prison and in great distress. Visiting him, she determines to improve his lot and redoubles her efforts at Coxtart's brothel, sending the money she earns to Lancelot. Just as she learns that he is planning an escape, Fanny encounters at a masquerade party Lord Bellars, who, unaware of her real identity, falls madly in love with her. Although she plays Bellars along, she believes her fate, and that of her babe, is with Lancelot. When she learns of his imminent escape, Fanny decides to journey with him to the New World.

Her plans, however, are discovered and betrayed by a jealous whore from the brothel, and she is imprisoned in her room while Lancelot sets sail. Distraught and worried for the future of her unborn baby, she gives in to Lord Bellars' generosity and allows herself to be kept in a handsome cottage, all the while remaining disguised to him. There she bears her child most painfully and is saved only by the tender ministrations of Isobel, who has miraculously reappeared as midwife. Her milk embittered by the very potions that saved her life, Fanny is forced to employ a wet nurse, Prudence Feral, whose gluttonous habits and uncaring attitude make life difficult for everyone. Prudence kidnaps the infant, Belinda, and sets sail for parts unknown aboard the *Cassandra*. Horrified but determined, Fanny and her servant Susannah give chase, bribing their way aboard the *Hopewell*, where they learn many lessons, most of them unpleasant, about life at sea. Forced to perform perverted acts for Captain Whitehead, Susannah despairs and jumps overboard to her death while Fanny remains determined to find her missing child. When the *Hopewell* is attacked by pirates, Fanny is delighted to learn that her rescuers are none other than Lancelot and what remains of his Merry Men. Lancelot, still determined to find his utopia, has become a pirate. While he remains physically aloof to Fanny, he promises to pursue the *Cassandra* and Fanny's child.

It is in the South Atlantic that Fanny encounters the beautiful and clever female pirate, Anne Bonny. Until this time, having performed as well as any man, Fanny has regarded herself as unique among pirates. When she comes face to face with a competitor, she is immediately jealous. Only when Anne Bonny reaches out to her, during one of the many lustful revels that punctuate the novel, does she come to admire and respect her as a true woman of the world. They part fast friends, amid much hugging and well-wishes for the future. It is only after she has gone that Lancelot realizes he has been taken for a fool, for Bonny's men have emptied their ship of booty and disappeared. Furious, Lancelot nevertheless continues his pursuit of the *Cassandra*, finally overtaking the ship during a great storm. Belinda is rescued but in saving the child, Horatio is killed, plunging Lancelot into grief and shattering at last his dreams. Tired and bereft, Lancelot and Fanny journey back to England and Lymeworth, where Fanny learns that Lord Bellars has died, along with her stepbrother, Daniel. A letter from the late Lord Bellars reveals him to be Fanny's actual father, and Isobel, once again in the right spot at the right time, as her natural mother. Shocked and more than a little horrified that her daughter is the product of an incestuous coupling, Fanny is nonetheless made heiress of Lymeworth. There, her love for Lancelot continues to blossom, and although they never marry, she settles on the estate and into a successful career as a writer, finding happiness and fulfillment as a woman at last.

Fanny, as a novel, is every bit as ambitious as its heroine. Vastly entertaining, it captures the tumultuous time of its setting through a deft mixture of language, detail, and predictably satisfying twists of plot. Above all else, it is the language that dominates the style of the book; written in 18th-century style the language establishes a tone and humor that run true and consistently throughout the novel. Fanny's amorous adventures, which are both plentiful and explicit, are puckishly rendered, the language itself lending a playful licentiousness that would not have been possible through conventional prose. As a bawdy tale it succeeds, the lustful obsessions of the characters made all the more understandable in the harsh and sometimes swiftly cruel times Jong so artfully presents.

What is less artfully presented, although certainly of central interest in the novel, is the unceasing feminist yearnings of Fanny. The reader is reminded throughout of the difficulty a woman has of getting ahead in a man's world, as well as Fanny's determination to do just that and more. In this, Fanny stands a little unfairly above her contemporaries —except perhaps for Anne Bonny—in a most astounding, and somewhat unrealistic, way. Fanny and her ambitions, however laudable, seem anachronistic in the times in which they are portrayed, making her contemporaries, male and female, seem all the more boorish. While it is all great fun, and certainly cleverly done, Fanny seems a little miscast as a feminist.

Still, her recounting of the ordeal of childbearing and of female biology in general is often illuminating and filled with some undeniable truths, not the least of which is a woman's unique ability to bear children ("because she, not they, must bear the Great Belly that assures all Humankind of its Survival!"). Similarly, Fanny's (and Isobel's) belief in a Goddess rather than a God, as well as her insistence in amending Lancelot's code to include women as well as blacks, serves to emphasize the unrelenting theme that a woman's lot, while inexorably cast with the lots of men, is unique and infinitely more complicated.

David Alvarez

THE FIFTH HORSEMAN

Authors: Larry Collins and Dominique Lapierre
Publisher: Simon & Schuster (New York). 478 pp. $13.95
Type of work: Novel
Time: The present
Locale: New York City, Washington, D.C.

A novel about an attempt by nuclear terrorists to blackmail the United States with the threat of the destruction of New York City

Principal characters:
THE PRESIDENT OF THE UNITED STATES
MUAMMAR AL-QADDAFI, President of Libya
ANGELO ROCCHIA, a New York City detective
LAILA, beautiful Palestinian terrorist
KAMAL, her brother, another terrorist
WHALID, their brother, a scientist

The Fifth Horseman opens with the President of the United States, who although unnamed clearly resembles Jimmy Carter, evidently early in a second term, as he begins Sunday dinner in the White House. He is interrupted by a call from Jack Eastman, the President's assistant for national security affairs, who brings him a disturbing document: a transcript of a tape recording delivered that day to the White House gate. The voice on the tape identifies the speaker as Muammar al-Qaddafi, President of Libya. His message is terse: Libya has developed a nuclear bomb and smuggled it into Manhattan. If the United States does not compel Israel to remove its settlements from the Arab lands seized in 1967 within forty-eight hours, he will cause the bomb to detonate. Attached is a design of the device itself. Eastman reports that the voice has not as yet been confirmed to be Qaddafi's. However, a report on the bomb plan shows its design to be viable.

Meanwhile, Laila Dajani, the woman who delivered the tape, is flying from Washington to New York. She is a Palestinian terrorist, traveling as a buyer for a luxurious Mideastern fashion shop. Having insinuated herself into the New York jet set, she is able to travel unsuspected and now returns to an obscure Manhattan warehouse where her brothers, the scientist Whalid and the militant fanatic Kamal, are at work. After establishing radio-beam contact via satellite with Qaddafi's command center in Libya, the trio have completed work on the detonation device—it may be detonated either from the site or by remote control by Qaddafi.

In Washington, the National Security Council holds an emergency meeting to consider the situation. It has been determined that the design sent was not that of a simple atomic bomb, but of a hydrogen bomb capable of destroying nearly the entire city. This claim is met with incredulity, for an H-bomb is simply too complex for any nonindustrial country to develop. A second communication from Qaddafi proposes to prove his boast; if the United States will focus attention upon a certain point in the Libyan desert at midnight Washington time, they will receive the confirmation they need. As the council watches the site through the television camera of a spy satellite orbiting above, the fireball of a thermonuclear explosion blooms upon the desert floor, confirming their worst fears.

The novel then moves in a flashback to Paris a year earlier, where President Giscard D'Estaing announced to his cabinet that French physicists have created a pioneering technique to produce a controlled fusion reaction. Then the scientist who developed the process is found murdered; the plans he was carrying have vanished.

The reader then learns the story of the three Dajanis, born in Palestine but now scattered in different countries. Kamal, a terrorist working under Libyan direction, recruits sister Laila. She, in turn, is to gain the cooperation of their elder brother Whalid, who has become a successful physicist and is living peacefully in France. Whalid, although opposed to violence, is at last coerced into helping to steal plutonium from a French nuclear installation. They are caught, and all three are deported. Whalid's French wife, despairing at the news, throws herself out of a window. Kamal cunningly convinces Whalid that she had been murdered by the French police, thus gaining his cooperation in their later efforts to build a bomb.

The scene returns to Washington, where the President has decided that America's European allies, the U.S.S.R., and above all Israel deserve to be apprised of the situation. He informs Menachim Begin of Qaddafi's threat and demand, and Begin immediately convenes his own security council. They swiftly resolve not to let considerations of New York's fate affect their own vigilance in defending themselves and decide after some debate to launch an immediate and massive nuclear strike against Libya. A high-ranking Israeli officer tips off the United States, however, and only minutes before Israeli jets are to fire their nuclear missiles, a message is received from the U.S.S.R. that it will annihilate Israel should the Israelis go through with their strike. In the final moment, Israel backs down.

In Washington, the President and his aides consider the situation. It is decided that an attack on Qaddafi's command center would not be advisable: it is too likely that the hidden bomb is set to explode unless a countermanding order is sent from Qaddafi. For the same reason, they cannot rely on jamming any radio message coming from Libya. The full complement of America's security forces—the military, the

FBI, and the New York City police—is mobilized to locate the bomb as rapidly as possible. As Qaddafi has threatened to detonate the device if any mention of its presence is made in the news or if he learns of any attempt to evacuate New York, the President decides to conduct these efforts in utmost secrecy. Although military specialists are aware of the situation, the New York police are not—they are told that a canister of chlorine gas has been hidden in New York and must be located.

Angelo Rocchia, a veteran detective of the New York City police, middle-aged, a widower, and father of a retarded young girl, is among the detectives dispatched to follow leads concerning the means of arrival of the bomb into New York without knowing what it is he is seeking. As helicopters and unmarked vans are dispatched throughout Manhattan, searching with radiation-detecting devices for tell-tale emissions that would reveal the presence of a thermonuclear device, detectives move quietly through the docks of Brooklyn and the Bronx, checking ships' manifests of recent cargo arrivals from the Mideast for records of unusually heavy or suspicious shipments. Angelo and the young FBI agent he is working with, an earnest Midwesterner named Rand, begin going through recent records. Angelo finds one shipment that, although it does not seem heavy enough to be what they are seeking, appears suspicious to him. Over his partner's protests, he checks the license number of the van that picked the shipment up, and discovers that it was rented with a stolen credit card.

The President makes contact by video phone with Qaddafi, but is unable to sway the cool dictator by appeals either to reason or to mercy and finds his efforts to stall for time or instill doubts in Qaddafi easily deflected. The Soviets, however, are able to gain one single concession from Qaddafi: he agrees to extend his deadline by six hours. When Qaddafi sends the radio signal cancelling the detonation command to the bomb, it is picked up by the Americans.

With the dubious Rand in tow, Angelo Rocchia follows his lead down a trail through the New York underworld, talking to pickpockets, mob-controlled dock loaders, fences, and male prostitutes as he seeks any information he can find on the rented truck that carried the bomb from the docks to its hiding-place. They are able to narrow the area where the van could have gone to a large rectangle within Greenwich Village. The entire area is cordoned off and flooded with agents, who conduct a house-to-house search with geiger counters.

The three terrorists meanwhile have retreated to a safe house in upstate New York to await the detonation. When the original deadline passes with neither explosion nor news of an Israeli withdrawal from Palestine, Kamal flies into a rage, guessing correctly that the peace-loving Whalid had done something to prevent the bomb from detonating. Before their sister's horrified eyes, he kills Whalid with a vicious karate chop. He finds in Whalid's pocket a cassette that Whalid removed from the detonating system. He and Laila race back to New York City in their car, intent upon restoring the cassette and detonating the bomb by hand.

The climax of the novel is a second-by-second chase between the terrorists and the police. Kamal gets through the cordon by stealing an ambulance, but he is seen by Angelo, who pursues him to the warehouse containing the bomb. In a final shoot-out Angelo kills Kamal as the terrorist is preparing to rearm the bomb, but Rand is killed as he comes to Angelo's aid.

The Fifth Horseman is the first novel by two celebrated writers of nonfiction, a thriller of the type that means to suggest "This could happen tomorrow." It relies less upon internal logic and consistency than upon its resemblance to the "real world" of today and upon the shock the reader should experience upon reflecting how easily the book's events could really happen. Despite the authors' reputation for serious historical works (including *Is Paris Burning?*), *The Fifth Horseman* is remarkably similar to unabashedly commercial novels of intrigue and near-war. The novel's composition is glib and schematic, reminiscent of other candidates for best-sellerdom in such respects. Most of the story's subplots and secondary conflicts are sentimental and freighted with clichés, such as Angelo's girlfriend, a beautiful, tough-minded investigative reporter for *The New York Times* who is carrying Angelo's baby and who eventually stumbles upon the secret of the government's covert bomb-hunt. Other ingredients, such as the world-weary cop's reflections on his early days of idealism and vigor, or the element of exotic sex in the world where crime and high society converge, confirm the novel's essentially commercial nature. Nevertheless, *The Fifth Horseman* is undemanding and well-researched.

Gregory Feeley

FIRE IN THE STREETS

Author: Milton Viorst
Publisher: Simon & Schuster (New York). 591 pp. $14.95
Type of work: History
Time: 1956–1970
Locale: The United States, especially in the South and on college campuses

A history of social protest in the United States during the 1960's, told through the experiences of some of the major black and student activists in the struggles for civil rights and against the Vietnam War

Principal personages
> E. D. NIXON, an organizer of the 1955–56 Montgomery bus boycott
> JAMES FARMER, the leader of the first Freedom Rides in 1961
> TOM HAYDEN, a Students For a Democratic Society leader and ideologue
> BAYARD RUSTIN, the planner of the 1963 March on Washington
> STOKELY CARMICHAEL, an advocate of Black Power and leader of the Student Non-violent Coordinating Committee
> JERRY RUBIN, the leader of protests at the 1968 Democratic convention

Fire in the Streets chronicles the protests of those Americans who found the established governmental institutions unresponsive to their needs and concerns. Blacks and college students were most visible in the demonstrations of the 1960's, and Milton Viorst focuses upon their activities. Viorst devotes his first chapters to the "new expectations" of blacks and the "new values" of students that developed during the 1950's.

The 1954 Supreme Court decision in *Brown* v. *Board of Education* ruled that segregation in the public schools is unconstitutional. Blacks hoped that decision would abolish the remaining barriers to racial equality in the United States. The hopes sparked by the 1954 decision were dashed when it quickly became clear that neither the courts, nor any other governmental organ, would enforce the equal rights of blacks. E. D. Nixon was head of the Montgomery, Alabama, chapter of the National Association for the Advancement of Colored People. Nixon believed that rights could only be won through the use of organized strength on the part of blacks. He organized a boycott by blacks of the segregated Montgomery buses, enlisting the support of Martin Luther King, Jr. The boycott brought a brutal reaction from Montgomery whites, finally forcing federal government intervention. The strategy of nonviolent resistance, developed by King and Nixon in Montgomery, proved to be a useful tactic for enlisting support from white liberals and for goading the courts into upholding and enforcing the constitutional rights of blacks.

At the same time that blacks began to challenge segregation, some young whites, mostly middle-class college students, opposed the conformity and emphasis upon material success prevalent in the 1950's. The writers of the Beat Generation portrayed a lifestyle that was adopted by students on a mass scale a decade later. The beatniks of the 1950's were for the most part apolitical. The influence of the civil rights struggles and the horror of the Vietnam War forced white students to look beyond their own lives and challenge the political priorities of their government.

Most of the tactical developments in 1960's protest were pioneered by those involved in civil rights. John Lewis, a student in Nashville, organized sit-ins at the lunch counters of department stores. Those stores refused to serve blacks or to hire blacks for any but the most menial jobs. Lewis's actions aroused the hatred and violence of many Nashville whites. However, scenes of blacks peacefully sitting-in and being arrested or subjected to mob violence became regular features on television news programs. The pattern was repeated when James Farmer, the head of the Congress of Racial Equality, led groups of whites and blacks on Freedom Rides throughout the South, challenging the segregation of interstate travel. President Kennedy had been reluctant to use the power of the federal government to enforce court orders outlawing segregation. The Kennedy administration finally acted, in large part from the fear that failure to protect the Freedom Riders would hurt America's image in the Cold War competition with the Soviet Union.

The 1963 March on Washington brought 250,000 people to the Capitol in an interracial demonstration of support for civil rights and the principle of nonviolent protest. The momentum created by the march and by President Kennedy's assassination led to the passage of the 1964 Civil Rights Act. After that success, attention of the Johnson administration turned increasingly to the Vietnam War. Liberal support for strong laws to end segregation did not continue with equal force to support economic equality for blacks. Despair and anger led to riots in many American cities. Black students of the Student Nonviolent Coordinating Committee focused on registering black voters in the South. Stokely Carmichael saw the organization of Black Power, able to press political and economic demands, as the best strategy to replace nonviolent protests, which had become less effective.

White students were influenced by the civil rights movement. Early student protests concentrated on modifying restrictive college rules. Radicals, such as Tom Hayden, were critical of liberals for what they saw as passive support of Southern racism and other cruelties of an

American power elite. The Port Huron Statement, the manifesto of the Students for a Democratic Society (SDS), utilized Marxist theory to point to the limits of American democracy and to argue for a broadening of political and economic rights to challenge the rule of the narrow power elite of businessmen, military leaders, and government officials.

The arguments of Hayden and other SDS organizers became meaningful for many students as the Vietnam War expanded and they were faced with the danger of being drafted. Most campus demonstrations were directed against the government's escalation of the war. However, American actions in Vietnam convinced some students of the validity of the larger radical critique of American society. Some of the most effective protests were planned by Jerry Rubin. He sought to combine violence with a satirical attack on American militarism. Rubin's protests in Chicago, at the 1968 Democratic convention, provoked the police brutality he had predicted. Less militant opponents of the war, already disappointed that the campaign to deny Lyndon Johnson renomination had led to the choice of Hubert Humphrey, who also supported the war, saw the police at Chicago as further reason to despair of American electoral politics.

Fire in the Streets concludes with the shootings at Kent State University. Viorst argues that the killing of four student demonstrators by National Guard troops signaled an unwillingness of the government to tolerate further dissent. The anti-war movement, already plagued by ideological schisms and weakened by the ending of the draft, which removed the personal interest students had in halting the war, declined in the face of government repression. Black militants had already been the objects of police murders. The Nixon administration rejected further civil rights advances in favor of "benign neglect" of blacks and veiled appeals for support from racists in both the North and the South.

Viorst effectively presents the sources of black and student protests. He analyzes the precedents that influenced radicals of the 1960's and explains the reasons why the civil rights and anti-war movements evolved as they did. Viorst is at his best in presenting the biographies of the individuals he chose to represent the many who work to change American society. His history allows the protesters to speak for themselves, revealing the meaning and value of their actions.

Richard Lachmann

FIRESTARTER

Author: Stephen King (1947–   )
Publisher: Viking Press (New York). 428 pp. $13.95
Type of work: Novel
Time: The present
Locale: Various parts of the United States

Eight-year-old Charlie McGee and her father, both of whom have unusual psychic powers, are pursued by a U.S. government agency called the Shop

Principal characters:
CHARLIE MCGEE, the firestarter
ANDY MCGEE, Charlie's father
VICKY MCGEE, Charlie's mother
"CAP" HOLLISTER, head of the Shop
JOHN RAINBIRD, the Shop's chief assassin
NORMAN and IRV MANDERS, a couple who befriend the McGees

Firestarter is the story of eight-year-old Charlie (Charlene) McGee, her father Andy, and their involvement with a near-autonomous U.S. government agency, the Division of Scientific Intelligence, fondly called the Shop. The Shop is interested in Charlie and her father because they both possess various psionic powers—telekinesis, mental domination, telepathy, and precognition. But most important, the Shop wants Charlie because she is able to start fires simply by thinking about it. She is a pyrokinetic.

As college students Charlie's parents took part in a government-sponsored program monitoring the effects of a drug known as Lot Six. Both Andy and Vicky McGee came out of the experiment with enhanced psychic abilities: Andy is able to "push" people into doing what he wants, and Vicky has the ability to know beforehand when some things are going to happen (precognition) and the ability to move objects with her mind (telekinesis). The McGees first become aware of Charlie's power when Andy "*felt* it pass him—the invisible, incredible bolt of death from his daughter's mind. It felt like the backwash of warm air from a highballing subway train, when it's summertime. A soft soundless passage of warm air and then the teddy bear was on fire."

Over the years the Shop has kept tabs on those who took part in the Lot Six project. Most of the other participants are dead, many from suicide, or have gone mad, and now the Shop is particularly interested in Charlie. Cap Hollister, the Shop's director, wants Charlie so that she may be studied, her power harnessed "for the good of the country," and to provide leverage with stubborn Senate appropriations committees. The Shop will stop at nothing to get hold of Charlie. In one of its first attempts to kidnap her from her Ohio home, her mother is brutally tortured and murdered, and Charlie is taken. Andy rescues Charlie after following her abductors and using his power to push people. For the next two years he and Charlie are on the run.

In a small town outside of Albany, New York, with Shop agents closing in, Andy decides that he and Charlie should hide out at a remote cottage that his grandfather once owned in southeastern Vermont. They are helped by a farmer and his wife, Irv and Norma Manders, and finally are able to elude Shop agents only after Charlie is forced to turn her attention toward them. "For a moment he [the Shop agent] was all there, screaming silently under a transparent caul of flame, and then his features were blending, merging, running like tallow. [He] was a flaming scarecrow." But Charlie finds that she is not able to control her terrible power sufficiently and she also feels guilty about using it.

Driving a jeep supplied by Manders and traveling on back roads, Andy and Charlie bypass the Shop's roadblocks and get to Tashmore, Vermont, where they spend the winter. Charlie turns eight and Andy has some time to think about their predicament and what to do about it. But the Shop is everywhere, and Andy's and Charlie's whereabouts are discovered. The Shop intercepts Andy's letters, among them one to *The New York Times,* and makes plans to capture them both. Cap Hollister has realized after the Manders Farm incident that for the present Andy McGee is just as important to his plans as Charlie is.

Hollister assigns his most deadly and effective agent, John Rainbird, to capture the McGees. Rainbird is a one-eyed, six-foot-ten-inch, half-Cherokee Indian, who is interested in death. As spring comes and the McGees prepare to leave Vermont, they are drugged by Rainbird and his crew and taken to Shop headquarters in Virginia, where they are kept on drugs and coaxed into giving demonstrations of their particular abilities. Charlie, however, refuses to start fires and Andy finds that the push has left him, at least temporarily.

In the meantime Rainbird has become fascinated with Charlie McGee. He blackmails Cap to agree that he will give Charlie to Rainbird when the Shop is through with her because Rainbird has plans of his own for her. Rainbird desires to kill Charlie while "looking carefully into her eyes all the time. And then, if her eyes give him the signal he had looked for for so long, perhaps he would follow her." In his twisted way Rainbird also loves Charlie.

During a power blackout at the Shop, Andy realizes that the push has returned and he is able to push himself away from the drug dependency that has been cultivated by the Shop. He begins planning to rescue Charlie who is kept in separate quarters. Meanwhile, Rainbird has been able to gain Charlie's confidence by posing as an orderly who cleans her living quarters. He convinces Charlie that she should allow the Shop's scientists to study her so that she may eventually get to see her father.

Andy is able to work his push on Cap Hollister. He finds out about Rainbird and also gets Cap to arrange for Andy and Charlie to leave. Charlie does perform several experiments and finds that she is now able to control her power better. Andy gets word to Charlie about his plans and about Rainbird's treachery. Unfortunately, Rainbird realizes that Cap is being pushed by Andy. The climax takes place in the Shop's stable, where Rainbird waits in hiding for Charlie, her father, and Cap Hollister. Rainbird shoots and kills Andy. Charlie in her anger sets fire to Rainbird and then proceeds singlehandedly to destroy the Shop's headquarters through a dazzling display of firepower. In the confusion and destruction Charlie escapes. Eventually, she makes her way to the Manders farm, where she remains while recuperating. The Shop, under a new chief, covers up what happened and the word is sent out that Charlie is to be killed. She is tracked once more to the farm but before the Shop's agents arrive, Charlie is off again; this time to tell her story to the one newspaper willing to listen—*Rolling Stone*.

In *Firestarter,* his best novel to date, Stephen King follows closely the spirit of his successful earlier novels, *Salem's Lot* and *The Shining,* in which the main protagonists are a child and an adult bound together in combating some dreadful outside force. In *'Salem's Lot* Paul Mears and Mark Petrie, the young boy, struggle against the vampiric power taking over a small Maine town. *The Shining* is the story of five-year-old Danny Torrance and his mother in a winter of terror snowbound in the Colorado Rockies. King, as he has consistently in all his work, deals in *Firestarter* with what may be called the other dimension of reality. His characters either naturally or through some accident of man have extraordinary abilities that take their toll on the possessor but may be used for good. While King may not be concerned with morality as such, he is, in terms of his writing, a very moral man. Good and evil are his elements, as well as the basic ingredients of good storytelling. He keeps the reader enthralled and experiencing a range of emotions; feeling the urge to jump in to help or shout a warning as unexpected danger suddenly appears. Willingly or not, the reader becomes a participant in the action. As he has shown in his short stories in particular, King has the knack for drawing his audience into the story.

One of the enjoyable aspects in Stephen King's work is his humor.

It is found in characterization or in the situation in which characters find themselves. The incident in the Albany airport when Charlie accidentally sets a young man's shoes on fire is funny because of the notion that King projects of a giant hotfoot and of the awkward situation that follows as the young man puts out the fire and as he tries to explain to the police what happened. Another distinctive aspect of King's style is the use of the commonplace to heighten the feeling in his story. His descriptions of everyday events and occurrences are very much on the mark.

Firestarter is a first-rate story. It has many sympathetic characters, a score of villains and other miscreants, and enough of the ring of reality. In the light of recent history, the establishment of a monolithic government agency like the Shop is very possible. Only at the very end of the story does King's tale falter, for he does not seem to be able to end it convincingly. It is a little hard to accept the fact that, after her escape from the Shop in Virginia, Charlie, although she is a remarkable child, makes her way alone to a small town hundreds of miles away. Also, the reader is somewhat skeptical when Charlie on her own again arrives at the *Rolling Stone* office in New York City ready to tell her story. Although it makes sense, the ending is a little too cute. This problem is minor compared to the excitement, action, and genuine interest that King generates in *Firestarter*.

Louis Sasso

THE FORBIDDEN EXPERIMENT

Author: Roger Shattuck
Publisher: Farrar, Straus and Giroux (New York). 220 pp. $10.95
Type of work: Social science
Time: 1800–1828
Locale: Aveyron and Paris, France

The life and attempted education of Victor, otherwise known as the Wild Boy of Aveyron

> *Principal personages:*
> VICTOR, the wild foundling who is the center of much attention and the object of Itard's efforts at recivilization
> JEAN-MARC GASPARD ITARD, the young, idealistic doctor who spent five years trying to educate Victor
> MADAME GUERIN, Itard's assistant and maternal model to Victor, later his guardian for the rest of his life

The story of the Wild Boy of Aveyron begins with his sudden and dramatic appearance in the village of Saint-Sernin in southern France. Naked except for the tatters of a shirt, appearing to be about eleven or twelve years old, he was found digging up vegetables in the garden of a tanner. The tanner captured the boy and turned him over to the local commissioner, Constans-Saint-Estève. The commissioner quickly discovered that the child could not speak and was, by all appearances, a savage. He was brought to a local orphanage in Saint-Affrique. While there, news of his discovery traveled quickly, bringing his case to the attention of the priest and naturalist Pierre-Joseph Bonnaterre. Bonnaterre obtained custody of the "savage" through the Central Commissioner of Aveyron and proceeded to record his first observations. Bonnaterre noted that the boy's body was scarred, suggesting either early mistreatment or the hardships he must have endured in the wild. It appeared that the boy had lived on his own in the wilderness for at least three years, and possibly as many as six. His senses seemed to function normally, though their order of importance was apparently modified. The boy relied first on his sense of smell, then on taste, and lastly, touch. Nothing interested him except food and sleep. His actual needs were seen to by an old peasant gardener named Claire. Although there seemed to be a bond of affection between the two, there is no record of Claire's having attempted to apply any systematic program of reeducation.

The Wild Boy had the good fortune to have appeared during a period of relative enlightenment, namely, the turn of the 19th century. Very quickly he became the talk of Europe. As his fame grew, he attracted the interest of a number of scholars, one of the more notable being

Sicard, the celebrated director of the Institute for Deaf-Mutes in Paris. A directive from the new Minister of Interior ordered Bonnaterre to deliver his charge to the institute for study. Despite his eagerness to observe the boy, Sicard, a very busy man, virtually abandoned him during his first months in the institute. The boy was housebroken, became very fat, and expressed a love of being tickled. He avoided boys and girls of his own age. Pinel, an influential doctor reporting on the Wild Boy for The Society of Observers of Man, declared him to be "an incurable idiot." It seemed more likely than ever that the boy was destined to spend the rest of his days in an insane asylum.

In the summer of 1800 a new character appeared: the young doctor Jean-Marc Gaspard Itard. Employed as an assistant to Sicard, Itard, aged twenty-five, took an immediate interest in the boy and, a month later, was appointed as resident medical officer of the institute. Although no papers were signed, Itard in effect became the Wild Boy's foster father. Since no one else was interested in assuming responsibility for the boy, Itard was given a free hand.

Betting against the learned assertions of both Pinel and Sicard, Itard was determined to restore the Wild Boy to his rightful place as a civilized human being. Realizing that he would need help, Itard hired Madame Guerin to assist him. She would prove to be an invaluable mother-figure, devoting herself to the boy's welfare for the next twenty-seven years of his life.

Itard had five goals in his plan to reeducate the boy. He wanted to help him respond to other people, to train his senses, to extend his physical and social needs, to teach him to speak, and to teach him to think clearly. Over the next five years, a few of these goals would be realized, but most would not. Nonetheless, the efforts of Itard contributed greatly to what is known today about deprived individuals.

Within three months, under the persistent and sympathetic care of Itard and Madame Guerin, the boy was taught to wear clothes without tearing them off, to use a chamber pot, and to sit at a table in order to eat. He no longer had to be kept on a leash. Within a relatively short period of time, the Wild Boy had acquired the status of a well-behaved pet. What would elevate him to full human status, and what Itard strove mightily to achieve over the next five years, was the ability to speak. Through repeated and often taxing exercises, the boy, named Victor by this time, managed to learn the significance of a few letters, going so far at one point as to construct, spontaneously, the French word for milk: lait. Vocally, he managed a few utterances. Itard was overjoyed and, in his earliest reports, expressed the idea that "education is all," believing completely that Victor's eventual triumph would have great implications for the future of mankind.

But this was not to be. Instead of progressing onward after his promising start, Victor never achieved the ability to speak. His outlook on life remained a very selfish one, still centered around eating and sleeping. Throughout his training he retained a love for the wild, staring out often into the woods in which he had survived for so long. By 1805, Victor could read and write several words, but it is doubtful that he saw these words as a real attempt to communicate. For reasons never known, Itard never taught Victor sign language.

Having started with high hopes, Itard was reluctant to admit defeat. He pressed forward, achieving results that would prove to be more significant with time. Victor, despite his indelible streak of wildness, proved capable of fond friendship, the desire to please through good behavior, and sincere remorse over bad behavior. He learned to write some signs and, thus, communicate sparingly with people around him. He had come a very long way, but not as far as had been hoped.

With puberty and the onset of both unpredictable and antisocial behavior, Itard realized that he could do little more to advance Victor's place in the world. He discontinued the training program to which he had devoted so much of his career, and Victor spent the next seventeen years of his life living in a small house near the institute with Madame Guerin. He created no scandals or complaints, but never learned a trade or the ability to communicate verbally. He died mysteriously, at the age of forty, a forgotten man.

Roger Shattuck's *The Forbidden Experiment* derives its title from the long-held desire scientists have had over the centuries to isolate a human being from birth and see just what is learned and what is innate. The experiment has been conducted several times over the course of history with inconclusive results, but with it too the stigma of moral cruelty. The Wild Boy seemed to represent a perfect set of circumstances through which man might learn much about himself without actually having to conduct "the forbidden experiment."

As a straight narrative of the Wild Boy's life, *The Forbidden Experiment* is meticulous and entertaining, drawing primarily upon Itard's own notes, as well as the observations of the most learned minds of the time. Throughout his account historical perspectives are amply provided, underscoring how Victor's fate might have been different had he appeared in another time. Finally, the methods and motives of Itard himself are thoroughly examined and compared to modern psychological knowledge. A detailed appendix at the end of the book deepens the reader's understanding of the Wild Boy's case through a description of similar and not so similar cases of human deprivation.

More than anything else, however, *The Forbidden Experiment* presents a tantalizing series of questions. Was the Wild Boy of Aveyron really an idiot? Could he, with the knowledge available today, have acquired the ability to speak, or was he the victim of an undiscovered physical impairment? Was Itard wrong in the methods he used? Was Victor, after his long period of isolation, incapable of learning the basic language skills most people routinely master at an early age? Could these skills, having perhaps been learned once, have been forgotten? These, and a host of other questions are raised constantly throughout Roger Shattuck's moving account. They invite few definite answers. Still, their exploration represents an artful attempt to help understand and learn from one of the more bizarre and intriguing episodes in human history.

David Alvarez

FREE TO CHOOSE

Authors: Milton Friedman, Rose Friedman
Publisher: Harcourt Brace Jovanovich (New York). 338 pp. $9.95
Type of work: Social science

A critique of government involvement in the economy of the United States, emphasizing a defense of the "laissez-faire" tradition of Adam Smith's economic philosophy

Each of the ten chapters of Milton and Rose Friedman's *Free to Choose* is both expository and exhortative: on one level each seems to have been taken from a textbook primer on free-market economies; on another level each attempts to demonstrate how the textbook hypotheses are subverted by government involvement in economic affairs. The result, the Friedmans claim, is that American citizens are no longer "free to choose" the nature of their economy. The choosing, they assert, has been done for them by their government. They lay groundwork for the thesis that a society whose individuals are not free to choose the manner in which their economic markets are set up, the way in which the value of exchange of goods and services is established, is not a free society. Through historical examples and a discussion of 20th-century American economic policies (focusing on government involvement in social welfare and regulation of business), they maintain that the ills of the contemporary American economy are the result of government bureaucracy and over-regulation.

The Friedmans begin with an examination of the market, an exchange system of goods and services that is predicated on cooperation through voluntary exchange. Individuals pursuing their own interests are able to achieve them in a free market while producing goods and services that satisfy the interests and goals of others. This is basically Adam Smith's principle of "the invisible hand." Free markets, the Friedmans assert, echoing Smith's economic philosophy, have the ability to regulate themselves. Prices of goods and services, for example, are a measure of this self-regulation. Prices perform three functions in a free-market economy: first, they transmit information (concerning the availability of a product or the demand for it); second, they promote the efficient use of resources and help to establish priorities for their usage; and third, they serve to determine the distribution of income—who gets how much of the product. It is government intervention, they claim, that distorts the economic system of prices.

The Friedmans explicate Adam Smith's view of the government's role in the economy, a view that states that government involvement should be limited to seeing that justice is done and that certain public works and institutions, the likes of which could not be developed by private enterprise because of large expense and little reward, are established.

Unfortunately, the Friedmans say, modern government has taken this as license for interference in the marketplace. Hong Kong is offered as an example of a place where limited government involvement has allowed the market to flourish profitably for all concerned. This statement is not strongly substantiated by the Friedmans, who take largely material factors such as "per capita income" and "standard of living" as indicators of the health of the economy.

Other points are made with reference to the control of trade. Tariffs, duties, and sanctions on both domestic and international levels act as prior restraints of a legitimate freedom: the freedom to engage in free trade activity. Both business and government find tariffs and duties defensible on the basis of the following, generally spurious, arguments: 1) national security would be endangered without them; 2) "infant industries" need governmental protection; 3) tariffs are needed to drive down prices that would-be monopolists would set; and 4) other nations set tariffs and duties, so we may as well. Of these four only the third argument has any merit, but, they caution, trusts and monopolies have a tendency to develop as much as a perverse result of government intervention as due to the lack of government intervention.

A comparison is made between Japan from the Meiji restoration to the present and India from its independence in 1947 to the present. Meiji Japan established a largely "laissez-faire" economy. Consequently, 20th-century Japan had a well-developed and robust economy to build upon. India, on the other hand, developed a centrally controlled planned economy that left little room for private initiative. The result is that India continues to be a backward and underdeveloped country while Japan is one of the economic giants of the world.

Although Americans do not admit it, the Friedmans say, we too have a centrally controlled planned economy. More than forty percent of our income is taken every year. Restrictions are rampant. Licenses are needed for everything from the practice of medicine to the driving of taxicabs. This creates profound effects on the personal freedom of Americans. Who, the Friedmans ask, dared to speak out against President Carter's "voluntary" wage and price controls? Most, they say, were silenced by the invidious effects of government. Economic freedom and individual freedom are fundamentally tied together.

The Friedmans then attempt to trace just how government became so entangled in the private affairs of citizens. In a discussion of the Great Depression they chart the rise of the Federal Reserve System and its control over the supply of money available to banks and discuss the rise of the "welfare state," in which government develops "cradle to grave" care for the lives of its citizens.

Fiscal mismanagement led to the Depression. Weak leadership and conflicting policies in the Federal Reserve System served to tighten the money supply at a particularly bad time. This, coupled with the Federal Reserve System going off the gold standard and government refusal to stop runs on banks by depositors, caused nearly a third of the banks in the country to fail. The results were devastating.

The ensuing efforts to put both the economy and the public on their feet resulted not in temporary efforts, but in efforts that created an entrenched bureaucracy and a maze of programs and regulations from which the American economy has never escaped. This, say the Friedmans, was the creation of the welfare state. They point to the Social Security system as the monster that has developed from misguided efforts and offer a counter-program to dismantle it, thus giving Americans access to the monies they earn and the freedom to do with it as they choose. They call for the immediate repeal of the payroll tax with the continuation of payments to all who qualify as beneficiaries under the Social Security Act. They also call for the immediate payment to workers of all the funds those workers have contributed to Social Security in the form of government bonds. In addition, they would seek termination of the entire program and would finance the remaining payments to be made with general tax funds and the issuing of government bonds. They offer this program for termination simply as an idea, expressing the belief that in today's society radical welfare reform has been precluded by the cultural, social, and bureaucratic entrenchment of the welfare system.

The problem of the welfare system, say the Friedmans, is that the very notion of equality has been misconstrued. Although equality of persons and equality of opportunity are fundamental aspects of personal liberty, equality of outcome (an explanatory quote is given from *Alice in Wonderland:* "Everybody has won, and all must have prizes.") is not. They note the inequity of taking from the rich to give to the poor. There is a difference, they explain, between ninety percent of the population taxing itself in order to support an impoverished ten percent and eighty percent of the population taking it upon itself to tax ten percent of the population to support another ten percent. In this inequitable scheme it is the tax collectors who become the privileged. Indeed, in terms of power they become a bureaucratic class. What is lost in this process is the ability of natural geniuses like the Fords, the Edisons to rise to greatness. At a time when there was no tax on income, there were incredible philanthropic efforts set forth by such people.

Along similar lines the Friedmans cast a vote for private over public education. Private education, they say, can be more responsive to the needs of communities and groups. Again, they offer a plan to remedy the current ills of the American educational system: extend the principles of the GI Bill voucher system to the entire educational system. This would allow individuals to choose the type of education they want; it would also make schools responsive to the needs of communities.

In each of two chapters dealing with the consumer and the worker the Friedmans point once more to the influx of governmental regulation. They find that workers' productivity declines as regulatory activity increases. They examine and compare the government-regulated railway system with the relatively free-market automobile production system. The former is grossly inefficient while the latter, a private industry, is responsive to the needs of the consumer.

It is the consumer, the Friedmans say, who usually loses when government steps in to regulate industry. When agencies like the Interstate Commerce Commission, the Food and Drug Administration, the Consumer Products Safety Commission, and the Environmental Protection Agency intervened, the cost of products to consumers rose greatly, the availability of alternative products decreased, mediocrity of products increased, and research and development of potential new products declined. They specifically advocate the abolishment of the Food and Drug Administration claiming that the market can effectively police the industry.

Beyond advocating many ideas that would radically change the regulatory capacities of government, the Friedmans also believe that unions in the workplace serve to limit consumers' and workers' freedom. For example, they hold that unions (including professional "unions" such as the American Medical Association) seek to reduce the number of available jobs and in so doing artificially raise demands for services and, of course, the wages for those jobs.

The minimum wage offers an example of how unions and government act in concert to drive workers out of the workplace while appearing to have the workers' best interests in mind. The incredibly high unemployment among teenage blacks demonstrates that the poor and unskilled are priced out of the job market by the minimum wage. The Friedmans have no doubt that a free market, without hindrances, would generate greater competition in industry and would create more jobs.

In the next to last chapter of the book, the authors discuss the nature of inflation. They say inflation occurs when the quantity of money rises more rapidly than production output. If output and money supply rose at an equal rate, prices would remain stable and there would be no inflation. One of the major problems today, however, is that there is virtually no limit to the potential money supply since gold reserves are no longer needed to support the value of paper money.

Three things, they say, have contributed to inflation. First, high government spending that is based on high taxation of the private sector of the economy is one cause. Second, the attempt to gain full employment results in arbitrary attempts to control demand. Finally, the Federal Reserve System, in an attempt to support government's full employment goals, increases loans to the private sector.

Inflation does have benefits to some, particularly owners of property, and it is in part because these benefits are cherished that inflation has not subsided. The one thing that would rid Americans of inflation is a reduction of the money supply. However, most people feel that the side effects of this cure, slow growth and high unemployment, are much too high a price to pay. One immediate step should be taken, the Friedmans say. Rents and loan rates should float with the rate of inflation. There would be a natural tendency to drive rates down, after which they would rise somewhat again, and then level off.

In the closing chapter the Friedmans propose "An Economic Bill of Rights." It is a radical statement including several principles. 1) Government taxing and spending powers should be greatly limited. 2) A constitutional amendment should be proposed that states that no tariffs or duties should be placed on imports or exports. 3) No restraints should be placed on the freedom of sellers of goods and labor to price their products and services. 4) No occupation should require licensure. 5) No infringements should be placed on the rights of individuals to buy and sell goods and services. 6) There should be a fixed tax rate not proportionate to income or population apportionment. 7) Floating rates of interest should be placed on all government contracts.

Although *Free to Choose* is a provocative book, it has two significant drawbacks. First, its sweeping claims lack adequate documentation. Second, the book seems designed to be provocative without being intellectually substantial. The Friedmans hammer away at their themes like boorish dinner guests. The layman is left to wonder why, if all these solutions are so simple and relatively immediate, nothing on this order has ever been attempted. The Friedmans offer solutions to economic dilemmas while only vaguely hinting at the chaos that would ensue if their proposed changes were put into effect. *Free to Choose* is a utopian book, a book that examines "what if" possibilities.

D. W. Faulkner

THE GIRL IN A SWING

Author: Richard Adams (1920–   )
Publisher: Alfred A. Knopf (New York). 339 pp. $11.95
Type of work: Novel
Time: May–July 1974
Locale: Newbury, England; Copenhagen, Denmark; Florida

The story of a young English dealer in ceramics and his beautiful and sensuous German wife whose mysterious past appears to bring a catastrophic end to their relationship

Principal characters:
> ALAN DESLAND, a sensitive, intelligent English ceramics dealer in his twenties
> KÄTHE, Alan's beautiful German wife
> TONY REDWOOD, an Anglican rector who is Alan's best friend

In the opening pages of Richard Adams' *The Girl in a Swing,* the narrator, Alan Desland, an Englishman in his late twenties, remarks upon the unusual clarity of the landscape surrounding his English country house. His mind is flooded with memories and he weeps.

In a stream-of-consciousness narrative, Alan begins the flashback from July 1979 that comprises the novel. The second child of loving parents who owned a china shop, Alan delighted in beauty at an early age. At Bradfield College he enjoyed fencing and swimming for the form, dignity, and rhythm of these activities. His competence in photography further revealed a definite aesthetic sensitivity.

Another aspect of his sensitivity was his clairvoyance, made evident several times at Bradfield. But these experiences, mingling sexuality, danger, and death, disturbed and frightened him.

Alan entered Oxford, and his years there were pleasant. He enjoyed long swims and had a few friends, none of them very close. He had, up to this point, rejected romantic love, considering himself ugly.

Upon his graduation he became a partner in his father's ceramics business. Finding his father a compatible partner, Alan immersed himself in his work. During that same summer, Alan's father died. Excessive grief may have been a factor in the next strange episode in his life. With his mother taking over the management of the retail side of the business, Alan went fully into antique and fine modern ceramics. During the first two years Alan experienced severe nervous strain, and almost consulted a psychiatrist. In one disturbing dream he was swimming with a woman who had taken part in his ESP experience at Bradfield. She enticed him to dive deeper where, amid the rubble of a china shop, he encountered the partially decomposed body of a young girl. He awakened screaming and sobbing.

By 1974, four and one-half years after his father's death, he had established himself as an international expert in ceramics. In May he visited Copenhagen, his favorite city, where he met Fraülein Wassermann, a woman recommended as a typist.

Enchanted with Käthe Wassermann from the moment he met her, Alan fell in love and proposed marriage after dating her for one week. Käthe was beautiful, but what dazzled him most was her detachment, her conscious command over those around her, and her innocence. Beyond having seen her in the park with a child and another woman, Alan knew nothing of her past, although there was a suspicion that the child might be hers.

Alan returned to England alone, leaving Käthe to settle her affairs and join him in England. The evening of her arrival in London, Käthe, Alan, Tony Redwood (Alan's pastor and best friend), and an American client dined together. Upon hearing of Alan's frustration at having to wait the required time for the marriage in England, the client offered to arrange their marriage in Florida.

Following the wedding, a humiliated Alan was unable to consummate the marriage. But when the couple took a leisurely three-mile swim down a river, two strong and graceful swimmers cavorting on the surface and along the bottom, Käthe became terrified at a log in the water that appeared to her to be a body. Alan comforted her, and as they rested on the sand, the newlyweds found a rapture of sexual fulfillment.

After two weeks, they returned to England. Alan's mother had gone to visit with Alan's sister Flick, a fortunate absence considering the spontaneous ardor of the two lovers. Alan's life was now taking its purpose from the joy of lovemaking. Content with the Käthe of the present, Alan did not ask her anything about her past, not even when she implied that it might hold a sinister secret. In a discussion of religion and morality with Tony, Käthe asked him if any sin could be forgiven. Tony assured her that it could if the sinner forgave himself.

Soon after this discussion, Alan began to have unsettling sensory perceptions. Even his visiting niece, Flick's daughter, normally not an excitable child, had a nightmare of being lost in water. After Flick and her child left, Alan found a stuffed green tortoise in the child's room. When he told Käthe that his niece left the toy, an upset Käthe insisted he saw no such thing. Returning to the room he found no tortoise.

After Käthe left him for a few days to visit his mother in Bristol, Alan awoke from a nightmare to hear the sound of water gushing. Finding nothing, he wondered if he had been hallucinating, but in the morning the gardener informed him that a water pipe had burst in the garden.

Upon Käthe's return two unusual facets of her complex nature came to light. She lured him into having sex on the kitchen table while their guests sat less than forty feet away in the drawing room. She demonstrated her business canniness with a porcelain statue she had bought at an auction, a piece of great value called The Girl in a Swing.

Alan went to London to consult a curator about the value of the statue. Returning home, he had a feeling of surreality when he found Käthe in the swing, naked, in the pose of The Girl in the Swing statue. The next morning, Alan dismissed the experience as the effect of the heat of the day and the excitement of discovering that Käthe's purchase was worth over £100,000.

Alan, calling a dealer in Copenhagen to share his good news, heard a child's voice on his line saying, among noises of water, that she was coming to her mummy. When Käthe tried to put through the call, she too was connected with the same child. Käthe became hysterical.

On the two-month anniversary of the day they met, Käthe told Alan she suspected that she was pregnant. In church that morning Käthe collapsed but regaining consciousness in the car insisted that she was not feeling ill. Alan, for the first time, asked her what was bothering her, but she made no response.

When Mrs. Taswell, Alan's secretary, arrived with some letters for him to sign, they both heard a child crying but found only a doll. In the bedroom Alan found Käthe under the covers. She begged him, "Oh, Alan, Alan, save me! You can save me—" The night was a torment of madness and fear brought about by the crying of the child, which they both heard. At one point Alan saw the toy green tortoise again.

The next morning Käthe asked Alan to take her away. While searching in her handbag Alan found a receipt for the purchase of a green toy tortoise bought in Denmark. They drove to the sea and, as they stood looking at the beach and the still gray water, Alan again went into a trance in which nothing seemed real. When Käthe asked Alan if he still loved her, he responded by making love to her. Suddenly they saw the calm waters ripple as a mutilated girl child surfaced and stumbled toward them.

Later, half mad and badly lacerated, Alan was found by a policeman. Käthe had already been found wandering naked and insane and had been taken to a hospital. The police and hospital personnel believed that Alan had raped and abused her. When they discovered that he was her husband, they allowed him to see her. Her beauty gone, she died, without recognizing him, of a ruptured fallopian tube. The doctor blamed an infection contracted during a previous confinement.

At the inquest, just as a confused Alan was about to testify, Käthe entered the courtroom in the guise of a reporter. Guided by her gestures and mental telepathy, Alan was able to offer a rational explanation. Later, when Alan looked at the reporter, she was no longer Käthe.

At the burial service, Alan felt that the Christian liturgy had nothing to do with Käthe. Convinced that Käthe had done away with her daughter before leaving Copenhagen, Alan imagined her taking the child to a deserted beach off the coast of Denmark. Feeling a small but essential part of her sin, he knew he would not have married her if she had had a child to bring along. But he could not wish anything to have been different if it would have prevented their loving one another. His reverie ends with an awareness that he has awakened to reality through his love of Käthe. He can now teach the world something about beauty and infinity.

The Girl in a Swing is a delectable gem. Abounding in literary, mythical, religious, and philosophical allusions, it is a minor masterpiece. Its success lies in the craft of the author. Unlike the utilitarian ceramic objects purveyed by Alan Desland, this literary treasure entertains more by its form and decorations than by what it holds.

Gothic in its foreshadowings of death, the novel is psychological in its implications. Never is the reader sure whether Käthe has actually murdered her child or whether Alan has misconstrued a much lesser unknown sin of her past.

Alan's impressions shape the plot. These impressions, derived from clairvoyance, dreams, poetry, history, sexuality, and supernatural occurrences, convince Alan that he has arrived at a higher level of consciousness. He believes that his will and his predestined role have become one.

The confluence of illusion and reality is a dominant theme of the novel. The reader wonders if Alan and Käthe have experienced that rare symptom of schizophrenia in which two closely related people have the same hallucinations. Aside from Mrs. Taswell's hearing the child and Alan's finding the receipt for the toy tortoise, almost every supernatural event is explained in terms of natural causes. Alan has warned the reader that his story must be understood in the light of his sexual rapture, so perhaps the receipt and Mrs. Taswell's visit were imagined.

Lesser themes of the book are the impermanence of beauty and the collusion of good and evil. It is not Adams' intent to develop fully these themes or to resolve them as philosophical problems. He seems, rather, to be satirizing these themes, particularly the one concerning good and evil.

Judith Sandstrom

GLITTER & ASH

Author: Dennis Smith (1940–   )
Publisher: E. P. Dutton (New York). 248 pp. $9.95
Type of work: Novel
Time: The present
Locale: New York City

An investigation of the firebombing of the posh Sophia Club, in which forty-three people die, reveals that the arsonist's crime has been facilitated by widespread social and political corruption

> *Principal characters:*
> TERRY AHEARN, idealistic New York fire marshal
> JOSE GILLESPIE, Ahearn's partner
> RODNEY LETTINGTON, deputy mayor
> PETEY AHEARN, Terry's father, armchair socialist
> MARCHESA DI TOTTI GAMBELLI, owner of the Sophia Club, an arson victim
> MELISSA REID, Terry's well-to-do girlfriend
> AGEL REID, Melissa's father, a lawyer
> LELAND QUINSBY, a socialite and arsonist
> LUCY HARTFIELD, an heiress and an arson victim
> JENKS MONROE, Quimsby's partner, another arson victim
> LT. SIRKIN, head of police Arson & Explosion squad

The opening of the Marchesa di Totti Gambelli's swank new disco in the basement of the Hotel Astor has a guest list that reads like a Who's Who of international society. The decor and the guests exude glitter, and the Marchesa's triumph seems assured. But the sparkling gathering is abruptly and tragically interrupted. A firebomb explodes just inside the entrance to the Sophia Club. Panic ensues. The Marchesa's silk-draped ceilings spread the fire within seconds. The sprinklers do not work because the Marchesa used her influence to circumvent that requirement; working sprinklers might go off spontaneously and ruin her ceiling murals. Further proof of her influence at City Hall, through Deputy Mayor Rodney Lettington, becomes plain when the stampeding guests discover there is only one emergency exit. Lettington procured a variance for the Marchesa so she would avoid the inconvenience of breaking through a wall for a second exit. Now Rodney's wife is among the forty-three people who are caught in the crush to get through the one inadequate exit and become victims of the fire.

Fire marshal Terry Ahearn and his partner, Jose Gillespie, are called in to investigate the Sophia fire. This fire is more than a routine case for them. The Bureau of Fire Investigation is in jeopardy. In an effort to economize, City Hall is considering a plan to turn all arson investigations over to the police department. The publicity surrounding the

Sophia fire could make or break the Bureau of Fire Investigation.

The carefully detailed, step-by-step account of Ahearn's handling of the case comprises the bulk of the novel. From evidence and testimony gathered at the site of the fire, Terry and Jose learn that the accelerant used by the arsonist in his Molotov cocktail was butyl nitrate, a highly flammable sexual stimulant favored by the gay community. They try to trace the sale of large quantities of butyl nitrate and also the trademark on a shard of glass from the bottle used for the bomb.

While investigating the Sophia Club fire, Terry and Jose also must deal with the less publicized, more common arson cases in New York, cases in which the victims and arsonists receive little or no attention from the public because of their poverty. Only the rich and the glamorous are interesting. Yet from his experience as a firefighter, Terry knows that the public's interest does not affect the tragic loss of human life, both among the victims of arson and the men who must risk their lives battling deliberately set fires.

In addition to the pressure Terry feels to solve the Sophia fire case and win favorable publicity for his endangered department, he is also under strain in his personal life. The son of lower-middle-class parents, Terry has been influenced by his father's socialist philosophy. He is involved with Melissa Reid, whose background is upper class. The social gulf between them is underscored when Terry learns that her parents were invited to the Sophia opening but decided not to go at the last minute. Melissa also knew one of the victims, Lucy Hartfield, who was one of Agel Reid's clients.

The net of investigation begins to yield results. Evidence points to Leland Quinsby, editor of the chic publication *Design and Discourse*. Quinsby's partner, Jenks Monroe, was planning to sell out his controlling interest in the publication to a British media mogul. Quinsby regarded this as a desecration of something he had worked hard to build. Although a homosexual, Quinsby forced himself to become Lucy's lover to influence her to buy out Monroe, but when the bidding got too high, Melissa's father talked Lucy out of the purchase. Quinsby was enraged and saw the Sophia opening as the perfect chance to avenge himself on all of his enemies at once. Lucy, Monroe, and Agel Reid were all on the guest list.

Time is running out for the Bureau of Fire Investigation. The deadline is nearing when it will be legislated out of existence. As Terry and Jose get closer to their man, they uncover many other interesting facts including Rodney Lettington's role in the Sophia's substandard safety measures; his father-in-law's huge Times Square real estate holdings, which would profit from arson; Lt. Sirkin's complicity with Lettington in exchange for political preferment; and the generally callous and indifferent attitude in high places toward arson.

Quinsby is preparing to strike again at Reid, choosing the crowded ARC Ball as the place. Quinsby does not know that Terry will be there, invited by Melissa. At the last moment, a desperate call from home to intervene between his father and sister almost prevents Terry's presence. Petey Ahearn, for all his preaching, is enraged that his daughter Maureen dates a Brazilian musician. Terry gets her safely to his apartment, then goes to the ARC Ball just in time to catch Quinsby at the moment he is about to throw his second firebomb. But due to Rodney Lettington's cowardice when he might have seized Quinsby, the arsonist escapes to the roof where he threatens to jump. Terry grabs him and both nearly fall as Terry ignores Jose's pleas to drop the arson-murderer and save himself.

Terry hauls Quinsby to safety. In custody, Quinsby demonstrates his obvious insanity. Terry brings the Bureau of Fire Investigation into the spotlight, as well as managing to embarrass Lettington at a press conference. He goes back to his apartment to find his father and sister reconciled and his own romantic future with Melissa assured.

Glitter & Ash is an odd but not unpleasing combination of elements. First there is the police procedural mystery novel given a new twist with the heroes as firemen-detectives. There is also the popular device of the *roman à clef,* in which no actual names of current celebrities are used, but the parallels between Smith's characters and real celebrities are obvious enough to allow the reader to draw conclusions. This device links Smith's fiction to reality in such a way that the reader is fully aware of the possibility of the action's really happening.

Finally a rather dated but still effective viewpoint is taken by the author. The lines of battle are drawn in black and white. Everyone in *Glitter & Ash* is either good or bad, with the chief villains primarily the faceless, heartless powers-that-be in City Hall. Terry Ahearn makes a perfect protagonist as the little guy championing a good cause, the cause of the people. Those fighting him are either rich and/or powerful, or eager to throw in their lot with the ruling classes.

Dennis Smith's attitude toward his crusading hero is understandable. He has seen the horror of arson and experienced the desperate conditions of New York's poor first hand. As a firefighter stationed in the Bronx, he knows intimately Ahearn's feelings of rage, sorrow, and occasional fear when called upon to do a job that is indispensable but seldom appreciated. *Glitter & Ash* is not his first work. His knowledge of firefighting and all aspects of the firefighter's life has already been demonstrated in *Report From Engine Co. 82* and other books.

Esther M. Friesner

GOING TO EXTREMES

Author: Joe McGinniss
Publisher: Alfred A. Knopf (New York). 285 pp. $11.95
Type of work: Travel
Time: Mid-1970's
Locale: Alaska

A look at Alaska during construction of the oil pipeline and a culture transformed overnight by technology

One evening in the mid-1970's, Joe McGinniss is sitting with an old friend who has recently returned from Alaska. As the mountains and the tales get taller, McGinniss finds himself entranced with the place. Not too long after he embarks on a trip that will take him away from his northeastern home to a state more than twice the size of Texas, with three major mountain ranges, one of which boasts the tallest mountain in the United States. *Going to Extremes,* the book that was inspired by this journey, recounts the life story of Alaska as seen through the eyes and deeds of random citizens, who exemplify many qualities uniquely representative of the state. In addition to Alaska's history, McGinniss tells a story of the people of Alaska. It is their growth and stagnation, their good luck and misfortune, that endow the bleak yet spectacular Alaskan landscape with its life.

Alaska, like a child that reaches six feet soon after shedding its diapers, is experiencing growing pains. The current growth has been spurred by oil companies and the construction of an 800-mile pipeline from the North Slope to Valdez. In fact, when the first oil trickles into a small town that has been entirely rebuilt since the 1964 earthquake, a crippled widow from Anchorage wins $30,000 for guessing the time it would take for the oil to travel south.

The rapid growth is having such an enormous effect on the culture that it has left few people untouched. Although regarding Alaska as "the last frontier" has become a cliché, there is nevertheless a full measure of truth to the statement. McGinniss, sensing the passing of a way of life, chooses to experience Alaska while the pipeline is still under construction—and before it is irrevocably changed.

McGinniss, outfitted in Seattle, finds himself waiting for the Alaska-bound ferry to cast off its lines. It is November. The tourist season is over, and no sightseers occupy the ferry. Duane Archer, who is in the restaurant and bar supply business, is a brash and raucous character. If he has a conscience, he does not let it get in his way. He sees Alaska as a woman to be slept with and discarded. The sky is the limit, and as long as Alaskan dollars continue to rain his way, he will applaud Alaskan progress.

There are others who make the passage north. Eddie the Basque is from Idaho and lassoes one of the two housewives who are returning from a shopping spree in Seattle. Eddie speaks with the same fiery language as Duane, and like Duane he hopes to cash in on the prosperity that the pipeline has brought. But Eddie's timing is off. He is so out of touch with the reality of Alaska that he thinks he can drive his truck from Wrangell to Ketchican, although no road has yet been built.

There is also Sandy, a 1960's flower child from Nebraska who has made her way up the coast from San Francisco to Juneau. Always gravitating toward action, she is nevertheless both aware of and afraid of Juneau's numbing, almost hypnotic power. The combination of the climate, the lack of mobility, and the heavy reliance on drugs and alcohol creates an atmosphere she fears will ensnarl her.

After riding to Anchorage with Duane, McGinniss calls up Tom Brennan, who with his wife Marni had moved to Alaska from Massachusetts ten years earlier. He and Joe are old friends. After Tom, a reporter, found he was spending most of his time writing about the oil companies, he decided to go to work for them at triple his former salary. Although Tom enjoys Alaska, the move there has hardly been an escape from the high-pressure world. Anchorage is booming with business, and the community is afraid "the music will stop." Tom works hard to keep it going.

New buildings are popping up so quickly in Anchorage that it no longer resembles the collection of tents it was sixty-five years ago. Indeed, the town is so young that the first white woman ever to live there is still alive. It is here, in the midst of a thriving boom town, that the government conducts hearings on the controversial Udall Bill, intended to exempt 114,000,000 acres from development.

Fairbanks lies approximately in the middle of the state, a day's drive, a twelve-hour train ride, or about a two-hour flight from Anchorage, if all goes well. There is ice fog everywhere, and visibility is extremely limited. Ice fog is produced when particles of pollutants freeze, or in cases of extreme cold, when the moisture in the air freezes. A day in Fairbanks with the temperature at 49 degrees below zero is not unusual. Fairbanks people, and Alaskans in general, are proud of the cold. It is one natural resource that is abundant. To the casual tourist the cold can be fun, but every Alaskan knows it can also be dangerous.

Fairbanks, which grew from 12,000 to 60,000 inhabitants in three years, is the stopping-off place for oil men going to and from the North Slope. The only sign McGinniss can make out through the ice fog proclaims "Girls Girls Girls" in bright neon. As he had been told on the ferry, Fairbanks is no longer a town—it is an open wound.

McGinniss meets an oilman, and they ride out to take a look at Pump Station Eight. The donut-eating manager explains the miracle of modern technology. Eighteen months later a man neglects a valve, a backup system fails, and a spark blows the place sky high. One man is killed, several are injured, and 1,000 gallons of oil are deposited on the tundra.

McGinniss and Tom head for the North Slope to take a look at the oil operation there. Life in Prudhoe Bay moves at a snail's pace; yet, paradoxically, here were these imported creatures living in ultramodern accommodations, sticking great lengths of iron into the ground, and sending ripples of cultural and economic change to the far corners of the world. Some are making more than $2,000 a week and complaining when they are not fed steak and lobster on the same night.

Barrow, the northernmost Alaskan settlement, has 2,000 people and is experiencing racial turmoil. Barrow's high school has 300 students and an athletic budget of $250,000, primarily for travel expenses. During winter Barrow's residents do not see the sun for more than three months, and they increase their alcoholic consumption accordingly.

In Nome, the dominant theme is also alcohol, with plenty of violence to supplement it. The town is populated with a colorful cast of characters who see themselves as the romantic descendants of the gold prospectors. In a remote Esquimo village in southwestern Alaska a father interrupts his daily routine of making fish traps to watch a favorite television program. In Bethel, the principal town in the southwest, mother-to-be Bev Hoffman has returned home with a contingent of long-haired friends from California, who bring both their culture and considerable talents to the small town.

At Halibut Cove, Clem Tillion and Tom Larsen are two Alaskans who measure success not only financially but also in terms of the rich experience the state has afforded them. To the north, in the Matanuska valley, the town of Palmer is the site of a thriving produce industry. In Talkeetna, the closest town to Mt. McKinley, the residents, hoping to keep their town small and independent, are fighting the proposed capital at nearby Willow. Glacier pilot Cliff Hudson skillfully maneuvers climbers to the base of Mt. McKinley. One of these climbers, Jack Hebert, recounts a fascinating story of the winters he and his wife Beth spent in a tiny cabin in the Arctic wilderness. McGinniss' narrative ends with the thrilling account of a hike through the Brooks Range, led by one of Alaska's foremost outdoorsmen, Ray Bane. Ray and his wife Barbara had once sledded from Hughes to Barrow.

Reading *Going to Extremes* is almost as good as being there, perhaps even better if you are sitting by a warm stove. McGinniss' tales are indeed chilling, frequently in the literal sense, and quite often in the human behavior they describe. *Going to Extremes* is a vivid portrayal of a culture made up of many independent subcultures. In part, the geography and climate demand self-reliance, but McGinniss portrays Alaskans as a breed apart, one that has little in common with the inhabitants of the lower 48 states. Shrouded in paradox, Alaskans are at once contemporary and primitive, intrepid and unstable, greedy and generous.

McGinniss has a knack for identifying the essence of a person or place and for allowing it to reveal a basic truth. He spreads the Alaskan panorama before the readers' eyes in a narrative filled with awe and drama. His final trek through the Brooks Range brings the story full circle in more ways than one. It is the fitting culmination of his commentary on a state whose greatest assets are its brute natural forces. Those who return from Alaska have had a notable experience; those, like Joe McGinniss, who can translate the experience into words, have a tangible memory of which they can be proud.

Cyrus Quinn, Jr.

GOODBYE, DARKNESS

Author: William Manchester
Publisher: Little, Brown & Company (Boston). 401 pp. $14.95
Type of work: Memoir
Time: 1945 and 1978
Locale: Sites in the Pacific Theater, from the Solomon to the Ryukyu Islands

Manchester revisits the Pacific islands where, as a Marine during World War II, he led a group of young men through the horrors of battle

William Manchester, biographer, historian, novelist, is perhaps best known for his earlier works *The Death of a President* (1967) and *The Arms of Krupp* (1976). Thirty-five years ago he served as a Marine sergeant in the Pacific and was very seriously wounded at Sugar Loaf Hill on Okinawa. In 1978 he decided to return to the scene of his wartime experiences. *Goodbye, Darkness* is a memoir of his two Pacific tours and the confrontation between the mature writer of the present and the young soldier he was during World War II.

As background material for *Goodbye, Darkness,* William Manchester briefly describes his childhood in Springfield, Massachusetts, an introduction of "myself to myself." Yankee on his father's side and Southern on his mother's, Manchester as a boy lived among family legends that portrayed keenly both the romance and the horror of war. His own sense of combat, however, remained strictly intellectual. He was a cowardly, bookish boy who never seemed able to stand up for himself. At the same time he followed the rise of Nazism and the gathering war in Europe with the bright eye of the soldier joyfully ready to make the ultimate sacrifice for the sake of all that is good: "I was really an eager Saint George looking for a dragon." The bombing of Pearl Harbor by the Japanese on December 7, 1941, and the immediate entry of the United States into the war came none too soon for Manchester, then a sophomore at the University of Massachusetts. Within weeks he was desperately downing bananas and milk in an attempt to make the weight requirement of the Marine Corps.

The Corps had been on his mind for a good many years. His father had served with the Fifth Marines in France during World War I, was gravely wounded in a shrapnel burst, and was left by doctors to die in a "moribund ward." When he was discovered alive after having been left unattended for five days, his life was saved but his right arm remained permanently crippled and his health was impaired. Despite the callousness and incompetence that had contributed to his calamities, the elder Manchester never relented in his identification of himself as a Marine. His two sons were raised in an environment permeated by

Marine lore, language, and, in many instances, discipline. But their
father did not live to see his sons enlist. He finally succumbed to his
lingering frailties early in 1941.

In his return to the Pacific, Manchester in retrospect sees his father's
experiences and his own as part of a single mechanic. Like his father,
he was wounded by shrapnel fire and left for a time for dead. Also like
his father, he imagines, he realized that the rhetoric of war is not a
language of passion but of calculation, designed to manipulate the best
in young men for the worst aims. But also like his father, he finds
himself unable to repudiate his Marine experience, unable to deny
what he was or why. Unlike his father, however, Manchester attempts
to dispel his nightmare by reliving it, by revisiting scenes of death and
finding that they have life after all.

In this Manchester is not entirely successful. Although he finally
achieves some reconciliation with the young sergeant he once was, his
reconciliation with the Pacific world of the present is far from complete. He believes that the sufferings of American servicemen in the
Pacific have not been remembered. The fault lies not, he feels, with the
native populations, who still nurture a mystical awe of American servicemen. In the Philippines, New Guinea, the Solomon Islands, and
Guam, Manchester finds an abiding reverence for the United States
and its war effort against the Japanese. The residents prize war relics
and weave legends around the battle sites. However, the war memorials in the U.S. possessions are poorly maintained and in some instances no longer exist. Manchester suggests a variety of explanations
for this neglect. Among them are the overshadowing of the Pacific war
by that in Europe, the propaganda of the war years, still affecting our
view from the 1980's, which emphasizes successes in the Pacific while
underplaying the losses, and a queasiness on the part of American
society as a whole in confronting the actual suffering of the soldier.
This suffering encompassed not only wounds, death, and constant fear,
but also the more mundane though equally devastating privations of
persistent infection, undernourishment, filth, heat, infestation, loneliness, boredom, and humiliation.

He contrasts the condition of American war memorials, to him representative of the American attitude toward the war effort and the men
who were a part of it, to their Japanese counterparts, which are well
maintained and conspicuous, visited often by Japanese tourists, many
of whom have come particularly to pay homage to the war dead. Regular delegations from Japanese families and communities come to the
Pacific islands to claim the bones and relics that are constantly
unearthed. More nagging than the superior memory of the Japanese is
the superior influence that the Japanese now enjoy in their lost territo-

ries. Everywhere Manchester notes signs of Japanese economic power, which he considers a final victory for Japan over the fallen Americans who are now forgotten by their own people. Citizens of the Pacific, he avers, feel the same resentment at Japanese economic influence that he does, yet, like him, they find it irresistible.

Manchester's primary concern, however, is not with polemic but with a reliving of the experiences of himself and his fellow "Raggedy Ass Marines." He had originally been marked for officer's training at Quantico, but before long it became apparent that he was neither temperamentally nor socially suited to officer status. Insubordination was finally his ticket out of the program, and he arrived at Guadalcanal as a sergeant. Without apparent irony, he was classified as an "intelligence specialist;" he was part of a section within his battalion assigned to "estimate enemy strength on the battalion's front, to identify enemy units by the flashes on the tunics of their dead, to patrol deep behind enemy lines, to advise our junior officers who were having trouble reading maps, and to carry messages to company commanders whose field radios were out of order." Manchester was joined in these tasks by a group of talented young men who for one reason or another had been denied entry into the society of officers.

> We called ourselves "the Raggedy Ass Marines." The rest of the battalion called us "the bandits." Whatever the name, I was this odd lot's honcho.
> We were in fact very odd. Most of us were military misfits, college students who had enlisted in a fever of patriotism and been rejected as officer candidates because, for various reasons, we either despised the OCS system openly or did not conform to the established concept of how officers should look, speak, and act.

One had the voice of a Wagnerian soprano. One thought military discipline was ridiculous. One was wall-eyed. One admired Japanese culture. One was built "close to the ground, like a cabbage." One had a grotesque facial tic. Others had simply never been to college, including a genius who added columns of four-digit numbers from the left and had worked as a stockboy before the war, and a confidence man who convinced the Marine Corps that he could read and speak Japanese, which was completely untrue.

Manchester's relationships with this group were often painful, since his fear of confrontation made leadership difficult for him. But ultimately the Raggedy Ass Marines became the matrix for his entire war experience. His memories of their antics, achievements, and fates frame the narratives of both his 1945 and 1978 tours. No detail is too crude or gory to be included, and toward the end of the book, in an imaginary roll call he coolly and meticulously notes the final escapes and near-escapes of his men, letting absurdity speak with its own voice. Manchester, it is clear, has a sharp vision of the senselessness of his own survival, stumbling through the maze of enemy snipers and artillery, the creeping dangers and diseases of the jungle, and the miscalculations and tunnel vision of the American military planners. That so many of his fellows did not complete the tour is, for Manchester, yet another part of the darkness to be dispelled.

If Manchester finds little in the modern Pacific to comfort him, he is also less than comfortable with modern American society. He suspects that the typical American reader will experience no flash of recognition in reading his memoir, and he is probably right. In his honest portrayal of his own sentiments, his ideas often emerge as contradictory. He hated the way Marine life was managed, but loved the Marines as an institution and cherishes his identity as a Marine. He claims to resent the Japanese but not to hate them, illustrating his point with a polite encounter with a young Japanese woman at the memorial of a Japanese general. His revulsion against war is complete, yet he entertains no political ideas that might parallel his sentiments. At the same time he clearly feels bemused by contemporary society after his close immersion in his own past. His students at Wesleyan University in Connecticut now inform him that some of his favorite poetry is sexist.

Despite his own experiences, he still is not convinced that modern skepticism of the military is justified. He clearly recognizes that internationalist sentiment is common in contemporary America and that the Japanese are respected as a nation of economic and technological accomplishment, yet he apparently is unable to give up the language of enmity; the Japanese to him are "Nips," "Nipponese," or "Japs." He repeats the conviction of his contemporaries that the atomic bombings of Hiroshima and Nagasaki by the United States were the only conceivable means of avoiding the huge American military and Japanese civilian losses that would have occurred in an invasion of the main Japanese islands. And perhaps most poignant, he is convinced, without saying why, that all sense of pride in American identity has been lost: "Without having the haziest idea of what combat would be, we wanted, in a phrase which sounds quaint today, to fight for our country. Subsequent generations have lost that blazing patriotism and speak of it, if at all, patronizingly. They cannot grasp how proud we were to be Americans."

Manchester has contributed a movingly guileless memoir, in which he seeks neither to justify, analyze, or, indeed, order his past. He has the courage to recall experiences profoundly at odds with his sense of how the world should work and yet makes no attempt to hide the fact that he is not a man whose view of the past has been significantly transformed by a society that prides itself on the fitful progressiveness of its ideals. His is the authentic testament of a man somehow indelibly marked by his own youth and the experiences of war. It is invaluable reading for people in the present.

Pamela Kyle Crossley

GREEN MONDAY

Author: Michael M. Thomas (1936–   )
Publisher: Wyndham Books (New York). 414 pp. $12.95
Type of work: Novel
Time: The present
Locale: United States, London, Paris, the Middle East

The ministers of a small OPEC nation, Qu'Nesh, attempt to change the economic and political structure of the United States and the entire world

> *Principal characters*:
> DAVID HARRISON, independent investment banker
> ALI KHAFIQ, unofficial member of the ruling family of the kingdom of Qu'Nesh
> THE MINISTER OF QU'NESH
> PRINCE ALRAZI, Prime Minister of Qu'Nesh
> FULGER BAXTER, President of the United States
> HERDON DUNSTABLE, Texas politician
> ERNEST CLEVELAND JONES, a computer expert
> DEVON LINDE, investment analyst and girl Friday
> JOHN JORDAN, former ambassador to Qu'Nesh and Republican nominee for president of the United States
> ALEX CAMRAN, investment analyst

On a sunny afternoon aboard the yacht of a mutual friend, David Harrison, an independent investment broker, was voicing his disenchantment with the world situation in general and the political and economic condition of the United States in particular. Listening rather impassively was Ali Khafiq, whose acquaintance Harrison had made during the Aegean cruise. Khafiq, an unofficial member of the ruling forces of the Kingdom of Qu'Nesh, listened to Harrison's strategy to bring off an economic about face with a mind that was alert to every detail and that absorbed every word.

Harrison's plan was basically simple. He suggested that the Kingdom could turn the world money market around by making a substantial cutback in the price of its crude oil to $10 a barrel. Such an action would serve to strengthen the dollar, which would, in turn, make the foreign reserves held by the Kingdom, as well as its loans in dollars to other Third World countries, more valuable, along with reducing the rate of inflation of products and systems that the Kingdom imported from industrial nations.

The Minister and the Prime Minister of Qu'Nesh, one of the Organization of Petroleum Exporting Countries (OPEC), had been cautioning their OPEC neighbors to curb the rising oil prices. The other countries, however, refused to listen, and, as the Kingdom's ministers had predicted, friendships with the United States were being priced out of existence.

Khafiq, intrigued by Harrison's plan, approached the Minister. Together they modified the plan somewhat prior to presenting it to the Prime Minister. Harrison had alluded to the fact that the Kingdom could literally handpick the next President of the United States if it were suggested that secret negotiations had brought the reduction in the price of oil. Although the Kingdom disliked the current President, Fulger Baxter, they intended to imply that he had been privately involved in the negotiations to lower the price of oil. Since John Jordan, a former ambassador to the Kingdom, was truly their "favorite son," they intended to have him nominated by the Republican party. It was then agreed that three weeks prior to the election an announcement would be made to the effect that since the Baxter administration had broken the agreements that had brought about the reduced oil rate, the price cut would be rescinded. The American public, reeling in disbelief, would unanimously elect Jordan.

When the plan was presented to the Prime Minister, he modified it even further, suggesting that since the Dow Jones average would certainly go up a minimum of one thousand points, they could increase their own portfolios by investing $5 billion "borrowed" from the Kingdom's holdings. As the King was only interested in the study of the Koran and the building of a spectacular mosque, he would hardly be aware that the money was missing. Furthermore, if the money was returned within a reasonable amount of time, the risk was negligible.

Once all of the details were worked out, the Minister, through his friend Khafiq, hired David Harrison, who had completely forgotten about the conversation aboard the yacht, to invest the $5 billion inconspicuously. The only stipulation was that it had to be done before the announcement reducing the price of oil, scheduled to be made on Good Friday. Using many aliases, Harrison contracted with an expert to design a computer program that could effectively handle all of the financial transactions. With the help of Ernie Jones and Devon Linde, who were hired by the Kingdom to run the computer and to help Harrison set up accounts in over one hundred banks, $4.8 billion was funneled into the stock market.

On Good Friday, at the end of an energy convention, the momentous announcement was made. As predicted, the stock market went wild and, at the same time, Harrison was advised to begin the slow liquidation of assets. Fulger Baxter's popularity, due to cleverly placed leaks in the media, soared, and although he was as bewildered as everyone else by the chain of events, he allowed himself momentarily to bask in his enhanced reputation.

Meanwhile, Alex Camran, a young investment analyst employed by

Certified Bank, was aware that great sums of money had been invested in the stock market and that most of the equities had already been sold. Disturbed because Certified Bank had received none of this business, he resolved to find out why. He discussed the matter with a friend in Washington who brought it to the attention of a friend in the Treasury Department. The department's probing revealed that $9 billion had been realized, and it was then that the matter was revealed to Fulger Baxter. Baxter, suspecting a connection between the $9 billion and the reduction of the oil prices, enlisted the aid of Herndon Dunstable, a powerful Texas politician, to expose what appeared to be a political and financial scheme.

After eliminating all other possibilities, Baxter and Dunstable deduced that the original money had probably come from Qu'Nesh, that the King was probably unaware of what was happening, and that the ministers certainly had something else planned as their negative feelings about Baxter were well documented. They correctly surmised that some sort of announcement would probably occur at the next OPEC meeting, which was planned for three weeks prior to the election in the United States. Suspecting that the announcement was designed to destroy Baxter politically, they invited the Minister to a meeting at Camp David under the guise of a security problem. There, Baxter discussed the recent occurrences in the stock market and the Minister, of course, feigned ignorance. Baxter then left the rest of the meeting to an extraordinarily capable Dunstable. Dunstable presented the facts to the Minister and let it be known that if anything unusual happened at the OPEC convention, the United States would be forced to dynamite the King's mosque and expose the fact that his money had been used to increase the personal wealth of the ministers. Lest the Minister think that Dunstable was bluffing about the mosque's accessibility, he was shown a film of the decapitation ceremony of his brother, which had occurred approximately eighteen months earlier. After conferring with the Prime Minister via telephone, the Minister assured Dunstable that nothing unusual would take place at the OPEC convention.

Baxter was reelected to a second term. Shortly after the inauguration, his vice-president contracted a rare disease. Ill health forced him to resign from office, and Herndon Dunstable was chosen to take his place. Baxter, in an effort to tie up all of the loose ends of his maneuver, managed to send to John Jordan the tape recording of a conversation between Dunstable and others that, if necessary, would ruin Dunstable's political career.

Dunstable and the ministers also tied up loose ends by methodically eliminating everyone involved from the beginning of the plan. All, that is, except for Harrison and Devon Linde who, escaping assassination, were eventually assured that there would be no further attempts.

Michael Thomas, an investment banker himself, brings a thorough grasp of the stock market and international finance to his first novel, *Green Monday*. It is frightening in concept, not only for its suspense and excitement but also because it is eminently possible. There is little in the novel that could not happen, or perhaps already has. The realist, feeling the pinch of inflation and concerned about the economic and political situation in the United States and all over the world, is made chillingly aware of this fact by Thomas's thriller.

Susan Floman

HEARTSOUNDS

Author: Martha Weinman Lear
Publisher: Simon & Schuster (New York). 413 pp. $12.95
Type of work: Memoir
Time: 1973–1978
Locale: New York City; briefly, Provincetown, Massachusetts

A journalist's memoir of her husband's struggle with progressive heart disease

Principal personages:
DR. HAROLD (HAL) LEAR, physician and heart patient
MARTHA WEINMAN LEAR, his wife, a journalist and author
DR. MOSES SILVERMAN and DR. PETER MASON, cardiologists

In this memoir of her husband's long struggle with progressive heart disease, journalist Martha Weinman Lear is writing about the most personal and difficult of subjects: impending death and the effect it has on two people who love each other very much. Out of this painful experience, she has created a book that is stunning and fascinating—beautifully written, brutally candid, containing piercing criticisms of the medical profession and sensitive insights into the nature of marriage.

When Dr. Harold Lear had his first heart attack at the age of 53, his initial reaction was that of most victims: disbelief. Yet within minutes his professional instincts took over and he was responding with the cool urgency of an experienced physician. Alone in his New York apartment, he dialed 911, only to be told that his particular request—that the operator call his doctor—did not come under the jurisdiction of the emergency service. So, rapidly growing weaker and dizzier, he managed to get to the elevator and down to the lobby, where he alerted the doorman as to his condition and was taken to a nearby hospital. The undignified, desperate quality of this incident was to characterize Hal's entire illness—he would request help, the request would be refused, and he would be forced finally to help himself, at great physical and emotional cost.

His wife Martha immediately flew home from France, where she had been working on an article, and the Lears faced the crisis together. That crisis, while chillingly sudden, was not wholly unexpected. There was an ominously high incidence of heart disease in Hal's family, he had been smoking three packs of cigarettes a day, and for the past few years he had been under intense professional stress. Several years earlier, he had given up a thriving private urology practice in suburban Connecticut to set up a human sexuality center at a New York City hospital. Once in New York, he found the hospital administration to be uncooperative. Yet, he gradually built the program to a position of national prestige. Then the hospital demoted him to associate director and installed as director a less experienced man. The situation had become intolerable, humiliating, and Hal had no real outlet for his anger and frustration. The strain was too much for his heart.

After a short hospital stay, Hal was released and the Lears began the awesome task of accommodating their lives to the restrictions imposed by his illness. There was no question of his returning to work. He had to rest most of the time and was still bothered by chest pains. Although encouraged to exercise, he found a one-block walk an ordeal. As he grew stronger, the resumption of sex proved even more difficult for both Hal and Martha, as each struggled to conceal from the other the fear that he might have another heart attack brought on by lovemaking. Hal was also having trouble quitting smoking. And worst of all, both Hal and Martha felt the strain of constant dread and ignorance —would he ever be the same again? Would he have another attack? Was he healing as he should? These fears were compounded by the fact that neither of them felt very comfortable with Hal's cardiologist, Dr. Roberts, who was remote and vague and seemed unconcerned when Hal reported that he was having increasingly severe chest pains. Hal decided to get a second opinion and consulted Dr. Moses Silverman, a prominent cardiologist. Silverman found that Hal was experiencing heart failure, which should have been immediately apparent to Roberts. Hal then decided to make Silverman his regular doctor and, shortly afterwards, had his second heart attack. This one, though milder than the first, left him with the excruciating pain of angina.

He underwent an angiogram, and the doctors discovered that the damage to the heart was far more severe than they had guessed. Hal needed immediate open-heart surgery: a double coronary bypass.

The operation was apparently successful. The painful angina disappeared, and Hal was able to walk again and even work out a little in the gym. But the surgery also brought about what was for Hal the most devastating effect of his whole illness, an unexplained, nightmarish memory impairment. He would read the newspaper and seconds later would be unable to recall what he had read. Simple, short words seen on a page were incomprehensible to him. Ordinary conversation baffled him; a trip to the grocery store was a walk through a labyrinth. Worst of all, his doctors refused to acknowledge that anything was wrong with him mentally; they joked and said he was just beginning to feel his age. Hal, enraged at their condescension, finally underwent a series of tests with a psychologist, who confirmed what Hal had suspected all along; the surgery had left him with permanent minor brain damage. Even if he were to heal physically, he would never be able to function as a doctor again, and just functioning in everyday life would be difficult.

The Lears had another worry at this point. Hal's physical health was not what it should have been, a year after the surgery. Hal several times made suggestions to Silverman as to possible modes of treatment, but Silverman barely listened. More and more the senior cardiologist was referring Hal to his junior partner, Peter Mason. Although Mason was an excellent doctor, Hal was insulted and hurt that the senior man no longer had time for him.

Delving into the medical facts of his own illness, he discovered that he had had another heart attack, during the open heart surgery two years earlier, and no one had told him. No wonder his physical condition was still so poor. The knowledge that everyone, including Martha, had concealed this from him added to Hal's frustration and rage. How could he monitor his own case if he was not kept informed about what was happening to him?

Martha resented Hal's loss of power, both physical and professional, and her fears for his future (and for her own) caused her to nag at him frequently. Hal, accustomed to a sharp mind, a strong body, and a challenging professional life, found the loss of these things hard to accept. Martha Lear is as honest about the effects of these losses as she is about everything else. Despite the incredible strain and fear, the Lears' marriage remained strong and loving.

They spent that summer in their house in Provincetown, where Hal grew strong again and enjoyed a period of miraculously good health. By the time the Lears returned to New York in the fall, however, Hal was weak and exhausted once again. He continued to worsen through the fall and winter, and finally, in April, had to enter the hospital once more. There, one horrifying night, Hal lay gasping for air, and not one hospital staff member paid any attention. The intern on duty refused to check on Hal; he was too busy reading the newspaper. Later, as Hal's condition grew critical, the intern had gone to bed, and the nurse refused to wake him up for fear of losing her job. Finally, at eight o'clock, Mason came to look at Hal and immediately rushed him down to intensive care, where he suddenly was regarded as an acute emergency case. What Martha Lear cannot get over in the telling of this incident is the absurdity of it: total neglect all night in an institution of healing, and then specialized emergency care to counter the crisis brought about by that neglect. Through it all she remained passive, afraid that if she made too big a fuss they would throw her out of the hospital.

Although Hal recovered from this crisis, Martha now had to begin facing the fact that he would die soon. They went to Provincetown once more, and the last chapter ends there. In an epilogue, Martha Lear tells briefly of Hal's death over a year later and of her own efforts to begin a life without him.

In American literature there are a number of thoughtful, sensitive memoirs written by bereaved relatives. Yet Martha Lear's *Heartsounds* stands alone in its relentless probing of the darker side of love that is exposed in extreme and prolonged crisis. It is also unique in its rage. In John Gunther's *Death Be Not Proud* and in Doris Lund's *Eric*, parents eloquently tell the stories of their sons' battles with terminal cancer. For Martha Lear, Hal's death is not an inexplicable abstraction; she is not writing in an attempt to find meaning in his death. On the surface, she appears simply to be recording and analyzing the events of his illness. But there is much more going on.

As well as being a highly personal memoir, *Heartsounds* is also an angry indictment of the medical profession—of the unspeakable blunders, colossal egotism, and insensitive errors committed routinely by doctors. She is in a unique position to make these criticisms; having been a doctor's wife, she has seen the medical profession from both sides. When Hal was well, she had a sense of vicarious omnipotence watching him hold human lives in his hands. When he fell ill, she felt completely helpless watching him decline steadily under the haphazard ministrations of his physicians. Hal himself was horrified at the implications of the inconsistent medical care he received, and spent much time reexamining his own years as a doctor, looking for possible instances in which he might have failed his own patients. Both the Lears became increasingly aware of the plight of the layman. Hal was able to ask shrewd questions about his treatment and to protest against errors in health care, but someone who knew nothing about medicine would be completely at the mercy of doctors and nurses.

For all of its bitterness, however, *Heartsounds* is also a loving story of a good man and a good marriage. Martha Lear's portrait of her husband and their life is so vivid that when Hal dies the reader is fully aware of what is lost. It takes courage to read this book. One can only guess at the courage needed to write it.

Joan Barrett Wickersham

HELEN AND TEACHER

Author: Joseph P. Lash (1909–)
Publisher: Delacorte Press/Seymour Lawrence (New York). 811 pp. $17.95
Type of work: Biography
Time: 1866–1968
Locale: The United States, particularly Alabama and New England

A biography of the blind, deaf, and mute woman Helen Keller, and her teacher, Anne Sullivan Macy, detailing the lives of each as an individual, but focusing on their symbiotic relationship, in which one perceived the world largely through the senses of the other

Principal personages:
ANNE MANSFIELD SULLIVAN, teacher, constant companion, friend, and mentor of Helen Keller
HELEN ADAMS KELLER, who overcame her handicaps to become one of the most celebrated women of her time
MICHAEL ANAGNOS, educator, head of Perkins Institution for the Blind
JOHN MACY, secretary to Helen and Annie, later Annie's husband
POLLY THOMSON, secretary to Helen and Annie
PETER FAGAN, Helen's suitor
NELLA BRADDY HENNEY, friend of both Helen and Annie, collaborator with Helen, author of Anne's biography

Anne Mansfield Sullivan was born in 1866 in Agawam, Massachusetts, to impoverished Irish immigrants. Her father, Thomas, was a brawler and a drunk; her mother, a gentle woman, was crippled. Annie was the eldest of five children, all but one suffering from some physical disability. She, herself, contracted a disease when she was about five, which left her half blind.

At the death of her mother, when Annie was close to eight, she was sent to a relative; then, with a crippled brother, to the Tewksbury Almshouse. Jimmie died there; Annie remained, unschooled, until an appeal to a trustee of Boston's Perkins Institution for the Blind brought admission to that school. There, her hot temper frequently got her into trouble, yet she did well enough in her studies to be recommended to Captain Arthur Keller when he sought a "governess" for his daughter, Helen.

The Kellers lived graciously but modestly in the small Alabama town of Tuscumbia, where Helen was born in 1880. At the age of nineteen months, the child was stricken with an illness that left her deaf and blind. Undisciplined, untaught, she was little more than a savage when Captain Keller turned for help to the Perkins Institution, where a similarly handicapped child had been taught to communicate through the spelling of words into her hand. And so Anne Sullivan arrived in Tuscumbia in 1887 to take charge of educating Helen.

The teacher's first task was to establish control over Helen; that accomplished, she could teach her to associate words with things—to communicate. The moments at which Anne Sullivan succeeded in these endeavors—when she demanded obedience before permitting Helen to eat, and when she held one hand under a gushing pump and spelled out "water" into the other—have become classics in both pedagogy and literature.

Helen proved to have a remarkably receptive mind and an overwhelming curiosity. That combination, along with Annie's genius for teaching, soon worked what the world would call "miracles." Helen learned the manual language and thereby to "speak." Soon she learned to write and to read. Her thirst for knowledge seemed insatiable. Moreover, her sweet disposition endeared her to everyone she met or corresponded with. Their number was legion.

Through Michael Anagnos, director of Perkins, knowledge of Helen's accomplishments spread rapidly, and she encountered many of the greats of the day, among them Mark Twain, Oliver Wendell Holmes, and John Greenleaf Whittier.

Remarkable though her progress was, Annie Sullivan—or "Teacher"—felt she needed other children, and Helen was enrolled at Perkins. She took all Boston by storm. Interest in Helen continued to grow; magazines and papers featured articles about her. Some were written by Helen herself.

She was eleven when a story she sent Anagnos as a birthday greeting was published, with fulsome praise of the author, in a small magazine. It was, however, very similar to one read to Helen a few years before, and its appearance caused an uproar. Helen was accused of plagiarism, and an "investigation" was conducted. But Annie bore the brunt of the criticism. Anagnos called her a "humbug;" many who had characterized her as a "miracle worker" now implied she was more of a ventriloquist, putting words into Helen's mouth.

The storm blew over quickly, but Annie never forgave Anagnos. Further, she resented any credit he—or Perkins—took for Helen's success; it was, she made plain, to be hers alone. Anagnos was only one of many with whom Teacher quarreled over Helen. Annie stayed in the background, pushing her charge into the limelight, but she was jealous of any who might usurp her own place. If Helen was dependent on Teacher, Teacher was dependent on Helen. Mark Twain summed up their relationship with "It took the two of you to make a complete and perfect whole."

With Teacher beside her Helen mastered English and went on to

French and German. Later she would learn Latin and Greek. And at the age of twenty, she entered Radcliffe. She graduated *cum laude,* a disappointment to Annie who had hoped for a *summa cum laude.*

While still in college, Helen, with the help of John Macy, an editor and an instructor at Harvard, wrote and published her first book, *The Story of My Life.* With a business sense they lacked, Macy became indispensable to them. He began, as well, to court Annie, ten years his senior, and in 1905 they were married.

John was a Socialist and a pacifist, and Teacher strongly disapproved of his political views. Helen, however, adopted them with enthusiasm, to the dismay of her friends. It was fitting that such a woman as Helen should be a suffragist. But to be a Socialist was unthinkable, to support the International Workers of the World an outrage.

Helen was deeply committed to her ideals, though, and published a book of socialist writings, *Out of the Dark.* She had learned to speak, but was barely intelligible. With the incentive of spreading her ideas, she now concentrated on improving her voice.

Teacher's marriage, which had begun well, had soon deteriorated. John was brilliant, but a heavy drinker. Moreover, he depended on Helen and Annie for financial support. After nine years John, complaining that he had "married an institution," left Teacher. With his departure, a young Scottish woman, Polly Thomson, was hired as a secretary. She was called home briefly and was replaced by a young man, Peter Fagan, who had been John's assistant.

Fagan, who was twenty-nine—Helen was then thirty-six—knew the manual language and could read Braille. And he was as devoted to radical causes as Helen. They fell in love, but told no one. Word leaked out, though, that they planned to elope; they had, in fact, taken out a marriage license. At that point, Kate Keller, Helen's mother, moved to put an end to the affair, driving Fagan away from the family home with a shotgun. It was a pathetic finish to Helen's only romance.

Helen had no private life; her personal life was also her public life. She devoted it largely to campaigning on behalf of the blind and the deaf. Her financial situation was precarious. Captain Keller had lost his job, for political reasons, while she was still a small child; he died when Helen was sixteen. Many of her needs were then met by gifts from wealthy benefactors, some of whom set up trust funds for her and Teacher. She had some income from her writings, as did Annie and John Macy, and lecturing brought more. An arrangement with the Federation for the Blind provided a salary and expenses while she was on fund-raising tours. Often, too, Helen and Teacher went on the "lecture circuit." They went into vaudeville, too, where Helen was a hit, speaking first, then answering questions from the audience. A movie based on her life, *Deliverance*, was a financial disaster, and friends again came to their aid.

As the years went on, Helen's fame grew. She and Teacher traveled around the world, received by heads of state. Honors, including honorary degrees, were heaped upon them. Then, the ultimate disaster overtook Helen: in 1936, Teacher died.

Polly Thomson, the Scottish secretary, took over Annie's responsibilities, but she could not take her place. Nella Braddy Henney, who had collaborated on Helen's book *My Religion* and was now one of her closest friends, devoted herself to the woman.

But Helen's life went on. There was a visit to Japan and the publication of a book, *Journal*. World War II was in full swing. Helen, a pacifist, had opposed American participation, but she was needed by the wounded, especially the blind. She toured the military hospitals, bringing cheer and hope to thousands.

With the war over, Helen, now with Polly, traveled once more; Japan again, South Africa, the Middle East. In 1948, however, Polly suffered a stroke. Recovering, she accompanied Helen on more tours: India, Latin America, the Scandinavian countries. There were more honors. A documentary film based on Helen's life, *The Unconquered*, was released; in 1955, she received an honorary degree from Harvard, the first awarded to a woman. That year also saw publication of Helen's book about Annie, *Teacher*.

In 1957, Polly suffered a cerebral hemorrhage, and now there was almost no one on whom Helen could depend. Polly had, like Annie, been jealous. But Annie had shared Helen with others; Polly had driven others away. Nor were there many old friends still alive. The one bright spot that year was the first production of William Gibson's now classic play about Helen and Annie, *The Miracle Worker*. Otherwise, Helen seemed to retreat into her shell, seeing few people, but still reading voraciously.

Polly Thomson died in 1960; the following year Helen Keller also suffered a stroke and retired from public life. When she died, in 1968, a memorial service was held at the National Cathedral in Washington, D.C. Later, her ashes were placed next to those of Polly and of Teacher.

Few characters in the recent past have better lent themselves to the art of the biographer than Helen Keller and Anne Sullivan Macy, Helen's "Teacher." Their story of courage, and the ultimate triumph over seemingly insuperable odds, is one of high drama. There is the element of tragedy in a small child's cruel affliction and of pathos as well. Inevitably, it has prompted innumerable articles, along with hundreds of books. But it would be hard to find a better one than that which Joseph P. Lash gives us in *Helen and Teacher: The Story of Helen Keller and Anne Sullivan Macy.*

Lash, best known for his prize-winning biography, *Eleanor and Franklin,* has brought the same skill to his treatment of these two remarkable women that he brought to that of Roosevelt and his wife. His approach is sympathetic, but never sentimental. His writing is clear and concise. His research seems to have been inexhaustible, and he has unearthed important information in documents that have been previously unknown. The result is a deeply moving book that, for all its length, is never dull, never lags for a moment.

It is, however, the author's deep psychological insights that makes *Helen and Teacher* so outstanding. Lash has, of course, based his book on the actual lives of each of the protagonists and told the story of each. His real subject, though, is their relationship, that of one human being who is dependent, to the most extraordinary degree, upon another. The needs, the conflicts, the fears, and the desire—all the emotions they experienced, fascinate the author. As he explores them, he makes them just as fascinating to the reader.

Seen through Lash's eyes, new pictures of both Helen and Anne Sullivan Macy emerge. Helen Keller is usually thought of, quite properly, as the embodiment of courage. Lash also reveals the terrors that lay beneath the surface. He shows both Teacher's genius and the insecurities that shaped both her life and her pupil's.

In *Helen and Teacher,* Joseph Lash wipes away the sentimentality that has shrouded both these women for so long. They are seen as living, breathing human beings, which is a welcome relief from the sainthood so often thrust upon them. *Helen and Teacher* is a most welcome book.

Vivian Werner

HE/SHE

Author: Herbert Gold
Publisher: Arbor House (New York). 213 pp. $9.95
Type of work: Novel
Time: The 1970's
Locale: An unspecified city

A *husband and wife endure the difficult process of their marriage coming* apart

> *Principal characters:*
> HE, the husband, an assistant principal at a local school
> SHE, his wife
> CYNTHIA, their daughter
> HAL, the wife's lover
> LESTER, a problem student at His school
> PAUL and PAULA, Gestalt therapists
> JEHANE, therapist at Dream Dharma Academy
> UWE, Norwegian educator, His associate
> LAUREN, Uwe's ex-wife

He/She attempts to deal on a general level with a problem that, in its many individual cases, has provided material for a host of novelists. It details the gradual, painful dissolution of a marriage. The protagonists are kept nebulous and nameless throughout the book, and at first the reasons for their split appear to be just as intangible.

She announces her wish to free herself from her role as His wife and mother of their small daughter. He is shocked and grieved by this. He loves her, he says, and he demands fuller explanations from her for her decision. According to her, his love is not enough. She is unsatisfied, although they enjoy what most would consider an excellent sexual relationship. She wants to take a lover, but on her first attempt at adultery, she spends the whole time being sick in the bathroom.

Now, as unsure of the rightness of taking a lover as she was sure of the rightness of leaving her husband, she agrees to try family therapy. They go to Paula and Paul, a pair of unlicensed, untrained therapists who might be the prototypes of all pop-culture analysts in America. Therapy yields no solution.

In spite of the conflicting emotions devouring him, he goes on with his job as assistant principal. He becomes involved with Lester, a fatherless black boy, eleven years old, who deals with his own frustrations and griefs by spitting. He feels a sense of kinship with Lester and takes him under his wing. He also, in the course of his job, meets again an old friend, Uwe. Uwe is a Norwegian educator who has brought his ex-wife Lauren with him on this trip to the States. Their relationship gives him a chance to see how others are dealing with a marriage that has come apart. He tries to indulge in a little adultery of his own with Lauren, but it goes no further than a vaguely adolescent cuddle in the park.

The marriage continues to dissolve. She alternates between raging at him for trying to bind her to him with his sorrow and viciously provoking that sorrow. She cannot stand his insistence on his love for her, nor his preoccupation with making her explain precisely what she wants and why she is ending their marriage. She says that she never loved him. For all of that, they still continue their sexual relationship. She decides that it was a virus rather than guilt that ruined her first try at an affair and determines once more to take a lover. When he demands to know who it is, she remains obstinately silent.

The war of emotional attrition continues. He moves out of their house and takes an apartment. He flirts with the idea of death. He feels that he cannot go on living without her, but he shies away from suicide, preferring to daydream about having a fatal accident, death without responsibility. He is, he reflects, too used to being married, protected by a strong woman, to face life unarmed.

He encounters her lover, Hal, by chance when he comes to pick up their daughter for an outing. There is a violent scene, but no actual violence. He transfers his love to their daughter Cynthia, but still he longs for his wife. He tries to get free through the ministrations of Jehane of the Dream Dharma Academy, whose therapy is largely sexual. He compares notes with other newly single fathers and begins to think he will survive after all.

In the meantime, she is not enjoying their separation as much as she thought she would. She remains plagued with doubts. Her habits of dress become erratic indicators of her inner moods. She goes from the hard self-sufficiency of jeans and work-shirts to the exaggerated femininity of long skirts and filmy blouses. Together they continue having occasional sex, but he never stays the night, at her insistence.

There is never any cleanly delineated break between them. They divorce, but the slang for divorce, "split," does not seem to apply. It is too clean a word for what is an almost organic pulling apart. Their marriage does not break, it tears, and the tear is a wound that he appears to feel more than she does.

He starts to take an interest in other women. He imposes a stern program of self-discipline that involves not thinking about her, not remembering the good times they once shared. He classifies the emotion he feels as homesickness for a place in time, when everything seemed to be settled for him. He had a wife, a child, and a steady job, the three requisites for happiness in American society. Now that he has no wife and only a half-share in a child, his job remains the one sure thing to which he can cling. In fact, the job saves him from mental collapse. She has no such rock and must rely entirely on her own certainty for support.

In the end he becomes numb. He can see her without pain. For him she has become less of a person, and although they still make love, there is no love in it for him any more. When she invites him to stay the night, it is he who declines. Even though he continued to think of her as his wife after the divorce, now she has sunk below the label of ex-wife to that of simply meat, an anonymous body that he pleasures and from which he receives some pleasure.

In analyzing the dissolution of a marriage, Herbert Gold has tried to make a statement about the dissolution of marriage in general. He uses very few specifics in terms of time, place, characters, or even motivation. A passing reference to Kissinger, Watergate, and the passed 1960's is the closest the author comes to fixing the time. As for locale, he selects a city that has poverty and pretty parks, but nothing more definite. That the main characters of the drama never have proper names speaks for itself. Gold wishes to give the reader an *Everyman* of marriage, separation, and divorce.

Gold's characters have problems that are vague but agonizing. She defines her wants in terms of negatives: not to be married, not to be hampered with a child, not to have to explain. Although a lover of truth-telling and compulsive about being sure of things, she realizes that she is not sure exactly of what she wants or if it will make her happy. Her strivings are made harder by the fact that she cannot break free of marriage. Marriage is a membrane that clings and hinders her. The magic word "divorce" does not break the spell of involvement.

His desires are also based on uncertainty and negativism. He wants not to be alone, not to be unprotected by the womb of family life. He fears uncertainty as much as she does, and by her insistence on divorce she is forcing him to face a new life filled with uncertainty. Yet, throughout it all, the two of them cannot completely give each other up. She finds it hard to live with him and just as hard to live without him. He thinks he can never live without her, but learns that if he must, he can. The divorce decree is not a sharp enough edge to sever them completely. There is no neat resolution in this book, just as there are few neat cuts in the separations of real life.

Esther M. Friesner

INNOCENT BLOOD

Author: P. D. James
Publisher: Charles Scribner's Sons (New York). 311 pp. $10.95
Type of work: Novel
Time: Summer and early fall 1978
Locale: London

An adopted girl, seeking her biological mother, discovers much about her own identity and her ability to love

Principal characters:
> PHILIPPA PALFREY, an 18-year-old adopted girl who plans to become a writer
> MAURICE PALFREY, her adoptive father, a sociologist
> HILDA PALFREY, her adoptive mother
> MARY DUCTON, Philippa's biological mother, a convicted child-murderer
> NORMAN SCASE, father of the murdered child
> GABRIEL LOMAS, Philippa's casual boyfriend

In *Innocent Blood*, P. D. James, departing from her customary murder-mystery format, presents an intricately-woven plot that details the long-term effects of a heinous crime. After the brutal rape and murder of a child, the surviving family members are psychologically changed. The novel begins many years after the crime was committed.

Immediately following her eighteenth birthday, Philippa Palfrey reports to the Registrar General in London requesting the names of her biological parents, information to which she is legally entitled under the British Children's Act of 1975. Philippa wishes to discover her identity, to give substance to the fragmented fantasies that have been familiar recurrences in her dreams since childhood.

Philippa's adoptive father, Maurice Palfrey, is a prominent sociologist and university lecturer. Her adoptive mother, Hilda (Maurice's second wife), is a timid, colorless, pathetic woman whose one pleasure is cooking. After Maurice's first wife, Helena, and their son, Orlando, were killed, Maurice married Hilda. Philippa reflects that her relationship with her adoptive parents is not one of love; instead, she believes they suit one another.

Philippa was raised to believe that her real mother was dead. She seeks her real father at the address provided by the Registrar and finds an empty house. Neighbors tell her that Martin John Ducton died in prison while serving a sentence for the rape and murder of a little girl named Julie Scase. They also inform her that Mary Ducton, her mother, is alive and still in prison.

Philippa is stunned by this information. She rushes home and confronts Hilda, demanding, "Why didn't you tell me my mother was a murderess?" Hilda admits that she concocted Philippa's previous fantasy about her origin to protect her. Maurice now informs Philippa that her mother is due to be released from Melcombe Grange Prison in a month's time.

Acting impulsively and defiantly, Philippa discards her plans for a vacation in Europe prior to entering Cambridge, and writes to her mother, inviting her to share a flat she plans to rent in London. Maurice labels her plan stupid and dangerous. Philippa retorts, "She can give me a past, help me find out who I am."

Concurrent with Philippa's story, P. D. James traces the movements of Norman Scase, father of the child who was raped and murdered by Martin and Mary Ducton. Chapters detailing Scase's activities are interwoven with those involving Philippa and her mother.

Norman Scase retires from his job as an accounts clerk. He is a mild, unassuming man whose outward demeanor never hints at his innermost thoughts: "I have to retire early because there is something I must do in the next few months, a task which will take a great deal of time and planning. I have to find and kill the murderess of my child." He promised his wife on her deathbed that he would kill Mary Ducton, and he has already begun his preparations.

Scase engages a detective to determine exactly when Mary Ducton will be released from prison. He sells his house and uses money from his office retirement party to buy a kitchen knife, binoculars, a canvas rucksack, protective gloves, and a white transparent mackintosh. He is now fully equipped for murder.

Meanwhile, Philippa visits her mother in prison and tries to analyze her emotions concerning this first encounter. "Here was a balance between excitement and apprehension, a euphoria which had nothing to do with the mind's quietude. Contentment, perhaps. Now at least I know who I am. I know the worst, I shall know the best. Above all, a sense that it was right to be here . . . an end and a beginning." Mary Ducton agrees to live with Philippa once she is released. Then Philippa begins an extensive search for a suitable flat, finally locating a two-room apartment at 12 Delaney Street.

Norman Scase begins his vigil to discover where Mary Ducton will go once she is released from Melcombe Grange. His entire existence is focused on tracking her; he is never parted now from his knife which becomes a "familiar and potent extension of himself." On the day of Mary Ducton's release, Scase watches as Philippa meets her mother. Scase does not know Philippa, but he carefully notes the name tag dangling from her travel bag. He follows both women to the train station but loses them on the crowded underground platform. Frustrated, Scase returns home to plan a systematic search of London for his prey. He calls all of the Palfreys listed in the phone book, using the story of a lost book as a ploy, until he reaches Hilda Palfrey. She innocently confirms that Philippa had resided at 68 Caldecote Road. Scase then rents a room at the Hotel Casablanca, located in sight of Caldecote Road. Here he maintains his vigil, waiting for someone to lead him to Philippa.

Philippa and her mother quickly establish a pleasant routine at 12 Delaney Street. Mary gives her daughter a hand-written account of the murder, which she wrote while in prison. It details the circumstances of the rape and murder. She asks Philippa to read it but not to tell her when she has done so. Philippa complies and feels satisfied that she has been given all that she would ever need to know about that segment of her mother's life. Both women begin to enjoy a free existence: work, dinners in front of the television, long excursions to explore London.

Scase is also lulled into a form of complacency at Hotel Casablanca. He befriends Violet, the blind girl who operates the switchboard, and on a Sunday afternoon takes her walking in Regent's Park. There, entirely by chance, he encounters Philippa and Mary. Scase freezes; then, sick with disappointment at his lost opportunity, he hardens his resolve to find Mary's new home. Sixteen days later, Hilda Palfrey unwittingly leads him to Philippa's flat. Scase's opportunity for vengeance moves closer.

Scase secretes himself in a vacant lot between buildings on Delaney Street and watches Philippa and Mary until he is familiar with their daily routine. Meanwhile, at an art gallery, Philippa and Mary encounter Gabriel Lomas, a casual boyfriend of Philippa's. Philippa introduces Gabriel to her mother but offers no further explanation. Gabriel, his curiosity piqued, phones Hilda to find out the truth about Mary.

Scase, with an expertise developed over weeks of careful observation and practice, steals the keys belonging to the grocer whose shop occupies the street-level space at 12 Delaney Street. With these keys, Scase finally gains access to the building. He spends one eerie afternoon rehearsing his murder plans. He dons his gloves and mackintosh but cannot enter Philippa's apartment because he has no key for that lock.

That evening Philippa and Mary are visited by a reporter sent by Gabriel. Philippa uses a chisel to break the lock on her front door, then threatens to call the police and blame the reporter. This frightens him away, but for Philippa and Mary the peaceful existence is irreparably shattered. They decide they must flee from London to avoid exposure.

Philippa leaves to visit her Caldecote Road home. She intends to steal some silver that she can convert into cash for their flight. Instead,

Philippa confronts Maurice at home. Once he hears of her intention to throw away her education at Cambridge and her whole future, he angrily tells her one final fact about her adoption. "You've assumed that Hilda and I adopted you after the murder, that your mother let you go because she was serving a life sentence, had no real choice. . . . Your adoption order went through exactly two weeks before Julie Scase was killed, and we'd had you as a foster child for six months before then. The truth is quite simple: your mother let you go because she didn't want you." Crushed by this revelation, Philippa runs to Delaney Street and confronts her mother, saying, "I wish you were dead!"

Philippa then leaves the flat and wanders the streets of London in confusion. Finally she realizes that throughout this experience she has thought only of herself. She begins to explore other perspectives. Recognizing that she does love her mother, she returns to the flat.

When Philippa enters the Delaney Street apartment, she discovers Scase in the bedroom, standing over her mother's body. Scase is awkwardly twisting a knife in her neck, muttering to himself, "She won't bleed." Philippa picks up a suicide note: "If God can forgive her death then he will forgive mine. These five weeks have been worth every day of the last ten years. Nothing is your fault. Nothing. This is the better way for me, not just for you. I can die happy because you are alive and I love you." She tells Scase, "I got to her before you. The dead won't bleed." Philippa gently pushes Scase out of the apartment; his mission is done. She calls Maurice and the police.

P. D. James has carefully explored the deep emotions and complex psychological reactions of an adopted girl and a grief-stricken father. Philippa is portrayed with a credible mixture of teenage cynicism and rebelliousness and of vulnerable romanticism. She rejects the familiar support of her adoptive family; she fantasizes that her real parents are starcrossed lovers in a Victorian garden. Her growth toward identity and an understanding of love is painful and believable. Norman Scase is consumed with grief, rage, and an obsessive, calculating desire for revenge. He is also lonely and pathetic. James delineates these subtle emotional facets with skill.

James also delights the reader with her attention to physical detail. She writes of a "smudged sun high above the lake like a great white moon, and the willow fronds slowly shedding their pale lances onto the water," and of "patches of early snow (which) had lain between the clumps of grass like the discarded litter of the dead summer." Sections of London become familiar because of her vivid descriptions.

Marilynn Malin Hufcut

JOSHUA THEN AND NOW

Author: Mordecai Richler (1931–   )
Publisher: Alfred A. Knopf (New York). 435 pp. $11.95
Type of work: Novel
Time: the 1950's and the present
Locale: Montreal, London, Paris, Ibiza

Reviewing his life, a middle-aged Canadian writer of Jewish descent searches for lost integrity as an artist while attempting to piece together the complex puzzle of his identity as a man

Principal characters:
JOSHUA SHAPIRO, a Jewish-Canadian journalist and television commentator
PAULINE HORNBY, his wife
REUBEN SHAPIRO, his father, a former prizefighter
ESTHER SHAPIRO, his mother
JANE TRIMBLE, Pauline's closest girlhood friend
JACK TRIMBLE, Jane's husband
KEVIN HORNBY, Pauline's brother
SENATOR HORNBY, the father of Pauline and Kevin

Although they grew up in the same city, Pauline and Joshua Shapiro come from completely different worlds. Pauline Hornby, daughter of a Canadian senator, is the product of Westmount, Montreal's wealthy English enclave, and McGill University. Joshua Shapiro's father is a former prizefighter and a lovable crook, but Joshua has escaped the demeaning poverty of Montreal's Jewish ghetto via journalism and television. Pauline and Joshua, who met and married in London, return to Montreal many years later with three children, determined to confront the corrosive prejudice of Westmount's decadent Wasps and nouveau riche Jews. Joshua, by selling his talent down the river of slick journalism and glib television commentary, has paid a price for his social elevation. Pauline has relinquished her feisty idealism for the emotional security of a family. As the book opens, both are struggling to come to terms with their peers, their past, and their personal disappointment in themselves.

Being Jewish is for Joshua the stigma he cannot eradicate, and rather than attempt to do so he turns his ethnic heritage into a weapon. A self-made, middle-aged celebrity, he is the token Jew among Pauline's Gentile social set, but it is to his credit that he refuses to act out a stereotypic role. Joshua's old high school friends, once aspiring and now also successfully established in Westmount, are victims of their own insecurity and the pretensions of their milieu. Although he may have compromised himself as an artist, Joshua strives to maintain his personal integrity as a man, a husband, and a father.

Joshua's past surfaces and re-surfaces (Joshua *then*) as the story of Joshua *now* unfolds. Joshua now is a man of principle who ardently avoids living off his wife's considerable financial resources. An important component of his new life is the commitment to his marriage and his children. Joshua spurns the sexual advances of Pauline's girlhood friend Jane Trimble with the same resolve he employs to maintain his own identity during summers on Lake Memphramagog amid the loose drinking and debauchery of Pauline's lifelong friends. Holding himself aloof while they ritualistically prey upon one another, Joshua watches and remembers, hoping Pauline will remain loyal to him.

Joshua then was a boy who idolized the renegade father who deserted him on mysterious trips to Ontario or across the border into the United States during the 1920's and 1930's. Reuben Shapiro, ex-prize-fighter, has been reduced to making "deliveries, sort of" and working as a henchman for a mobster. By sharing his love for the Old Testament, telling Joshua that God did not keep records on a person but was willing to forgive, Reuben tried to teach his son what it means to be a Jew while cheek-by-jowl explaining the proper protocol to be used when visiting a brothel. The absent father entrusts his only child with a safety deposit box key, which Joshua wears around his neck like the keys to the kingdom. He will only avail himself of the treasure in time of dire need. Joshua learns to be a man very early, for while his father is running gin or running from the law, Joshua's mother runs around with a local gangster. Tough, lewd, and bitter, Esther Shapiro does not hide the fact that she considers Joshua a liability who has placed a sizable crimp in her independence.

Joshua now is a man who feels threatened by the sudden appearance at the lake of Pauline's brother, Kevin. Kevin Hornby is athletic, graceful, and handsome—everything that Joshua is not—but he is also deceitful and desperate. Kevin's presence fills Joshua with fear and foreboding, the implication being that Kevin has some kind of inexorable claim on his sister, with the suggestion that they have committed incest. Joshua has usurped Kevin in Senator Hornby's esteem, and the two rivals for Pauline's love circle each other warily to the amusement of the others on the lake. Joshua is not the only man on the lake who feels threatened by Kevin, the once golden-haired boy who was humiliated for cheating on his exams at McGill and finally banished to Bermuda by his own shame. Jack Trimble, the pseudo-Englishman who is married to Jane, realizes that the passion she once had for Kevin is still smoldering, and he hatches a plot to ensnare the reckless charmer while bringing about his final humiliation.

As a boy, Joshua compiled a scrapbook on the Spanish Civil War.

Determined to become a writer by starting with a newspaper, Joshua the young man hones his skills by rewriting articles for the *Gazette* and finally serves his apprenticeship as a cub reporter. Once in a position to realize his youthful dreams, he goes to Spain with the intention of researching and writing a book on the Canadian volunteers who fought against Francisco Franco. On vacation in Paris and later Ibiza, Joshua tries to find himself as a writer. In Ibiza, he meets a crowd of influential although uninspiring scoundrels, including the sinister German, Dr. Dr. Mueller, a double PhD who has a penchant for baiting Joshua with a shake of the dice and the question, "Are you a man or a mouse?" As with Kevin Hornby, Dr. Dr. Mueller elicits an embarrassing response from Joshua by making him feel insecure. Joshua must prove his manhood at the risk of his own destruction. In both instances, it is a Pyrrhic victory for Joshua then and now.

Jack Trimble makes Kevin Hornby a partner in his stock brokerage, astonishing everyone with this gallant gesture. Working for Jack will enable Kevin to reinstate himself in the eyes of the old crowd in addition to allowing him to free himself of Pauline's financial assistance, on which he has depended during the years of exile in Bermuda. It appears at first that Kevin has a knack for making money, and soon the old crowd is getting into the stocks he recommends and quickly realizing an enormous profit. Then disaster strikes—the stocks plummet, and many fortunes are ruined. About to be investigated by the securities commission, Kevin crashes his plane and kills himself. Having made a trip to Ibiza against Pauline's wishes, Joshua returns to Montreal to find that Kevin's suicide has pushed Pauline over the edge. She is in the Royal Victoria hospital under heavy sedation. Filled with remorse and self-reproach, realizing that had he not gone to Spain Pauline might not have collapsed, Joshua sits daily by her bedside pleading for her recovery. Pauline regains her stability only to tell him that she has lost herself and must leave him and the children because her need for them eclipses her own sense of self. Lashing out at him, she accuses Joshua of having taken the easy way out by marrying her instead of testing his limits as a writer. He has made her and her friends ashamed of themselves, she tells him, by acting better than they have. The bitter and ironic truth is that Joshua has always wanted to be a regular fellow with a normal life.

Soon afterwards, Pauline disappears from the hospital. Trying desperately to find his wife and restore their lives together, Joshua returns to the lake that summer with his children. Joshua has had a car accident and is wearing a cast, but he strives to maintain a normal family life in the hope that somehow Pauline will feel these vibrations and be drawn back to him. As Jack Trimble is relating his own past to Joshua, justifying his treatment of Kevin because of his long years of poverty and social ostracism as a barber's son, Joshua looks out the window and sees Pauline working in the garden. Their children approach her cautiously, and finally Joshua goes out to her.

In his best-known novels, *The Apprenticeship of Duddy Kravitz* and *St. Urbain's Horseman*, Mordecai Richler paints an unglossed portrait of Montreal Jews in which their driving ambition to overcome poverty and achieve a parity with the Wasps of Westmount makes them both rapacious and repugnant. Richler could never be accused of flinching when it comes to showing us this darker side of the human soul, but in *Joshua Then and Now* he presents for the first time a character who can be admired almost without reservations.

Joshua Shapiro struggles valiantly to hold onto his humanity in a world where he seems to be the only one called upon to prove himself. It is a hallmark of Richler's ability as a writer that he can make apparent the humanity of an unlikable character. Richler chooses to write mostly about disagreeable people such as the cocky entrepreneur Duddy Kravitz. Joshua Shapiro is not readily likable, and yet looking at the Joshua of then and now, the reader feels a growing compassion and finally acceptance of him, Joshua, for himself.

Richler's greatest strength as a writer is his humor—it is a humor that dignifies and adds dimension to many of his characters. Without this comedic element, the people he writes about would fail to come alive. In this novel, however, the only person to come to life in this way is Joshua's father, Reuben Shapiro; many of the other characters and scenes have no purpose other than comic relief. The meetings of the MacKenzie King Memorial Society, for example, present clowns who do and say funny things but have no reason to be in the story except for the fact that they are from Joshua's old high school. These characters are trotted out on stage to keep the audience awake. None of the principal characters comes across as a real person.

Although it is entertaining and sometimes poignant, *Joshua Then and Now* does not hold together as an organic, seamless work of fiction convincingly told. It is not really a novel in the sense of a developing story with people who react with one another, but rather it is a slide show of the scenes of one man's life. The reader is able to watch and laugh at the slapstick but ultimately yearns for people to care about more.

A. S. Maulucci

KENNEDY AND ROOSEVELT

Author: Michael R. Beschloss (1955–)
Publisher: W.W. Norton and Company (New York). 318 pp. $14.95
Type of work: History
Time: 1932–1945
Locale: The United States and England

*A study of the political relationship between Franklin Delano Roosevelt and
Joseph P. Kennedy*

> Principal personages:
> FRANKLIN DELANO ROOSEVELT, President of the United States
> JOSEPH PATRICK KENNEDY, millionaire businessman, one-time
> Ambassador to England

Joseph Patrick Kennedy and Franklin Delano Roosevelt sprang from
two very different American traditions. The Roosevelts' New York
Dutch heritage rooted them in a long tradition of wealth and power,
and by the mid-19th century the family promoted the notion of public
service. "You know you were created for better things," Isaac Roosevelt preached to his son James, FDR's father; "we live for God—for
the good of our fellow men—for duty—for usefulness." Franklin was
reared with this conception of service, with not only his father and
grandfather as models, but cousin Theodore as well. After education
at Groton and Harvard, and a frustrating stint at the law, FDR entered
politics, serving as New York state senator in 1911, campaigning for
reformer Woodrow Wilson in 1912, and joining his administration as
assistant secretary of the Navy. FDR's work in the Democratic party
forced him to come to terms with New York City's Tammany machine
and the rough self-interest of urban politics, and his *noblesse oblige*
was tempered by a superb acumen for practical politics.

The Kennedys were in many ways the antithesis of this comfortable
nobility. Joseph's father was an Irish immigrant's son, a successful and
prosperous saloonkeeper and a Democratic ward boss. The avenue of
politics as advancement conflicted sharply with the reformism of the
Roosevelts. According to John F. Fitzgerald, father of Joseph's future
wife, Rose, reformers were "in the main a band of hypocrites." Joseph's father took every opportunity to advance the interests of his
son. Education at Boston Latin School and Harvard: the father's plan
for his son was to acquire the power and prestige denied the Irish
masses. At twenty-five Joseph had used his father's political connections and his own ambitious energy to become the nation's youngest
bank president. By World War I, Joseph was already a wealthy man,
serving the country as an assistant manager of the Fore River Shipyard

in Boston. It was here that the twenty-nine-year-old Kennedy and the thirty-five-year-old naval secretary had the first of their numerous confrontations.

When Roosevelt asked for delivery of some Argentine naval vessels before payment had been completed, Kennedy resisted, demanding full payment before delivery. Roosevelt sent in armed marines and simply commandeered the ships. Power prevailed as it would throughout their relationship; and throughout it was FDR who held the power.

Kennedy and Roosevelt were not to meet again in the 1920's. Throughout the decade Kennedy successfully played the role of financier, speculator, and stock market wizard. He was particularly successful in risk-capital ventures like Hollywood productions and theaters. Roosevelt, on the other hand, lost several small fortunes in his unsuccessful attempts at New Era capitalism. FDR worked at the notion of business as a kind of public service, and tried to organize within the trade association movement—experiences that would culminate in his New Deal programs for economic management. Business was not an end in itself for FDR. In fact, he stayed closely involved with Democratic politics and in 1928 was elected governor of New York. But for Kennedy, speculation was a career, a way of earning security and stature for his family.

What the two men did have in common was a fascination with politics. Kennedy inherited this from his father. In 1932 he jumped on the bandwagon for FDR. Kennedy offered Roosevelt a conduit to the financial world of Wall Street and big capital; for Kennedy, FDR offered the opportunity for national power and prominence. Privately, Kennedy expressed the conviction that the United States required "drastic changes in economic system." FDR was a man who could save the country for "my own security and the security of our kids." Kennedy played an important role in the campaign—contributing substantially from his own funds, raising contributions, opening doors to business associates. He played a minor role in bringing William Randolph Hearst into the Roosevelt camp. Kennedy expected to play a major role in the New Deal.

He expected appointment as secretary of the Treasury but was not called to any office. Always impressed by his own importance, Kennedy was flabbergasted and hurt. On the campaign trail he had been frank with Roosevelt, but ushered into the Oval Office for the first time in 1933 he was flustered in the face of power. FDR kept Kennedy waiting for office in a fashion typical of the Roosevelt ability to control men. Finally, in 1934, Kennedy was tapped as chairman of the newly created Securities and Exchange Commission. Stock manipulations were Kennedy's stock-in-trade, and many more liberal New Dealers cried foul at the appointment, but FDR answered that he had "set a thief to catch a thief."

FDR admired Kennedy's ability to handle the office, to reconcile opposing factions, to get things done. By 1935, Kennedy was one of Roosevelt's closest business advisers, often visiting the White House three or four times a week. By this time the aura of the presidency had lessened for Kennedy, and he prided himself on his ability to talk frankly with the President. Kennedy continued in his role as envoy from Roosevelt to the business community and to difficult but powerful personalities like Hearst. In 1935 he also tried, unsuccessfully, to bridge the gap between FDR and the fascist radio priest, Father Coughlin. During the 1936 campaign Kennedy published a piece of propaganda, *I'm For Roosevelt,* spoke for the President on national radio, and generally played the role of the most prominent businessman and Catholic in the New Deal.

Kennedy was by no means universally popular within the administration. His goal was frankly conservative—recovery of the old order. His greatest fear was of a social and economic revolution that would challenge the basis of his and his family's privilege. Kennedy was, in short, a conservative insider, FDR's connection to big business, and as such, increasingly uncomfortable with the "liberal" direction of the Second New Deal. In 1937 he told Roosevelt that he would like to leave government: "there's a lot of money to be made in the market. I'd like to skim off my share of the profits." But the recession of 1937 kept him in the New Deal, this time as chair of the Maritime Commission, where he established a reputation as a tough, antilabor bargainer.

His disquietude with the direction of the administration, however, gave Kennedy cause for complaint, which he exercised freely in private conversation. Late in 1937, FDR, in what was a typical move, kicked Kennedy upstairs and out of the country by appointing him ambassador to England. At a dinner party at Hyde Park someone questioned the wisdom of sending "that awful Joe Kennedy" to London. FDR replied that sending an Irishman to London was "the greatest joke in the world."

Kennedy's term in London from 1937 to 1940 was the high point of his career in government and the period of his greatest controversy. From the beginning, he established his point of view as an isolationist and opponent of confrontation with fascism. Before 1939, Kennedy found a friend to his views in Neville Chamberlain, but after the Polish invasion even Chamberlain came to think of Kennedy as an opponent of the Allied cause. Kennedy's greatest fear was that war would bring a revolution promoting communism. U.S. entrance into the conflict, he believed, would necessitate pulling back on democratic ideals in order to protect the social order. According to FDR, Kennedy was convinced that the United States would have to "come to some form of fascism." "Joe Kennedy, if he were in power," Roosevelt confided to Harold Ickes in 1938, "would give us a fascist form of government." Kennedy proposed a kind of fortress America, an accommodation with the fascists, a world divided into "spheres of influence."

Why did FDR tolerate Kennedy, with such views, for so long? According to the Washington observer Drew Pearson in 1939, "Roosevelt wants him to stay because he'd rather have Joe in England than here on his neck." Roosevelt simply bypassed his ambassador on important negotiations and collaborations with the British, using Kennedy to keep his options open to the conservative, isolationist, even semifascist right wing, while pursuing interventionist options of his own. FDR used Kennedy in his well-known political manner.

In 1940, Roosevelt believed that "Joe has been an appeaser and will always be an appeaser," but continued to be intent on using his relationship with Kennedy for his political advantage. He flew Kennedy to the White House for a confrontation over their differences in international perspective. The President had not listened to his advice, Kennedy complained; he had been mistreated, abused. FDR adroitly *agreed*. The State Department was at fault, he claimed. Yet by cleverly manipulating Rose Kennedy, present for the interview, by dangling the promise of political support for a Kennedy presidential bid in 1944, and by suggesting support for Kennedy's ambitious sons, Roosevelt was able to convince Kennedy to swallow his opposition to the administration's approach to the world crisis and endorse the third term. After the election, with Kennedy still publicly crying for accommodation and preaching British defeat, FDR cut his renegade loose. After a meeting at Hyde Park, Roosevelt angrily told Eleanor, "I never want to see that son of a bitch as long as I live. Take his resignation and get him out of here!"

After Pearl Harbor, Kennedy tried to reenter the administration, but although FDR never completely shut the door to him, Kennedy remained a bitter outsider. In a 1944 visit Kennedy told Roosevelt that his liberal advisers were all "Jews and Communists" who would "open the way for the Communist line." Kennedy had "left a bad taste" in his mouth, Roosevelt admitted. That same year Kennedy asked Truman, "Harry, what are you doing campaigning for the crippled son-of-a-bitch that killed my son Joe?" Truman responded by threatening to throw Kennedy out of his hotel window.

Beschloss's appraisal is that Kennedy's politics were characterized by a fear of social chaos and a consequent decline in his family's fortunes. This brought him to the New Deal, where he was used by Roosevelt for his own ends. Kennedy had a weakness for the powerful and was susceptible to "presidential hand-holding." Certainly the outstanding conclusion that one may draw from Beschloss's discussion is the crafty and skillful way in which FDR shaped and used power and men like Kennedy.

The study, interesting in its own light, is, in the end, unsatisfactory. The very notion of the "relationship" between Kennedy and Roosevelt distorts the picture, for it becomes increasingly clear that Roosevelt *used* Kennedy for his own purposes. The differential of power is the crucial ingredient to understanding the relationship of the two men, yet Beschloss's approach asks the reader to see the two men in equal terms. The focus, the whole conceit of the study, then, would seem misplaced. The two men can be better understood in their own separate stories: reading, for example, Frank Friedel or Arthur Schlesinger, Jr., on FDR, Richard Whalen or David Koskoff on Kennedy.

Most disturbing is Beschloss's unwillingness to come to terms with Kennedy's politics. Perhaps the most interesting and yet untold story of the New Deal is the politics of corporatism and semi-fascism that motivated many on the right. Kennedy was particularly articulate (many at the time would have said "loud-mouthed") on this, and he provides an opportunity for an evaluation of these politics. Unfortunately this opportunity must be left for others.

John Mack Faragher

KENNEDY FOR THE DEFENSE

Author: George V. Higgins
Publisher: Alfred A. Knopf (New York). 225 pp. $9.95
Type of work: Novel
Time: August 1978
Locale: Boston

A story about a Boston criminal lawyer and the clients he represents, who interrupt his vacation continually

Principal characters:
JERRY KENNEDY, a criminal lawyer
"CADILLAC TEDDY," a professional car thief
TROOPER HUDSON, a state police officer
DONALD FRENCH, a mechanic who fixes smugglers' boats and has just enough sense to know he is in trouble
JILL, his girlfriend, an FBI informer
HARRIS, an FBI agent
EMERSON TELLER, a spoiled fop, arrested on a morals charge
RICHARD TELLER, his father, eager to use his wealth to avoid a hint of scandal
COOPER, another lawyer, an ex-FBI agent, whose advice and connections Kennedy often seeks

The setting of *Kennedy for the Defense* is Boston in August 1978. The narrator of the story, like author George V. Higgins, is a Boston lawyer, and although the events are fictionalized, they are drawn from Higgins' own legal experience.

The story opens with the case of "Cadillac Ted" Franklin, a car thief of extraordinary ability. He has been stealing Cadillacs on a full-time basis for seventeen years, without ever being convicted. He has, however, a lengthy arrest record and is known throughout New England for his hot-Cadillac business. To irk the authorities further, Teddy and his wife have legally registered Cadillacs of their own, trading them in every few months. The state troopers detain Teddy frequently, necessitating a lawyer on a regular basis. He will have no other counsel but Kennedy and calls the lawyer at the summer cottage where he is vacationing.

Teddy Franklin has been arrested at nearby Dedham, for driving without a license. He explains to Kennedy that he had a temporary license but the state trooper swallowed the paper and then arrested Teddy for driving without a license. With this preposterous defense, Kennedy requests and gets a continuance.

On the way back from court, Kennedy stops at his office, where Donald French and Jill Candelaria are waiting, without an appointment. They seem unwilling to discuss why French wants to see a

lawyer, and Kennedy leaves the reception room on a pretext, to eavesdrop on their conversation.

It is apparent that French is employed as a speedboat mechanic, and
one speedboat is outfitted in such a way that it could only be used for
cocaine smuggling. Chris, a go-between, will reveal no names, and
French does not ask. In addition, French is being overpaid, in cash, by
an unknown source. Jill tells him not to think about it, that he is in no
legal trouble himself, and complains about a delayed drug pickup.
French is in love with the girl, but she will have none of it. Kennedy
can get little else from French and advises him to call back if any real
trouble arises.

Two days later, Kennedy's vacation is interrupted again by a phone
call from Roger Kidd, a civil lawyer and long-time friend who often
refers criminal cases to him. Kennedy goes to Roger's office and meets
Richard Teller, a wealthy businessman, and his son, Emerson. Emerson, uncommunicative throughout the consultation, is an elaborately
attired man, who is unconcerned with the legal difficulties that resulted
when he made homosexual advances toward a state police officer. An
appointment is set up for the next day, and Kennedy leaves hurriedly
in response to another call, from "Cadillac Teddy."

"Cadillac Teddy" Franklin and his wife Dotty are both in the Dedham jail. He has not been charged, but his wife is accused of operating
a vehicle without a registration. Again, Trooper Hudson is the arresting officer. Dotty claims that Hudson pulled her over, ate the temporary registration paper, and arrested her. Teddy, in a rage, calls his
lawyer from the jail, and then is arrested himself. Kennedy arranges
bail for them and later that night, after discussing the case with Dotty,
concludes that the two could not have made up the same story, since
they have nothing to gain by lying. In addition, the same state trooper
is involved in both arrests. But Kennedy is worried about how they
will behave in court, after the display they put on in jail.

Later that night, Kennedy's daughter Heather comes home from her
job at the local fast-food stand, upset over her friend and coworker,
Margie. Margie is involved with Joe, a young troublemaker with a
prison record. Margie says she may be pregnant. Heather feels sorry
for her and would like to help somehow.

The next morning, Kennedy meets Emerson Teller, and after an
initial denial of guilt, the boy finally discusses the particulars of the
case.

Donald French has been waiting in the reception room, again with
no appointment. Saying he needs legal counsel, he places $6,900, in
cash, on the lawyer's desk. He mentions Chris Lynch, the owner of a
bar near the marina where French works, who is the middleman be-

tween French and the owner of the speedboat. He adds that a man named Warren Gould has been looking for him at the marina. French wants Kennedy present when Gould finds him, and apparently French has sold cocaine to pay for this service.

Weldon Cooper, a lawyer from an adjacent office, is a valuable source of information. Kennedy and Cooper often go to lunch to discuss their cases. Kennedy takes Cooper to lunch that afternoon to make sense out of both cases. Cooper refuses to discuss the Teller case, but the former FBI man provides a fresh viewpoint on the French case. Cooper thinks the girl is an informer, a government plant. The authorities will probably wait until they have enough evidence to arrest everyone involved, including French, the middleman, and the supplier. Then French would be expected to turn state's evidence in return for clemency if he is not killed by the drug smugglers to silence him. The irony of French's dilemma is that he was never in trouble until he got directly involved by selling cocaine to pay his lawyer's fees.

The next day, the man calling himself Gould comes to the marina, asking French many questions about the boat and its owner. Kennedy, observing, goes unnoticed by Gould. Cooper identifies him as an FBI agent named Harris, when Kennedy calls him with a description of the man.

That night, in Chris Lynch's bar, Kennedy sees the man again, and once again he is asking about speedboats. Lynch refers Harris to Donald French as a boat expert. Kennedy is in a location where Harris cannot see him, and the lawyer is able to eavesdrop when Jill, French's supposed girlfriend, joins Harris at the table. Kennedy gathers that Harris has been using Jill to get information, but that French knows nothing of any value to them. Kennedy, still unseen, then leaves.

Cooper still has friends in the FBI, who confirm for Kennedy that Harris is on such a case, and furthermore that he is a dangerously impulsive man, liable to shoot his way out of trouble.

That night, in the parking lot of the fast-food stand, where Kennedy is waiting for his daughter, he is accosted by Joe, Margie's boyfriend. Heather tells her father that Margie is pregnant and that Heather is giving Margie money for an abortion. Joe, who will not marry her, nonetheless wants her to keep the baby. Margie has said she will get the abortion money by prostitution if Heather cannot help. For once, Kennedy is at a loss for an answer.

"Cadillac Teddy" has been doing some investigation on his own, and he calls Kennedy late that night. Trooper Hudson is a man with an unsavory past who got his job with the state police with the help of Richard Teller. Kennedy hires ex-cop "Bad Eye" Mulvey to gather enough information to build a case, then gets Richard Teller's corroboration. The state police, eager to rid themselves of a corrupt officer without undue publicity, agree to drop the charges against Emerson.

The Donald French case is not so tidily solved. Harris, with a number of federal agents, has Chris Lynch's bar surrounded. French, at the bar for a nightcap, sees Harris and flees, fearing a raid. Harris, with a John Doe warrant, finds no drugs, and eager to arrest someone, goes out looking for French. French, in his van, expects to be ambushed, and as Harris approaches the van, gun in hand, French shoots and kills the agent. French is immediately arrested by the remaining officers. Coming home late from the federal courthouse, Kennedy is warned by a neighbor that there is trouble inside the house. He enters and finds that Joe, seeking revenge, has tied up the lawyer's wife and daughter. Kennedy overwhelms the young thug and holds him for the police. In an epilogue, Donald French pleads guilty to a reduced charge and receives a five-year sentence.

Kennedy for the Defense is a rousing novel. Its characters are portrayed with a seamy realism that pervades the book. From "Cadillac Teddy," the outraged car thief, to the incompetent Judge Fathead, hated by prosecution and defense alike, Higgins endows his characters, both major and minor, with lives of their own.

The character of Kennedy is deep and revealing. He may not like all his clients, but he does all he can, and more, to earn his hefty fees, even at the cost of his much-needed vacation. Ever the professional, Kennedy hires specialists whenever he feels someone else can do the job better. Thus, Cooper is called in to help on a narcotics case, and "Bad Eye" Mulvey is used to ferret out a cop gone bad. Thanks to Kennedy's legal skills, very few of his cases ever come to trial, but when they do Kennedy is there, even during the month of August.

Once his characters appear on the page, the plot unfolds, seemingly by itself. In the interrelated vignettes centered around the narrator, cops and robbers alike move naturally through the world Higgins created. The addled French is an all-too-real portrait of a loser—his boss is a pusher, his girlfriend an informer, and his idea of keeping out of trouble is to sell only enough cocaine to pay his lawyer's bills. He is bound to do something stupid like killing a federal agent.

Higgins is, additionally, a master storyteller. Kennedy's vacation is doomed from the outset, and it is superbly entertaining to see what crisis the harried attorney will be called on to attend to next. Skillfully blending earthy humor with gripping suspense, Higgins takes the reader through the grimy maze of the world of the criminal lawyer.

Thomas McCue

THE KEY TO REBECCA

Author: Ken Follett
Publisher: William Morrow & Co. (New York). 381 pp. $12.95
Type of work: Novel
Time: Summer 1942
Locale: Egypt

A British intelligence officer tracks down a German spy in Cairo during World War II

> *Principal characters:*
> MAJOR WILLIAM VANDAM, British intelligence officer
> ALEX WOLFF, German spy
> SONJA EL-ARAM, famous belly dancer and Wolff's occasional mistress
> ELENE FONTANA, young woman hired by Vandam to entrap Wolff
> MAJOR SANDY SMITH, British officer seduced by Sonja
> SUPERINTENDENT KEMEL, Cairo police detective
> BILLY, Vandam's son

It is the summer of 1942, and the Germans are attempting to wrest control of North Africa from the British. British security is tight, and no one gets in or out of Egypt unobserved. No one but Alex Wolff, that is. As Ken Follett's newest thriller opens, Alex Wolff, German spy, has defied the limits of human endurance to complete a two-month-long, solitary trek across the Sahara from the Libyan coast. He is determined to get to Cairo, where his mission is to steal British military secrets and radio them to German forces in the African desert. He has been chosen for the job not only because of his successful espionage record, but also because he has spent much of his life in Cairo and should be able to surface there without arousing suspicion.

On his way into Cairo, Wolff runs into trouble and has to change his plans. He is casually questioned by some British soldiers, and when one of them seems dangerously close to discovering his occupation, Wolff unhesitatingly slits the soldier's throat. Since he has given his true name and address in answer to the other soldiers' questions, he can no longer stay in his Cairo home but must enter the city as a fugitive from the British.

For Wolff, British justice will soon be represented by one man—Major William Vandam. When a routine report of the murder of a British soldier by a man named Wolff crosses Vandam's desk, he immediately suspects that Wolff is a spy. He wants to question Wolff, but first he must find him.

Meanwhile, Wolff has set up a parasitic sort of housekeeping with

Sonja, his former mistress and the most famous belly dancer in Egypt. Sonja gives him sanctuary in her houseboat, and they resume their sexual relationship.

It is the owner of the Greek market, where Wolff buys delicacies for Sonja, who tips off Vandam, enabling him to lay a trap for Wolff. He hires Elene Fontana, a 23-year-old Jewish beauty, to go to work in the grocery. When Wolff comes in, Elene is to find out where he lives so that Vandam can arrest him. It seems a natural assignment for Elene, who has been a kept woman for much of her life. But Elene, attracted to the upright Major Vandam, suddenly finds her own lifestyle disgusting. Nevertheless, since Vandam is counting on her, she agrees to go through with the assignment.

Meanwhile, Wolff is using Sonja in a similar manner. He knows that certain British officers carry military strategies around in their briefcases, so he has Sonja seduce one of them, Sandy Smith. While Sonja goes to bed with Major Smith in one end of the houseboat, Wolff is in the other end rummaging through the major's briefcase. He is able to gather detailed information about British plans for a counterattack at Tobruk on June 4. That evening, he wires the information to Rommel's forces in the desert, using a code constructed around Daphne du Maurier's novel *Rebecca*. The information is enough to give the Germans a victory, thoroughly stunning the British.

Vandam realizes that Wolff's spying is somehow responsible for the German victory at Tobruk, and he steps up his search. He believes that success is near when Wolff finally makes another appearance at the grocery store, meets Elene, and asks her to meet him the following evening for dinner. Vandam plans to stake out the restaurant and arrest Wolff when he shows up.

However, Vandam receives another piece of luck that evening, when Wolff and Sonja are seen dining together. Vandam arrives just as they are leaving. Wolff runs, Vandam pursuing him. A wild chase follows, ending in a scuffle. Wolff slashes Vandam's cheek and then escapes into the night.

Vandam has now connected Wolff with Sonja. He asks Superintendent Kemel of the Cairo police to stake out the houseboat. Unknown to Vandam, however, Kemel is an ardent Egyptian nationalist, ready to ally with anyone who can help him overthrow the British. He soon confirms Vandam's suspicion that Sonja may be harboring Wolff. Instead of arresting Wolff, he approaches Sonja with a proposition. He will keep her secret if she helps him gain access to Wolff's radio so that he can bargain with the Germans.

Vandam, unaware of this treachery, is still counting on trapping the spy when he keeps his date with Elene. But Wolff, with some inexplicable sixth sense, stays away from the restaurant; instead he sends a taxi for Elene, and she has no choice but to climb into it as Vandam and his backup men watch helplessly. Wolff takes her on a moonlight picnic and treats her like a lady all evening, which puzzles her, since she knows of his reputation for ruthlessness. What Elene does not know is that Wolff plans to seduce her into going to bed with him and Sonja. This is one of Sonja's fantasies, and Wolff has agreed to act it out in exchange for her silence. For the moment, at least, Wolff bids her goodnight like a perfect gentleman; Elene is left to wonder at his true motives and to enjoy Vandam's ill-concealed jealousy as he questions her about her evening with the spy.

Several days later, Wolff sends a note to Elene asking for another date. Elene knows that Vandam will want to see the note and takes it to his home, which she has never visited. While there, she meets Vandam's ten-year-old son, Billy, who, like his father, falls instantly in love with Elene. When Vandam comes home and finds Elene waiting for him, all of his reserve falls away, and they confess their love and spend the night together.

The next morning, Vandam returns to his office and is told to burn any sensitive information in his files; the British risk losing Cairo to the Germans. The situation is desperate. It is no longer enough simply to capture Wolff; Vandam needs to get hold of his code to impersonate the spy, and to radio a message to the Germans that will steer them into a British trap.

Everything comes to a climax on the night of Elene's second date with Wolff. Vandam, seeing the spy take Elene onto the houseboat, sends an Egyptian to fetch more British intelligence officers. Instead, the Egyptian reports to Kemel, who shows up, knocks Vandam out, and ties him up in the bushes.

All that Elene knows is that she must delay Wolff from sending his usual midnight message. She participates in the sexual threesome, driving the German so wild with desire he forgets all his other responsibilities. The next morning, she is searching the houseboat for the radio and the code when Wolff discovers her. She runs away, but Kemel catches her and returns her to Wolff in exchange for the radio.

Wolff now needs his second radio, which he has left with his desert cousins near the town of Assyut. Taking Elene with him, he then kidnaps Billy, and the three of them board the train to Assyut. Vandam meanwhile has freed himself, questioned Sonja and Kemel, and figured out Wolff's plan. He knows that he could stop the train and arrest the spy, but that would destroy any chance of obtaining the radio and the code. So instead he rides his motorcycle to Assyut and waits at the train station disguised as a cab driver. Wolff hires him, and they drive out to the spot where Wolff's nomadic cousins are camping, while Elene and Billy, both aware of the deception, remain silent.

On the way back to town, Billy finally gives the game away. In the ensuing struggle, Elene knocks out Wolff as he is about to kill Vandam. The false radio message is sent; the German movement to seize Egypt is crushed; the spy goes to jail; and the lovers and the British army both see a bright future ahead.

The Key to Rebecca is a good, gripping spy novel. The story moves smoothly and swiftly, with enough suspense to keep the reader interested. Although the characters are stereotypical in many ways (the suave, ruthless spy; the proud cruel belly dancer), Follett skillfully controls the reader's response to them. During the first part of the book, Wolff is presented as being agile and attractive, a sort of James Bond-like figure, while Vandam is slow and always seems to be bumbling along several steps behind the spy. The battle is between a boring good guy and an attractive bad guy, and loyalty is divided. As the book progresses, however, Wolff's cruelty begins to eclipse all of his Continental charm, and by the time he murders the unfortunate Major Smith in an agonizingly long scene, the reader has grown to hate him as much as Vandam does. Conversely, Vandam's reticence and quiet intelligence begin to take on heroic proportions as he proceeds to outwit Wolff, saving the woman, child, and country he loves in the bargain.

Although *The Key to Rebecca* is supposedly based on a true incident, Follett's attempts to introduce real historical figures are gratuitous. He basically reduces the contest between the British and the Germans to a cat-and-mouse game between two men, Vandam and Wolff. For all of its worldly characters and complicated plot, *The Key to Rebecca* is a somewhat naive book, a melodrama in which a hero singlehandedly defeats the powers of evil. Perhaps it is this ultimate simplicity, this optimistic conclusion that one decent man can change the course of modern history, that makes Follett's books so popular.

Joan Barrett Wickersham

LIFE BEFORE MAN

Author: Margaret Atwood (1939–   )
Publisher: Simon & Schuster (New York). 317 pp. $11.95
Type of work: Novel
Time: October 1976 to August 1978
Locale: Toronto, Ontario, Canada

The story of the bafflement and pain found in the break-up of a modern marriage

Principal characters:
ELIZABETH, wife to Nate
NATE, husband to Elizabeth
LESJE, lover of William and Nate
WILLIAM, lover of Lesje
JANET and NANCY, Elizabeth's and Nate's daughters

Margaret Atwood, in *Life Before Man,* delves into the lives of three characters, Elizabeth, Nate, and Lesje, in a story of the fatigue and miseries of marriage and relationships. The story is presented in chapters entitled simply "Elizabeth," "Nate," and "Lesje," along with the date of the action. Each chapter of *Life Before Man* is a first-person monologue or third-person narrative description of what each particular character is feeling or doing on the same day. The days are sometimes consecutive, at other times separated by weeks or months. And Atwood reaches deep into each of their pysches to retrieve the reasons, like somber pearls, for what will bring them together and what keeps them forever separate. In the first chapter, Elizabeth is lying on her back, her clothes unrumpled. It is as if she were laid out at a wake, and her psychological state is deathlike. Elizabeth is a woman on the verge of breakdown. She is distraught over the recent suicide of her ex-lover Chris, who killed himself because of her, and she mourns for herself. Her husband of ten years, Nate, soon breaks an invisible thread across her doorway, one that she puts there in her mind to keep him out.

Nate has either forgotten what love is or he has never known. He is a bumbler, apologetic from too many years spent in a broken marriage, still trying to assuage a wife he can no longer appease. Nate gave up practicing law to make wooden toys. It suits him better and is easier, although not as lucrative. They remain together because of the children, and there is an understanding between them that they may take lovers.

Elizabeth works in the city museum where she is a director of special projects. She is competent, businesslike, and urbane. Her ex-lover, Chris, worked there also. The affair was simply physical for Elizabeth, but it had a deeper meaning for Chris.

As for Lesje, who also works at the museum, her passion is dinosaur bones. Ever since she can remember, in school, she could always spell the names of dinosaurs like pteranodon. In her adolescent daydreams she walks in Cretaceous swamps observing various species such as a Gorgosaurus. Lesje thinks her breasts are too small, her teeth too large, and her nose too long. She has problems in dealing with the world.

Lesje's choice of a lover reflects her shortcomings in real life. William is blonde, well scrubbed, and from a good family. Lesje is ashamed of her family. Her grandmothers actually raised her; one was Jewish and the other Lithuanian. Although they never met, they hated each other, and of course never approved of their children's marriage. Lesje, angular and fragile, feels protected by William with his rich kid smile, college boy manners, and stuffy smoking room charm. For William, Lesje is non-confronting, safe, someone whom he can intimidate if he would like.

Nate asks Lesje to show his children, Janet and Nancy, around the dinosaur exhibits one Saturday. She thinks this a bit odd and believes he has ulterior motives. To Lesje, Nate seems more mature than William, and to Nate, Lesje is feminine, beautiful, young, another chance at life and love. Lesje is tired of William's pomposity and childish antics. Nate is tired of affairs with pasty-faced secretaries from his old law firm, and of trying to pay his share of the rent by chiseling wooden giraffes. They are both tired of their lives. They have something in common, and they become lovers.

Elizabeth's reaction to Nate's new affair is vituperative and hostile. She could understand Nate's predilection for washed-up clerical workers, but she is jealous about Lesje. Lesje, the awkward and shy beauty, is a personal threat to Elizabeth, who needs Nate to keep everything running smoothly for the children. Nate's leaving her for Lesje is the cataclysmic event that could shatter her life.

The thing to do, Elizabeth decides, is to tell William what is going on. But her plan backfires. William's boyish pride is bruised by Elizabeth's eye-opening revelation, and he is hysterical. After Lesje comes home from work on the afternoon that he has learned of her unfaithfulness, he rapes her. She frees herself from him, locks herself in the bathroom, and moves out the next morning after he leaves for his job. She is determined to convince Nate to live with her, to leave Elizabeth and his children.

Nate worries over whether to leave Elizabeth and the children. Little Janet is already copying her mother's polished manners, and crybaby Nancy is constantly tugging at his pants. He has never been very decisive but has let the decisions make themselves. Through Lesje's obvious commitment, he feels forced to join her, yet he procrastinates about moving.

As frightening as the thought of a broken family is to Elizabeth, Nate's vacillation is too much to bear. Elizabeth grits her teeth, faces the situation, and gives Nate a push in Lesje's direction, but not without demanding child support, even though she can easily support them.

Elizabeth's fear of the family break-up and concern for the children originates from her own tortured childhood. Her mother was an alcoholic, who died from burns received while smoking in bed obliviously drunk, and her father was a ne'er-do-well. She and her sister were raised by their aunt, a tyrannical holier-than-thou, white-gloved religious fanatic. Elizabeth survived her upbringing with her instinct intact, but her sister had a mental breakdown and later committed suicide. This is one of the many unhealed wounds that Elizabeth bears. For Elizabeth's and Nate's children, there are no such denouements. They live during the week with Elizabeth and on the weekends with Nate, who has had to resume his law practice to make ends meet. But the children's visits do not suit Lesje well. They become for her a part of Nate's former life and Elizabeth's treachery.

Lesje succumbs more and more to her regressions, considers suicide but lacks the courage. Nate continues to believe that she is a princess, a feminine wonder. Lesje demands more understanding from Nate than she receives. To get even, she throws away her birth control pills, deciding to have a child by Nate without his knowing and believing this might force Nate to pay more attention to her.

At the conclusion of *Life Before Man*, the characters are left with their unresolved struggles. They are like three solitary dancers on three separate stages, the action subtly stopped, the spotlights dimming. They are still mired in their own lives, and they have gone in circles searching for meaning. Their lives have been altered, but everything seems to have remained the same. Like marionettes, their positions have just changed a bit, nothing more.

Margaret Atwood, the author of three other novels, seven volumes of poetry, and one of literary criticism, continues to write in *Life Before Man* with the same poignancy that characterized her previous works. This is a tightly-knit story, a modern tragedy, and one that confronts the reality that one out of every two marriages ends in divorce. Atwood presents the sorry replica of contemporary life and love with astringent clarity. She writes powerfully and with wisdom.

Wally Swist

LITTLE GLORIA . . . HAPPY AT LAST

Author: Barbara Goldsmith
Publisher: Alfred A. Knopf (New York). 650 pp. $15.95
Type of work: Biography
Time: 1860's to the present
Locale: Europe and New York

A biography of Gloria Laura Vanderbilt, concentrating on the trial for her custody that took place in 1934

Principal personages:
GLORIA MORGAN VANDERBILT, wife of Reginald Vanderbilt and mother of little Gloria
REGINALD VANDERBILT, son of Alice Gwynne and Cornelius Vanderbilt II
GERTRUDE VANDERBILT WHITNEY, Reginald's sister and Gloria Morgan Vanderbilt's opponent in little Gloria's custody trial
THELMA MORGAN CONVERSE FURNESS, Gloria Morgan Vanderbilt's twin sister
LAURA KILPATRICK MORGAN, Gloria Morgan Vanderbilt's mother
EMMA SULLIVAN KEISLICH, little Gloria's nurse
CHIEF JUSTICE JOHN FRANCIS CAREW, the presiding judge at the custody trial
GLORIA LAURA VANDERBILT, daughter of Gloria Morgan and Reginald Vanderbilt, known as "little Gloria"

The custody trial for little Gloria Vanderbilt captured the imagination of the nation. On one side stood her aunt, Gertrude Vanderbilt Whitney, a haughty society matron whose worth was estimated at $78,000,000. On the other was little Gloria's mother, Gloria Morgan Vanderbilt, a famous beauty with no money of her own "who numbered among her friends the most impressive titles in Europe." But the case's real attraction lay in its ironic twist. The story of little Gloria, the quintessential "poor little rich girl," offered victims of the Depression the rare opportunity of feeling sorry for an heiress to $2,500,000.

Gloria Morgan's marriage to Reginald Vanderbilt marked her entrance into what could be considered an American royal family. Established by Commodore Cornelius Vanderbilt in the mid-19th century, the Vanderbilt financial empire was legendary by the 1920's. But as Reggie's uncle, William Kissam Vanderbilt, once observed, "Inherited wealth . . . is as certain death to ambition as cocaine is to morality." Reggie's obsession was not making money but spending it; in fourteen years he went through nearly $25,000,000. By the time he met Gloria, his fortune had all been spent, except for an inviolable $5,000,000 trust fund established by his father.

In his proposal Reggie admitted not only that his sole income came from this trust fund, but also that he was seriously ill with cirrhosis. Neither point seemed to worry Gloria, who could not imagine a situation in which there would be no one to protect her. Reginald Vanderbilt and Gloria Morgan were married on March 6, 1923. Less than a year later, on February 20, 1924, she gave birth to a tiny Vanderbilt heiress named Gloria Laura. Not long afterward, Reggie's health began a rapid decline. A European cure was attempted, but Reggie was apparently powerless to stop drinking, the only thing that could save him. On September 2, 1925, he died.

Reggie's death revealed the true state of the Vanderbilt fortune. For years tradespeople had been extending credit, and upon his death they converged to collect. The only untouchable asset was the $5,000,000 trust fund his own father had left him, which was now to be divided between Cathleen Vanderbilt, his daughter by a previous marriage, and little Gloria. Gloria was not only penniless but unable to serve as her own child's guardian, being legally under age. Her legal counsel, George Wickersham, was named as guardian for little Gloria.

Gloria's only legal claim to the estate consisted of her dower rights, which entitled her to one third of the revenues yielded by the sale of Reggie's houses. There was one other possibility, however. Little Gloria's trust came under the jurisdiction of Justice James Aloysius Foley of the New York Surrogates' Court. Gloria's counsel appealed to Foley to grant her $4,000 per month of the income from little Gloria's trust, for the support of the child. Foley knew that the money requested for the child represented Gloria's only means of financial support beyond her right of dower, and although he disliked the subterfuge involved, he immediately granted the request.

In May 1926, Gloria departed for Europe with her mother Laura, little Gloria, and nurse Keislich. Here she spent her time with the most dazzling members of the international set, leaving her daughter to the care of grandmother and nurse. Her life style drew criticism from all sides, particularly after the beginning of her association with Prince Hohenlohe. Laura Morgan insisted that if Gloria married the penniless Hohenlohe, he would murder little Gloria for her money; she even accused Gloria of wanting to murder the child. Little Gloria's guardians were apprised of the situation and were soon issuing warnings that little Gloria's money could not be used to "finance a second marriage." The affair with Hohenlohe was broken off, but similar financial pressure was exerted when Gloria showed reluctance to return the child to America for schooling. Gloria resisted for as long as she could, but in March 1932 was forced to capitulate.

When little Gloria returned to New York it was found that she needed an operation for her tonsils and adenoids. Gloria was anxious to return to Europe and was greatly relieved when Reggie's sister Gertrude offered to let the child recuperate at her country estate. A year later Gloria's income was cut because the child was in residence at another household. Gloria requested that little Gloria be returned to her, but her lawyers were convinced that Mrs. Whitney was a healthier influence. The child had arrived at her estate weak and fearful and had since shown much improvement.

Gloria still had no legal standing in regard to her daughter, never having taken steps to become her legal guardian after coming of age. She hired Nathan Burkan, an aggressive and successful lawyer, to represent her. After a long delay due to lack of funds, they managed to set a guardianship hearing for July 1934. It was far from routine: Gloria's petition was challenged on the grounds of her unfitness as a guardian, a charge brought by her own mother and supported by Mrs. Whitney.

"The Matter of Vanderbilt" was brought to court on September 28, 1934. The conservative Justice John Francis Carew, whose judgment alone was to decide the trial's outcome, was shocked from the beginning by the allegations against Gloria. Nurse Keislich bitterly hated Gloria for her treatment of little Gloria during the European years and painted a damning picture of immorality and parental neglect. The most compelling point was the attitude of little Gloria herself. In a session closed to the public, little Gloria affirmed that she had hated and feared her mother since she had been old enough to talk. The child had essentially decided the case: Carew could hardly force her return to a mother of whom she was terrified.

Little Gloria's fear of her mother remained a mystery to the court, but Goldsmith believes that she was powerfully influenced by the wave of kidnappings that went on in the 1930's. Little Gloria herself had been under heavy guard at her aunt's estate after threats had been made against her life. In an attempt to regain control of little Gloria about a year before the custody hearing, Gloria had intercepted the child and nurse Keislich on their return from the Whitney camp in the Adirondacks, and Keislich had told the child they had been kidnapped. As a small child she had heard her grandmother accuse her mother of wanting to murder her for her money. In little Gloria's mind these facts assembled themselves into an overpowering fear of her mother.

On November 21, 1934, Justice Carew issued his decision: Little Gloria was to be a ward of the Supreme Court of New York, under the custody of her aunt Gertrude. Gloria was to have the child on weekends, in the hope of wooing her back. Carew's decision came under heavy criticism, which proved justified; little Gloria's visits to her mother were too fraught with publicity to be of much value, and she had soon learned to play one side against the other to achieve her own ends. Once the issue had been settled, Mrs. Whitney left the child in the care of servants just as she had done with her own children, and little Gloria grew up largely unsupervised. At sixteen she chose to live with her mother in California, soon afterward beginning a series of unsuccessful marriages. Her relationship with her mother was tinged with bitterness for years, but tensions eased somewhat later. When Gloria died at age 60, although little Gloria was unable to attend the funeral, her lawyer made sure reporters understood that the breach with her mother had been healed.

The amount of research that went into *Little Gloria . . . Happy at Last* is impressive. Goldsmith began by studying over 7,000 pages of trial transcript, from this assembling a meticulous chronology of the lives of the principals. Study of these chronologies revealed a great deal about the development of events leading to the trial. Unfortunately, the plethora of legal detail can be confusing, particularly when combined with Goldsmith's flashback technique.

The list of secondary sources shows that Goldsmith's research into the period was painstaking. Her account of the Vanderbilts' rise is particularly incisive; a sympathy for the family shows through, not a slavish adoration of the rich but an understanding of the peculiar circumstances of their lives. Virtually all of the Vanderbilt women were thwarted by their wealth. Reggie's mother, Alice Gwynne Vanderbilt, devoted her life to grim social competition with her sister-in-law Alva. Gertrude Vanderbilt Whitney, who was strongly attracted to the bohemian world of the artist, was restricted to patronage of other artists by the Vanderbilt need to remain "irreproachable." The more conformist Gloria found herself violently criticized for living as all her friends did, leaving their children in the care of servants in order to pursue their own desires. Trite though it may seem, little Gloria Vanderbilt was indeed the "poor little rich girl" of the newspaper headlines. Goldsmith's accounts from little Gloria's viewpoint are full of pathos, showing a child in mortal fear of kidnapping and death but unable to communicate the nature of her fear to her elders. Fought for in a blaze of notoriety, she was then largely ignored, and much of her adult life has been spent in a search for the love and self-confidence she never received as a child. Now a successful businesswoman, she has to some extent made peace with herself, but mused in 1976, "Sometimes I wonder, at fifty-two has success come too late? I needed it more in my 20's and 30's."

Lisa Halttunen

LOON LAKE

Author: E. L. Doctorow (1931–   )
Publisher: Random House (New York). 258 pp. $11.95
Type of work: Novel
Time: The 1930's
Locale: The Adirondack lodge Loon Lake; an automotive plant in Indiana

*An inventive novel of power and deceit as shown through the life and for-
tunes of a man who is transformed from a Depression victim into a person of
money and prestige*

> Principal characters:
> JOE, the protagonist
> F. W. BENNETT, industrial magnate, head of Bennett Autobody
>   Works
> CLARA LUKÁCS, Bennett's mistress, Joe's lover
> LUCINDA BENNETT, wife of F. W. Bennett, famous aviatrix
> WARREN PENFIELD, sometime poet-in-residence at Loon Lake
> RED JAMES, worker in an Indiana automotive plant
> SANDY JAMES, Red's teenage wife
> TOMMY CRAPO, underworld figure in Bennett's employ, once
>   Clara's lover

Loon Lake opens with Joe, a young boy from a lower-class family in
Paterson, New Jersey. His parents consider him a burden, and he
breaks with them to go to New York City, where he becomes a grocery
delivery boy. Joe, in spite of his limited opportunities, is ambitious and
willing to connive and cheat to get ahead. After his stint as a delivery
boy, he joins the Hearn Bros. Carnival where he is able to refine his
connivances into confidence games and to see an even seamier side of
life. At the end of the summer Joe is on the road again, this time with
a respectable sum of cash.

Stumbling along a single track railroad in the Adirondacks of upstate
New York, Joe sees a private train rumbling through the autumn darkness. He is mesmerized by its opulence and by a blonde woman standing naked, holding a dress to herself before a mirror. The train spins
off into darkness, but this vision of the beautiful woman has changed
his life. He follows the train track to its end, a large estate, and,
wandering in the darkness, is savagely attacked by wild dogs.

Upon regaining consciousness, Joe finds he is at Loon Lake, the
Adirondack lodge of F. W. Bennett, the millionaire automotive mag-
nate. Loon Lake is frequented by the cream of society. The guest
register is signed by such world-renowned personages as Charlie Chap-
lin and King Leopold of Belgium. Joe looks for a signature that might
indicate who the blonde woman is but finds none. He does strike up a
friendship with Warren Penfield, an aging, drunken poet who lives at

Loon Lake.

As Joe convalesces, he is allowed to earn his keep by working on the grounds of Loon Lake and becomes a frequent audience for Penfield's drunken and melancholic rantings. It seems that Penfield has been at Loon Lake for seven years and has become something of a toy for Bennett and his wife, Lucinda, a world-renowned aviatrix. Joe, oblivious to the lack of quality of Penfield's work, is overwhelmingly impressed by this man of letters.

He also finally locates the blonde Venus of his vision, Clara, who is either Penfield's or Bennett's lover. Joe goes to visit Penfield's cottage where he finds the poet and the beautiful Clara drunk and morose. Both speak despondently of their feelings of imprisonment at Loon Lake. Joe realizes that Clara is Bennett's lover and that Penfield suffers from both an unrequited and paternal love for her. We soon find out that Clara was "passed on" to Bennett by Tommy Crapo, Bennett's gangster hireling. Joe is impressed by the genuineness of Penfield's innocent and impotent love.

Upon his return Bennett singles out Joe as a worker with intelligence and imagination. Clara, meanwhile, spends her nights with Bennett at the main house. When Bennett's wife Lucinda returns, landing her own seaplane on Loon Lake, Clara is returned to her cottage, a toy put back on the shelf.

In a daring plan, Joe decides to steal a car and run off with Clara. Penfield approves and aids their escape, knowing that his love for Clara will never be realized. Although Bennett has offered Joe a job as a groundskeeper, Joe refuses, telling Bennett he would rather strike out on his own. Bennett, who has come to admire Joe, gives him the number of Loon Lake to call if he ever has a problem.

With money from Penfield and a stolen car Joe and Clara head west. The two end up in Indiana where Joe takes a job assembling automobiles at the Bennett Plant. Love has blossomed between the two on their journey, and they settle into a life of working-class drudgery redeemed only by their love. Joe hopes to make enough money by spring to take them to California.

Clara reveals how she was snatched from oblivion by the gangster Tommy Crapo, and Joe's jealousy casts a shadow over their otherwise happy relationship. The young couple befriend their next door neighbors, Red and Sandy James, a young couple with a baby. Clara and Sandy forge a strong feminine and maternal relationship centered on the care of the infant.

Red gets Joe involved in the incipient union movement at the plant. Joe follows willingly, more out of fascination with Red's character than with the values of the movement. Joe finds out the hard way that Red is a company operative planted to break the union strike that is being planned. Red has befriended Joe in order to set him up as the fall-guy for the other union members. As they walk home one night the two are jumped in an alleyway. Red is murdered, while Joe is brutally beaten and his arms broken.

Sandy is beside herself with grief when she hears of the killing of her husband. Joe realizes that it is probably Crapo who is responsible. Joe realizes that he, Clara, Sandy, and the baby must get out of town as quickly as possible because they know too much. When Clara resists the idea, Joe cruelly suggests that she might want a reunion with Crapo.

Plans for their speedy escape are foiled when Joe is picked up for questioning by the police. Sandy and Clara, who have nowhere else to go, come along. After Joe is sequestered, he sees through a window a man whom police identify to him as Crapo. He is headed for the waiting room where Clara and Sandy are sitting. Joe screams, but to no avail. By the time Joe is finally freed, Crapo has left with Clara. Joe does not know if she has gone willingly, but he never sees her again.

To extricate himself from the police interview Joe concocts a story that seems plausible. He claims that Red was not only a company operative but also a double agent working for the union as well, feeding misleading information to company agents to protect plans for a much larger strike elsewhere. Joe insists he is a company operative dispatched by Bennett himself to check on the loyalty of Bennett's hired strike-breaker, Crapo. He claims that he is Bennett's son and that Red James was killed by his own agents in order to silence him. Joe produces Bennett's telephone number at Loon Lake and asks them to call him. Bennett, Joe is certain, will be willing to play along with this ruse. After the police seem to have made the call, they free Joe. With some money from Red's insurance policy, Joe, Sandy, and the baby head for California both to escape and to find Clara. In New Mexico, as they prepare to board a train for Los Angeles, Joe thinks he sees Clara on a train heading the other way. With the mother and child asleep aboard the train, Joe leaves them his money, jumps from the train, and begins his trek back to Loon Lake.

Joe is hoping he might see Clara again, but as Loon Lake comes once more into view, he realizes that it is the place itself that has drawn him back. He finds Bennett living as a recluse, Bennett's wife having disappeared on an around-the-world flight. Penfield, now dead, has willed all his papers and writings to Joe who, as Penfield notes in his will, will surely return to Loon Lake. Both the house and Bennett seem to be crumbling.

In conversation with Bennett, Joe is surprised to find that the police never called Loon Lake that night, and that his motive for staying on at the estate, a feeling of duty or gratitude, is unwarranted. Perhaps drawn by Bennett's power and wealth, Joe chooses to stay in order to revenge all of Bennett's wrongdoings by, paradoxically, giving the crumbling old man a sense of hope, humanity, and a reason to live.

The story ends with a one-page biography of Joe. After enrolling in Williams College and graduating *cum laude,* he joins the OSS during World War II and is decommissioned a major. He works for the CIA, is twice married and twice divorced, and retires in 1975 from the State Department with the rank of ambassador. Having assumed all of Bennett's board positions and club affiliations, and legally changing his name to Bennett, Joe is finally "Master of Loon Lake."

For all the complexity of its exposition and shifts of scene, time, and narrative voice, *Loon Lake* is surprisingly easy to follow. It rewards the expectations of each of the story-forms it cultivates. It is a novel of the working-class boy made good. It is a detective thriller. It is a novel of obsession.

Like Loon Lake itself, it has a strange majesty coupled with a deep gloominess. The two together create a pervasive cinematic mood, not unlike that of Orson Welles' *Citizen Kane.* What is the obsession that drives both Joe and Bennett, that leads them to meld into one character? The reader looks for some answer, but there is none. By now, Doctorow seems to feel, there are no answers. "You are thinking it is a dream," Doctorow writes in the voice of one of his characters toward the end of the novel. "It is no dream," he says. "It is the account, in helpless linear translation of the unending love of our simultaneous but disynchronous lives."

D. W. Faulkner

LYNDON

Author: Merle Miller
Publisher: G. P. Putnam's Sons (New York). 645 pp. $17.95
Type of work: Biography
Time: 1908–1973
Locale: United States

A review of the life of Lyndon Baines Johnson as seen through the eyes of his friends, supporters, and opponents

Principal personage:

LYNDON JOHNSON, the passionate, unpredictable, flamboyant 36th President of the United States

As majority leader in the U.S. Senate, he could recite the drinking, sexual, and voting habits of each and every senator. His stories and jokes were notorious for four-letter expletives ranging from earthy to vulgar. He drove his cars as if they were cow ponies, gave a press conference in his pajamas, and once tested the echo qualities of the Taj Mahal by giving a Texas yelp. In 1960 he ran not only for vice-president of the United States but also for reelection as the senator from Texas, winning both races. He threw temper tantrums frequently, berating his staff one minute and lavishing them with praise and affection the next. When Lyndon Johnson was bad, he could be brutal; when he was good, he dazzled.

Johnson was born August 27, 1908, in Pedernales, Texas. His mother Rebekah used to tell the story that he was called "baby" for three months until one morning she refused to cook breakfast for her husband, Sam Johnson, Jr., until he agreed to a name. Although Lyndon Johnson liked to recall in later years that he had come from a very poor family, that was not exactly the case. His father was a farmer and Texas legislator, and although neither occupation was highly paid, the family lived comfortably. Sam Johnson was known as a "Texas rebel;" he supported farmers over the interests of the wealthy ranchers. Rebekah Johnson was the granddaughter of George Washington Baines, who was, as she liked to remind everyone, once president of Baylor University. She had given up a promising career in journalism to marry young Sam.

The milestones of Johnson's career are reminiscent of a novel by Horatio Alger. While a student at Southwest Texas State Teachers' College, Johnson not only edited the school newspaper and headed the debate team, but also taught a course in freshman government, carried seven courses, and had a date practically every night. Later, as a young teacher in a poverty-stricken Mexican-American school in the southern part of Texas, Johnson quickly turned schoolyard brawls into organized music lessons, a softball team, and dancing. In 1930, although barely 22, he left for Washington to run the congressional office of newly-elected Richard Kleberg of Texas, who much preferred golf and the social life of Washington to the time-consuming duties of his congressional office. During this time, Johnson met Claudia Taylor. He proposed to her on their second date and three months later married the woman who became known as "Lady Bird." He also met Sam Rayburn, Speaker of the House of Representatives and an old friend of his father's. Rayburn and Johnson would be like father and son, ruling over the House and Senate for the decade between 1951 and 1961.

In 1935, as the country was digging out from the Depression, President Roosevelt, who had his eye on the energetic young congressional staffer, appointed him the Texas director of the newly formed National Youth Administration. Three years later, Johnson was elected to Congress; by 1948 he was a senator; and in 1954 he became the youngest majority leader in the Senate's history.

As Senate majority leader, Johnson moved confidently on both sides of the aisle, forging alliances between Republicans and Democrats. He mended squabbles within the party between northern liberal and southern conservative Democrats, at least enough to win the votes needed for his legislation. Even critics of Johnson respected his style. Barry Goldwater, Senator from Arizona and presidential candidate in 1964, recalled that "when Lyndon Johnson said 'This is going to be legislation,' you knew you were not going to leave until it *was* legislation."

Johnson's philosophy was "if you haven't got the votes, wait and maybe you can pick them up." In early 1952 when Senator Joseph McCarthy began using his government-operations subcommittee to hunt for Communist conspiracies among a number of prominent Americans, Johnson was urged to denounce McCarthy. Johnson refused, saying, "If you're going to kill a snake with a hoe, you have to get it with one blow on the head." He privately told Hubert Humphrey, his young Minnesota colleague, that it would only be a matter of time before McCarthy and his subcommittee would violate the rules of the Senate—meaning that when McCarthy picked on a conservative senator, he would be through. In 1954, McCarthy attacked a close friend of the powerful Virginian senator Harry Byrd. Within a month, Johnson had organized a full-scale investigation of McCarthy, who was later "condemned" by the Senate for his actions.

While some historians would argue that Johnson was as much a political opportunist as a liberal humanitarian, there could be no doubt of his power and legislative genius in the Senate. In 1956 a number of anti-civil rights bills had been introduced by southern conservatives in order to restrict the power of the federal courts to enforce school desegregation. Johnson advised his liberal colleagues that if they wanted to defeat the bills, they should put all of them into one bill for consideration by the Senate, noting that some conservatives would like part of the conglomeration but that nobody would like it all. Liberals, including Humphrey, ignored the advice and chose to vote on each measure as it came up. When the liberals were defeated on the first measure, however, they quickly followed Johnson's advice, repackaged the bills into one, and defeated it as Johnson had predicted.

A large part of the Johnson success on the Senate floor lay in his behind-the-scenes maneuvering—somewhere between an artful movie director and a head football coach during the playoffs. Humphrey once complained to a friend that when Johnson wanted him to push certain legislation, he would grab Humphrey by the lapels and say, "Now, Hubert, I want you to do this and that and get going," and with that he would kick him hard on the shins. Humphrey apparently pulled up his trousers to reveal numerous scars.

William Jorden observed: "When he talked to somebody, Johnson used to get right up close . . . he would poke you in the chest with his finger, cock his head under and look up at you and talk, all at the same time." Ben Bradlee, executive editor of the *Washington Post,* compared the "Johnson treatment" to having a St. Bernard lick your face for an hour and paw you all over.

As vice-president, Johnson was unable to translate the successes of the Senate into his new role; he constantly stumbled trying to make the transition. One reason was that Johnson, the powerful "work horse" (as he called himself), was uncomfortable as a diplomatic "show horse." He found it very hard to fit the urbane and witty image projected by the Kennedy administration. Friends observe that during his vice-presidency he "got fat and drank a lot." And on his frequent trips on behalf of Kennedy, his free-wheeling Texas style infuriated and embarrassed the State Department.

In early 1963, as plans were beginning for the next year's presidential elections, Johnson, according to several friends, wanted to return to his Texas ranch and to his mushrooming radio and television empire in Austin. The assassination of John F. Kennedy in November changed those plans.

In recalling the performance of Johnson as he assumed the presidency after Kennedy's assassination, Hugh Sidey, chief of the Washington bureau of *Time* magazine said, "Johnson in my judgment was probably the only man in the United States who could have handled that transition. He'd been in Washington since 1937. As an administrative aide, House representative, senator, vice-president, he'd lived through virtually every crisis in politics this country had had. He knew instinctively what to do."

From the beginning of his presidency, Johnson had a sense of urgency about accomplishing his Great Society legislation. During his presidency, he introduced over 60 bills on education and sponsored bills on low-income housing, Medicare, women's rights, civil rights, and job training, which jumped from an enrollment of 75,000 under Kennedy to over 1,500,000 under Johnson. Programs such as VISTA, Head Start, and the Office of Economic Opportunity were created.

Shortly after reelection in 1964, Johnson observed, ". . . I'll have a good chance to get my programs through . . . But after I make my recommendations, I'm going to start to lose the power and authority I have because that's what happened to President Woodrow Wilson, to President Roosevelt and to Truman and to Kennedy. Every day that I'm in office and every day that I push my program, I'll be losing part of my ability to be influential, because that's the nature of what a president does. He uses up his capital. Something is going to come up, whether something like the Vietnam War or something else where I will begin to lose all that I now have."

In 1965 the Reverend Martin Luther King began a voting rights drive in Selma, Alabama. Federal troops were called in to protect the marchers. In February of that year, Johnson made a critical decision about Vietnam. He authorized systematic bombing and a commitment of ground troops on a major scale. According to the *Pentagon Papers,* in April 1965 the "mission" to Vietnam had been changed; there was no more talk of Americans as advisers.

By the end of 1966, racial riots had occurred in New York, Chicago, Cleveland, Los Angeles, San Francisco, Atlanta, Detroit, Dayton, and Oakland. At the same time, hundreds of thousands of young men were drafted into military service, and two thirds of them went to Vietnam. By the beginning of 1968, demonstrations against the escalation of the war had reached major proportions. On April 4, 1968, the Reverend Martin Luther King was shot and killed, setting off more violence than ever before in the history of civil rights. Rioting and looting throughout the country affected over 125 cities in 28 states. At one point, over 711 fires burned in Washington, D.C., alone. Johnson's prophecy had been fulfilled. A few days before Martin Luther King's murder, Johnson had announced to the nation that he would not seek reelection.

His retirement years were lived with the same energy and drive that he had given to his political career. He supervised every detail on the management of his ranch, ran his radio and television operations in Austin, and oversaw the construction of the Lyndon Baines Johnson

Library in Austin. One of his employees in Texas tells the story that whenever she couldn't find him on the ranch, she could call to his birthplace home (now part of the National Park Service), and there he would be selling copies of his memoirs.

Merle Miller's *Plain Speaking: An Oral Biography of Harry S Truman* received wide public attention. In *Plain Speaking,* as in *Lyndon: An Oral Biography,* taped interviews with the people who knew these men are presented in written forms as they were recorded, with a minimum of editing. The author fills in historical information when necessary to provide continuity between speakers.

Miller spent five years researching and editing *Lyndon.* He concluded that "no one was ever neutral about LBJ," and that an oral biography was perfect for this man because "LBJ almost never stopped talking." The result of Miller's effort is a graceful, witty, funny, and sometimes poignant look at this unusual man. And while it is filled with the recollections from those who were his friends and supporters, the book will nonetheless be a useful tool for historians, providing valuable and conflicting insights into a remarkable period of history.

Whether Johnson was tragically caught in historical circumstances beyond his control or whether he provoked circumstances that went out of control, the jury of history is still out. Mark Twain wrote, "It is not what they don't know that hurts people, it is what they do know that isn't so." This applies to Lyndon Johnson. After more than a decade, the events of the late 1960's—Vietnam, Civil Rights, the Great Society, the War on Poverty—still provoke among many a sense of confusion, anger, and disappointment. To many, Johnson remains partly saint, partly Satan.

Those who knew him saw a bit of both. John Connally said of him: "There is no adjective in the dictionary to describe him. He was cruel and kind, generous and greedy, sensitive and insensitive, crafty and naive . . . as a matter of fact it would take *every* adjective in the dictionary to describe him."

As Hubert Humphrey observed: "Just keep in mind that he had all the weaknesses and strengths of a big man. He loved women, he loved to take a drink, he loved a good earthy story . . . He was an All-American president. He was really the history of this country with all the turmoil, the bombast, the sentiments, the passions. It was all there. All in one man."

Martha Paddick

MANAGING IN TURBULENT TIMES

Author: Peter F. Drucker
Publisher: Harper & Row (New York). 239 pp. $9.95
Type of work: Current affairs
Time: Present and future

A guide for corporate managers to the demographic and technological changes transforming the world economy, and advice on how to confront successfully this turbulence

The "managerial revolution" in American capitalism brought with it a group of pundits eager to describe the contours of the revolution and to prescribe a ruling philosophy for the managers of the modern corporation. For the last half century or more, intellectuals and academics from Adolf Berle to James Burnham to John Kenneth Galbraith have aspired to the title of "Marx for the Managers," a phrase coined by C. Wright Mills. Perhaps no one has come closer to achieving this preeminence in the eyes of the managers themselves than Peter F. Drucker, whose latest book, *Managing in Turbulent Times,* offers ruling elites in capitalist societies a guide to the dangers and opportunities ahead in a future of great economic, political, and social turbulence.

Drucker has published sixteen books, all of which have been marked by a combination of common sense, fruitful speculation, and artful advocacy. He has won the respect of corporate managers throughout the world, and is perhaps one of the most influential intellectuals alive today.

Managing in Turbulent Times might best be described as informed speculation in which Drucker forecasts the future of industrial society and offers advice to those managers who hope to retain their power in the face of this future. For capitalist societies, Drucker argues, an era of tremendous turbulence lies ahead, "a period of rapid innovation, a period of fast and radical structural shifts." His book aims to tell managers what to do in order to make the best of this unsettling future.

If their organizations are to survive in a period of rapid change, Drucker insists that managers must pay attention to some "fundamentals" that are too often ignored. It is imperative that enterprises constantly adjust their accounts for inflation and maintain adequate liquidity if they are to be successful. In turbulent times, Drucker observes, "management has to put financial strength before earnings." The task of managers is to increase the productivity of the resources at their command and to ensure that their organizations can not only meet current operating costs but also the costs of doing business in the future.

In order to meet the opportunities as well as the dangers of the future, Drucker argues, managers must develop flexible strategies of growth and innovation. This means practicing "corporate weight control" through a willingness to abandon those uses of resources that are obsolete or unproductive. Managers should abandon one less promising or less productive program for every new venture they take on. Drucker calls upon business managers to distinguish carefully between right and wrong kinds of growth, between growth that is the consequence of increased productivity and growth that is simply an increase in volume without increased productivity. Managers should also be aware of technological change and be prepared to take advantage of the opportunities afforded by technical innovation. Drucker believes a period of dramatic technological change, based on the advances in basic research of the last fifty years, is ahead. Innovation will be particularly striking in communications, health care (genetic engineering), and the integration of computers into production tools.

According to Drucker, the most important cause of turbulence in the future will be the effects of dramatic demographic change throughout the world. As he says, "in the last decades of the twentieth century, population structures will be the least stable and most drastically changing element in economics, society, and world politics, and probably the single most important cause of turbulence." This demographic change is a two-edged phenomenon, affecting "developed" and "developing" nations in quite different ways. Developed countries such as the United States have in recent years seen a decline in the rate of population increase (a "baby bust"), an increase in life expectancy, and a steady increase in the educational attainments of the population. The developing countries, on the other hand, have been experiencing a baby boom, attributable in large measure to a dramatic decline in the infant mortality rate.

These demographic changes have had and will continue to have important effects on the economics of both developed and developing countries. In the former, population dynamics and educational growth have made for a shortage of "traditional workers for traditional jobs," that is, young, male workers employed full-time in industry. At the same time, the nontraditional (female and part-time) service sector of the work force has expanded rapidly. Moreover, the labor force in nations such as the United States is "a labor force in which an increasing number of the young people have had an advanced education and are simply not available for the traditional jobs, almost irrespective of pay." Conversely, in developing countries, the problem is a shortage of unskilled and semi-skilled jobs for a population freeing itself from the blight of infant mortality.

As Drucker sees it, this pattern of demographic change presents corporate managers in the developed world with the opportunity for orchestrating a major shift in international business strategy. The problem of labor shortages in the developed nations and labor surplus in the Third World will be solved, he argues, through a new form of "transnational integration," which he terms "production sharing." In production sharing, the abundant labor force in developing countries available for traditional jobs will be brought together with the markets and purchasing power of the developing countries under the direction of skilled managers in the United States, Western Europe, and Japan. Such production sharing, Drucker notes, will involve very little capital investment by developed countries in developing countries, for it would work through partnership arrangements with Third World subcontractors. Tomorrow's multinational corporations will be quite different from those of today. They will be smaller, more flexible enterprises, built on marketing power rather than investment power. Unlike most of today's multinationals, which have shown relatively little interest in investing in the developing countries, tomorrow's "transnational confederations" will make an earnest effort to utilize the rich labor resources of the Third World.

The key nations in the world, Drucker argues, will be the "almost developed" nations, and he urges managers to concentrate their production-sharing efforts on countries such as Brazil, Mexico, Taiwan, and South Korea. These are the nations "whose success or failure to attain full economic development will largely determine the success or failure of the entire world economy in the next decades."

Drucker does not hesitate to point to the many obstacles that will stand in the way of managerial success in the turbulent times that lie ahead. Managers must face a world that is increasingly integrated economically but increasingly fragmented politically. Thus, corporate managers must not only learn to think transnationally as business people, but they must also develop the political skills necessary to deal with politicians, labor leaders, and other groups that will inevitably resist the effort to rationalize the international division of labor.

One of the most difficult and interesting problems to which Drucker points is that which managers in developed countries face in controlling a highly-educated, professionalized labor force of "knowledge workers." These workers, who regard themselves as autonomous, skilled professionals, are resistant to managerial control, and their integration into corporate bureaucracies poses the threat of the "double-headed monster"—organizations divided between managerial authority and demands for professional autonomy. Drucker recommends that managers handle their professional workers with care, delegating as much responsibility to them as possible for the design and control of their own work without impinging on managerial control of key decisions.

Managing in Turbulent Times is a book written for managers, and non-managers will perhaps be struck most by the implicit and explicit assumptions of Drucker's discussion, assumptions that are invariably supportive of the power of managerial elites. According to Drucker, "there are no profits; there are only the deferred costs of staying in business." He acknowledges that his vision of international "production sharing" will create an integrated world economy firmly controlled by corporate managers in the developed world, yet denies that the ensuing imbalance of power is in any sense imperialistic. For him it is simply a response to the fact that "the standard of living of the developed world can be maintained only if it succeeds in mobilizing the labor resources of the developing world." Drucker's book is a guide for those with decision-making power in advanced capitalist societies, and he does not question the right of managers to exercise this power. He reserves his sharpest barbs for those who challenge this power and hence increase the level of "turbulence" in the modern world.

If Drucker does not question managerial power, he does admit that this power has yet to be legitimatized. Drucker's greatest strength as a social analyst is his recognition that corporate power coexists uneasily with the democratic political traditions of nations such as the United States. However, this legitimatization problem is one to which neither he nor any other managerial theorist has provided a solution. Those who will undertake the challenge of managing in turbulent times will, as Drucker shows in this book, confront a host of new opportunities and difficulties, but they will also confront the problem of managing men and women, at home and abroad, who remain wedded to old-fashioned notions of democracy and self-management.

Robert B. Westbrook

MANCHU

Author: Robert Elegant (1918–   )
Publisher: McGraw-Hill (New York). 560 pp. $12.95
Type of work: Novel
Time: 1624–1652
Locale: China, Portuguese Macao, and the Manchu capital at Mukden

The adventures of an English soldier of fortune in China before and after the Manchu victory over the Ming dynasty in 1644

Principal characters:
>FRANCIS ARROWSMITH, soldier of fortune, protagonist of the story
>FATHER GIULIO DI GIACCOMO, Jesuit missionary stationed in Macao
>DR. PAUL KWANG-CHI HSÜ, a senior Ming official
>FATHER ADAM SCHALL, ranking Jesuit at the Ming court
>JOSEPH CHOU-SZE KING, Arrowsmith's slave and secretary
>MARTA SOO, Arrowsmith's Chinese wife
>BABUTAI (BARBARA), Arrowsmith's Manchu concubine
>DOLORES ANGELA DO AMARAL, Macao heiress who became Arrowsmith's second wife
>TSAO CHUN-HUA (Known as the BLACK PREMIER), chief eunuch officer at the Ming court

The story of *Manchu* takes place within three major time frames—"The Artillery of Heaven" from 1624 to 1632; "The Wrath of Heaven" from 1632 to 1644; and "The Mandate of Heaven," from 1645 to 1652. Although these section titles refer to the dynastic cycles of China, the story begins in the Spanish provinces of France where Francis Arrowsmith, an orphan, has been studying for the priesthood at the English College of St. Omer, a college run by Jesuits who had fled the persecution of Catholics in England. His father, who took refuge in Spain following the confiscation of family lands in Lancashire, had died in a battle with Protestant forces just four months after the birth of his son. Before her death a few years later, his Spanish widow had put their child in the care of the Jesuits, with the admonition that the boy become a priest, a man of God, rather than a man of blood like his father.

Young Arrowsmith was a fervent Catholic who had sat entranced as a visiting Italian Jesuit, Father Giulio di Giaccomo, made an appeal for the Mission to China—a glorious enterprise to convert some 150,000,000 pagan Chinese—but in 1624 the fathers of St. Omer's had to expel their unruly charge for carousing with the soldiers at a nearby post of the Spanish Guard. After a couple of years in the army of King Philip learning the use and manufacture of artillery, Arrowsmith offered his services to the Mission to China, arriving in Macao in 1628.

Under the sponsorship of Father di Giaccomo, by now also in
Macao, Arrowsmith eagerly joined a Portuguese expeditionary force
requested by the Ming emperor to help fend off the Manchus (Tartars)
threatening the capital. It took almost two years for the expeditionary
force to reach the environs of Peking. There Arrowsmith got his first
real lesson in the ways of China when a detachment of the Imperial
Infantry literally cut a path for the expeditionary force through a mass
of people clogging the road in their flight from the warfare in the capital. Moving into the throng with spears and maces, these personal
soldiers of the emperor had toppled carts carrying women and children, sliced off heads and arms at random, smashed skulls, and pushed
the bloody rubble to the sides. Before the foreigners could complete
their journey, however, word came that the Chinese forces were re-
treating from a Manchu assault on Peking and would make a stand at
Chochou to the south. Turning back to assist at Chochou, the expeditionary force sent the Manchus flying in terror with blank fusillades
from their strange weapons.

The victory that elated the Portuguese artillerymen also elated one
faction in the Ming court while dismaying another, and Arrowsmith
became the unwitting prize in their intrigues to control this marvelous
new instrument of power. The dismay belonged to Tsao Chun-hua,
known as the Black Premier, whose evil influence over the emperor
would be in jeopardy if the foreign artillery brought to Peking at the
behest of the conservative mandarins and the Jesuits were to be employed in their cause. The Black Premier, the chief eunuch officer, was
a mock eunuch, having eluded castration by bribing the examiners and
presenting as the requisite proof of his eligibility the testicles of a male
prostitute. His leverage at court was founded on a lifetime of chica-
nery, a homosexual relationship with the emperor, and the command
of two dreaded organizations—the Flamboyant Cloaks (security) and
the Divine Skein (secret police). The other faction, intent only on
saving the Ming dynasty and bringing the Catholic faith to the Chinese,
had persevered under the leadership of Father Adam Schall, the rank-
ing Jesuit in Peking, and Dr. Paul Hsü, a senior mandarin and a Catholic.

Arrowsmith went to Father Schall and Dr. Hsü for instructions on
furthering the Mission to China. His initiation into the devious and
intricate strategies by which the Chinese advanced their interests followed quickly. As part of his scheme to outmaneuver the Black Premier and to bind the Englishman to China, Dr. Hsü arranged for
Arrowsmith the command of a special battalion to be trained in the
new technology, the services of Joseph King (scholar, Christian, and
Ming loyalist with the status of a slave), and a marriage to Marta Soo

(Dr. Hsü's grandniece). The Black Premier, for his part, arranged to have his spy Simon Wu made adjutant to Arrowsmith. By 1631, Arrowsmith found himself relieved of command in favor of Simon Wu and in virtual exile in Tengchou with the rest of the expeditionary force, ostensibly for the defense of this outpost from Manchu attackers. Playing both sides, the Black Premier masterminded the capture of Tengchou in 1632 by "rebels" and the delivery of Arrowsmith and his slave Joseph King to the Manchu capital of Mukden.

Four years in China had taken the edge off Francis Arrowsmith's innocent idealism, so the Manchus rather easily convinced the cannon expert that his fortune lay in serving the Manchu emperor. Among the inducements were a military command and permission to trade on his own account with Macao. Arrowsmith had been surprised at the vitality of Mukden—obviously the center of an empire in the making—and rationalized his disloyalty to the Ming dynasty as a higher loyalty to the Mission to China. Following the Jesuitic logic, Arrowsmith would make himself one with the Manchus, the new rulers, to advance the conversion of China.

The Manchus confounded his conscience, however, by insisting that Babutai, daughter of a Manchu nobleman, be accepted as his wife in token of good faith. His reluctant marriage to Marta Soo for a similar purpose remained valid according to the Catholic creed, though after initial sexual ecstasy and the birth of a daughter their union had shriveled to a formality. But Arrowsmith finally took Babutai as his concubine and for a while enjoyed her simple ways and feral ardor.

In 1640, growing weary of the barbarous life of the Manchus and fearing the long arm of the Divine Skein (in his precarious link as a double agent), Arrowsmith got Manchu approval for a journey to Macao, the pretext being to improve his skills there as a cannon maker and to buy new cannon for shipment to Mukden. For nine years Joseph King and his master drifted with the tides of war, setting up a trading operation in Macao and returning briefly to Peking before and after the Manchu takeover in 1644, traveling to the Southern Ming stronghold in the coastal province of Fukien. Their wanderings confirmed the disarray of their old dreams. Dr. Hsü, the Black Premier, Marta Soo, and Simon Wu were all dead. Father Schall was casting cannon for the Manchus.

Marriage to the wealthy Dolores Angela do Amaral in Macao in 1650 brought a kind of contentment that was new to the aging English adventurer, but there was to be one more military effort, the defense of Canton for the Southern Ming. The battle ended in disaster when Arrowsmith collapsed at the critical moment with a severe attack of malaria. The following year Arrowsmith nearly succumbed to "black-

water fever'' and was warned that another attack of the endemic mal-
ady would be fatal. Weakened by the ills of Asia, his hopes of glory
dissipated in the convolutions of a mysterious empire, Arrowsmith
sailed for Europe in 1652 with Dolores and their newborn son ''to bask
in the sunshine of a Lisbon plaza remembering ancient battles for other
dotards.''

The parallels between *Manchu* and James Clavell's *Shōgun* are interesting. Both Francis Arrowsmith and John Blackthorne were middle
class English youths who went to Asia in the 17th century—one to
China, the other to Japan—to seek their fortunes. Both were drawn
into the intrigues surrounding a political upheaval—the overthrow of
the Ming dynasty by the Manchus in China, the emergence of Tòranaga
from a deadly rivalry as the new ruler in Japan. Both were tutored in
the language and the culture by highborn ladies in an aura of romantic
entanglement. Yet these parallels and others may simply indicate the
adaptation by two authors of a story line hallowed in the literature of
adventure.

The differences may be more illuminating. *Manchu* is less solidly
based on scholarship than is *Shōgun*, reflecting in part the inherently
greater difficulties of research on China and in part the divergent approaches of a former foreign correspondent (Elegant) and a former
academic (Clavell). Elegant admits that *Manchu* was harder to write
than his bestseller *Dynasty,* which owed much of its ring of authenticity to his personal knowledge of sources. A corollary of his dependence
on elusive historical records seems to be breezy style. *Manchu* also
tends to ramble, the many subthemes sometimes blurring the focus.
But perhaps for a long adventure in a sprawling empire this is art
imitating nature.

Anyone looking primarily for a rousing tale is quite likely to dismiss
such observations as quibbles, for *Manchu* quickly catches the imagination with exploits in a faraway land and time. Furthermore, for the
many people newly curious about China there is a wealth of incidental
instruction in Chinese history and culture. As amply demonstrated in
his earlier books, Elegant has a genius for evoking the sights and
sounds of Asia and has developed a keen insight into the subtleties of
the Chinese character. These talents have been put to good use in
Manchu, which offers an enjoyable way to become better attuned to
China.

Adrienne Suddard

MAN IN THE HOLOCENE

Author: Max Frisch
Publisher: Harcourt Brace Jovanovich (New York). 120 pp. $7.95
Type of work: Novel
Time: The present
Locale: Switzerland

The story of the mental and physical disintegration of Herr Geiser during a storm that cuts him off from the outside world

Principal character:
HERR GEISER, a lonely and eccentric pensioner

Herr Geiser, a seventy-four-year-old pensioner, lives alone in a village in the Swiss canton of Ticino. *Man in the Holocene* charts his thoughts and experiences over a four day period of continuous rainfall. The village in which Geiser lives has been cut off from the world by a landslide, and Geiser too is cut off, isolated by the weather and by his own mental disintegration. Frisch's narrative describes this reality from his only character's perspective, and, through Geiser's fragmented thoughts, the reader gains an understanding of the process of mental collapse.

In the first pages of the novel, the reader becomes aware of two crucial themes—Geiser's physical and intellectual isolation, and the continuous storm that dominates his imagination during the next several days. Frisch writes that "Geiser has time to spare." He lives alone; his wife, Elsbeth, has died several years earlier. He recalls having had guests to his house—his daughter Corinne, his grandchildren whose names he cannot remember, and a solar astronomer and his wife who visited him and brought him books over the summer. Yet he does not converse with anyone, and he reminds himself throughout that nobody will ever know what he is thinking and how he is spending his time.

Geiser's intellectual isolation is even more apparent. No longer working, he has come to the canton of Ticino, a remote region in the Alps, to retire. He spends his time reading the encyclopedia and trying to remember what he has just read. At first, he writes the information on slips of paper, which he pins to the paneled wall in the living room in order to remind himself of those facts. He tires of this, however, and begins to cut paragraphs out of the books, which he tacks or tapes to the wall. When the wall space at eye level has become too crowded, he removes the portrait of his deceased wife to make room for the clippings. Ultimately, he decides that the illustrations are as important as the text, and these he cuts out for his walls as well. In decorating his house in this bizarre manner, Geiser admits that he does not expect others to see what he has done to his books and his wall; he does not expect anyone else to share in the knowledge that he has collected. Furthermore, as Frisch writes, "Geiser finds himself wondering what he really wants to know, what he hopes to gain from all this knowledge."

Virtually all of the notes, excerpts, and illustrations that Geiser has collected pertain to the prehistory of the earth and of man. They symbolize most clearly the main character's own intellectual regression. Geiser is fascinated with the Holocene, the geological period in which modern man first emerged. He pursues also the history of the Ticino valley, which was carved out of glaciers and first populated during the Ice Age. As he remains in his house over the next few days, Geiser becomes obsessed with the primitive animals—lizards, dinosaurs, salamanders, and ants—that preceded man on earth. Interspersed with the paleontology, however, are items pertaining to Geiser's image of destruction. He investigates the causes and different types of thunder and the periodic floods and landslides that have plagued the Ticino region. At the very end of the novel, he begins to encounter scraps of information announcing his own demise. One clipping discusses the weakness of memory that accompanies senility; the final clipping diagrams and describes the symptoms of apoplexy, that is, the most complete loss of brain function.

The never-ending storm serves as the background of Geiser's obsession with regression and disintegration. At the beginning of the novel, the power is out and all the roads to Geiser's small village are blocked because of the rain. Aware of the region's history of landslides and avalanches, Geiser imagines that the mountain will collapse and bury everything. He has packed a knapsack, although he knows he cannot escape. When he goes outside, he notices that a small stone wall behind his house has fallen to the ground. He interprets this as a sign that he and his house will be the next to go. Having convinced himself of impending doom, Geiser examines everything in the house according to this logic. The food that spoils as a result of the power failure and the lizard and ants that enter through the flooded basement remind Geiser that his entire world is disintegrating, reverting to its most primitive natural state.

Geiser's interpretation of the storm and its dire consequences reflects his own sense of personal disintegration. As the novel progresses, he becomes less capable of understanding and assimilating the information he collects. He begins to hallucinate, to the point that he cannot distinguish the real damage caused by the storm from the massive geological transformations described in his reading. At one point, when the rain has stopped, he goes to the tavern for matches, but, once there, he forgets what he has come for. Later, driven by his insane logic, he tries to make an escape over a mountain pass in a steady, soaking rain. He reaches the other side, naps for a couple of hours, and decides, for no apparent reason, to return to his house. He gets back at midnight and is completely disoriented, unable to remember how various items in the house got there. He, and consequently the reader, is only dimly aware of what happens next.

At one point, after his return from the trip across the mountain pass, Geiser finds himself lying on the floor. Presumably he has fallen, but he cannot recall how and when. Afterward, he gradually becomes aware of a numbness on the left side of his face and a squeezing pain above his right temple—the first symptom of a stroke. Since his abortive journey across the mountains, he has ceased to care what happens to himself and his house. For the first time, he takes no interest in the salamander that has entered the house. The telephone rings repeatedly; although he hears it, he makes no attempt to answer it. At this stage, Geiser has begun to accept the impending doom that he perceives in nature and that he feels is happening to him. Throughout the novel, he has interpreted all of prehistory and all of nature according to his own obsessive vision of regression and disintegration. Yet, his final thoughts separate for the first time the reality of nature and his own disturbed mental processes; Frisch writes that "The ants Geiser recently observed . . . are not concerned with what anyone might know about them; nor were the dinosaurs, which died out before a human being set eyes on them. All the papers, whether on the wall or on the carpet, can go. Who cares about the Holocene? Nature needs no names. Geiser knows that. The rocks do not heed his memory." It is here, at the point of his stroke, that Geiser's pursuit of knowledge, and, in fact, his ability to know at all, ends.

Geiser's partially coherent thoughts take the reader into a fantasy world from which there is no escape. Gradually, the reader becomes unable to distinguish between the real storm outside and Geiser's projection of his thoughts upon it. The final thirty pages are the most confusing, as Geiser's thoughts become even more cloudy and disturbed until his mind dissolves in a single flash of lucidity. Afterwards, Frisch presents the reader with a description of the village, which "stands unharmed." The mundane unchanging lives of the people within contrast sharply with the hallucinatory visions of the deceased Geiser, and through this final scene, Frisch provides another perspective.

Frisch's narrative style accurately portrays his principal character's mental collapse. The third person narrative describes Geiser's thoughts and actions, and the relationship between them. At the same time, the gaps between short passages and Frisch's use of the third person narrative mimic his main character's disturbed mental processes. Interspersed with the narrative are the copied lists, excerpts from texts, and illustrations that paper Geiser's wall. These bits of recorded information echo Geiser's own obsessions and in turn help to release other fantasies and memories. They are important also for the course of the story. From the first items on the history of floods in the Ticino region to the final matter-of-fact description of apoplexy, the clippings on the wall serve as the sole connection with objective reality.

The greatest strength of *Man in the Holocene* lies in its graphic portrayal of Geiser's disintegrating thought processes and the way in which the doomed pensioner brings history and the external environment into his own subjective experience. Frisch effectively involves the reader in Geiser's internal world. Gripped by his vision of certain catastrophe, the reader finds it difficult to follow what is taking place on an objective level. As Geiser sinks deeper into his hallucinations, his actions and the real events that happen to him seem even more confusing. Geiser apparently recognizes his mental disintegration. At various points, he wonders what the meaning is of all his isolated and disconnected studies. Geiser realizes as well that he is completely alone in the world—his wife has died, the solar astronomer has departed, his daughter has not come to visit, and he cannot communicate with anyone else in the village. This sense of total physical and mental isolation lies at the foundation of Geiser's demise and ultimately gives *Man in the Holocene* much of its emotional and intellectual power.

Richard Lachmann

MAN, WOMAN AND CHILD

Author: Erich Segal (1937–   )
Publisher: Harper & Row (New York). 244 pp. $9.95
Type of work: Novel
Time: Summer 1978
Locale: Cape Cod and Boston

The innocent harmony of a close-knit family is disturbed by an unsuspected reality, and man, wife, and children must become reacquainted on more solid ground

Principal characters:
> BOB BECKWITH, a 40-year-old family man and professor
> SHEILA BECKWITH, Bob's wife
> JESSICA, their 12-year-old daughter
> PAULA, their 8-year-old daughter
> JEAN CLAUDE GUÉRIN, Bob's 9-year-old son by another woman

Man, Woman and Child recounts the eventful summer when a man tells his wife that he wants to bring his son by another woman into their home. The man is Bob Beckwith, a professor at M.I.T. His wife, Sheila, is an editor at Harvard University Press. They have two daughters, Jessica and Paula. Their summer vacation is ruined by the death of a French woman. She had a son, and Bob Beckwith is the boy's father.

Until the accident, the existence of the child, Jean Claude, is completely unknown to Bob who hardly remembers that ten years ago in France he had a brief extramarital affair. Jean Claude, the child of this affair, is nine years old and homeless. His mother's executor calls Bob to ask if he will keep the boy while a permanent home is found for him in France. The Beckwiths enjoy the rapport and satisfactions of a close-knit family. Bob, devoted to his wife and daughters, is fully aware that the news of Jean Claude could destroy their happiness. Unfortunately, there are no alternatives, and Bob must tell his wife about the affair and Jean Claude. When he does tell her, Sheila reacts with fear and anger. All of her belief in Bob, their marriage, and her own self-worth are undermined. For her, Bob's one lie about the past falsifies their entire relationship. Because she also fears that Bob might abandon her, however, she allows him to invite his son for a one month visit on Cape Cod. Bob, overwhelmed by his wife's generosity and more in love with her than ever, is curious to see what his only son is like.

Jean Claude arrives, a meticulously well-bred and self-possessed child of nine. Jean Claude's responses to Bob's first questions convince him that the boy has no idea who his father really is. Jessica and Paula vie for the visitor's attention, but Sheila can hardly manage to look at him. She is caught between pretending that everything is normal and fearing that nothing is the same and she becomes ever more aloof and distant.

In a flashback to happier times, the story of Bob's and Sheila's courtship and marriage is told. He was a math student at Yale; she went to Vassar. They met at a dance, and after their first kiss, Bob knew that he wanted to marry Sheila. When they did get married, their relationship was the envy of all their friends.

In the present, the Beckwiths are pretending to enjoy the summer the best they can. Bob is torn in two directions. Every day his affection for Jean Claude increases, and yet he also values his marriage. Nothing he does reassures Sheila, and the only thing that might work—sending Jean Claude back to France—is out of the question for Bob.

To postpone making a final decision about leaving Bob, Sheila goes to Boston to visit her best friend, Marge, confiding to her the entire story. At the same time, Bob is telling his best friend, Bernie, who, it turns out, is not at all trustworthy.

In spite of the widening rift between husband and wife, the children are becoming fast friends and enjoying a fine summer. Jean Claude helps Jessica and Paula prepare supper one night, and he impresses them considerably by whipping up a perfect vinaigrette sauce. The dinner, calculated to cheer up Sheila on her return from Boston, is not successful, and Sheila remains despondent. That evening she goes to Jean Claude's room. At the sight of the sleeping child, Sheila sees clearly for the first time that this child is completely innocent, regardless of his parents' illegitimate affair. For a moment her heart goes out to him. But, when she notices a picture of Jean Claude's beautiful mother on the bedside table, Sheila's heart hardens once more.

Bob Beckwith continues his efforts to cajole his family into a unit. He suggests a trip to Provincetown. The day spent touring the town is a great success, and Sheila seems happier. That afternoon Jean Claude beats Bernie's son, Davey, at a game of soccer. Bob, utterly thrilled with his son's victory, realizes how much he cares and how dangerous his growing affection may be.

Soon after, Sheila discovers that she is not immune to temptation herself, when she meets Gavin Wilson, a Washington lawyer. She is working with him in Boston on a manuscript. He is handsome, intelligent, and attracted to her. Sheila is deeply flattered, and the encounter restores some of her self-esteem. Marge urges her to take advantage of the situation, telling Sheila that she has a right to some good times. Sheila is not that calculating, but she cannot deny her attraction to

Gavin Wilson.

Meanwhile the summer calm is blasted once and for all when Davey, who having overheard his father talking about Jean Claude's true identity, takes his revenge by telling Jessica who her family's visitor actually is. Soon Paula knows too, and the floodgates of their emotions are flung wide open. Bob comes home that evening, unaware of disaster, to find his daughters locked in their bedroom and his wife more alienated than ever. Bob knows now that he must either send Jean Claude away or lose his family.

Jean Claude, accepting the brutal change of events, quietly packs his bags. Bob drives him to Boston that afternoon. While they are gone, Gavin Wilson calls Sheila. Hearing the strain in her voice, he immediately drives up from Boston to see what he can do. Sheila is both alarmed and comforted by his concern, and when Bob calls to say that Jean Claude missed the flight to Paris, Gavin Wilson is right there to hold Sheila in his arms when she is most in need.

Jean Claude did not miss the plane by accident. He knows now that Bob is his father. "I hoped that maybe my father might be someone like you." Bob is touched by the child's trusting love, and he cannot let him go. They spend the night in Boston and the next day celebrate by doing all the things a dad is supposed to do with his son. Jean Claude misses the plane again that night. They go instead to a jazz concert and fireworks display on the Charles River. Despite the rain, they have a marvelous time, and Bob does not even notice when Jean Claude begins to shiver. Within a short time, Jean Claude is very sick. Bob has to call Sheila and ask her if he can bring Jean Claude back home. By the time they reach Cape Cod, Jean Claude is unconscious.

Catastrophe has struck, and the entire family puts aside personal griefs in their concern for Jean Claude. The doctor tells Bob that Jean Claude's appendix has burst and he must be operated on immediately.

Bob collapses in the waiting room. In his mind he returns to 1968 in southern France. Bob is attending a conference in Montpellier amid student riots and unrest. He ventures out into the streets only to be roughed up by the police, who think he is a French student. Nicole Guérin, a doctor, comes to his rescue and tends to a small cut on his head. The times are exciting; to Bob, France is another world, and Nicole offers herself to him with no strings attached. After that weekend he never sees or hears from Nicole again. Bob's memories of Jean Claude's mother overwhelm him as he waits for news of their son now on the operating table.

The operation is a success, and Jean Claude will recover. The Beckwiths reach out for each other with relief, thankful that they do have each other. Jean Claude comes back to recuperate at the Beckwiths', who welcome him with open arms. The crisis is past, and for the rest of the summer the whole family, including Jean Claude, lives in harmony. Jean Claude is now a part of their lives, and when the time does come for him to return to France, they ask him to stay. To everyone's surprise, Jean Claude wants to go back where he will live with his mother's friends and study to become a doctor. He is much happier now, knowing he has a father and a family that cares for him. When they all must say their farewells at the airport, it is Bob who is afraid that his son will forget him.

The story of *Man, Woman and Child* is simply told. Erich Segal has created a situation of rich dramatic potential and invested it with deep-felt tensions. He has not, however, told his story with the complex subtlety necessary to transform that tension into something more than melodrama. Nor has he created characters whose experiences and convictions might have enduring meaning for the reader.

Although the story is full of detail about summertime on Cape Cod and the Beckwith home and their habits, the lack of perception on the author's part leaves the impression that the book and the people in it are shallow. Instead of insights into what the experience of marital betrayal really means, Segal has over-simplified reality to make things happen in the way he wishes they would. For the reader, a sense of unreality and fantasy undermines the threat that something irrevocably bad might happen. Sheila seems more the idealized version of a wife, the kind that any man in Bob's position would wish to have, than a real woman facing disillusionment. Also, Bob's thoughts never get beyond the anxious and regretful meditations of a confused mind. The stock responses found in *Man, Woman and Child*—confusion, indecision, and self-pity—do not achieve the self-reflection that could make this a story of consequence.

Segal does not see easily into the emotions of his own characters. The reader is left with the nagging sense that Bob, Sheila, Jean Claude, and the girls might be thinking and feeling something more than the predictable things they say. In a moment of true perception, Sheila says, "When words fail, comfortable clichés are always nice to fall back on." *Man, Woman and Child* contains a plot worth investigation, but for Erich Segal words have failed. He has written only a minor bedtime tale full of stock characters and reliable clichés.

Julie V. Iovine

THE MARRIAGES BETWEEN ZONES THREE, FOUR AND FIVE

Author: Doris Lessing (1919–)
Publisher: Alfred A. Knopf (New York). 244 pp. $10.00
Type of work: Novel
Time: Sometime before the Marriage between Ben Ata and Al·Ith
Locale: Zones Three, Four, and Five in the galactic empire of Canopus

Science fiction work in which marriages between zone rulers Ben Ata, Al·Ith, and Vashti offset the limitations of awareness within each zone and offer salvation among all zones via shared understanding and flexible boundaries

> *Principal characters:*
> AL·ITH, princess of Zone Three
> BEN ATA, ruler of militarist Zone Four
> JARNTI, commander of Ben Ata's troops
> DABEEB, Jarnti's wife
> MURTI•, Al·Ith's sister and future ruler of Zone Three
> VASHTI, warrior princess of Zone Five
> ARUSHI, Ben Ata's and Al·Ith's son

With *The Marriages Between Zones Three, Four and Five,* book two of *Canopus in Argos: Archives,* Doris Lessing continues the saga of *Shikasta.* The Chroniclers of Zone Three narrate a thinly disguised allegory wherein different zones represent different political, economic, and cultural systems.

Marriages opens with the impending marriage of Zone Three ruler Al·Ith to Zone Four ruler Ben Ata. When Ben Ata's men come to bring Al·Ith to Zone Four, the disparities between zones becomes evident. Zone Three is a populous and busy land; it is antimilitarist in ideology and has no soldiers. One figuratively descends into Zone Four, a degradation symbolized by the flatness of the terrain. Zone Four appears to be a nation with nothing but a standing army. A ballad echoes this sentiment: "Three comes before Four. Our ways are peace and plenty. Their ways-war!" Zone Three people are free spirits, looking to the stars, while their "slavish" Zone Four brethren are forbidden to gaze. There is a clash of ballads—those of Zone Three sing of loving friendship, while those of Zone Four express death and sorrow.

The relationship between Ben Ata and Al·Ith begins inauspiciously when he rapes her. This underscores his lack of awareness of planned conception as well as his displeasure with how little Al·Ith resembles the eternal feminine. Yet this violent episode releases the tension between them, allowing for a tender reconciliation and an open discussion about the problems of both zones. It appears that the birth rate is down among animals, symbolizing the relative "infertility" of both systems. This sharing is interrupted, however, when Al·Ith is ordered home to Zone Three.

Al·Ith journeys home, where she meets a representative denizen, Yori, in a border town. More of the customs of Zone Three are revealed, particularly the difference between gene fathers and mind fathers. In Zone Three one can father a child biologically or spiritually. The Zone Three basis of knowledge is also disclosed: an extremely anti-individualist philosophy that does not allow for notions of individual guilt or wrong-doing. Zone Three is truly a collectivist society. Through her conversation with Yori, Al·Ith sees how her foray into Zone Four has already begun to influence her way of thinking.

Ben Ata sends Jarnti's wife Dabeeb to fetch Al·Ith in an episode that adds further depth to the picture of Zone Four. Dabeeb means literally "something that has been made soft by beating." While Dabeeb is an illustration of a strong woman who has never thought of rebelling, she is also a positive figure, emblematic of Zone Four virtues of acceptance and humor.

The marriage between Ben Ata and Al·Ith is finally consummated, and a drum begins to beat, symbolizing their togetherness. This drumming is constant, yet its source remains elusive, and the characters are continually on the verge of understanding. Al·Ith becomes pregnant, and there is a more open exchange about the militaristic nature of Zone Four. For the first time Zone Five is mentioned. Al·Ith points out the poverty of Zone Four, blaming it on the prolonged war with Zone Five. All the wealth of Zone Four is depleted in this war. She also relates the war economy to the need for hierarchy. Zone Four is dependent upon the appurtenances of rank; Ben Ata must wear special clothes to set him apart from his people. There is no corresponding need for Al·Ith.

Ben Ata again attacks Al·Ith, who tries to escape, but cannot breathe the air in Zone Four and has to be rescued by Ben Ata. She then goes to visit her sister Murti• and glimpses the sapphire air of Zone Two en route. The novel's universe has now expanded on both frontiers, foreshadowing later plot developments. Al·Ith gives her report on Zone Four: the irony of a country built for war, but with no real war to fight. While they ponder the meaning of this contradiction, the economic structure of Zone Three is outlined. Opposed to the barren war economy of Zone Four is a balanced economy, which does not rely on any single commodity. One quarter of the population are artisans and one quarter are merchants. None of its wealth goes to the waging of war. The bellicose nature of Zone Four people is shown to reside in the contradiction mentioned previously.

Next comes a period of intimacy and sharing between Ben Ata and Al·Ith. While Ben Ata is on a campaign, his son Arushi is born. The memories of Zone Three begin to fade for Al·Ith. While her previous births were personal events, almost independent of society, marking her strength and purely personal evolution, she now begins to see the child as a symbol of salvation. Moreover, Arushi is seen as Ben Ata's son and not her own as well. She is merely the vehicle for its birth. This is the first time a child was directly related to ownership.

Ben Ata has also evolved. During his campaign, he begins to reflect about the poverty of his country. He has discovered that he can no longer use women as he did previously. He returns from his campaign, and Al·Ith is angry with him. He begins an affair with Dabeeb and also starts to participate in the care of his son. Meanwhile, Al·Ith has increasingly become the Zone Four woman. She even begins to dream Zone Four dreams. She weans her child and turns her new-found energies into her married life. No longer passive and needy, Al·Ith restructures her relationship with Ben Ata into a passion between equals. This bliss is short-lived, however, as Al·Ith is ordered home and Ben Ata is ordered to marry the warrior princess of Zone Five, Vashti.

Al·Ith feels displaced in what was once her homeland. She has been usurped as ruler by her sister Murti•, and there are hard feelings between them. Dabeeb, back in Zone Four, takes care of Arushi and is raising him as her own son. Arushi is to spend six months in Zone Three each year. Ben Ata instructs Zone Five with his new-found knowledge of Zone Three. Zone Four plunders Zone Five's farmland and wastes its resources. Just as Al·Ith represented a model of collective agriculture, so Vashti is the incarnation of another utopian ideal of female society as an Amazon warrior. Vashti argues for anarchy, license, and unrestrained freedom in all domains just as Al·Ith argued for democracy. Both of these are opposed to the militaristic, hierarchic, and constraining male principle.

To Vashti, Zone Four's laws represent self-satisfaction and smugness. She is a tribal leader of several hundred people and dominates fifty poor tribes. Zone Five is rich, unproductive farm and trading country; its workers are lazy and self-satisfied and are hence easily exploited by Vashti. Meanwhile, Al·Ith has become critical of the complacency of her own people. Zone Four women make an unprecedented journey into Zone Three and are astounded by a peacetime nation. Al·Ith begins to live in exile. She does not return to Zone Four despite her increasing estrangement from her sister and her own people. Dabeeb sings her a new song from Zone Five symbolizing cultural and physical interpenetrations.

There is no salvation in the immediate fate of the protagonists.

Al·Ith, but cannot remain with her. Transcendence lies beyond individual fate—the continuous movement and fluidity between zones is the true offspring of the marriages between zones Three, Four and Five. The novel ends optimistically; "There was a lightness, a freshness, and an enquiry and a remaking and an inspiration where there had been only stagnation. And closed frontiers. For this is how we all see it now."

In *The Marriages Between Zones Three, Four and Five*, Doris Lessing presents and critically appraises three diverse political, economic, and critical systems. Zone Five is a rich trading country anarchically disorganized and thus exploited by a warrior princess. Zone Four's destructive war economy with its dependence on hierarchy and repressive laws is also lacking in vision. While Zone Three on the surface seems ideal—a democratic regime with a balanced economy—it too is plagued with shortcomings of complacency and lack of imagination among its citizenry. This "democracy" does not have room for its dissidents, and Al·Ith lives in exile rather than more directly experience the ostracism that would ensue. It is clear that for Lessing no substantive feminist utopia exists. Collective agriculture (and the democratic commune) as well as Amazon warriorship are rejected. For Lessing only continuous synthesis between different concepts, systems, and zones can produce a really viable alternative. Additional hope resides in generational change, which might come with Arushi, for example, who is raised in two zones by two different women, Dabeeb and Al·Ith.

Although narration in *The Marriages Between Zones Three, Four and Five* follows a more continuous pattern than *Shikasta*, it nonetheless marks a departure from Lessing's earlier, more realist fiction, exemplified by her first novel, *The Grass is Singing*, or her celebrated *The Golden Notebook*. This departure into science fiction was perhaps anticipated by the apocalyptical ending of *The Four-Gated City* and later experiments such as *Briefing for a Descent Into Hell*. It is becoming increasingly obvious that Doris Lessing feels her feminist ideals may be best expressed in the genre of science fiction. It remains to be seen if these works of science fiction become inspirational fiction or flatly transparent and didactic political treatises.

D. S. Rubenstein

MAUGHAM

Author: Ted Morgan
Publisher: Simon & Schuster (New York). 711 pp. $17.95
Type of work: Biography
Time: 1874–1965
Locale: Primarily England and France

The life of one of the most prolific and financially successful English novelists, playwrights, and short-story writers, William Somerset Maugham, told with candor

> *Principal personages:*
> WILLIAM SOMERSET MAUGHAM, English author
> ROBERT ORMOND MAUGHAM, his father
> EDITH MARY MAUGHAM, his mother
> HENRY MACDONALD MAUGHAM, his uncle
> SYRIE BARNARDO MAUGHAM, his wife
> GERALD HAXTON, his lover

William Somerset Maugham was born of English parents on January 25, 1874, in Paris. It was the apogee of the Victorian era in England. In France, the Franco-Prussian War had recently ended with the French defeated at the hands of the Prussians. Maugham's father, Robert Ormond Maugham, had set up a partnership in law in Paris in the late 1840's. In 1863 he married Edith Mary Snell, a delicately beautiful woman seventeen years his junior. When asked by one of her friends why she married such an "ugly little man," Edith replied that he was the only man who never hurt her feelings.

William Somerset was their fifth child. Their first born died in infancy as did the sixth and seventh of the Maughams' children. Edith had consumption, and it was thought at the time that childbearing could cure consumption. She died within a week of her last child's death.

William Somerset Maugham, who was eight at the time of his mother's death, never recovered. Her love proved to be the only unselfish love that was bestowed upon him in a lifetime that spanned nearly a century. As the youngest surviving child, and with his three older brothers, Charles, Henry, and Frederic at boarding school, his mother's affection had been concentrated on him. Her death was the single most tragic experience of his life. But this was not the only tragedy of his early years. Two years after the loss of his mother, Maugham's father died of cancer, and he was sent to live with his father's only living brother, Henry MacDonald Maugham, a church of England clergyman, in Whitstable, near Canterbury, England. With an inheritance of 150 pounds a year and a nurse to accompany him across the channel, Maugham left French soil, the country of his birth, as an orphan at the age of ten.

Speaking "fractured French"—French peppered with English phrases—Maugham arrived unhappily in Whitstable. He was ill-prepared for a strict and parsimonious household ruled by his uncle. Henry MacDonald Maugham, who was later portrayed harshly in one of his nephew's most famous novels, *Of Human Bondage,* was fond of such maxims as "Only ask those people to stay with you or dine with you, who can ask you in return." Maugham spent seven years in his uncle's household, and when his taste for literature was whetted with classics like *Alice in Wonderland* and *The Arabian Nights,* he would have to satisfy his addiction on the sly, for his uncle disparaged him for reading so many books.

When Maugham was eleven, he was sent to the King's School in Canterbury. Here Maugham escaped the bullying of his classmates by winning prizes in music, divinity, history, and French, despite his poor showing in athletics and, above all, the stammer that he developed shortly after his arrival at his uncle's.

After acquiring the respect of his classmates with his academic achievements, he still longed for popularity and a way out of his singularly lonely existence. He would choose a boy to whom he took a particular fancy, make believe that he threw his spirit into the other boy's body, speaking with his voice and laughing with his peers in imaginary conversations. Only in this way did he find any happiness at the King's School, because despite his excellence in his studies, his stammer precipitated harassment and undeserved punishment.

Maugham left the King's School in poor health and at loose ends. To the disappointment of his uncle, he decided not to go on to either Cambridge or Oxford. Maugham secretly desired to become a writer, although in Victorian England being a writer was not considered a respectable way of earning one's living; a belief held by his uncle. His aunt, however, suggested that he spend a year in Germany with her relatives, which proved to be a turning point for Maugham.

In Germany he attended lectures at Heidelberg University, became acquainted with the works of Ibsen and Schopenhauer, and lost his virginity to a young "homosexual esthete," Ellingham Brooks, who remained a friend for the rest of his life. Maugham became convinced that he should carry out his dream of becoming a writer. Still furtively hiding his deepest convictions from his uncle, he returned to England and at his uncle's suggestion enrolled in medical school. This gave him the opportunity to write in his spare time, unhampered, and to see life first hand, in the raw. St. Thomas's Hospital, where he spent five years, was located near Lambeth, one of London's most notorious slums.

At first, while studying for his medical degree, he wrote short plays in the manner of Ibsen that portrayed the troubles of the spirit and that delved into the heaviness of the heart. Obsessed with women who bear stillborn children or who die in their effort to bear children, like his mother, his first published work was a novel, entitled *Liza of Lambeth*. It was an old-fashioned "potboiler," in which the heroine has an affair with a neighbor's husband, becomes pregnant, miscarries, and then dies herself when the doctor does not arrive in time. The book's only distinction was that it depicted life in a London slum to a degree that assaulted the tastes of the Victorian reading public that preferred lighter novels. He was in the company of George Gissing and Arthur Morrison, who prior to Maugham, published novels about slum life that caused enough of a stir to inspire a few attempts to reform some of the more impoverished areas. *Liza of Lambeth* paled in comparison to the novels of Gissing and Morrison, but it launched Maugham's literary career, in 1897, at the age of twenty-three.

It would be another decade before Maugham would receive even the first glimmer of recognition. In this period he finished six full-length plays, six novels, and a volume of short stories to ambivalent reviews and countless rejections. His travels took him to Capri, Paris, and Spain in search of material. On the continent he hobnobbed with the famous portrait painter Gerald Kelly, the occultist Aleister Crowley, who serves as the model for the main character in his novel *The Magician,* and his old friend Ellingham Brooks. In England, he made the rounds of the cocktail circuit and kept up appearances by courting the ladies, despite the fact that his true affections lay elsewhere. The Victorian era ended and a new age was ushered in. The motto for social survival in the Edwardian era was: "Do anything you please as long as you don't scare the horses."

Maugham's long-awaited success came in 1908 with his first hit play, *Lady Frederick*. The play, a comedy about a widow who survives a financial crisis with the help of a former suitor, was one of four plays written by Maugham that ran in London's illustrious West End in the same season. A cartoon of Shakespeare biting his fingernails while a caricature of Maugham looked on, appeared in the advertising spots on the broadsides of triple-decker buses. His fame, despite many caustic reviews of his work, would no longer be in doubt in his lifetime, nor after his death. And his fortune grew with his fame. Maugham grossed over $4,000,000 with his pen.

Shortly after his rise to literary stardom, he became involved with a young divorcée, Syrie Barnardo, whom he married in 1917, primarily because she was carrying his child. Their marriage served as a veil for

his homosexuality and eventually ended in divorce. His "real marriage" with Gerald Haxton, a fellow ambulance driver he met during
service in World War I, although thinly disguised, was kept hidden for
nearly three decades.

Haxton was Maugham's companion on his many excursions around
the world in his fervent search for material to use in his writing. Although Haxton's alcoholism, which largely contributed to his prema-
ture death in 1944, was a nuisance, he was garrulous, outgoing, and
confident—the exact opposite of Maugham, who often could not speak
on the phone because of his stammer. It was Haxton, not Syrie, who
accompanied him on his exploits to the South Seas, where he wrote
one of his most famous short stories, *Rain,* dealing with the relationship between a prostitute and a priest, and to Tahiti, where he wrote
The Moon and Sixpence, a novel based on the life of Gauguin. During
his years with Haxton he did his best creative work and found a joy
that was second only to his mother's love.

Through the ever-increasing sales of his books and the eventual sales
of movie rights, Maugham built a home, a tribute to himself, on the
French Riviera, that he called Villa Mauresque. Villa Mauresque was
the site of high society parties that were frequented by Lord Beaver-
brook, Sir Winston Churchill, Noel Coward, Garson Kanin, and a bevy
of others who were flamboyant, glamourous, or titled.

In spite of the wealth Maugham accumulated, the avalanche of fan
mail he received, and, at times, encouraging reviews of his work, he
felt that he was a second-rate writer. Many of his contemporaries, such
as D.H. Lawrence and Edmund Wilson, shunned him, partially because of his outrageous success. Haunted by the belief that he never
realized his full potential, and ailing severely from senile dementia,
Maugham died ignobly at Villa Mauresque in 1965 at the age of 91.

Neither severe nor ignoble, Ted Morgan's biography of Maugham is
an impressive work of scholarship. Of the dozen or so biographies and
partial biographies extant, his is the most comprehensive and coherent.
To investigate and research a life that embraces as much as
Maugham's, a man who fought tenaciously to keep his life a secret, is
an achievement of high praise. It is worthy of the praise that its subject
deserved in life but never received.

Wally Swist

MAYBE

Author: Lillian Hellman (1905–   )
Publisher: Little, Brown & Company (Boston). 102 pp. $7.95
Type of work: Memoir
Time: The present and recent past
Locale: United States and France

A memoir by author Lillian Hellman, focusing on Sarah Cameron, an intriguing and elusive woman who appeared repeatedly in Miss Hellman's life although the two were never close friends

> *Principal personages:*
> LILLIAN HELLMAN, playwright and author
> SARAH CAMERON, an acquaintance
> CARTER CAMERON, Sarah's husband
> SOM CAMERON, Sarah's and Carter's son
> FERRY DIXON, a friend of both Sarah and Hellman

Lillian Hellman, the successful playwright and more recently the author of three volumes of autobiographical memoirs, has again reached back into her memory to produce *Maybe*. *Maybe* is woven from the fragments of recollection about the author's experiences with Sarah Cameron. As these encounters are infrequent and confused by the passage of time, *Maybe* is more a story about the nature of relationships and memory than about a woman's life. The opening lines of the book convey this:

> It was always with Sarah this way and that way all over the place, or maybe I never saw enough to understand. At a few points I know what happened, but there's a good deal I don't, because of time or because I didn't much care.
>
> It's not easy. But not much is easy because as one grows older, one realizes how little one knows about any relationship, or even about oneself.

This ambiguity is a central theme of the book. It characterizes Sarah's and Hellman's contrasting recollections of their first meeting. Hellman remembers meeting Sarah in Paris at the Fourth Republic restaurant: Sarah maintains they met earlier at a *New Yorker* magazine anniversary party. Hellman recalls Sarah's helping her place her order in French and seeing her a week later with her baby, Som.

A much later recollection of Som follows. While a student at Princeton, Som calls Hellman to say he is in trouble, and asks to see her. After putting off the meeting, she receives a call from a friend of Som's saying that Som is at the Royalton Hotel, and cannot pay his bill. By the time Hellman arrives at the hotel to help, Som has gone.

Soon after this incident, Hellman goes to dinner with Ferry Dixon, an old school friend of Sarah's, and her millionaire husband. In the course of a drunken dinner at "21," Ferry mentions Hellman's first lover, Alexander. This reminder triggers a long reminiscence of Hellman's first sexual experience. Hellman is nineteen and Alexander a few years older. They sleep together four times, and after the fourth time he tells her that she has an offensive odor. An inexperienced Hellman is shattered by the criticism, which has had a lingering impact on her.

Years after her affair with Alexander, when she and her husband are staying in a small Paris hotel room, their downstairs neighbors complain that they are using too much hot water taking three baths a day. Confronting the facts for the first time, Hellman realizes how tremendously anxious she is about how she smells, although she does not connect this with her experience with Alexander. She struggles to overcome this obsession by limiting herself to one bath a day. After a few weeks of increased anxiety, she decides to take a trip. At a hotel on a lake, she sleeps with an Englishman as a sort of test for herself. There she also spots Sarah in the hotel's cocktail lounge, but the two do not speak.

The author does not arrive at the source of her neurosis until much later, and it is Sarah who effects the "cure." On the occasion of Hellman's introduction to Sarah's husband, Carter, Sarah and Hellman sit together on a couch and Sarah reveals that she was involved with Alexander after his affair with Hellman. She adds that Alexander had told her that she, Sarah, smelled. Sarah had blithely ignored Alexander's criticism because she knew it reflected more poorly upon him than upon herself. For Hellman, Sarah's attitude is illuminating, and she realizes that it is Alexander's malice that has haunted her all these years.

The story then moves back in time to another meeting with Ferry, a few years after the "21" dinner. By chance Hellman runs into her at an inn in Stockbridge, Massachusetts. Ferry's millionaire-alcoholic husband is a patient in a nearby sanitarium. Ferry's own shaken mental health is apparent as the two stay up all night drinking and talking. Bitter and drunk, Ferry complains about her unhappy life and her intolerable husband. The next day, after a visit to her husband, Ferry is hysterical and, Hellman thinks, on drugs. In her rambling, she explains that her life could have been much better if, instead of marrying for money, she had married the man she loved—Alexander. She scornfully turns on Hellman, telling her that Alexander told her that they slept together and that Hellman smelled. When Hellman counters with her information that Sarah had gotten the same line, Ferry becomes more hysterical, accuses Sarah of constantly lying, and says that Sarah has never even met Alexander.

In a gossipy phone call from Ferry, Hellman learns that Ferry's husband has killed himself and that Alexander has written a book with an uncomplimentary treatment of Hellman. Irritated by Ferry's attempts to make trouble, Hellman abruptly hangs up.

A short section of italics marks the transition to the second major section of the book. In this italicized section Hellman discusses, in a foggy romantic style, the passage of time and the changes that occur.

Hellman mentions Sarah's involvement in a shooting scandal, but, before giving the details of the story, she relates her recollections of two other encounters with Sarah. Once, when they were both twenty-five, in a restaurant in Harlem, Sarah's shoulder straps fall off, revealing her breasts. The other meeting occurs in France, where Hellman is staying at an inn. Taking a walk at dawn she wanders away from the inn, and, discovering that she has lost her way, she stops at a house to ask directions. On a terrace behind the house, she finds Sarah sitting with a man and a woman. Sarah drives Hellman back to the inn, and on the way their conversation is baffling. Sarah tells Hellman that she is no longer married; Hellman finds out later from Carter that this was not the case. She also says that the man on the terrace is her son, Som, and that the woman is Lady Ottoline Morrell. Hellman knows the middle-aged man is not Som, and finds out later that Lady Morrell has been dead ten years.

Hellman, in another passage in italics, comments on her memory and her reasons for writing about Sarah:

> What I have written is the truth as I saw it, but the truth as I saw it, of course, doesn't have much to do with the truth. It's as if I have fitted parts of a picture puzzle and then a child overturned it and threw out some pieces.

Hellman recalls running into Sarah and her husband at a Hollywood party, after which the Camerons give Hellman a ride home. A few days later Sarah returns to Hellman's house, saying she is in trouble and needs Hellman's help. Sarah goes on to recount an intriguing, but often incoherent, story of her involvement in a gangland murder. Hellman's mind is elsewhere, and she recalls: "I was only half listening. There was no other way because there was no coherence."

Sarah remembers waking up naked in a strange all-purple penthouse with no recollection of where she was or how she got there. Wandering about trying to find her clothing and a clue to her whereabouts, she stumbled upon this scene: Two men were confronting a third man seated at a desk. They were demanding money. One of the two men became more threatening and as he drew his gun, the seated man—MacPherson—pulled a gun himself and shot the other two.

She recounts the ensuing trial and the scandal of her involvement.

When she goes on to explain that as a result of the scandal her husband divorced her and gained custody of their son, Hellman realizes, to her surprise, that these events must have happened quite a while ago. Hellman's surprise turns to incredulity when Sarah tells her that the papers were full of it and that MacPherson was eventually acquitted of the murder charges on the basis of Sarah's testimony that he had acted in self-defense and had become the owner of a nightclub that Hellman and Hammett frequented.

The loose ends of this bizarre story are left hanging; Hellman's memory moves to her last encounter with Sarah in Rome in 1960. On the roof of the Hassler Hotel, Hellman sees Sarah seated with a group of people. Hellman greets her, but Sarah replies in Italian that her name is Signora Pinelli, that Hellman must be mistaken. Convinced that "she was still at the old loony stuff," Hellman does not pursue it.

Returning to the late 1930's, Hellman describes her friendship with Frank Costello, the gangster. After passing several dinners in awkward conversation, Hellman finally asks Costello what he knows of the MacPherson murder trial. Not surprisingly, nothing that Sarah has said about MacPherson's life is accurate, and Costello knows nothing of the events Sarah has recounted. Hellman is never able to lift the veil of confusion surrounding the story, but she remains convinced of Sarah's involvement in some scandal, as her acrimonious divorce and loss of custody of Som testify.

Many years later, Hellman becomes close to Sarah's ex-husband, Carter. They meet by chance on a plane to New Orleans and begin a casual and passionless relationship that lasts seven or eight years. They drift apart after their first and only discussion of Sarah, when Carter's bitter memories of their marriage and Hellman's inability to understand his feelings create a distance between them.

Sometime after the relationship has ended, a time that Hellman describes as "about five or six years ago," she runs into Som at a wedding. Her description of him is frightening: "The man was somewhere in his forties, but the face was of an old pervert waiting to be fixed in a funeral parlor. Certainly it was dope. But dope does not always cause such havoc. The havoc in his face and body was, to me, unidentifiable." He is antagonistic and insulting to Hellman about her liaison with his father. He tells Hellman a sad tale of Sarah dying a pauper in Italy, of Carter refusing to bury her and demanding that Som never call him again.

A few weeks later Hellman sees Carter again and he refutes Som's account. Carter knows that Sarah is not dead because he has seen her since the phony funeral in Italy. He knows few of the details, but apparently Sarah had taken out a large insurance policy with Som as the beneficiary. When he needed money they had opened the grave of an Italian peasant and faked an automobile accident, in order to collect on the policy. Sarah then left the country with a false passport—bearing Ferry's name.

There is a strain on their meeting, and when Carter hints at a renewal of their relationship, Hellman is offended at his falseness. A few months later, in an especially bad humor, she sends him this mysterious telegram:

> There are missing pieces everyplace and everywhere and they are not my business unless they touch me. But when they touch me, I do not wish them to be black. My instinct repeat instinct is that yours are black. Lillian.

When Western Union calls to say they cannot locate Carter, Hellman tries to call him herself. The man who answers the phone says he is a housepainter and has never heard of Mr. Cameron. Hellman concludes *Maybe:* "I hung up."

Maybe is an odd and somewhat intriguing story. A streak of inconsistency that pervades it, however, prevents the reader from being fully involved in the mood that Hellman seeks to create.

Hellman's persona, established in her previous memoirs and present here as well, is tough-talking and tough-feeling, independent, and irritable. Her approach to Sarah, both as a character, from hindsight, and in their actual contact, as Hellman relates it, is similarly tough. Her sense of detachment prevents her from admitting that Sarah interests her, and this detachment seems almost studied.

Hellman is bored and "only half listening" when Sarah relates the story of the murder. However, when Hellman describes her dinners with Frank Costello, her attitude is wholly different: "I would eagerly wait for any small piece of information about a murder . . ." So strongly does Hellman convey her lack of interest in Sarah that the reader is left wondering why she chose to write about her at all.

As a study of memory and recollection, *Maybe* is similarly unsatisfying. Hellman is open and honest in her tone from the start. She wants to overcome the flaws in her memory, to explore the fragments of recollection about Sarah and her circle, and to try to piece them together. While ostensibly sincere in her purpose of discovering the truth, Hellman contributes to the confusion that is created by the failure of memory and Sarah's own elusiveness. This is especially evident in a chronology that simply does not make sense. Hellman's apparently deliberate clouding of the issue contradicts her stated intention of guiding her readers on a genuine quest to recapture the past.

Annie Talbot

THE MIDDLE GROUND

Author: Margaret Drabble
Publisher: Alfred A. Knopf (New York). 277 pp. $10.95
Type of work: Novel
Time: The present
Locale: London

The story of Kate Armstrong, a successful journalist, who is undergoing a largely unformed mid-life crisis

Principal characters:
> KATE ARMSTRONG, successful journalist, mother
> HUGO MAINWARING, her good friend, also a journalist
> EVELYN STENNETT, a friend of Kate's, social worker
> TED STENNETT, a doctor, Kate's ex-lover
> STUART ARMSTRONG, Kate's ex-husband
> MUJID, Kate's houseguest

Kate Armstrong, the central figure in *The Middle Ground,* is a tremendously successful journalist. By writing of her own very personal experiences of pregnancy, childbirth, young motherhood, and divorce, Kate helped to formulate and was in turn shaped by the growing women's movement, developing a public identity inextricably linked with the elevated feminine consciousness. But Kate has begun to feel constrained by her public image and fears that her own limitations as a journalist will prevent her from expanding. Her old friend Hugo Mainwaring diagnoses her plight as a mid-life crisis, and Kate cannot decide whether to find solace in this label or not.

Kate Fletcher was born in 1937, and brought up near London. She was not much of a student and, when the time came, she was sent to be educated among future secretaries and salesgirls. After graduation, she got a job in a photo shop. She also met Stuart Armstrong, a sensitive young painter with whom she fell in love. One of Stuart's relatives helped her get a job as a secretary for a women's magazine, and before long Kate's natural gift for writing started her on her way up the ladder. She and Stuart got married. When they had their first child, Kate, at Stuart's insistence, gave up her job. However, Stuart's inability to earn a reliable income prompted Kate to begin the public documentation of her life.

When her third child entered school, Kate went back to a full-time job, despite Stuart's protests. He took up with an art student, and they divorced. Kate was relieved to be on her own. She supported the family, and she and Stuart remained close.

When she was twenty-nine Kate became involved with Ted Stennett, the husband of a close friend. Ted's marriage to Evelyn was not particularly close. There were some awkward moments but Kate's relationship with Evelyn was never jeopardized. The affair lasted for six or seven years. Kate was very happy, her children thrived, and her career prospered.

Then a nebulous anxiety began to infect all aspects of her life: her worries and ill humor affected her relationship with Ted; she developed high blood pressure. She stopped taking birth control pills, became pregnant, and had an abortion. When she returned from the hospital, Evelyn visited her and told that for the past year Ted had been having an affair with another woman. This news widened the distance already created between them during the past months, and Kate broke off their relationship. She began to date other men, but none of the new relationships proved particularly satisfying.

The account of Kate's present picks up again about a month after her luncheon with Hugo. Two changes have occurred in her life. She has a new job making a TV film about women's choices when they leave school. And she finds herself entertaining an uninvited houseguest, a young Iraqi who is engaged to the daughter of a friend. Mujid is in London for a few months in order to learn English. Kate is intimidated by what she views as his political fanaticism. He is a Marxist, pro-Kurd, and vehemently wrapped up in causes that she, ashamedly, knows very little about.

The film and Mujid prompt Kate to examine her life in a way that was never necessary during her years of complacency. To make the documentary, she explores the town where she spent her childhood. She visits her old school, meets the new headmistress, and looks up some of her old classmates. This trip triggers in Kate much thought and helps her, ultimately, to reestablish a sense of connection with her past.

In another episode, Kate, Hugo, Mujid, Paul Armstrong (her ex-brother-in-law), and two Jewish friends of his all go out to the theater and dinner. Kate fears an outburst of vehement polemic from Mujid in response to the frivolity of this purely social occasion. But when Mujid enjoys the evening immensely, the experience serves to assuage some of the feelings of inadequacy that he has sparked in her.

Interspersed with Kate's ruminations are her friends, Evelyn, Hugo, and Ted, going about the business of their daily lives. Evelyn, while stuck in a traffic jam on her way to a day-care center, thinks about last night's dinner with an old school friend. The two had compared their lives, the decisions and compromises they had made along the way. Hugo, in a moment of frustration with his writing on the Middle East, writes a story about his friendship with Kate. The reader learns about his life, his mother, the dissolution of his marriage, his children, and his impressions of Mujid. Ted is flying from Bombay to London seated next to a beautiful woman he knows slightly. His thoughts move from questions about her life to Kate, to Evelyn, and to himself. It becomes clear that much of what Kate is going through her friends are experiencing as well:

> The middle years, caught between children and parents, free of neither: the past stretches back too densely, it is too thickly populated, the future has not yet thinned out. No wonder a pattern is slow to emerge from such a thick clutter of cross-references, from such trivia, from such serious but hidden connections.

Kate, realizing that she is not alone in her anxieties, is brought closer to her friends, even to Ted, with whom she had previously maintained an icy distance. Nothing much happens as the story unwinds, but slowly and subtly, Kate begins to exorcise her anxieties and to find again a sense of direction for herself.

In the final section of the book, Kate plans a party to celebrate her eldest son's birthday, to say good-by to Hugo who has decided to go to Iraq, and to welcome home Evelyn, who, after an accident, has been hospitalized for two weeks. In the midst of the preparations, the reader has a final glimpse of Kate, lively, happy, and excited with anticipation. She has rediscovered herself after a pause, a lull in her life. As she thinks about the evening ahead, trying to decide what to wear, Kate for the time being is back on track:

> Anything is possible, it is all undecided. Everything or nothing. It is all in the future. Excitement fills her, excitement, joy, anticipation, apprehension. Something will happen. It is all in the future . . . There is no way of knowing what it will be. It does not know itself. But it will come into being.

Margaret Drabble has a lively and entertaining writing style and an eye for bits of contemporary life. She is funny and her characters are too—charming, endearing, and sane. Kate has problems, serious problems, but she seldom loses perspective. There is no doubt that she will pull through; the reader is concerned for Kate, but never depressed. Drabble's depiction of contemporary London life is similarly vivid, describing what one would see on billboards, whom one would see in the subways, graffiti, advertising. This sense of time and place is fascinating and witty, while somehow not appearing trendy or faddish at all.

The Middle Ground suffers some on account of its plot, which at times is a little contrived. The overly long account of Kate's background comes in the first 100 pages, which are a chronological record of a fictional character for whom the reader has had no opportunity to develop any feeling. In addition, the limitations that Drabble imposes upon her life seem artificial. It is hard to believe that her life has not changed more since she left school at the age of sixteen. Her entire circle of friends has remained pretty much the same since the early days of her marriage. It is probably necessary for Drabble to limit Kate's experiences and scope in order to deal with her entire life from birth to present, but frequently this limitation seems unnatural.

Margaret Drabble's ninth novel, *The Middle Ground,* demonstrates the keen powers of observation, warm sense of humor, and deft writing ability that her fans have come to expect in the work of this young British novelist. As in her other works, Drabble has taken a narrow subject matter, three months in the lives of a woman and a handful of her friends, and endowed it with qualities so vivid and humane that it has become, if not universal, then at least accessible and evocative to her contemporary audience.

Annie Talbot

MORGAN'S PASSING

Author: Anne Tyler (1941–   )
Publisher: Alfred A. Knopf (New York). 311 pp. $9.95
Type of work: Novel
Time: 1967–1979
Locale: Baltimore and Tindell, Md.

Morgan Gower, who deals with the clutter and confusion of his life, embarks on a mid-life Odyssey, finding love without losing the conviction that life is full of delightful possibilities

> Principal characters:
> MORGAN GOWER, a middle-aged eccentric
> BONNY, his wife
> LOUISA, his mother
> BRINDLE, his sister
> LEON MEREDITH, a would-be actor turned puppeteer
> EMILY, Leon's wife, later Morgan's lover
> GINA, Leon's and Emily's daughter
> ROBERT ROBERTS, Brindle's childhood sweetheart
> JOSHUA, Morgan's and Emily's son
> MRS. APPLE, owner of Crafts Unlimited
> VICTOR, her son

Morgan Gower is a character who seems to have taken to heart the idea that everyone is really many different people living in the same body. On a prosaic level he is the father of seven daughters, the husband of easy-going Bonny, a fairly good son to his rambling mother, a tolerant brother to his reclusive sister, Brindle, and manager of one outlet of the Cullen Hardware chain, a job he acquired after his marriage to Bonny Cullen.

Morgan, however, is more than a series of prosaic images. His wardrobe bulges with a bizarre collection of hats and clothing that are more properly costumes. To Morgan, all clothing is costume, and he puts on his role for the day, his accent, his entire behavior in accordance with his whim and what he decides to wear. The hardware store is left in the capable hands of his clerk, while Morgan roams his small world as if searching for something.

One day, in the role of Dr. Gower Morgan, he is compelled to assume more than the title. At a church fair puppet show, "Cinderella" goes into labor and Morgan delivers the baby himself en route to the hospital. This impromptu delivery of their daughter Gina is his first encounter with Leon and Emily Meredith, but not the last.

Morgan's home life is as cluttered as his closets. With seven grown daughters, his mother, and his sister all sharing the same roof, life is chaos and confusion. The simplicity of Leon's and Emily's life is a welcome contrast. The two younger people met while in college. Leon's theatrical aspirations alienated his well-to-do parents. When threatened with having his college tuition cut off if his grades do not improve, Leon declares that he will go to New York and make it as an actor. Emily, in love, insists on going with him.

Their life in New York is short. Jobs are hard to come by. They join a group of like-minded contemporaries and go on the road as an improvisation troupe. This does not bring financial success. At last the troupe lands in Baltimore, lodging at Crafts Unlimited, which is owned by the mother of one of their number. Here they split up until only Leon, Emily, and Victor are left.

It is Emily's idea to give puppet shows as a way of earning money. The three of them make a good business of it until Victor, claiming he is in love with Emily, decides to leave. Leon and Emily continue the work, even after Gina's birth. If Morgan wears costumes that change on a whim, Emily and Leon wear uniforms. He is never seen without a soft white shirt and orange corduroy jacket, she is always clad in black leotards, dance skirts, and ballet slippers.

Morgan haunts Crafts Unlimited, follows them from a discreet distance, builds up his own fantasies of what life must be like in their less cluttered existence. Emily notices "Dr. Morgan" keeping an eye on them and wonders about his motives.

Morgan declares himself at last on the occasion of his eldest daughter's marriage. He feels aged by the experience, mourning the sweet toddler he once knew, wishing that time could stand still and his daughters remain babies forever. Leaving the hectic reception in his backyard, he goes to Crafts Unlimited. Although trying to maintain his mask as "Dr. Morgan," he gives in to Emily's demand for honesty and confesses his true identity.

The years pass with a growing bond of interaction between the Merediths and the Gowers. Leon's parents learn that they have a granddaughter and start injecting possessions and financial advantages into the Merediths' simple lives. Gina goes to private school and good camps, financed by her grandparents. Leon grows more staid, almost stodgy, and Emily feels that their relationship is stagnating, becoming dull and conventional.

In Morgan's household more daughters marry, leave home, have children. Brindle, survivor of a disastrous first marriage, is at last able to wed her childhood sweetheart, Robert Roberts, but her absence from the Gower house is to be only temporary. Robert is in love with the Brindle he once knew, she says, not with the person she is.

Loneliness draws Morgan and Emily toward one another. He loves as he once observed her, from afar, until she declares her love as well.

But their affair ends when Emily discovers she is pregnant. Leon seems unmoved by the news, tacitly accepting the fact that he will move out of Crafts Unlimited and go back to his folks while Morgan moves in. Bonny is not so calm. She dumps Morgan's wardrobe on the curb, later sending along his mother and sister too. Clutter invades, dogging Morgan even into his new life.

In desperation, Morgan assumes Leon's identity and takes a puppeteering job in a church-centered community, Tindell. He, Emily, and their son Joshua run away from their previous lives, leaving Bonny to pick up the pieces. Even Gina is left behind, although against Emily's wishes. She does come to realize that the girl will be happier in the conventional life Leon, now training to be a banker, can give her.

One last jolt from the past reaches Morgan in Tindell. On opening the local paper, he finds his own name in the obituaries, a wild parting shot from Bonny. She has made a new life without him and saw placing the obituary as a symbolic declaration of independence. Yet, for all her purported new freedom, she still calls Emily persistently to tell her what a loon she now has on her hands and how glad Bonny is to be rid of him. Still, as Emily, Morgan, and Joshua continue with their lives, the question remains whether anyone who has once known Morgan Gower will ever truly be free of him.

Chaos, clutter, confusion, and costumes, all seem to dominate *Morgan's Passing*. Not only is there chaos outside Morgan—in his house, in the rubbish-strewn streets of Baltimore, in the world itself—there is just as much chaos within. His search is a basic human one, to pare down the extraneous details of life in order to enjoy living. Morgan needs his costumes and his roles for the same reason. A doctor has a clearly defined part to play. He heals, and he delivers babies. When Morgan realizes that real doctors lead lives as confusing and scattered as his own, it is time to drop that role for a while and go on to another.

Emily represents the ideal life for Morgan, and it is hard to say how much is just a desire to move into the Quaker simplicity of her role. She is unchanged and unchanging, the set uniform as opposed to the wildly varying costume. Not even the socially acceptable costume-switch of following fashions changes her manner of dress. When he sees her once in running shoes instead of her usual ballet slippers, Morgan is violently upset.

There is the temptation to compare Morgan and Emily to another famous pair of contrasting characters, Don Quixote and his faithful squire, Sancho Panza. Morgan's fantasies and masquerades, Emily's down-to-earth pragmatism, at first glance do seem to echo the relationship of Cervantes' characters. But Morgan's flights are more complex.

Don Quixote chose one role and stuck to it, even when he discovered that being a knight was not as simple as in the books. Sancho lost some of his practicality, gaining the Don's imagination, and vice versa. There is no such trading of outlooks between Morgan and Emily. At bottom neither one of them wishes for it. It would destroy their relationship.

Through Morgan Gower, Anne Tyler voices our own desires to escape from the confusion of living, to get away from the picayune details that trip us up and eat away at our precious few days of life. Beyond that, she examines the nature of human relationships, turning the concept of love into a situation where lover and beloved stay together because each sees in the other some quality he or she lacks and needs. The need is strong, so strong that we may one day find ourselves minor versions of Morgan Gower, playing the role of Wife or Husband, Friend or Lover, Father or Mother in an attempt to clear away the clutter and get on with living. For life, as Morgan muses, can be "luminous and beautiful, and rich with possibilities."

Esther M. Friesner

MUSIC FOR CHAMELEONS

Author: Truman Capote (1924–   )
Publisher: Random House (New York). 262 pp. $10.95
Type of work: Reminiscences
Time: The present
Locale: United States

A celebrated author presents a series of dramatized reminiscences that re-
volve loosely around the theme of identity

In the Preface to *Music For Chameleons,* Truman Capote describes how his diverse literary activities over the years brought him, some years ago, to a severe creative impasse. He drew the conclusion at that time that "my writing was becoming too dense . . . . I was taking three pages to arrive at effects I ought to be able to achieve in a single paragraph." Feeling that none of his works attained the quality of which he was capable, Capote realized that the root of his difficulty was the fact that he had worked in many diversified areas of literary output (ranging from film scripts to novels and poetry) but had not yet blended together all the various skills acquired. "A writer ought to have all his colors, all his abilities available on the same palette for mingling." This phrase suggests that the writer, or more specifically, Truman Capote, should have at his disposal a range of colors that he can make use of as needed. In this regard he is like a chameleon, many of his literary colleagues and readers are like chameleons, and so are the characters in this book. They are men and women who exhibit a protective coloring that alters to the degree that their personal or professional situations alter. Thus the title, *Music for Chameleons,* for this is a collection by, for, and about those whose lives are defined by a defensive back-and-forth shifting of appearances, and sometimes, if they are lucky, a harmonious mingling of disparate roles and people.

Among these characters there is, for example, Bob Quinn of the book's novella, "Handcarved Coffins." Quinn is a Western rancher who, through his wealth, social position, and heroism during World War II and because of his all-around conviviality, is virtually idolized by the neighboring townspeople—even though it is almost certain that he has committed a series of particularly gruesome murders. Quinn has, as it were, the right protective coloring, something that is duly lacking in his antagonist, State Investigator Jake Pepper. Despite all the incriminating evidence Pepper can amass against Quinn, no one in the town will support him because he, unlike Quinn, does not *appear* to be one of them.

In "A Day's Work," Mary Sanchez, a cleaning woman, reveals by turns that she is professional about her work but can also be capable of irresponsibility on the job and yet is almost saintly in her concern for most of her employers. *Where* she happens to be cleaning has a great deal to do with *what* she shows herself to be. Sarah Whitelaw of "Mojave" is in one instance a sympathetic listener to the romantic worries of her hairdresser, in the next a tough-minded caller of the shots in her sexual liaison with her ex-psychiatrist, and in another a tender-hearted procuress for her husband, a wealthy older man whom she loves but with whom she does not have sexual relations because of her emotional problems. Marilyn Monroe, the person referred to in the title "A Beautiful Child," is scatterbrained or intelligent, reverent or profane, self-absorbed or self-forgetting. This characteristic is shown not just as she moves from one setting to another (a funeral home, a Chinese restaurant, a waterfront pier), but from one idea to the next, as evidenced by the conversation she carries on with "TC"—if not the real Truman Capote then his narrative persona—throughout their afternoon together.

"TC" himself, in the reminiscence "Derring-do," quite literally undergoes a protective transformation of appearance when, sought by San Diego detectives who have a warrant to arrest him for refusing to honor a court subpoena, he changes clothes with a young dancer in the entourage of Pearl Bailey, a famous friend who just happens to be passing by. (They are near the boarding gate of a flight bound for New York.) Survival, it seems, depends on being able to enact these quick shifts and transformations, although, as is suggested by the Marilyn Monroe account, the dialogue with convicted murderer Robert Beausoleil in "Then It All Came Down," and the monologue, in "Hello, Stranger," of a once-respected Wall Street man who became improperly involved with a twelve-year-old girl, a severe price sometimes has to be paid by those who lead multi-faced or deceptive lives.

Beausoleil, whom "TC" interviews in a maximum-security cell in San Quentin prison, claims that "Everything in life is good. It all flows. It's all good. It's all music." He, it seems, is not a chameleon figure; from the bland, accepting manner with which he speaks of his fate—a life sentence—one would think that the identity he presents is fixed, unchanging, undisguised. He describes himself as "A white man. And everything a white man stands for." Yet, in his constant reiteration, "Everything that happens is good," he displays a spiritual vacuity, a moral idiocy incapable of recognizing, and thus avoiding, evil behavior. "I was noticing how your face changes," comments TC immediately after registering astonishment at the prisoner's amoral viewpoint. "One moment, with just the slightest shift of angle, you look so boyish, entirely innocent, a charmer. And then—well, one can see you as a sort of Forty-second Street Lucifer." Lacking the capacity to distinguish between any form of right and wrong, Beausoleil is indeed "entirely innocent"—like a reptile. He is the book's ultimate chameleon, but unlike that harmless lizard he is adaptable to the point of being extremely dangerous to human beings.

The final piece of the book, "Nocturnal Turnings, or How Siamese Twins Have Sex," is written in the form of a bedtime dialogue between "TC" and "TC"—in other words, it is an interior conversation. One TC is serious, professional, rather melancholy; the other is catty, sarcastic, cynical. At one point, the professional TC gets out of bed to work on a magazine assignment to interview himself, and as we read what he writes, we encounter a further splitting of TC's selves, this time into interviewer and interviewee. When asked what one wish he would like to have granted, the interviewee answers, "To wake up one morning and feel that I was at last a grown-up person, emptied of resentment, vengeful thoughts, and other wasteful, childish emotions. To find myself . . . an adult." Here, rather poignantly, is a wish for wholeness, security, integration of selves: a state of being that precludes "wasteful, childish emotions." It is a call, on a personal level, for the same sort of harmonious mingling of colors or selves that, in the Preface, Truman Capote spoke of seeking on an artistic level.

After TC has finished writing his self-interview, he turns to his "alter ego," and the two "selves" have an intimate conversation, which ends "TC: I love you, too. TC: You'd better. Because when you get right down to it, all we've got is each other." The premise of this intimate conversation may strike the reader as overly cute, but what recommends it is the wit with which it is performed and the relevance it bears to the theme of fragmented personality that pervades the entire book.

As he has demonstrated over and over in the nearly four full decades of his somewhat-distinguished, somewhat-scandalous literary career, Truman Capote is a first-class storyteller. What makes a raconteur succeed more than anything else is his skill in getting his words to be believed; no matter how fascinating a story is, if the reader is doubting it while hearing it, the presentation has failed. Because of the first-person narration used in the Preface and thirteen of the book's fourteen reminiscences, the constant recurrence of the "TC" initials for the latter two thirds of the text, the minute specificity of time and place, the frequent inclusion of well-known names (Norman Mailer, John Kennedy, Pearl Bailey), and the mostly documentary tone, *Music For Chameleons* implicitly asks the reader to take every word of it as true —not simply "true-to-life," but rather "true-to-what-actually-was-said-and-done."

By employing the formal devices just mentioned, as well as by endowing his characters with plausible although often unaccountable behavior, Capote's tales attain the level of credibility that makes them succeed as attention-holding narratives. A reader might rightfully point out that gossip columns also hold attention. The difference is that, gossip aside, these stories/reminiscences provide insight into character (of a real or made-up Pearl Bailey . . . Marilyn Monroe . . . Truman Capote) and at the same time deal, rather subtly, with serious themes such as the resolution of fragmented identity.

"The best part of a writer's biography is not the record of his adventures but the story of his style," Vladimir Nabokov wrote. In *Music For Chameleons* there is both: the adventures of Truman Capote, however embellished, and the writing style of Truman Capote, verbally embellished here, stripped-down there, sometimes lyrical, often journalistic, and always in itself an attempt to bring resolution—a harmonious mingling—to its disparate stylistic elements.

David M. Lubin

MY MANY YEARS

Author: Arthur Rubinstein (1887–)
Publisher: Alfred A. Knopf (New York). 626 pp. $16.95
Type of work: Memoirs
Time: 1917–1980
Locale: North and South America, Europe, Africa, Asia, Australia

An autobiographical account of the great pianist's career and travels, from World War I to the present

Arthur Rubinstein is one of the most widely known, respected, beloved, and enduring classical musicians of this century. As a pianist, he is generally held in the highest esteem by colleagues, critics, and the general public. He played his last concert in 1975, at the age of 88, only when his eyesight began to fail him and he could no longer reliably see the keyboard or the gestures of the conductors who often performed with him. At that point he began writing this account of the 67 years since the close of the first volume of his memoirs, *My Young Years,* published in 1974.

My Many Years begins in Spain in 1917. The 30 years of Rubinstein's life up to this point had been largely a struggle for maturity and recognition. He was often without engagements, often impoverished and reliant on others for favors and financial help. What he did not lack was an unwavering conviction that he was going to be a success. The Spanish public were his first ardent fans (they have remained ardent all these decades). Rubinstein's affinity for Spanish music made him a privileged interpreter of Albeniz, de Falla, Granados, and other Iberian composers. The aristocracy adopted him, as the aristocracy and high society invariably did wherever he went, even though these contacts did not always guarantee him concerts with decent fees.

In one of the many strokes of good fortune that have punctuated his life when the going was bad or indifferent, an Argentine impresario, hearing of Rubinstein's popularity in Spain, invited him for a promising and remunerative tour of South America. Armed with a Spanish passport and the personal guarantee of King Alfonso, he set sail for Buenos Aires with his new manager, a ladies' man, rogue, and brilliant organizer named Juan Avila, for what was to be a turning point, the beginning of an almost steadily successful and brilliant career. South America loved him. His Spanish music was wildly applauded, his Chopin and Beethoven were approved, Ravel and Debussy hated (because they were French, not because of Rubinstein's performances). Young men exuberantly carried him through the streets on their shoulders after his performances, which terrified him at first but to which he became accustomed.

For most of Rubinstein's life until his marriage he was involved with a woman—at least one. At this time it was the volatile, highly erratic, but brilliant Italian contralto Gabriella Besanzoni, who was on her own operatic tour while at the same time forming a more or less permanent liaison with Rubinstein. Many of the famous personalities that always seemed to turn up in Rubinstein's presence were there in South America. He describes the moving concert in Montevideo he gave with Waslaw Nijinsky that turned out to be the dancer's last appearance before the public. Diaghilev was on tour with his company, and Anna Pavlova turned up unexpectedly at a roulette table in São Paulo. The French minister to Brazil, the poet Paul Claudel, and his secretary, Darius Milhaud, who was to become world famous as a composer, became close companions. The tour was financially successful, and Rubinstein, at his happiest, made music, attended endless parties and fashionable events, dined like an epicure, and was made much of by the social and artistic inner circles. Encouraged by the gratifying accumulation of gold pesos he had earned in fees, Rubinstein, accompanied by Besanzoni and his new valet Enrique, traveled north for concerts in Mexico and Havana, which were similarly successful, and then on to a series of less successful concerts in the United States.

Rubinstein had first toured the United States in 1906, when he was 19, and the response to his playing was indifferent and discouraging. This time, however, he went at the invitation of an unfamiliar New York manager, R.E. Johnson. Johnson turned out to be a good-natured, bibulous backslapper but not much of a manager. Most of the engagements Johnson arranged were for appearances at a curious cultural hybrid of the time, the "musicale," typically held in the lounge of a midtown hotel and attended largely by women shoppers eager to rest their weary feet. A Carnegie Hall recital, on which every musical artist pinned his hopes, was respectably received but disappointing. The reigning keyboard lions of the day were Rachmaninoff, Josef Hofmann, and Paderewski, a trio leaving no room for competition. This, coupled with the critics' tendency to recall with condescension Rubinstein's undistinguished debut of 1906, embittered him. He left Johnson's management and the United States to sail for Europe, vowing never to set foot there again.

Europe after World War I was full of renewed hope and excitement. It was an environment in which many artists flourished, but Rubinstein in particular seemed to come into full bloom, not just because he was in steady demand as a performer in England, France, Italy, and Spain, but because he partook so totally in living, in drawing so deeply on the minds and gifts of those around him; not just the musicians, but the painters, the poets and novelists, the politicians, the academics. The gifted seemed to sense his boundless curiosity and his responsiveness. Fluent in at least eight languages, familiar with people on all social levels, traveling constantly, watching and listening always, Rubinstein was like a synthesizer of the times. Stravinski, Prokofiev, Poulenc, de Falla, and many other composers were intimate friends and often sought his counsel and dedicated important works to him. He seemed to make it all work by dint of his generous personality, his frequently uproariously self-deprecating sense of humor, and his acceptance of life as it comes, of life as an endlessly interesting adventure. It becomes evident, however, that what chiefly pulled people to him and kept them close was his marvelous gift for making music. The celebrities—the Prince of Wales, Misia Sert, Picasso, Coco Chanel, H.G. Wells, the Rothschilds, Chaliapin, John Sargent, Elsa Maxwell, Beatrice Lillie—they all cherished him as an artist.

In his early forties, to the incredulity of many of his footloose, high-rolling friends, Rubinstein fell in love with and married Nela (Aniela) Mlynarska, the lovely and gifted daughter of his friend Emil Mlynarski, a distinguished Polish conductor. The marriage marked another turning point in his life. After the birth of their first child, Rubinstein quite spontaneously began a serious reexamination of his musicianship and found it deplorably wanting. Blessed from childhood with an abundance of musical gifts that made practice and serious study easy to ignore, he acknowledged to himself that his technique was slapdash and his concern with the text of his repertoire was in many ways superficial or cavalier; that the sheer bravura of his playing had disguised these faults and cheated his public of the meticulous performances they deserved.

Rubinstein began then, decades after the time when most pianists mastered all this, to practice his technique finger by finger, to restudy his pieces, and to enlarge the repertoire that for so long had been standing him in good stead. He ceased to be the tireless bon vivant and transformed himself into the dedicated musician for which he became celebrated for the next four decades.

It was at this juncture that the irrepressible impresario Sol Hurok providentially turned up in Rubinstein's life. Hurok, who found unintelligible the word no, arranged for Rubinstein's third trip to the United States, in spite of the pianist's grave misgivings. Rubinstein describes the return to this country in a leisurely fashion.By the time Rubinstein reached the stage of Carnegie Hall in 1937, and the tumultuous, triumphant welcome New York gave him, the reader is ready to stand up and cheer along with the long-ago crowd.

The rest was, for the most part, sublime. Three more children were born. There were countless tours across the United States and Canada; a successful, if hideously uncomfortable, tour of the Soviet Union; wonderful concerts in China and Japan, Java, and the Philippines; South Africa and South America again. He never toured Germany, however: nearly every one of Rubinstein's relatives perished in Poland in the Holocaust.

The Rubinstein family settled for a while in Beverly Hills, gloriously happy among the movie luminaries, with Rubinstein maintaining his dignity and his sense of humor dealing with Sam Goldwyn and Jack Warner. There were homes in Manhattan and Paris, but every place they went seemed home, full of love and music and friends. If his eyesight had not betrayed him, Rubinstein would no doubt be giving concerts to this very day. As it is, at 93, he is still receiving honors, writing, listening to new music, and planning to make films in New York, Spain, and Poland.

Rubinstein the writer resembles Rubinstein the pianist: he is in somewhat a class by himself. The personality, the warmth and intelligence, the marvelous humor, the zest for living, the integrity of the man boil out of the pages as they boiled out of the keyboard. Throughout this volume, as in the preceding one, Rubinstein has relied solely on his prodigious memory for events, places, people, names, financial transactions, details of meals long ago savored, or programs played. It is the same memory that allowed him to memorize, almost at sight, the most complicated solo work or demanding concerto. The reader's astonishment at the wealth and particularity of this recalled information comes not, however, from its mere recitation, which could be tedious, but from the way in which Rubinstein uses it to convey the excitement of a life and career that page by page becomes more challenging, suspenseful, and satisfying. With this kind of characteristic gusto and endurance, Rubinstein might just delight the reader with a third volume of memoirs.

Robert B. Costello

NAMING NAMES

Author: Victory S. Navasky
Publisher: Viking Press (New York). 482 pp. $15.95
Type of work: History
Time: 1940's to present
Locale: Hollywood, Washington, New York

A comprehensive and compassionate exploration of the moral issues that faced those who named names to congressional committees investigating Hollywood during the 1950's

Whittaker Chambers' accusations against Alger Hiss signified the beginning of the anti-Communist hysteria that swept the United States in the 1940's and 1950's. Victor Navasky chronicles the forays of the House Committee on Un-American Activities (HUAC) into the entertainment industry.

From 1936 on, the Communist Party had actively recruited in Hollywood, seeking prestige, substantial financial resources, and the possibility of using the movies for propaganda. This effort was successful because many people were disillusioned with World War I and by the bloodbath it had engendered. The Communist Party stood for social security and the rights of the unemployed, minorities, women, and colonial countries. The Soviet Union had been the first government to oppose fascism.

The first hearings investigating Hollywood in 1947 centered on ten people who were known as the Hollywood Ten. Alvah Bessie, Herbert Biberman, Lester Cole, Edward Dmytryk, Ring Lardner, Jr., John Howard Lawson, Albert Maltz, Sam Ornitz, Adrian Scott, and Dalton Trumbo all based their refusal to cooperate on the First Amendment guarantee of free speech. All ten were cited for contempt by Congress and sentenced to prison for terms of up to a year.

The hearings resumed in 1951 after a suspension that had allowed the Hollywood Ten to appeal, unsuccessfully, their decision. Larry Parks opened the new testimony by admitting that he had been in the Communist Party from 1941 to 1945. He pleaded "Don't present me with the choice of either being in contempt of this Committee and going to jail or forcing me to really crawl through the mud to be an informer." His plea was rejected. Congressman Donald L. Jackson explained, "The ultimate test of the credibility of a witness is the extent to which he is willing to cooperate with the Committee in giving full details as to not only the place of activities, but also the names of those who participated with him in the Communist Party."

The names were important to the preservation of national security, claimed HUAC, yet Navasky shows that from 1936 to 1945 the Los Angeles Communist Party had given membership lists yearly to the Los Angeles Police Department and that HUAC had copies. The naming names procedure was ostensibly a ritual that would allow informers to prove that they had broken irrevocably with the Communist Party. Instead, it served as a punitive, degrading ritual and sowed distrust within the entertainment community.

The Fifth Amendment failed to provide an adequate defense, for in 1948 the Supreme Court ruled that once a witness made any statement about himself he "waived the privilege" and could not refuse to name names. "Taking the Fifth" exempted the witness from testifying but was "interpreted as the ultimate evidence of conspiracy," resulting in unemployment through the blacklist. Thus, whereas the committee punished those who took the First with a "contempt" charge, the community itself provided the punishment for those who pleaded the Fifth. Organizations such as the American Legion, the Catholic War Veterans, and Hollywood's Motion Picture Alliance for the Preservation of American Ideals enthusiastically made lists of "Reds" and pressured studios to fire questionable employees. Ward Bond, Adolphe Menjou, and John Wayne were some who participated in the purge.

Those witnesses subpoenaed faced three options: they could refuse to testify on the grounds of the First Amendment and face jail; they could refuse to testify on the basis of the Fifth Amendment, implicitly incriminating themselves; or they could testify and name names. Those who cooperated with HUAC were often encouraged to do so by their doctors, lawyers, priests, and therapists.

Navasky interviews a number of informers to determine why they did what they did. Budd Schulberg says, "My guilt is what we did to the Czechs, not to Ring Lardner. I testified because I felt guilty for having contributed unwittingly to intellectual and artistic as well as racial oppression." Elia Kazan refuses to discuss his reasons for informing. Despite Navasky's obvious compassion for the informers, he prints Abe Polansky's statement that "If you wait till they put a gun up against your head, it's too late to claim that you're doing it for moral-political reasons."

Myriad specific reasons for testifying were given, but Navasky reduces them to four general ones. Many ex-Communists turned against the party. "They Deserved What They Got" was a reason frequently cited. "I Was Acting in Obedience to a Higher Loyalty" was cited by ex-Communists who did not want to suffer for a cause they no longer believed in. Many equated refusal to cooperate with HUAC with support for Stalin, his death camps, and Soviet anti-Semitism. By claiming

"I Wasn't Responsible for My Actions," still others implied that they were acting under the pressure of forces beyond their control. The fourth claim—"I Didn't Hurt Anybody" or "I only named those who were already named"—often was simply not true. Whatever the reason, every cooperative witness reinforced the strength of HUAC.

Navasky acknowledges that the 1950's were the time of the organization man, the silent generation of standard distrust of "the foreign, the different, the strange, the subversive." The victims of this hysteria were many. The intended victims were those who were named, some of whom even "seemed to die of blacklist," like John Garfield, Canada Lee, Mady Christians, Philip Loeb, and J. Edward Bromberg. Another victim was the Hollywood community at large. The quality of movies declined and so did Hollywood's economic well-being. Even the informer was a victim. Initially, informers suffered from mild feelings of guilt and a loss of self-esteem as a consequence of their cooperation with HUAC. Since then, an even greater social penalty has been paid, and continues to be paid, by those who named names. The correspondence between Hollywood Ten victims Albert Maltz and Dalton Trumbo on the subject of the informer as victim expounds different points of view. Trumbo's view, set forth in 1972, is that since this is "a country which, after a reasonable period of punishment, returns murderers and rapists to society on the humane theory that it is still possible for them to become decent and even valuable citizens, I have no intention of fanning the embers of justifiable hatred which burned so brightly twenty-five years ago." Maltz's attitude is that "a virtuous man keeps a decent distance from the carriers of social evil."

Navasky sees an even wider effect of McCarthyism in the weakening of American culture and government. He blames it for a declining morale within the civil service and argues that the purge of the foreign service, in turn, led to the Southeast Asia debacle. The nuclear arsenal build-up is a direct result of anti-Communist hysteria, according to Navasky. McCarthyism destroyed the faith of the liberal young and led them away from the Democratic Party and into the civil rights and peace movements.

The ultimate questions raised in this book are those of morality, of knowing what to do in a time of disruption and shifting values. "Morality, we are told, is a voice of conscience from within in harmony with a voice of authority from without. We have seen what happens when the citizen delegates his conscience to the state."

Naming Names is a comprehensive, well-researched chronicle of a difficult period in American history. Victor Navasky has presented a balanced view of the informer using the experiences of many people.

Navasky puts "the Hollywood informers in context . . . not to relieve them of responsibility for the consequences of their actions but, rather, to locate that responsibility more precisely."

Dalton Trumbo felt that the burden of guilt for McCarthyism should rest on HUAC alone, but Navasky places it with those who cooperated and those who stood by and allowed it to happen. Just about everyone allowed HUAC its premise that it could require the naming of names. The few who objected were condemned as Communist sympathizers. The liberal organizations that should have been the first line of defense against such repression themselves required loyalty oaths. Liberal publications suffered failures "not merely of courage but in many cases of perspective."

Throughout the book Navasky makes effective use of scientific and historical contexts. One particularly interesting discussion considers the blacklist in light of the recent controversial investigations into the manipulation of individuals in a group context. Solomon Asch proved that 32 percent of his subjects would change their opinion about the length of a line when it is unanimously contradicted by their fellow subjects. Stanley Milgram showed that individuals will inflict real pain on others under the orders of an authority figure. In both experiments the introduction of an ally into the situation freed subjects to follow their best instincts.

There is a vast store of information in *Naming Names*. Navasky has organized it carefully and offered all the rationales the informers could possibly ask for. Then he has equally well set forth the moral failures of the cooperators, collaborators, name-namers, and silent spectators —and the effect that their failure has had on all of us. *Naming Names* is a fascinating story "about the conditions under which good men do things they know or suspect to be wrong, about a political system that puts people in a position where they are encouraged to violate their values, about a republic that asks its citizens to betray their fellows."

Pamela Murfin

NEIGHBORS

Author: Thomas Berger (1924–   )
Publisher: Delacorte Press/Seymour Lawrence (New York). 275 pp. $9.95
Type of work: Novel
Time: The present
Locale: Suburbia

Earl Keese, fat and forty-nine years old, is subjected to various forms of harassment by his new neighbors, Harry and Ramona

Principal characters:
    EARL KEESE, a settled, overweight, middle-aged man
    HARRY, an attractive blond man who brings violence into Earl's world
    RAMONA, an attractive woman whose sexuality disrupts Earl's life
    ENID KEESE, Earl's nondescript wife
    ELAINE KEESE, Earl's college-aged daughter

Earl Keese—forty-nine, overweight, and subject to hallucinations —has lived a comfortable life with his wife, Enid. When Ramona, his new neighbor, introduces herself in a blatantly sexual manner, life begins to change for Earl. Ramona makes herself at home in Earl's house, drinks all his wine, tells Earl he is fat, and generally abuses him. Nevertheless, Earl invites her to stay for dinner. When he informs Enid, she tells him they have only frozen succotash in the house. Earl returns to the living room to invite Ramona out to dinner but she is gone.

As Earl contemplates her departure, a hungry Harry appears. Suggesting a take-out dinner, he prepares to go get it. Earl goes to his bedroom to get his car keys and is stunned to see Ramona lying on his bed wrapped only in a bath towel. With Earl's $32, Harry departs driving Earl's car to pick up some Italian food at a restaurant not yet open. Earl walks next door and sees, through the kitchen window, Harry cooking spaghetti.

Insulted by Harry's deception, Earl decides to roll Harry's car into his own driveway, since Harry has Earl's car and keys. The car rolls out of control into the creek at the end of the street. When Harry brings the spaghetti to Earl's house, Earl confronts him with his knowledge that Harry has cooked it himself. Before the ensuing argument ends, Harry informs Earl that it is actually Earl's "gas guzzler" that has rolled into the creek. Ramona accuses Earl of trying to rape her, and Earl, in a frenzy, orders them both out of his house. Moments later they reappear, laughing at how they have fooled Earl into believing Harry rolled his car into the creek. Earl now feels obliged to confess that he actually has sunk Harry's automobile.

To confirm it, Earl and Harry go to inspect Harry's car in the creek and inevitably get into a fist fight in the mud. Earl goes to his basement to clean up and, stepping from the shower, is met by Ramona. He manages to lock Ramona and Harry in the basement; then, in desperation, Earl calls several friends to help him deal with these intruders but is answered with varying negative responses. Harry, who has been eavesdropping on Earl's conversations on an extension phone downstairs, offers an apology. Earl lets Ramona and Harry out of the basement but, in the maneuver, he finds himself locked in instead. After working fruitlessly on the hinges of the outside door, he discovers that the door leading to the kitchen is open.

Earl emerges cautiously to find the local mechanic, Greavy, towing Earl's intact car out of the driveway. Suffering from "loss of will" and exhaustion, Earl decides to go to bed—Enid seems already to have done so. He turns on the light and is shocked to discover that he has crawled into bed with Harry and Ramona.

Ramona tells Earl that Enid has offered them the master bedroom since their own beds are not assembled. Nevertheless, Earl makes them leave. In the guise of a friendly handshake, Harry crushes Earl's right hand. Earl rushes after him to retaliate, but when he opens the front door he finds his daughter, Elaine, home from college.

Earl goes upstairs to tell Enid, who shows a sudden shift in attitude by expressing relief that Harry and Ramona are gone. Downstairs, Elaine realizes she has left her suitcase on the front doorstep. Earl goes out to get it. Instead of the suitcase he gets a punch in the stomach from Greavy, who is furious at being called to tow away a car in perfect working order. When Earl returns to the house, he finds that Harry has brought in Elaine's suitcase. In the following discussion, Harry takes sides with Elaine and Earl alternately. However, when he makes advances toward Elaine, Earl punches him and Enid and Elaine praise him. All decide to go to bed. Earl checks the front door to see if it is locked and finds Ramona seated on the front step. He talks to Ramona through the keyhole, in the hope he can convince her to go home. Enid tells Earl that Elaine has been expelled from college for stealing a ring.

When Earl goes to Harry and Ramona for consolation, Harry shoots at him, claiming that he mistook Earl for a prowler. Earl and Harry enjoy a friendly interlude until Harry accuses Earl of murdering Ramona. Harry swings at Earl but Earl ducks the blow while delivering a swift kick to Harry's groin. Outside, Earl confronts the dawn and his car, which now has the word "pimp" painted on the left side.

At home, Enid, Earl, and Elaine consult on Elaine's alleged act of thievery. It seems that it was not Elaine who stole the ring after all.

Earl suggests that the ring be returned anonymously. Elaine agrees and telephones her roommate, to whom she relays the terse message "Mail it back." When he finds Ramona asleep in his bedroom, Earl generously lets her stay. He goes outside to wash the insult off his car. While he is working, Harry arrives and, after a short but vicious tussle, they work together amiably.

Greavy and his son tow Harry's car out of the creek. It starts up and seems to run well, but Harry wants a new paint job, paid for by Earl. They then disagree over who will paint the car. Just when that issue is settled, Harry tells Earl he is moving away. Earl tries to convince Harry not to move, finally saying that Ramona does not want to go. Harry says he is leaving Ramona to Earl.

Earl returns to his house to find Elaine packed and ready to escape the neighborhood disasters. Earl keeps her from calling a taxi by surreptitiously unplugging the telephone. He then goes upstairs to advise Ramona that Harry is leaving her. She invites Earl to get into bed with her. Earl complies, only to be startled by Harry's pounding on the bedroom door. Harry's house is on fire and he needs Earl's car keys to drive to the fire station, since his own car has a broken axle and Earl's telephone is out of order. Earl calls the fire department, and when they arrive the fire is out of control. Harry accuses Earl of setting the fire; Earl accuses the Greavys. Harry tells Earl that Ramona and Elaine are compromising themselves in the master bedroom. Earl asks Harry to handle the situation.

In the kitchen with Enid, Earl suggests that they move, leave their house to Harry and Ramona, and not reveal their new address to Elaine, but Enid refuses. Their conversation is interrupted by the fire chief, who indicates that the Greavys saw Harry throwing matches by a can of paint remover. Even the thought that Harry deliberately burned down his own house fails to dampen Earl's warm feelings toward him. Upstairs Earl finds Harry, Elaine, and Ramona playing hide-and-seek. Earl joins in. After a long search he finds only Ramona. She tells him Harry has gone off with Enid and Elaine, leaving her for Earl.

Harry, Enid, and Elaine eventually return laden with food. As they eat, Earl learns that Harry never owned the house he burned down. Earl washes the food down with rum and achieves a mellow state that is interrupted slightly by the realization that Harry and Ramona intend to live with him. Despite this, and the fact that Harry paid for all the food with Earl's checkbook, Earl retains positive feelings toward Harry. "Every time I see you as a criminal, by another light you look like a kind of benefactor," Earl says wonderingly.

Earl asks Harry and Ramona to stay, suggesting ways in which they might contribute to the family. They decide to leave even though Earl offers them the master bedroom. He gives them his car, and they drive away. Enid and Elaine immediately begin berating Harry and Ramona, but Earl misses his neighbors. When they return to take Earl with them, he joins them. As the car drives off, Earl suffers a fatal stroke. Ramona says, " 'Earl, it could happen to anybody.' "

Neighbors, Thomas Berger's tenth novel, is so filled with absurdities and slapstick routines that a synopsis cannot do justice to the story. For a comic novel, however, there are a great many disturbing themes to the book. Berger's own unpublished subtitle for the book is appropriate: "A Tale of Harassment."

Earl Keese is Everyman coping with one impossible, humiliating, violent situation after another. Earl's peculiar antagonists, Harry and Ramona, represent the darker side of human nature. The sexual nature of Ramona is apparent from the outset. Her character is revealed by constant sexual innuendo and bedroom encounters. Harry matches her sexuality with brutality.

Earl initially resists these primitive newcomers to his everyday life. Yet, because he has long felt a sense of loneliness and isolation unrelieved by his wife and his superficial friends, he gradually comes to accept and even appreciate their baser natures. They seem somehow to satisfy his longing for a more vital connection with life. The fundamental paradox the book explores is the fact that vitality, because it is rooted in anarchy, imperils survival.

Berger sets the novel on a dead-end street and makes a neighborhood of two houses. The action takes place in a 24-hour period. Greavy and his son play all the incidental parts: mechanic, tow truck operator, fireman, mover. Enid and Elaine serve as shifting backdrops to Earl's ongoing battle with Harry and Ramona.

Early in the story, Earl feared that "he was to be denied all nourishment this night. He was not to be allowed even the basics of human life! Would they even find some way to prevent the air from reaching his lungs?" Sadly, the answer is yes, for Harry and Ramona come as death comes to Everyman. It can only be fought, cursed, and delayed.

There remains the question of the credibility of this morality play. At the beginning, Berger tells us that Earl Keese saw visions and was forced to "consistently reject the evidence of his eyes." Since Earl is the protagonist, can the reader believe what he sees? The best way to view this beautifully crafted novel, however, is suggested by the last line of Berger's novel *Arthur Rex:* "King Arthur . . . was never historical, but everything he did was true."

Pamela Murfin

THE NINJA

Author: Eric Van Lustbader
Publisher: M. Evans & Co. (New York). 442 pp. $12.95
Type of work: Novel
Time: The present, with flashbacks to World War II
Locale: New York City, Long Island, Japan, and China

The story of a man who must try to end the murderous rampage of a powerful Japanese warrior who wreaks havoc on a defenseless contemporary community

> *Principal characters:*
> NICHOLAS LINNEAR, an ex-adman who must invoke his Japanese heritage to confront the diabolic *ninja*
> SAIGŌ, Nicholas's boyhood rival who later becomes the *ninja*
> RAPHAEL TOMPKIN, the oil magnate who is the *ninja's* ultimate target
> JUSTINE TOMPKIN, Nicholas's girlfriend, daughter of Raphael Tompkin
> LIEUTENANT CROAKER, the New York detective assigned to the *ninja* case

For the setting of *The Ninja,* the activity shifts between present-day New York City and a Long Island suburb and the Far East, first in China and then to Japan. The central character, the son of a British military officer and a Japanese survivor of World War II, moves to the United States, where the opening scene finds him quitting a lucrative position in an advertising agency.

From the beginning of the novel, where Nicholas literally runs into his soon-to-be-girlfriend Justine, moments after he sees a body being plucked from the sea, the common denominator is murder, as performed with as much intrigue as the *ninja* can muster. This practitioner of the ancient art of *ninjutsu* has mastered all the martial arts, adding to his craft an element of sorcery that makes him lethal. That first day on the beach, as Nicholas reads the telltale signs on the corpse, he knows that there is a rampant, murdering *ninja* who will defy traditional western police investigation. The dominating conflict is set: Nicholas will have to find this man and give him a dose of his own medicine.

A rash of murders ensues, all with the unmistakable signs of the *ninja.* Doc Deerforth, the Long Island medical examiner who looks over the bodies, knows from his experience in the Philippines during World War II that he is up against no common criminal, and he informs Nicholas, as well as a New York City medical examiner, Vincent Ito, of his suspicions. The action shifts back to New York City, where

Nicholas goes when Terry Tanaka and Eileen Okura, owners of an establishment where resident Japanese can practice various forms of the martial arts, become the most recent victims. On his way to meet Lieutenant Croaker about their murders, Raphael Tompkin, Justine's father, picks up Nicholas. Raphael reveals information indicating that he is the ultimate object of the *ninja,* no doubt because of his shady business deals in Japan.

At various points the narrative is interrupted by flashbacks to Nicholas's adolescence in Japan, where he excels in martial arts. His parents had met in China, where his father was an influential military dignitary, and his mother, Cheong, is recovering from the war. By means of an emerald fortune inherited from her foster father, Cheong and the colonel are able to buy a comfortable house in Japan, to which Cheong has been drawn in a dream by Itami, the sister of Cheong's first husband. When the colonel and Cheong arrive in Japan, Itami, who has never seen either of them and has not received information about their arrival, is waiting for them.

Saigō, the son of Itami and Satsugai, becomes Nicholas's rival at the school for martial arts, where Nicholas spends years studying various disciplines. When Satsugai is threatened by his political rivals, the colonel, at Cheong's urging, intercedes to save him. But the two men, both in temperament and tradition, waste no love on each other, although Satsugai does not demonstrate the extent of his dislike because of his obligation to the colonel.

When Nicholas defeats Saigō in the equivalent of a final examination at the school, the latter is shamed and seeks revenge, both for himself and his father. He begins to study *ninjutsu,* and lures Nicholas and his girlfriend Yukio to the mountains, only to run away with her and physically humiliate Nicholas. Feeling vanquished on both fronts, a distraught Nicholas flees to America to begin a new life. It is shortly after his emigration that the narration of the novel begins. Saigō, having poisoned the colonel, contrives a plan to eliminate Nicholas, just as he has already killed Yukio.

Back in New York, Vincent and Doc become the latest victims, as Nicholas goes to work for Raphael to protect him. Up to the time that he is hired by Raphael, Nicholas has been in close contact with Lieutenant Croaker, hoping to educate him in the devious and unorthodox ways of the *ninja*. The two go through periods of mutual respect and reproach. Croaker, who by this time is all too aware that he is not up against a traditional urban psychopath, keeps looking for the clue that will break the case. But just as Nicholas has found himself torn between his love for Justine and his dislike for Raphael, Croaker finds himself caught between his professional desire to apprehend the *ninja* and his unmitigated hatred for Raphael.

Raphael has been implicated in a case Croaker has been working on for months, in which the famous model Angela Didion has been murdered. Feeling certain Raphael is the culprit, but keeping this hunch to himself, Croaker lacks conclusive evidence that would stand up in court. On the verge of securing the necessary proof through a surprise witness, he is unexpectedly pulled off the case. This action only increases his suspicion that someone with political influence, like Raphael, has indeed been involved.

At this point the various themes begin to converge, although their resolution remains elusive. Nicholas is motivated by a rekindled desire to defend his family's, as well as his own, honor using the skills he spent years acquiring. He realizes that Saigō is the *ninja* and that the attack on Raphael is merely a ploy to engage him in mortal combat. This battle is a continuation of the one their fathers fought. There is a lot at stake, and Nicholas, increasingly aware that time is running out before the *ninja* will strike his final blow, awaits the encounter with both confidence and trepidation.

In his efforts to pinpoint the *ninja's* attack, he neglects to detect one microphone in Raphael's car. This device represents Saigō's wild card, and just how he will play it will determine his chances of success.

Then the break comes. Raphael's other daughter, Gelda, is pulled into the police station for being at a party where drugs are confiscated. She provides the link that indicates where the *ninja* is living, and within hours, Nicholas and Croaker are attempting to ambush him. Croaker prevails on Nicholas to use the former's plan of entrapment, and the *ninja* escapes with ease.

This episode convinces Croaker to rely on Nicholas's judgment. Hours later, as Saigō stalks the office building teeming with policemen, Croaker lets Nicholas direct the operation. In a climactic ending, Saigō makes his way through bulletproof-vested policemen, leaving them strewn by the wayside like so many spent bullets, only to disappear into nowhere and return to meet the next adversary. Realizing that he has mere seconds in which to kill two men and unwilling to compromise his plan, he crashes through the plate glass window of the office, presumably falling to his death. After Nicholas leaves the office building with Raphael, their limousine ride is interrupted dramatically as Saigō bursts through the windshield. Saigō has saved himself by hiding on a window ledge after he jumped through the office window. In a dramatic sword fight in the streets of Manhattan, Nicholas vanquishes Saigō for the last time, decapitating him with a final blow.

With the major conflict resolved, few questions remain unanswered. Ever eager to prove Raphael a liar, Croaker embarks on a trip to

Florida in quest of the one elusive witness in the Didion case, disguising the trip as a vacation. Raphael offers to keep Nicholas on the payroll, but he declines, saying that he has had enough action for a while. But when he hears of Croaker's death in an accident in Florida, Nicholas recalls that one of Raphael's bodyguards had recently been sent there, and immediately the connection becomes clear. Outraged, he telephones Raphael and tells him he has decided to work for him after all. As the novel closes, the reader is confident that Croaker's death will be avenged.

As *The Ninja* approaches the climactic scene, the reader is aching for a dramatic ending, and author Van Lustbader provides a satisfactory outcome. He stimulates curiosity by never letting on just how much information about each other Nicholas and Saigō possess. Within the realm of intrigue Van Lustbader is able to maintain a tempo as well as a tension that keeps the reader involved until the last page.

The Ninja goes to great pains to give the reader sufficient cultural background to appreciate fully the motives and actions in this contemporary thriller. The contrast, however, between a moral Japan, where years are spent studying intangible concepts, and a materialistic United States, does not always enhance the drama on which the book thrives. Although central to the background of the drama, the Japanese interludes often seem to beg for the upbeat tempo of the present.

Van Lustbader shrouds his villain in satanic mystery and thereby endows the drama with a metaphysical dimension. The fact that one man is capable of superhuman tasks could not be presented plausibly were it not for this unique feature. Van Lustbader manages to conjure up a captivating creature who somehow straddles the line between the possible and the superhuman.

Cyrus Quinn, Jr.

THE OAK AND THE CALF

Author: Aleksandr I. Solzhenitsyn (1918–)
Publisher: Harper & Row (New York). 568 pp. $15.95
Type of work: Memoirs
Time: 1963–1974
Locale: The Soviet Union

Russian novelist Aleksandr I. Solzhenitsyn's account of his conflicts with the Soviet authorities and the official literary establishment over his right to publish his works freely within the Soviet Union

Principal personages:
> ALEKSANDR I. SOLZHENITSYN, Russian novelist, now living in exile in the United States
> ALEKSANDR TVARDOVSKY, Russian poet, journalist, and editor in chief of the prestigious Soviet literary journal *Novy Mir;* Solzhenitsyn's editor, friend, and patron

As writer and as a man, Aleksandr I. Solzhenitsyn has helped to change the course of history by serving the cause of truth and justice, by standing firm, by fighting unfalteringly against the forces of totalitarianism. Yet, Solzhenitsyn admits that he drifted into literature unthinkingly, writing in camps and exile, committing his words to memory. Without incarceration he might never have achieved greatness. In his latest book, *The Oak and the Calf,* Solzhenitsyn sets down for the record the chronicle of his emergence from underground to the luminous heights to which he has ascended.

In the camps, where a single line could have cost him his life, Solzhenitsyn began committing many thousands of lines of verse to memory by using beads and broken matchsticks as tallies. Soon he was writing down prose on scraps of paper, committing the words to memory, and destroying the incriminating evidence. At the end of his prison term, as much as one week per month was needed to recite his oeuvre from memory. After prison and the camps came exile and cancer. Solzhenitsyn's life reached its nadir when, in autumn 1953, he was told that his malignant tumor would kill him within three weeks. In a state of panic that his works would perish with him, Solzhenitsyn, working as a teacher and kept awake at night by pain, copied out all he had memorized on paper rolled into tight cylinders and squeezed into a champagne bottle that was then buried in his garden. Someday, he thought, the world will discover the contents of that bottle.

Miraculously, Solzhenitsyn survived his cancer, and the life that was given back to him was reinvigorated with a new sense of purpose. Living alone and writing out everything now without having to destroy it, Solzhenitsyn learned how to put manuscript pages on microfilm, which was then sent to Tolstoy's daughter, Aleksandra Lvovna Tolstoy, at her farm in the United States. When he was released from exile, Solzhenitsyn moved to Ryazan in Central Russia, where he taught mathematics, married, and continued his underground literary production. Writing in minute script on both sides of onion skin, he produced *One Day in the Life of Ivan Denisovich* and *The First Circle* as well as a film script, *Tanks Know the Truth,* during this period. Solzhenitsyn's writing meant that he had to adapt his entire life to the rigors of tight security, and he made certain that he heeded the advice of the Russian proverb: "The woodpecker could hide in the forest but for his beak."

For twelve years, Solzhenitsyn was a quiet but assiduous woodpecker, sustained by the belief that he and others like him writing underground, the former "zeks" (prisoners) intent on truth, were the true writers, the hope and salvation of Russian literature. Armed insurrection, he felt, could only bring disaster, but a solitary writer recording the truth of Stalin's death camps could breach the concrete wall of the Soviet regime. Isolation had its drawbacks, however, and chief among them was a feeling of suffocation and self-consumption. In 1960, Solzhenitsyn began to experience a compelling desire to air his works, a need to move around and stretch himself. Then came Khrushchev's Twenty-second Congress, in which Stalin was publicly vituperated. Winds of change were blowing across Russia, or so it seemed at the time, and Solzhenitsyn filled his lungs with air and swelled out his chest. He could breathe again, the time was right, and he was strong enough at the age of forty-three to come out from hiding and face the enemy in a hand to hand combat aboveground, without the need for subterfuge.

Solzhenitsyn decided to submit *One Day in the Life of Ivan Denisovich* to the prominent Soviet journal *Novy Mir* because of his personal admiration for its editor, the accomplished poet Aleksandr Tvardovsky. The manuscript was brought in by one of Solzhenitsyn's prison friends while Solzhenitsyn waited anxiously in a Moscow hotel. The manuscript reached Tvardovsky through the cleverness of an editorial assistant who thought the book spoke with the voice of Russia. Tvardovsky, a poet of peasant lineage, was sensitive to the voice of the Russian people, as was Khrushchev himself. In his hotel room, Solzhenitsyn fretted, not as a novice author but as a former prisoner who had informed against himself. In due course, however, *One Day in the Life of Ivan Denisovich* was published in a lightened version in *Novy Mir* with the sanction of the Kremlin. Solzhenitsyn, once the quiet woodpecker, had leaped irrevocably into the limelight of the Soviet political and literary arena.

Aleksandr Tvardovsky, the poet-editor of *Novy Mir,* was a man divided against himself. His profound inner conflict arose from the fact that his loyalty to the state was incompatible with his allegiance to Russian literature. Tvardovsky wept over Solzhenitsyn's book, but years of Communist party indoctrination prevented him from believing the book's implications. Solzhenitsyn had hoped for a friend and ally in Tvardovsky, but the man lived in fear of official censorship and rebuke, and the best he could do for Solzhenitsyn was to admonish him against antagonizing the top people in the regime. By allowing *Novy Mir* to publish *Ivan Denisovich,* Solzhenitsyn agreed to the magazine's right to a first reading of his subsequent works. This agreement ultimately led to the rift between Solzhenitsyn and his editor. When Tvardovsky refused to bring out *The First Circle* but submitted it to the Central Committee, which had in turn begun to circulate it without his approval, Solzhenitsyn decided to retaliate with his ultimate weapon—*samizdat,* or Russian-language publication in the West.

Solzhenitsyn's position was extremely precarious at this juncture. *Ivan Denisovich* had squeaked by the censors as a fluke—the Soviet regime's iron door of secrecy had opened an inch under Khrushchev but when Khrushchev toppled, the iron door shut tight again. From then on, Solzhenitsyn's only hope was to take the offensive, striking blow after blow without giving an inch, and his only weapon was samizdat publication and English translation in the West. Emboldened by the fact that time after time he had stuck his neck out and the axe had not fallen, Solzhenitsyn released *The First Circle* and then *Cancer Ward* to the West through clandestine channels. He also began working surreptitiously on his most potent explosive: the *Gulag Archipelago* books, the unglossed history of Stalin's camps. But Solzhenitsyn realized that he was playing with dynamite—*Gulag* was certain to wake the sleeping giant.

Why was the giant sleeping, especially since there was such a noisy woodpecker in the forest? With one eye open, the Soviet regime waited for Solzhenitsyn to advance further and further until the ice became so thin that he fell through, but Solzhenitsyn was too clever for them. He consolidated his position in the West by giving interviews to foreign correspondents. Whenever he was summoned before the Writers' Union, a secretariat, or a committee, he took notes, read prepared statements, and issued open letters and documents through samizdat that turned up the following day on the BBC and in Western newspapers. The Soviet bureaucracy seemed caught in a paralytic seizure. No one had ever stepped forward to do battle with them in this fashion. Their own tactic of removing Solzhenitsyn's sting by circulating his works in pirated editions had backfired—giving him justification for publishing his works abroad.

Aleksandr Tvardovsky, credited with discovering Solzhenitsyn, was to bear the brunt of the government's wrath. *Novy Mir* had become Tvardovsky's life blood, and when the government took away his magazine, they struck a fatal blow to his heart. Although Tvardovsky and Solzhenitsyn were ideological adversaries, they had shared many moments of triumph and despair. Without his beloved journal, Tvardovsky lost the will to live, and Solzhenitsyn made several valiant attempts to rescue him from gloom. Solzhenitsyn thought that Tvardovsky would be revived by an interest in his new work, *August 1914,* but by the time it was completed, Tvardovsky was too ill to appreciate it.

For ten years Solzhenitsyn had confounded his enemy, the state, but he now sensed that his immunity was wearing out. What he needed to do was to consolidate his position further. By 1973 he realized that without the protection of an international spotlight, he would be swallowed without a trace.

Solzhenitsyn was working on *August 1914* in seclusion in a restricted area at a dacha that belonged to the cellist and conductor Rostropovich, when the announcement came through that he had been awarded the Nobel Prize for Literature. The West had come through in the nick of time, for without the prize, Solzhenitsyn was sure he would have perished. Although Solzhenitsyn would have been allowed to leave Russia in order to attend the Nobel ceremonies, as was expected of him, he knew that once he left the country the way back would be forever barred. He did not mind expulsion, but he preferred to fight his cause at home—there was no honor, he felt, in abusing the regime from the safety of the West. The attention of the world was now focused on him. This was the moment to speak and tell the world the truth, but protocol intervened. The Nobel banquet was not the place to discuss politics. The furor died away, the Soviet facade remained unruffled, and Solzhenitsyn's life passed into a twilight zone.

Later that year, a nuclear physicist became a central figure in the dissident movement by holding a press conference in which he inveighed against the Soviet Union, calling it "one great concentration camp." Solzhenitsyn followed up the press conference with his *Letter to the Leaders.* A government crackdown turned up a copy of *Gulag,* spurring Solzhenitsyn in turn to release it immediately to the West. But the dissident movement lost its momentum when Andrei Sakharov announced his plans to emigrate to the United States.

Rumors now began to spread in Moscow that Solzhenitsyn would not be allowed to walk around much longer. Indeed, Solzhenitsyn began to feel the ground trembling beneath his feet. To their campaign of harassment, which included discrediting Solzhenitsyn abroad, slowing his divorce from his first wife, investigating his background, and slandering him in the press, the regime now added hate mail and obscene phone calls. During the course of a weekend in June 1974, he was visited by intelligence operatives twice, once in his country hideaway and once in his Moscow apartment. The first time they asked him questions, the second time they had orders to bring him along by force if necessary. Solzhenitsyn cooperated—he had his wife, children, and manuscripts to consider—he was told he would be back in an hour. He was taken to prison and treated well, but he knew that another prison sentence would kill him. All his works were in a repository in the West, many had been published, it was not a bad time to die, and he would rather die than give them any information that might cause others harm. But the next day he was driven to an airport, put on a plane, and flown to West Germany, where he was met by a welcoming committee including government officials, the press, and his friend and sponsor, the German writer Heinrich Böll. His wife and children joined him later in Switzerland.

The calf had butted the oak, and his horns were still intact.

Written in 1967, with supplements added that year, as well as in 1971, 1973, and 1974, *The Oak and the Calf* is an extraordinarily detailed account of Aleksandr Solzhenitsyn's struggle to speak the truth while preserving his life inside the world's most viciously totalitarian state. The exhaustive documentation includes an index, a glossary, textual notes, and an appendix of salient documents referred to in the text. More than a factual record of maneuvers and counter-maneuvers, *The Oak and the Calf* is full of life and drama and suspense. It is a robust literary memoir told with the unfailing command of a truly great novelist and a man worthy of unqualified admiration.

A.S. Maulucci

OFF CENTER

Author: Barbara Grizzuti Harrison
Publisher: The Dial Press (New York). 305 pp. $9.95
Type of work: Essays
Time: 1974–1979
Locale: United States

A collection of book reviews and essays, some autobiographical, all dealing with current and often controversial topics or figures

During the latter half of the 1970's, the essays of Barbara Harrison appeared regularly in American periodicals. Those ranged from the politically-oriented *The Nation* and *The New Republic* to the popular women's magazine *McCall's,* from *Ms.* to *Esquire.* Her book reviews appeared in *The Washington Post* and *The New York Times Book Review,* two leading establishment papers. Twenty of her best have been collected in this volume.

The diversity of the publications indicates the diversity of Harrison's topics. In *Off Center* she deals, among other subjects, with the emancipation of her adolescent son, women's lib, and Dick Cavett. She explores each with deep insight, bringing both sensitivity and sensibility to her subject. She sees them from the unique perspective of the reflective, rather than the reflexive, liberal. Harrison is never dogmatic, never rigid. She may be unorthodox, but she is never extreme. She avoids the fringe and remains, happily, only "off center."

The book is divided into four sections, beginning with that headed *Self and Others,* where the first essay is the poignant *"Write the Truth," My Son Said, "Write About Me."* Doing so, Harrison writes the truth about herself when she is faced with the boy's departure to spend a year in India with his father. She is painfully aware of her need for him—he has no such need for her—and is burdened with guilt at her possessiveness. It is the child who assumes the role of the adult, the son who comforts the mother.

In *Growing up Apocalyptic,* Harrison recalls her days as a member of the Jehovah's Witnesses, where her station was almost that of a servant, ministering to the domestic needs of the men in the group. She neatly sums up the sect in one sentence: "Because all their longing is for the future, they are bound to hate the present." *Going Home: Brooklyn Revisited,* in the same section, describes the author's return to her own high school, the scene of recent racial violence. Appalled by the prejudice of the instigators, she nevertheless can understand them, can even see the inherent goodness of those who do evil, those who, as she unhappily concludes, "have the courage of their contradictions."

Contradiction, paradox, ambivalence, these themes recur constantly. They are especially marked in the book's second section, *Feminism and Individuality,* where one of the essays is called *Moral Ambiguity.* It is a critique of Linda Bird Franke's book *The Ambivalence of Abortion.* In her essay Harrison addresses herself to the dilemma of those who cannot reconcile their dedication to the freedom of the individual with their abhorrence of abortion, those who can neither condone the act nor condemn its perpetrator. In another essay in this section, *Consciousness Raising: Truth and Consequences,* she describes her experiences with a group of women bent on that objective. Sometimes it was harrowing, but they succeeded because "we all used the group to grow up—to grow into ourselves." Finally, "Out of all that was bad, came so much good."

Because she has come to terms with the ambivalence in the human condition, Harrison has little patience with those like Adrienne Rich, whose *On Lies, Secrets and Silence* she reviews in her next chapter and whose ideas she considers parochial. It is bad enough that Rich is so enthralled with feminism that she can "contend that only women's concerns are of universal importance." It is worse that Harrison finds her "boring . . . and possibly corrupting . . . boring to hear witches praised . . . to read casual references to matriarchal societies . . . to hear more whining about ironing." With the sardonic wit that enlivens her writing throughout she adds, "Ms. Rich's excesses provoke me to my own: why the hell doesn't she just buy drip dry?"

The British writer Dorothy Sayers, the subject of another essay, is to Harrison "the most austerely intelligent, the wittiest, liveliest practitioner of the tidy art of detective fiction. . . ." Although Sayers died in 1957, before the feminist movement came into its own, her novels embody its principles. In the world Sayers created, men and women *were* equal. Moreover, they understood this. Lord Peter Wimsey, the protagonist of her most famous novels, is, says Harrison, "one man who does not believe that it is every woman's secret desire to be raped." Moreover, Harrison believes that Peter's "un*macho* character . . . is a calculated feminist statement," not just "a fortuitous artistic shot in the dark."

The final essay in this section is *A Troubled Peace,* a review of the collected letters of the American poet Louise Bogan, and a paean of praise to a courageous woman and an immensely talented writer. Never a cult figure, Bogan was plagued by poverty and was alone for much of her life; she suffered depressions so severe she was incapacitated. Yet her works and her letters shine with joy, with a spirit of "fun." Bogan inspires, says Harrison, something better than hero worship: she inspires love.

It is Marlon Brando (in an essay in the opening section of *Off Center*) who inspires hero worship. The hero worship largely results from Harrison's nostalgia for the 1950's, a period she still sees through starry eyes.

Nostalgia also colors Harrison's view of Roseland, the New York City dance hall frequented, in their salad days, by a host of celebrated dancers, and well into later life by the lonely and dispirited. *The Subject is Roseland,* one of five essays in the part called *Culture Heroes,* was prompted by a visit there to watch the making of a film. Prepared to scoff at it as camp, at the setting as kitsch, she discovers that the regulars find it a source of happiness, of fulfillment of their admittedly middle-class dreams, and is deeply touched by the revelation.

An interview with Dick Cavett is warm and amiable. He emerges as surprisingly profound—the eminent philosopher Paul Weiss was his teacher at Yale—with a wit "both playful and bleak." Characterizing him as "gentle, sensitive," Harrison writes a gentle, sensitive piece, liberally sprinkled with samples of Cavett's own brand of humor.

Jane Fonda, though, fares less well at Harrison's hands. She is a mass of inconsistencies, an aristocrat pretending to be plebeian, a superstar playing the role of housewife—she ostentatiously washes her own dishes, carries out the garbage—a political activist who is condescending. In Harrison's eyes, she is a phony. But Harrison reserves her sharpest barbs for the writer Joan Didion. "She makes it a point of honor not to struggle for meaning," she says of Didion's writing: "her 'style' is a bag of tricks." Although Didion is the antithesis of Adrienne Rich, and almost antifeminist, she, too, "whines." Harrison's major complaint is that Didion "refuses to forge connections between the personal and the political, the personal and the transcendental." Consequently, making no social commitment, "she reduces politics to personalities." As to her politics, Harrison says, "let us at once call her a reactionary." This essay, *Only Disconnect,* is devastating.

In the fourth section, *Panaceas,* Harrison looks at cults—est, the Moonies, and such purveyors of salvation as Billy Graham and Bernard Lefkowitz, author of *Breaktime: Living Without Work in a Nine-to-Five World.* Lefkowitz promotes something akin to welfare chiseling, getting something at the expense of others. Graham uses his religious position only to serve the powerful and wealthy; he is the ultimate hypocrite. As for est, it is both "silly and sinister . . . as if the Wizard of Oz had set up business in Dachau and invited victims to pay . . ." The Reverend Moon's Unification Church also degrades: Harrison's description of the Helander family whose daughter, Wendy, was caught up in it, is as heartfelt as it is heart-breaking.

The book concludes with a short section, *Final Things,* consisting of two essays. *The Profound Hypochondriac* is a light-hearted account of Harrison's own ongoing bout with hypochondria, compounded, she says of "guilt and grief and narcissism." And *The Facts of Life and Death* is both a review of the book *The View in Winter* and a loving tribute to its author, Ronald Blythe. He has treated the subject of aging —and of dying—with such lucidity, such compassion, and with such profound insights that Harrison calls the book a "treasure" and predicts that it is "bound to become a classic." So sure is she of this that she compares the book to Muriel Spark's *Memento Mori,* its fictional counterpart.

Barbara Harrison is a superb writer; wise, witty, often wonderful. She is a master of the felicitous phrase; on every page there is a line, a description, a comment that delights. Her work, though, is far from being merely clever. Her subjects may be controversial, but they are never shallow. She is a person concerned with the welfare of her fellow human beings and with the matters that touch them, that change their lives. Harrison is both a passionate defender of freedom and a champion of human rights.

Barbara Harrison's essays are far more subjective than most; she is more involved personally and is more emotional than other writers. She is alternately gentle and sardonic, tender and trenchant, even sentimental and scathing. Incensed by some affront to the dignity of man —or, more likely, of woman, although she would deny this—she lays about her with a pen until the enemy is demolished. Stumbling upon a pure and snow-white soul, she is overwhelmed with admiration and has the ability to make most readers share it. Those who find her viewpoint inimical to theirs will nevertheless find Barbara Harrison thought-provoking. They, too, should find *Off Center* pure pleasure.

Vivian Werner

THE OLD NEIGHBORHOOD

Author: Avery Corman
Publisher: The Linden Press/Simon & Schuster (New York). 219 pp. $10.95
Type of work: Novel
Time: 1944–1980
Locale: The Bronx and Manhattan, New York City; California

Steven Robbins, a self-made success in advertising who is not happy with his life, returns to his old neighborhood in The Bronx to find contentment

> *Principal characters:*
> STEVEN ROBBINS, an advertising man
> BEVERLY, his wife
> SARAH and AMY, their daughters
> BERNARD ROBBINS, Steven's father
> SYLVIA ROBBINS, Steven's mother
> GEORGE and CINDY HILLMAN, Beverly's parents
> SAM GOODSTEIN, the neighborhood bookie
> RAY TOLCHIN, Steven's partner

The Old Neighborhood is the story of Steven Robbins' journey from an unpromising and unpretentious childhood in The Bronx to success in California and Manhattan, then back again to The Bronx in quest of what went wrong with his life along the way.

In the 1940's life for Stevie and his pals seems good despite World War II. He realizes that his parents do not get along, but they stay together because divorce is simply unthinkable. His father is a mediocre salesman who is not aggressive enough, and his mother does not get a job because women do not work. Instead she concentrates her hopes for better things on her son.

The 1950's find Stevie interested in basketball and girls, but with no clear idea of his future. It is drummed into him that he must have some plans, and he finally settles on getting a business degree at City College of New York. There he manages to fulfill his dream of losing his virginity as well as his parents' of a college education. However, he soon finds that New York advertising agencies are bastions of Ivy League graduates. There are no jobs for him. When he finally does secure a job in advertising, it involves a move to California, the end of the earth as far as his parents are concerned.

In California he meets and marries Beverly Hillman, whose father George owns a ranch and whose speech is sprinkled with incredibly garbled Yiddish words. This is not the kind of Jew Stevie is used to. He and Beverly have two daughters and seem to be the perfect family. While he is in California Stevie's mother dies, and his father remarries. His new wife is a rich widow, and together they become globe-trotting senior citizens.

Meanwhile, Beverly has begun to feel restless. She has a useless degree in art history and no way to apply it until she comes up with the idea of starting a children's art playgroup in her home. When a tempting bid from a New York ad agency brings Steve and his family back to the East Coast, Bevvy transplants her playgroup idea to Long Island.

Things appear to be going remarkably well for the Robbins family. Their daughters are growing up into beautiful women. Bevvy's playgroup thrives and escalates into a full-fledged school. Steve earns many awards for creativity in advertising and goes on to establish his own agency in partnership with Ray Tolchin. In terms of success both of the Robbinses seem to be doing very well.

Yet, underlying the financial success story there is a price that both of them must pay. Their separate interests are pulling them apart. They no longer confer about major decisions regarding money, or, for that matter, anything else. He has no time to share her triumphs, nor does she have time any more to accompany him to award banquets. Little by little their jobs erode their marriage until the only thing they share apart from the children is a common mailing address.

Marriage counseling does not help, and in any case they do not have the time to spend on it. Bevvy announces she wants a separate vacation to think things over and try to find herself. When Steve jokingly says he is relieved that at least she is not running off to have an affair, Bevvy admits that she has had "an episode."

Disgusted with life and with himself, alone in the house for the summer while Bevvy is on Montauk and the girls away at camp, Steve begins to go to pieces. The dishonesty of "good business" advertising has depressed him, particularly his latest client, who wants to capitalize on the homosexual market by creating fragrances especially for gays. Steve decides to take a leave from his own agency.

Something compels Steve to return to his old neighborhood before he suffers an actual nervous breakdown. The train from Long Island and the subway ride to The Bronx become his time machine. He finds the old neighborhood changed, but not too severely. Although now ringed by other, disintegrating neighborhoods, Steve's old turf remains about the same.

As a kind of rehabilitation therapy, Steve starts jogging and playing playground basketball—his old love—to get back into physical shape. He shuns the ad agency to help the owner of a foundering candy store. Charity alone does not motivate him; it is the very soda shop where he once created the perfect egg cream in the lost years of his youth. From president of his own ad agency to soda jerk, it is a backward step in some people's eyes, but for Steve it means salvation.

Tolchin, Steve's partner, is shocked at the way Steve is spending his summer. He is more shocked when Steve declares he wants to leave the agency. Steve's daughters are embarrassed by their father's shenanigans, plaintively wondering how they will ever explain such an unchic aberration to their friends. Their mother is just as dumbstruck as the rest. She agrees to accompany Steve on a tour of the old neighborhood, to try to understand what has drawn him there again after all these years. He squires her through his reconquered realm, shows her the soda shop, the men's baseball team from the local bar who have accepted him, even presents her to old Sam Goodstein, who has been the neighborhood bookie since the days of Steve's glory on the DeWitt Clinton High basketball team.

Every therapy must end when the patient is cured. Steve has gotten on his feet again and is ready to re-enter life. He does not go back into advertising, however, deciding to turn his love for things of the past into a new business. He opens an antique shop in Manhattan and calls it, appropriately enough, The Old Neighborhood. It specializes in memorabilia of the 1930's and 1940's, with items displayed in a home-like setting, the homes Steve fondly remembers. He faces his divorce calmly, maintains good terms with his ex-wife, continues to enjoy the love of his daughters, who find an antique dealer more acceptable than a soda jerk, and begins to make a few tentative steps into a new social life. Anchored in relics that symbolize the security of his childhood, Steve Robbins is no longer afraid that the world and life are slipping between his fingers.

In *The Old Neighborhood,* Avery Corman uses Steven Robbins as the symbol of the confusion and sense of nameless loss besetting so many people today. They have gone forth and conquered the worlds of fame and fortune. Their families are everything the press tells them a modern family should be. For all that, the day comes when they find their carefully planned lives crumbling and their diligently won goals worthless.

Through Steve, Corman attempts to offer one solution to the problems of living. It is not enough to treat the symptoms, as with ordinary counseling. Going back in time, in an almost Freudian manner, may identify when and where things started to go wrong. When did lives, so perfectly regulated in childhood, begin to get out of control? Whether or not living out fantasies of nostalgia is a cure-all must remain a subjective matter. Corman offers a very persuasive argument in favor of going back to the days when America fought the good fight for a clear reason, if only because the society of that time gave her children clear-cut roles to follow, freeing the individual from responsibility.

There is, Corman implies, a price that must sooner or later be paid for today's wider opportunities. A couple like Steve's parents need not suffer through years of unhappy marriage together, but divorce should not become too easy a solution for every small marital difficulty. A woman can work and make her own career as meaningful as that of her husband, but her marriage may suffer for it. There is no longer a social barrier to be crossed if a poor boy from The Bronx wants success in business, but he must be prepared to deal with the unsavory aspects of his success.

Fortunately *The Old Neighborhood* does not end with its hero permanently ensconced in his childhood world. What he has gained from his trip back in time might appear to be a desire to live forever in the past, but Robbins' situation at the end of the book is more complicated than that. He has not brought back an entire lost world, but only gleaned things of solid, durable value from it. Furthermore he has learned that the very word *value* has more meaning to it than in his simple dreams of financial success. The 1960's put forward the concept that youth is the only answer; the 1970's preached the gospel of fulfilling the self at any price. Perhaps what Robbins has ultimately found is that the real value of each individual life should not come from the prevailing popular causes and catchwords of a decade, but from within. No longer seeking to justify his life in terms of what is currently acceptable to society, yet not rejecting society either, Steven Robbins has found his own kind of happiness.

Esther M. Friesner

THE ORIGIN

Author: Irving Stone (1903–)
Publisher: Doubleday and Company (Garden City, N.Y.). 743 pp. $14.95
Type of work: Novel
Time: 1831–1882
Locale: England, route of the *Beagle* through the Southern Hemisphere

Biographical novel of the life of Charles Darwin, who challenged the foundations of Victorian confidence in a stable, unchanging nature by proposing the theory of evolution and natural selection

Principal personages:
> CHARLES DARWIN (1809–1882), father of evolutionary biology
> EMMA WEDGWOOD, his wife and first cousin
> REV. JOHN HENSLOW, Professor of Botany at Cambridge University
> CHARLES LYELL, father of modern geology
> JOSEPH HOOKER, botanist best known for studies of plant geography
> THOMAS HUXLEY, zoologist and paleontologist
> ALFRED WALLACE, botanist who, independent of Darwin, developed the theory of evolution and natural selection

In 1859, when *On the Origin of the Species by Means of Natural Selection* was published in London, the book was denounced in Sunday sermons, hotly debated in scientific journals, and, according to one astute observer, was "feverishly discussed over the dinner tables of Great Britain by those who had never read a line."

This uproar was over a remarkably clear, precise, and logical piece of thinking by a well-published, award-winning natural scientist, Charles Darwin. He proposed that the environment determines what species of life will survive or die in each generation of plants and animals, that species must continually change in adaptation to the environment and that by doing so will eventually evolve into new species. Darwin had proposed the theory of evolution and natural selection.

The theory challenged the existing Victorian view of the world: unchanging, benevolent, and most important, with man in control. Catastrophism, the official scientific doctrine, satisfied a number of prickly religious questions by explaining that the earth changed only through episodic cataclysms, followed by tranquility and creation of new life. But the last cataclysm, according to the doctrine, was the biblical forty days' flood. Since that time no new life had been created, destroyed, or changed. Life was immutable.

Darwin, who had trained for the clergy, assumed the role of scientific gladiator reluctantly. He was born in 1809, into a prosperous, intellectually curious family of five children. His father, Robert Darwin, was a popular physician. His grandfather, Erasmus Darwin, had also been a physician, a scientist, and a poet with some highly speculative theories of his own about evolution. Darwin's mother, Susanah Wedgwood, who died when he was eight, was the daughter of the famous potter Josiah Wedgwood.

As a child, Darwin was labeled a slow learner by his teachers. He was usually out collecting bugs rather than conjugating Latin verbs. Later, at the University of Edinburgh, where he was sent to study medicine, Darwin fell asleep in anatomy lectures and sickened at the sight of operations. He next studied theology at Cambridge, spending every possible moment with geology professor Adam Sedgwick and botany professor John Henslow. These two professors, who became his mentors, nurtured his untrained interest in natural history, teaching him species identification and classification. Since the natural sciences were only tolerated at Cambridge as a part of a gentleman's education, however, Darwin's career prospects at his graduation in 1831 were directed toward a quiet parish, Sunday sermons, and his avocation, bug collecting.

However, John Henslow had other plans for him. When Darwin returned home Henslow arranged for him to travel as the unpaid naturalist aboard the H.M.S. *Beagle,* a British Admiralty exploratory vessel, for an expedition to South America, the South Seas, and the Indian Archipelago. Armed with Alexander von Humboldt's travel narratives, and Cambridge Professor Charles Lyell's *Principles of Geology,* an innovative new book claiming that the earth was in continuous change, gradually but constantly reshaping the continents, Darwin settled in Plymouth, England, to wait for the *Beagle* to be refitted for her second voyage to the Southern Hemisphere. The *Beagle* sailed for the South American coast December 27, 1831.

The ports were a panorama of contrasts. Tenerife in the Canary Islands and Brazil's Rio de Janeiro, with brightly colored houses and gaily dressed people, are juxtaposed against the volcanic desolation of St. Jago, a mid-Atlantic island, and the crudely painted faces of the Fuegan tribes of Tierra del Fuego at the southern tip of the continent. As the *Beagle* meandered up and down the South American coast for the next several years, charting previously unexplored waters and rechecking nautical calculations, Darwin made frequent expeditions into the interior. He penetrated the Brazilian forest of Tucans and bee eaters, collecting hundreds of specimens, including a sample from a conical ants' nest 12 feet high. He rode with the gauchos across the Argentine pampas into southern Patagonia, collecting variations of the rhea (ostrich) and armadillo. Although he was bitten, stung, poisoned by an Indian wine called "chichi," and frequently seasick, he managed to collect thousands of specimens, mounting insects and plants, skinning birds, dissecting reptiles and marine animals for shipment back to England.

In May 1834 the *Beagle* crossed to the Pacific Ocean, docking at Valparaiso, Chile. In an expedition to the Andean Cordilleras, north of Valparaiso, Darwin found evidence that Lyell's theory of continual geological change was correct. He found trees thousands of feet in the Andes that carried remnants of ocean fossils. Later, in the Galápagos Islands, amid the giant tortoises and thousands of reptiles piled five and six deep, he found more evidence that the species were not immutable, that species varied even within areas of identical climate and physical characteristics. Local inhabitants told him that they could tell by sight from which of the Galápagos Islands each tortoise had come.

When the *Beagle* returned to Plymouth in October 1836, Darwin at 26 found himself a bit of a celebrity. His letters to John Henslow about the geology of South America had been read before the Cambridge Philosophical Society, and his thousands of priceless specimens were the talk of the London scientific clubs. Eminent naturalists like Richard Owen and John Gould were eager to write commentary for a five volume series of books on Darwin's zoological specimens that were to be published with a grant from the British Treasury. Darwin was also asked to abstract for publication not only his geological and botanical notebooks but his personal travel diary as well.

In 1839 he began a 43 year marriage to his first cousin Emma Wedgwood that would produce 10 children. With a pension from his mother's estate and the consent of his father to abandon a career in the Church of England, Darwin devoted his time to research and writing. Although plagued by frequent debilitating attacks of nausea and lassitude, which eventually forced a move from London to the quiet countryside of Downe, in Kent, Darwin read insatiably, recording his thoughts in a series of notebooks he called "Transmutation of the Species." In 1842 he had outlined his theory of evolution, and by 1844 he had completed a documented essay. Then he tucked it away to devote the next eight years to a study of barnacles that was published between 1851 and 1854. Although he never planned to publish his theory of the species, his plans changed when he read an article in 1855 by a young naturalist, Alfred Wallace, who, like Darwin, had drawn upon the theories of economist Thomas Malthus. Malthus had calculated that man would increase faster than the available food supply unless held in check. Applying the principle to plants and animals, Darwin and Wallace independent of each other had reasoned that some system of natural selection holds all species in check.

With the advice from his close friends, Charles Lyell, whom Darwin had met shortly after the *Beagle* voyage, and two younger scientists, botanist Joseph Hooker and zoologist Thomas Huxley, he set out to expand his essay for publication. Three years later, Darwin was still completing documentation for his work, which had now become book length, when Wallace sent him a completed monograph for review. Wallace's theory, although not as well documented, was identical to Darwin's. In June 1858, the work of Darwin and Wallace was presented at the annual meeting of the Linnean Society, a group devoted to the study of botany. The audience clapped politely and went home. The next year, *On the Origin of the Species* appeared in bookstores, and the furor began.

It was not until a decade later that Darwin completed the trilogy on evolution and natural selection. He published *The Descent of Man, and Selection in Relation to Sex* (1871), reminding his readers that he did not claim that man descended from apes, only that man's ancestors would be classified as primates, probably lower on the scale than apes. In 1872 he published *The Expression of Emotions in Man and Animals.* Darwin's sequels were prompted by his severe disappointment in both Charles Lyell and Alfred Wallace, who had published defenses exempting man from the evolutionary pattern.

Although Darwin will always be remembered as the architect for evolutionary biology, his geological and botanical research established new fields of study. In geology, he linked volcanic action and earthquakes to the formation of the Andes and the reshaping of the South American continent; he developed a new theory about coral reefs, presenting evidence from his *Beagle* journey that coral reefs were built on receding underwater mountain ranges, not rims of volcanoes as once believed. In botany, his studies of cross breeding and pollination established the link in generations of heredity. His study of plant growth patterns established the existence of growth hormones and plant sensitivity to light, leading to the future research of tropisms. His last study, completed with his son Francis, documented the fertilization and aeration of the soil by earthworms.

Darwin died in 1882, and despite the objections of numerous outraged citizens, he was buried in Westminster Abbey. At his death, Darwin had only begun to shake the foundations of Victorian religious and scientific certainties.

In its 731 pages *The Origin* provides enough ground for a candid look at Darwin, a survey of his ideas, and a historical scan of the Victorian mentality that so vehemently rejected his theories. Despite author Irving Stone's use of ample anecdotes and of a vigorous cinematic technique following Darwin from early manhood to his death, too much ground lies fallow. Darwin's observations on geology, zoology, and botany from the *Beagle* voyage are fragmented and difficult to connect to the eventual development of his theory of evolution and natural selection. His relationship to Alfred Wallace, with whom he corresponded for many years, is only touched upon, and Darwin as a character is never fully developed in the novel. He remains a stiff, two-dimensional figure who seems to walk and talk as if he were reading from cue cards.

Darwin is an ideal character for a biographical novel, and there is a great deal of information to draw upon. Numerous biographies have already been written about him. There is a rich assortment of geological, zoological, and botanical studies, as well as Darwin's travel journals, filled with perceptive, even poetic, observations. There is also *Darwin by Darwin,* an autobiography with additional letters, compiled by his son Francis. The autobiography was written for the amusement of his grandchildren and never intended for publication.

Irving Stone is the author of eleven biographical novels, four biographies, and assorted works for young people. His books are well researched and meticulously detailed, and they have both extensive and authoritative bibliographies. For *The Origin,* Stone has consulted the most respected sources on Darwin. What seems to be missing, however, is the full measure of the man, his humor and humility. Stone carefully provides endless linear and angular measurements, but they do not adequately delineate the whole spirit of Darwin or his age. Darwin's recurring illness is treated as the complaint of a hypochondriac with no indication that Darwin's nausea and intestinal problems might have been caused by the Argentine Benchuca bug (which was known to have bitten him) causing the disease Chagas. The antics of Darwin's sloppy maid Bessy are given importance equal to his agonies over the development of his theories. Stone is, to quote an A. E. Housman phrase, "a very democratic author. He gives no phrase preference over another."

Uninitiated readers who embark on this Darwinian journey should first consult an encyclopedia or biographical dictionary for a brief summary of his life and accomplishments. It will make the trek a little easier. For those who know Darwin's life, are familiar with his theories and studies, and are in the market for an easy reading novel, *The Origin* is good entertainment.

Martha Paddick

THE PANDA'S THUMB

Author: Stephen Jay Gould
Publisher: W.W. Norton and Company (New York). 343 pp. $12.95
Type of work: Essays

A collection of scientific essays covering various aspects of Darwin's theory of evolution; including its history, current form, and bearing on the natural world

The publication of *The Origin of Species* in 1859 rocked the scientific world, forcing thinkers in nearly all branches of knowledge to reexamine their most basic assumptions. Today, over a century later, Darwin's legacy forms one of the chief theoretical foundations of modern science. In *The Panda's Thumb,* Stephen Jay Gould—professor, critic, and advocate—reviews the history and current state of evolutionary theory and shows how it has organized our understanding of life on earth.

The Panda's Thumb consists of 31 essays loosely organized into 8 sections. The first section defines his major theme—that the most convincing proofs of evolution are not found in its most elegant syntheses of animal form and function, but instead in its half-solutions, its opportunistic second guesses, its tendency to make do with whatever materials are available, no matter how clumsy or inappropriate. He recalls a visit to the Washington Zoo, where he saw a Chinese panda strip a bamboo shoot of its leaves by drawing it between its paw and its thumb. Pandas eat nothing but bamboo shoots. However, this operation should have been impossible for a panda or for any kind of bear, because they all belong to the order Carnivora, a group of meat-eating mammals whose forelimbs are adapted for running, scratching, and clawing; the opposable thumb is an exclusive feature of the higher primates. Looking more closely, he saw that the panda had five claws in addition to its thumb. Therefore the thumb could not be a thumb at all, in the strict anatomical sense, since all mammalian paws share the same original five-toed design. So where did it come from? A search of the scientific literature yielded an answer.

The panda's thumb is actually a wrist bone that has been strengthened and enlarged to function as an extra finger. At some point in the evolutionary past the panda abandoned a meat diet and turned to bamboo as the chief food source. The need to strip the shoots of their leaves favored the development of an opposable digit. Thus, the animal acquired something very much like a thumb without resorting to the conventional method of modifying the first finger.

A divine creator, the author asserts, would not have settled for such an obviously improvised arrangement. But, in biologist Francoise Jacob's words, "Nature is an excellent tinkerer, not a divine artificer." The most important fact about the panda's thumb, in an evolutionary sense, is that it works. In the first section the author also examines sea turtles, orchids, and anglerfish as further examples of design by adaptation rather than adaptation by design.

This movement from fact to research to theory and back again continues throughout *The Panda's Thumb*. In the second section Gould distinguishes Darwin's system from those of some of his well-known precursors and disciples, such as John Baptiste Lamarck, the French biologist who recognized the fact of evolution decades before Darwin but believed mistakenly that it proceeded by the inheritance of acquired characteristics; or Alfred Russell Wallace, the young naturalist who independently developed the key idea of natural selection while recovering from malaria in Indonesia and whose letter to Darwin finally persuaded the timid genius to publish his conclusions. The modern idea of kin selection and Richard Dawkin's controversial book *The Selfish Gene* are also discussed.

The third section, devoted to human evolution, opens with a whimsical discussion of the transformation of Mickey Mouse from the long-nosed, ratty character of his early movies to the cuddly mouse of today. Along the way it incorporates both Lorenz's ideas about biological releasers and the important concept of neoteny, or evolution through progressive infantilization, of which the human race is a notable example. In the following essay Gould reviews the notorious Piltdown Man hoax and uncovers a possible new conspirator—the young Teilhard de Chardin, who later became well known for his efforts to reconcile evolution and Christianity.

Scientific villains, charlatans, and bigots dominate the next section. The author shows how Darwin's ideas were used to give a scientific patina to racist and sexist prejudices. Paul Broca, 19th-century founder of the Paris Anthropological Society, tried to prove the innate intellectual superiority of white men over women, non-Europeans, and apes by weighing innumerable brains he acquired from the Paris morgue. His prize piece of evidence was the cerebral remains of the great French taxonomist Baron Cuvier, which weighed in at a massive 1,830 grams. Broca's American follower, E.A. Spitzka, had trouble supporting the correspondence between large brains and large minds when Walt Whitman came in at a below average 1,282 grams.

Although evolution is the reigning scientific hypothesis concerning the origin of species, biologists do not agree on the rate at which it occurs. One group maintains that most changes occur slowly and deliberately as populations adapt to changing environments, while their opponents argue for long periods of relative stasis interrupted by short intervals of abrupt and rapid change. In the fifth section Gould summarizes the debate and places himself in the second group, basing his position on the evidence of the fossil record, which is rich in individual species but poor in transitional forms, or "missing links"—this, he asserts, is the "trade secret of paleontology." He expands his argument to include a history of the geological debate concerning the vast, eroded scablands of western Washington State, which were thought to be the result of thousands of years of erosion until aerial photographs confirmed J. Harlen Bretz's theory of a catastrophic Ice Age flood.

Sections six and seven focus on two difficult evolutionary questions: the first appearance of multicellular life and the place of dinosaurs on the evolutionary tree. Gould introduces the latest fossil finds and describes their impact on current ideas. In the process he illuminates a number of recent discoveries. For instance, primitive microbes have been found in rocks 3.4 billion years old. The oldest rocks known are only 400 million years older. Therefore, life has been present on earth for most of its history, and it existed in one-celled form for 3 billion years before the relatively recent appearance of more complex forms 400 million years ago. It is also slightly disturbing to learn that dinosaurs are still common in the modern world—they have feathers and are called birds.

The last section is devoted to aspects of scale in the living world. There is a direct correlation among size, heartbeat, and longevity; the larger the animal, the slower its heart rate, and the longer its lifespan. A species of marine bacteria demonstrates how evolution takes advantage of physical laws. Since an individual bacterium has almost zero mass, it is much too small to orient itself in relation to gravity. However, this particular species has evolved the ability to construct tiny iron magnets within itself. In the northern hemisphere, where the species occurs, the earth's magnetic lines of force have a vertical component, and the bacteria might use them to find their way down to the sea bottom, their preferred environment. This, at least, is a plausible hypothesis. The researchers know that these organic magnets exist; they are not yet sure what the bacteria do with them.

The final essay strays from biology into a discussion of the slowing of the earth's rotation caused by the friction of the tides. Physicists have determined that the average solar year lasted almost four hundred days in the prehistoric past. Paleontologists working with daily growth lines in fossil corals have found evidence to support this view. Apparently the tiny animals were keeping time with the sun 370 million years ago. As Gabriel said to Mary at the Annunciation, "For with God nothing shall be impossible." What does the Virgin have to do with

Darwin's theory? In Gould's words, "we resort to metaphor and image to emphasize just how long the earth has existed and just how insignificant the length of human evolution has been—not to mention the cosmic millimicrosecond of our personal lives."

All the essays in *The Panda's Thumb* originally appeared in *Natural History* magazine. The main difficulty in making a book out of a group of essays is that the repetition of a single, unvarying form at length can produce an effect of sameness; the reader will wish that some entries were longer and that others had been dropped entirely. *The Panda's Thumb* avoids this episodic, mechanical rhythm because all the essays revolve around a single idea—the theory of evolution. Each part is devoted to the elaboration of the whole. Certain ideas recur in different settings—the necessary distinction between homologous and analogous adaptation, for instance, or the various approaches to the problem of systematic taxonomy, or the definition of a species. These unifying themes contribute to a sense of a coherent purpose that transcends the boundaries of each essay. Together, they amount to a tour of the biological world, a critical history of a powerful idea, and a quick rehearsal of more than 3 billion years of planetary history.

Gould is a versatile scholar and combines a gift for apt quotation with the ability to draw from other disciplines—literature, philosophy, and economics in particular. In his prologue he promises to explain why evolution cannot be identified with progress in nature, but he never addresses the subject directly again. This is a noticeable loss since this topic is both crucial and fascinating. He also has an annoying habit of concluding his essays, on occasion, with a glib, aphoristic generalization. But anyone with an interest in natural history who reads this book will hope that he writes another soon.

Thomas Palmer

PETER THE GREAT

Author: Robert K. Massie
Publisher: Alfred A. Knopf (New York). 909 pp. $17.95
Type of work: Biography
Time: 1672–1725
Locale: Europe, particularly Russia and Eastern Europe

A biography of Peter the Great, the incomparable autocrat whose ruthless program of military, administrative, and economic modernization transformed Russia into a formidable power and altered permanently the international power structure in Europe

Principal personages:
PETER THE GREAT, Tsar and, after 1721, Emperor of Russia
SOPHIA, Peter's half-sister, regent until 1689
EUDOXIA, Peter's first wife
FRANCIS LEFORT, Swiss adventurer and officer, until his death in 1699, Peter's closest friend
WILLIAM OF ORANGE, Stadholder of Holland and William III of England, Peter's boyhood military hero
CHARLES XII, King of Sweden and Peter's antagonist in the Northern War
CATHERINE, Peter's second wife and, as Empress Catherine I, his successor
ALEXIS, Peter's son by Eudoxia and heir apparent

Peter was born on June 9, 1672, the son of the second wife of Tsar Alexis. His early childhood and perhaps his personality itself were profoundly influenced by the fierce power struggle that broke out after his half-brother, Tsar Fedor III, died in 1682. Against Peter and his mother were arrayed the family of Alexis' first wife, who intended to put Peter's half-brother, the sickly, feeble-minded Ivan, on the throne. Because he was both healthy and intelligent, the ten-year-old Peter was proclaimed tsar, provoking a furious uprising that ended only after several of Peter's maternal relatives and their adherents had been hacked to pieces within the palace itself. Peter and Ivan were then declared co-rulers, but power passed into the hands of Peter's half-sister Sophia, who became regent. Peter was shunted aside and allowed to grow up away from the court.

As a child Peter early displayed those traits that were later to distinguish him: a love of all things military, immense physical strength and energy coupled to a restless need for action, and a deep interest in and aptitude for manual crafts. During his adolescence he formed play regiments manned by his retinue and engaged in military drills and mock sieges. Quickly growing to his exceptional height of six feet, seven inches, he taught himself carpentry, masonry, and metalworking. When he was fifteen, he discovered an old English sailboat and became obsessed with sailing, a passion that would lead to the founding of the Russian Navy and the conquest of ports on the Baltic.

In 1689, Peter was married by his mother's arrangement to Eudoxia in order to produce an heir and undermine Sophia's power. False rumors of another uprising precipitated the inevitable confrontation between Peter and Sophia, whom he deposed and had locked up in a convent. Peter was effectively in power, but at seventeen he was content to let his relatives govern. He also deepened his knowledge of European ways by carousing, drinking prodigiously, and smoking with his European friends living near Moscow in the German Settlement.

Peter's military career and his personal reign began in earnest in 1695, when war between Russia and Turkey broke out. He participated in the first campaign by land against the fortress at Azov that prevented Russia from entering the Sea of Azov. After the Russians were repulsed, Peter rebounded immediately, constructed a fleet of war galleys on the Don, and succeeded in conquering the fortress in 1696. He then began the construction of a naval fleet and organized a diplomatic mission to secure European allies against the Turks.

Peter's "Grand Embassy" (1697–1698) was one of the most significant episodes in his reign. Although the mission failed to find allies for a Turkish war, it enabled Peter, as well as the more than 200 Russians he took with him, to see at first hand the commercial, technological, and administrative basis of the power of European states. Peter had, of course, already sensed the need to reform his government, modernize the army, and create a navy, but the months he spent actually training as a shipwright in Dutch and English shipyards, visiting workshops and arsenals, talking to scientists and craftsmen, dissecting cadavers, and learning to pull teeth had a galvanic effect on his resolve to remake his country. But before he completed his planned journey he was called back by a revolt.

By the time Peter returned to Moscow in the summer of 1698, the revolt had already been put down. Those rebels who had not been executed on the battlefield were in prison. Peter was nevertheless convinced that his old rivals had fomented the rebellion and that his throne would be insecure until he had discovered and destroyed the conspirators. None were found, despite weeks of torture that was judged unprecedentedly ferocious even by Russian standards. Peter himself was present at many of the gory examinations, and when the public executions finally began ordered some of his high officials to wield the executioner's axe. In all more than a thousand were tortured, mutilated, and executed, and many more were exiled.

Even this horrible repression was not enough to deter Peter from his program of reform. Immediately upon his return, he forbade the wearing of beards and subjected those unfortunate nobles within his reach when he made the announcement to a painful shave. He also directed that all officials adopt western dress. The traditional Russian New Year was abandoned for the European. As Peter himself said, these dramatic measures were designed "to sever the people from their former Asiatic customs." He also began the reorganization of local administration and the collection of taxes.

At the same time, he resumed his diplomatic and military designs. He turned his attention to the Baltic coast, then held by Charles XII of Sweden, the commander of an army that many believed invincible. The Northern War (1700–1721) was the great military drama of Peter's reign and his defeat of Charles a crucial turning point in Russian and European history. At first Peter was badly beaten at Narva in 1700 but, again displaying his indomitable will and immense energy, he worked, he later recalled, "night and day" to create an army along European lines and to marshal Russian resources. His triumph came in 1709 at Poltava, where he defeated Charles decisively. The war was to drag on until the Treaty of Rystadt (1721), but it was Poltava, as Massie writes, that gave Peter his Baltic seaport and permanently shifted "the political axis of Europe."

The demands of the Northern War had slowed but did not stop Peter's program of reform and modernization. After Poltava both the scope and the pace of change increased. In addition to the urgently necessary military reforms, Peter had to create a manufacturing base for his armed forces. Continuing a practice he initiated during the Great Embassy, he attracted foreign experts. He granted subsidies, extended privileges to businessmen, and invested capital. He replaced the administrative machinery he inherited from medieval Russia with one designed on a more rational European pattern. In 1711, for example, he created a central administrative organ, or Senate, consisting of nine appointed members. Later the departments of government were reorganized into bureaus directly modeled on those of Sweden. To encourage enterprise, skill, and service to the state, he promulgated his "Table of Ranks," which made advancement into the aristocracy possible to anyone, including men of business, who rendered service to the state. Finally, in 1721 he struck at the last potential rival to his autocratic power by abolishing the office of Patriarch of the Russian Orthodox Church, making the church an organ of government.

Despite these colossal accomplishments, the last phase of Peter's reign was profoundly marred by the tragic conclusion of his troubled relationship with his son Alexis. Resentful of his father's abandonment of his mother, Eudoxia, attracted to the old Russian ways, devout and a dissolute drunkard at the same time, bookish and lazy, Alexis could in no way measure up to Peter's expectations. He had neither the capacity nor the will to be a warrior. When Peter in exasperation commanded Alexis either to relinquish his right to the throne and enter a monastery or become a worthy successor, Alexis fled abroad with his mistress. Tricked into returning to Russia by Peter's agents, he was tried at Peter's orders, examined under torture, and found guilty of treason. Before the death sentence could be carried out, his son died in prison, probably from torture, in July 1718.

Peter's own end came a few years later. Worn out by years of surpassing labor and increasingly weakened by illness, he caught a fever after plunging into the sea in mid-November to rescue men from a shipwreck. He died in January 1725 and was succeeded by his former mistress and second wife, Catherine.

This lavish biography of the most extraordinary of monarchs in an age well supplied with extraordinary rulers will remain the most widely read study of Peter the Great for some time to come. Massie's book will in a certain sense deserve its success, for it is very good popular biography. His fluid and undemanding style, his ability as a story teller, his open and usually engaging affection for Peter, and, of course, the inherently fascinating character of the tsar combine to attract and hold the reader's attention through most of the book's 855 pages of text.

Peter the Great has two salient faults. It is self-indulgently long, and it fails to achieve real critical distance from its subject. Massie is a skillful writer, but he ought to have curbed his wordiness and fought more effectively against his weakness for the colorful anecdote. A writer who means "the English Channel" when he writes "the narrow strip of gray sea that separates the continent from England" takes his readers' stamina and good will for granted. Some of Massie's piling up of descriptive detail is necessary to resurrect Peter's world. But he carries it too far and at the expense of historical analysis. It also leads him into error. For example, his description of the intricate and ponderous etiquette at Versailles provides an illuminating contrast to his account of Peter's rambunctious, unceremonious household. However, what Massie meant to be the telling, piquant detail—the fact that fawning French nobles waited on their king as he "performed his natural functions" in public on a "chair with a hole in it"—is not true. Louis XIV was in fact only going through the motions. He performed his natural functions in private after the play acting. This is doubtless a small error, but it shakes our trust in an author who relies so heavily on this approach to history.

Massie's fascination with Peter constitutes part of the book's appeal, but it is also the source of the biography's most serious weakness. Peter so dominates Massie's view of "Peter's World" that his book must be judged misleading and quite at odds with recent serious historical work on the course of Russian history. The problem is not Massie's almost invariably sympathetic appraisal of Peter. This is an honest book. The reader is given more than enough documentary evidence to form his own, perhaps less admiring opinion of a man whose fury, anger, and disregard for others dismayed even contemporaries used to the harshness of 17th-century life. The fault stems rather from Massie's belief that Peter's undeniably herculean labors to force Russians to adopt modern western techniques in warfare, commerce, and administration were the result of a coherent program of westernization first conceived and then relentlessly pursued. Such a view far underestimates contacts with Europe before Peter and fails to recognize the extent to which anyone ruling Russia would have been driven by threatening neighbors to emerge from the political and military disorganization of Russia's Middle Ages. Above all, Massie misinterprets Peter's real aims. The tsar was obsessed not with making Russia a European state but in importing only those practices that could increase his own power and Russia's might. Peter himself knew that the European nations he most admired—Holland and England—could in no way serve as models for a despotic autocrat who could do with his subjects literally whatever he wished. "We need Europe for a few decades," he told his nobles, "and then we must turn our back on it."

Richard Bienvenu

PREPARATIONS FOR THE ASCENT

Author: Gilbert Rogin (1929–   )
Publisher: Random House (New York). 181 pp. $8.95
Type of work: Novel
Time: The present
Locale: Greenwich Village and Central Park West in Manhattan, Miami Beach, parts of Connecticut and Long Island

A comic study of a man reaching middle age, looking back to take rueful stock of his life before he faces his future

> *Principal characters:*
> ALBERT, both hero and anti-hero
> VIOLET, Albert's wife
> THE HUMAN DYNAMO, Albert's mistress
> DR. NEDERLANDER, Albert's and Violet's psychiatrist
> BARNEY, Violet's son, Albert's stepson
> ALBERT'S DAD
> ALBERT'S MOM

Albert, the protagonist of *Preparations for the Ascent,* is a kind of Everyman, strictly limited, however, both in scope and sphere. Rather than being a universal prototype, he represents only a minuscule fraction of humanity, that part which is male, middle-aged, intellectual, Jewish, and which inhabits Greenwich Village and its "suburbs"— Miami Beach, Connecticut, and Long Island.

Albert is descended from the *schlemiel* of Jewish folklore. Less a perpetual loser than a perpetual non-winner, he has been propelled from the ghettos of Eastern Europe to those of Manhattan and Florida, from the early 19th century to the late 20th. As he has moved on, his frame of reference has expanded; Albert no longer relies solely on the Torah for his wisdom but invokes Kant and Schopenhauer. Definitely an innocent, Albert is also a bungler. He lacks dignity—modern dental hygiene is beyond him and he finds himself hopelessly entangled in yards of dental floss—but never loses his integrity. A comic figure, Albert is never ridiculous.

His story begins as he asks his friend Lippholzer, a composer and arranger, to write music to describe his life. Albert envisages some symphonic work, scored for full orchestra. But Lippholzer demurs; Albert is to him only a wind quintet with the oboe ("What a pathetic instrument!" he exclaims, "I underscore it in your case . . .") predominating or even taking solos.

Albert's marriage is as pathetic as the other aspects of his existence. It is a disappointment that he has no children of his own, and his chief joy in matrimony seems to be his relationship with his stepson, Barney, who is soon to leave. In the emptiness that engulfs him, Albert takes what pleasure he can from a series of brief affairs with women who emerge from his past. Each seduction is a repetition of one a decade earlier, and each so meaningless that Albert is hard put to remember the name of his partner, let alone what she is doing in his bed.

Given a deteriorating marriage, it is inevitable that Albert should consult a psychiatrist. It is not, however, inevitable that he should consult Violet's. Nevertheless, he ends up on the couch of Dr. Nederlander, a man capable of expressing his feelings in only two ways—either by nodding or by closing his eyes.

Albert cannot bring himself to discuss his waning sexual drive, his diminished desire for Violet, and speaks instead of the sheep he tries counting at night. The sheep are no problem—"Albert knows sheep: Giotto did terrific sheep . . ."—but difficulties arise with the fence—Albert cannot string wire to it and must staple it in place—and persuading the sheep to jump it.

"The sheep, Albert, drop them. Try a more urban approach," Dr. Nederlander orders. And he urges him to stop postponing pleasure and to attend a basketball game, one of his own passions, in Violet's company, as well as to enjoy food, his other passion. "Tonight," he says, showing emotion for the first time, "eat Chinese." But even such simple injunctions defeat Albert, who sees the game with Barney and later, as usual, goes to a deli.

The marriage continues to deteriorate, and Violet moves from the bedroom they have shared to one of her own. She takes a lover, a New Realist sculptor, Owen, who seems to mock Albert with his late-night telephone calls. "The cuckold as comic hero may be derided," Albert protests futilely, "but not reviled."

Their parting is imminent, but both strive to preserve their former living arrangements. Albert checks with Violet as to the time for which he should set her alarm, although to do so he must reach her by telephone at one of the bars she now frequents. When he at last moves to his own apartment, it is one from which he can see Violet's. He continues to perform small services for her, picking up her laundry, walking her dog. Violet, in turn, attends to Albert's mail.

The negotiation of a separation agreement is entrusted to Albert's dad, a lawyer, and a man, unlike Albert, who accomplishes things. Albert expects some day to be in *Who's Who in America;* Albert's dad has been in *Who's Who in the Northeast* "for ages." Albert sees his life as "one long interruption between what I intended to do and what I never got around to doing;" Albert's dad does not procrastinate. He is a man who controls his fate. It could never be his lot, as it is Albert's, to buy a loaf of raisin bread in which there are no raisins, or to ex-

change it for a second loaf in which, also, there are none. Albert's dad
would never, like Albert, carry home an iris that refuses to open . . .
to "say 'Ah' " as the florist describes it, and so return it. Albert's dad
is a man who takes charge, and Albert is happy to let him.

While the agreement with Violet is still being worked out—one that,
typically, is satisfactory to neither party—Albert drifts into an affair
with the Human Dynamo, nearly twenty years his junior. The two are
completely different from each other. "You don't play tennis, you
don't snow-ski, you don't water-ski, you don't ride a bicycle, you're
the last one off the train, you *plod* across the parking lot. Albert, we
have nothing in common," she tells him. Nevertheless, the affair continues, and Albert visits her weekly. On each visit he carries a slice of
bread for his morning toast, since she, not eating bread, refuses to buy
a loaf. Such a clandestine act is, to him, thrilling.

Albert's life follows much the same course with the Human Dynamo
as it did with Violet. Albert worries about his virility and again consults
Dr. Nederlander; he has an occasional run-in with Violet and with her
first husband, to whom she gives Albert's cast-off clothes. He has
another with the landlord, who refuses to replace the hall light bulbs.
Always, it is Albert who is bested, Albert who remains at the bottom
of the heap.

Earlier, as he left the room of one of those amorphous women he has
bedded so briefly, so forgettably, Albert has met a man—presumably
his beloved's husband—and passes him on the stairs. He hears the
man murmur, "My life stands revealed as a Sisyphean ordeal, with
Groucho Marx as Sisyphus, a partly deflated beach ball for a boulder."
Albert might have uttered the words himself.

The suicide of Barney reveals a more impressive facet of Albert's
character. Sorrowed, burdened by his own guilty knowledge that his
stepson might have been saved, he makes a desperate effort to cling to
Barney, to evoke him by visiting the young woman with whom he has
lived. Barney slips away, as he must, and Albert overcomes his grief
to emerge shaken by the experience but not shattered.

Life goes on as it always has for Albert, eternally doomed, it would
seem, to live it entangled with Violet and the Human Dynamo although
already "the magic has gone out" of the relationship. Incompatible
though they are, he can no more break with her than he has been able
to break with his wife.

Just as the story began with another character in it depicting Albert's
life for him in music it ends with a character describing it for Albert's
benefit in words. Albert, as an editor and a published writer, has been
asked by an author to read a manuscript. He agrees but is less than
enthusiastic about the novel; the hero's life, he insists, is not very

interesting, the hero himself is too predictable. If it were only . . . but it is not. It is Albert, and it is Albert's life, although he is unaware of that.

Preparations for the Ascent is a brilliant and beautifully written novel. (Much of it appeared in a slightly different version in *The New Yorker*.) The book is unconventional in its form, lacking all but a rudimentary plot. Focusing on character rather than story line, it presents a picture of Albert that is full and rounded, and entirely believable. His vivid, alive portrait emerges from a series of vignettes, from brief but telling episodes. Borrowing the techniques of the impressionist painters, and more precisely that of the *pointillistes,* Rogin shows Albert through a series of sharp flashes of insight—like the splashes of color in a Seurat canvas—adding one to another until they delineate a man.

Rogin has avoided a major pitfall of the comic novel; he has not caricatured his protagonist. Even Albert's most outlandish foibles are credible; what befalls him could befall anyone. We believe in Albert and empathize with him; we are sorry for him. We like him. Rogin has also avoided a second pitfall. At a time when the comic Jewish novel —or the comic novel about a Jew—has become so common as to be trite, he has taken a fresh look at his subject. There are no stock figures. Albert's dad is easily recognized, but never a stereotype. Happily, Albert's mom, while both Jewish and a mother, is not that ubiquitous parody, the Jewish Mother. Albert, like an affectionate, overgrown puppy, is as endearing as his own dog, Josh.

Vivian Werner

PRINCESS DAISY

Author: Judith Krantz
Publisher: Crown Publishers (New York). 464 pp. $12.95
Type of work: Novel
Time: The 20th century
Locale: Russia, Switzerland, France, England, United States

The story of Princess Daisy Valensky, who as both a child and an adult displayed courage, toughness, and determination to maintain her freedom and her dignity

Principal characters:
> PRINCESS DAISY, daughter of Francesca Vernon and Stash Valensky
> DANIELLE VALENSKY, sister of Princess Daisy
> RAM VALENSKY, half-brother of Princess Daisy, son of Stash Valensky
> STASH VALENSKY, wealthy Russian polo player
> FRANCESCA VERNON VALENSKY, American movie star
> ANABEL DE FOURMENT, mistress of Stash Valensky
> FREDERICK NORTH, director of television commercials
> PATRICK SHANNON, president of a large conglomerate
> KIKI CAVANAUGH, Daisy's best friend
> ROBIN and VANESSA VALERIAN, high-fashion designers

Marguerite Alexandrovna Valensky, nicknamed Princess Daisy by an adoring press, is the daughter of Francesca Vernon, a famous American movie actress, and Alexander "Stash" Valensky, a wealthy Russian polo player. The novel begins by introducing Daisy, a producer of television commercials, then quickly flashes back to the events leading up to her birth. The reader is introduced to the parents of Francesca Vernon and Stash Valensky and is plunged into the lives of the St. Petersburg elite. Shortly after the birth of Stash Valensky, his mother contracts tuberculosis and the family, on the advice of her physician, leaves St. Petersburg for a warmer climate. Prince Valensky, having no idea if or when the family will ever return to Russia, duplicates their St. Petersburg palace in their new home, Switzerland. He sells most of his holdings in Russia and transfers his huge fortune to Swiss banks in order to facilitate his complicated business dealings. As a result of Prince Valensky's business acumen, the family fortune is not lost in the Russian Revolution.

The Valenskys' only child, "Stash," grows up in Switzerland surrounded by very wealthy and very sick people. His mother's failing health and the other invalids with whom she surrounds herself, foster in Stash an intense intolerance for anything less than physical perfection. Stash meets Francesca Vernon in Deauville during the final

matches of the polo season, and after a passionate whirlwind courtship, their marriage appears to have been made in heaven. Before long,
twin daughters are born to them. The first daughter, Marguerite
(Daisy), is an example of physical perfection. However, the second
twin, Danielle, who is born only a few minutes later, is found to be
mentally retarded from complications that occurred during her birth.
Stash Valensky cannot cope with this imperfection and places Danielle
in a foster home as soon as she is strong enough to leave the hospital.
He tells Francesca that the baby died and she, in a deep depression
after the births, does not question him. However, through a series of
circumstances, Francesca learns that Danielle is alive in a foster home,
and with the help of a faithful servant, she retrieves Danielle. Francesca leaves Stash and returns to California with the twins. They live
in a secluded cabin in California for several years, their privacy protected by friends, and although Stash is never told exactly where they
are, arrangements are made for him to visit with Daisy at regular intervals. Francesca dies in a freak automobile accident when the twins are
six years old, and they are taken to England to live with their father.
Stash whisks Danielle into a private institution for the mentally retarded and although he assumes financial responsibility for her, that is
the extent of their relationship. Daisy is devastated by this separation
and enters into a voluntary hunger strike until her father allows her to
visit Danielle at least once a week. Her young life is further complicated by her relationship with her half-brother Ram, Stash's son from
an earlier marriage. Daisy adores Ram yet he remains aloof toward
her. Unfortunately, she is too young to recognize that he is jealous of
her relationship with Stash, a relationship that he does not have with
their father. Furthermore, she is unaware that he has always dreamed
of someday becoming "the" Prince Valensky and completely controlling the family fortunes. Daisy is his adversary, and although he is
overwhelmed by her beauty and vitality, she is nonetheless an enemy
to be controlled. Ram finds himself in a love-hate relationship with
Daisy that is to consume him until his death.

Meanwhile, Stash has entered into a long-lasting relationship with
Anabel de Fourment. She and Daisy become very close and she is, in
essence, a surrogate mother. Daisy grows up to be a beautiful, intelligent, competent, vital woman. Unfortunately, because of an escapade
during her early teens, Stash alters his will. The new will leaves all of
the property and half of his valuable stock in the Rolls-Royce company
to Ram, and the other half of the stock to Daisy with Ram as executor
until Daisy reaches the age of thirty. However, when Daisy is fifteen,
Stash Valensky dies in an airplane accident. Anabel takes both Ram
and Daisy to spend the summer with her in France and it is there that

Ram first rapes Daisy. Daisy understands by this time that Ram both loves and hates her, but she is so grieved by the loss of her father that she clings to Ram for support. When she tells him that they cannot continue their relationship, he becomes violent and rapes her again. Desperate and deathly afraid of Ram, Daisy tells Anabel about the rapes. Anabel arranges for Daisy's early admittance to the University of California at Santa Cruz where her roommate is Kiki Cavanaugh, the daughter of good friends. At Santa Cruz, Daisy discovers that her artistic talents are valuable, particularly to the theater department. Adept and skillful, she learns the craft of scenic design exceptionally well. She hears from Ram occasionally, but his letters are businesslike and do not threaten her. Eventually the letters become more and more personal, and Daisy begins to throw them away without reading them. When Daisy receives a letter from Anabel informing her that because of the collapse of Rolls-Royce, she will be unable to continue supporting Danielle, a responsibility she assumed after Stash's death. Daisy writes to Ram requesting a full financial statement, learning by return mail that her fortune also has been lost. Although Ram had sold off his shares, he had taken his unanswered letters as a sign that she wanted to retain her part of the stock.

Daisy realizes that she must find work immediately. Ram is unaware of Danielle's existence, and Daisy cannot ask him to shoulder this responsibility. After Daisy finds a job with Frederick North, a director of television commercials, she and Kiki move to New York. To supplement her income, Daisy paints portraits of the children of wealthy people. During one of these weekend assignments she meets Robin and Vanessa Valerian, the darlings of the design industry, and Patrick Shannon, the president of a large conglomerate.

The Valerians are very taken with Daisy and arrange many commissions for her. Friends of Ram, they are secretly curious about why Ram and Daisy do not get along with each other. Daisy, who is quick to see that the Valerians are the type of people who will, in time, demand something in return for their favors, nevertheless accepts their assistance out of desperation. She must not fall behind on Danielle's payments. She herself does not know, and cannot articulate, why Danielle's existence must remain a secret. All Daisy knows is that she was born first, and she is convinced that somehow Danielle's affliction is her fault.

The initial introduction to Patrick Shannon results in Daisy's being asked to promote a line of cosmetics in an effort by Shannon's conglomerate to inject new life into a failing perfume business. Daisy refuses, wishing to preserve her privacy and not wishing to use her title in this way. However, an incident occurs that forces her to change her mind. The Valerians invite her to spend a long weekend on their yacht. Daisy accepts, unaware that they have also invited Ram. Their meeting is less than joyous, but before Daisy demands to be put ashore Ram tells her that Anabel has cancer. She has come to Ram for financial assistance, telling him about Danielle and explaining that she does not want to burden Daisy further. Ram agrees to pay Anabel's expenses as well as those incurred by Danielle if Daisy will give up her life in New York and come live in England with him.

Once ashore, Daisy contacts Patrick Shannon, telling him that she will promote a Princess Daisy line of cosmetics. She then writes to Anabel, assuring her that she will be cared for.

The Princess Daisy promotion goes into high gear, and Daisy is selected for a magazine cover story. Shortly before the magazine is released, Vanessa Valerian, who has never forgiven Daisy's behavior on the yacht, calls Ram, ostensibly to tell him of Daisy's good fortune and the cozy relationship that has developed between Daisy and Patrick Shannon.

Upon hearing this news, Ram goes berserk with jealousy and plots to destroy her. He drives to Danielle's school and calls a press conference in which he exposes Danielle as Daisy's twin. Believing that this exposure will completely destroy Daisy, he commits suicide on the day of the publication's release.

Daisy, who receives an advance copy of the magazine, is, as expected, devastated, and Patrick Shannon, one of the few people who knew about Danielle, attempts to protect her by scuttling the entire campaign. The promotion is not scuttled, however, because a curious thing has happened to Daisy. The exposure, which was meant to destroy her, has the opposite effect. By telling the world her secrets, a weight is lifted from Daisy's shoulders and she is finally free.

Like her earlier novel, *Scruples,* Judith Krantz's *Princess Daisy* is a novel about a woman in search of herself and of the power that women possess, with all of its problems and rewards. Daisy, Francesca, and Anabel are strong, determined women, demonstrating many of the characteristics that have heretofore been ascribed to males.

Princess Daisy reads like a soap opera. The plots and subplots are intricately woven to form the whole. Assuming that Krantz set out to write a commercial blockbuster, there is no doubt that she succeeded.

Susan Floman

THE REAL WAR

Author: Richard M. Nixon (1913–   )
Publisher: Warner Books (New York). 341 pp. $12.50
Type of work: Current affairs
Time: The present
Locale: The entire world, principally the United States and the U.S.S.R.

Former President Richard M. Nixon describes World War III, in which he believes the United States and the Soviet Union are currently engaged

"We are at war." This stark statement sets the tone for Richard M. Nixon's *The Real War,* a "cri de coeur addressed not only to our political leaders but to leaders in all walks of life—to take hold before it is too late, and to marshal America's strengths so as to ensure its survival." This is the second book by the former President that has been published since he resigned the presidency on August 9, 1974. As Nixon states in an author's note, his first book, *Memoirs,* looks backward; his second book, *The Real War,* looks forward.

That the United States and the Soviet Union are engaged in a struggle of sorts is a fact that must be obvious even to the most casual observer of the contemporary American scene. Few Americans, however, think of this struggle as being World War III. Yet, this is precisely how the struggle is characterized by Nixon. The shock that such a characterization visits upon the reader illustrates Nixon's central point: the specific objective of Soviet policy is conquest by any means, including the very real possibility of conquest without nuclear war. The American public, however, does not take this Soviet policy objective with a sufficient degree of seriousness, according to Nixon. The result has been a significant expansion of Soviet power and dominion since the end of World War II. The prognosis is continued Soviet expansion unless the American public can be infused with a sense of urgency concerning the threat posed by its adversary.

> The central thesis of this book is that the West, today, has crossed the threshold of a period of acute crisis in which its survival into the twenty-first century is directly at stake. We have the material capacity, the economic and technological strength to prevail—which means to maintain our freedom and to avert a major war. But the capacity alone is not enough. Sir Robert Thompson, the British expert on guerrilla warfare, has trenchantly defined national power as manpower plus applied resources, *times* will. We have the resources and the manpower. Have we the will to use them?

How have the Western nations gotten into a position where their very survival is at stake in the 21st century? Have they the will to use material resources to assure their survival? These are the principal

questions that Nixon addresses with clarity in each of the chapters of
The Real War. At first, the reader might quarrel with Nixon's opening
premise, that the Soviet Union truly set out upon a goal of world
conquest and dominion. When one finishes the book, however, there
can be little doubt about the correctness of that premise. Nixon makes
his case by carefully examining the historical record since 1945. Particular emphasis is placed upon Soviet action in Eastern Europe, Vietnam, Cuba, South Yemen, Angola, Ethiopia, and Afghanistan. This
examination of the record is complemented with appropriate quota-
tions from Lenin, Khrushchev, Brezhnev, and other Soviet leaders
and theoreticians. Typical is the following quote attributed to Lenin:
"Probe with bayonets. If you encounter steel, withdraw. If you encounter mush, continue." Finally, Russian history from the 13th century to the present is examined. Nixon concludes that "there simply is
no tradition in the Soviet Union of freedom internally or of non-aggres-
sion externally. Territorial expansion comes as naturally to Russia as
hunting does to a lion or fishing to a bear." The reader is left with little
doubt that the Soviet goal is indeed conquest and control.

Similarly, the reader might question the correctness of Nixon's other
major premise, that survival of the Western nations in the 21st century
is, in fact, at stake. Here, too, Nixon makes his case convincingly. The
declining American and Western European commitment to defense
spending, particularly nuclear defense spending, is well documented.
Equally well documented is the increasing Soviet commitment to defense items. An obvious consequence of this is that post World War II
nuclear superiority has been transformed to bare nuclear parity in
1980. "For a quarter of a century American nuclear superiority kept
the peace. Now that superiority is gone, and if present trends continue,
the Soviets will have strategic nuclear superiority by the mid-eighties.
. . . The greatest danger in a period of Soviet nuclear superiority is
defeat without war."

Special condemnation for the creation of this condition of military
insufficiency is reserved for Secretary of Defense Robert McNamara's
policy of "unilateral restraint," and for President Carter's decisions to
cancel production of the B-1 bomber and to slow deployment of the
MX missile. However, the real culprit is not assumed to be any one
person or policy. Rather, the real culprit is the sense of casualness and
naivete with which Western leaders have treated the Soviet threat
since 1945—the lack of will that has been demonstrated. "What America does suffer from is not itself a terminal illness, but rather a sort of
creeping paralysis that could become terminal unless treated. . . . The
nation that survives is the one that . . . has the wisdom to recognize
the threat and the will to turn it back, and that does so before it is too

late. The naive notion that we can preserve freedom by exuding good-will is not only silly, but dangerous."

Is the struggle inevitably to be lost? Certainly not. Western nations have the resources. All that is needed is the good sense and will to use them properly. This is the responsibility of Western leaders. They must act with a sense of immediacy and determination. "America and the West need to be jolted into a sense of urgency." Because the book is a "take action" book and because the action must be taken initially by leaders it is written, in many respects, as a textbook or teaching manual. A number of specific suggestions are made. They include the following: act as though the United States is at war, because it is; act as though the war can be won, because it can if the people have the will; dramatically increase the funds committed to defense and intelligence spending; use international trade selectively, for example, by granting Most Favored Nation status to a country like China whose interests currently complement those of the United States; recognize that an "ally" is someone who supports or advances U.S. interests; provide economic and military support to allies without insisting that they adopt American democracy as a condition for receiving that support; recognize that the vastly superior productivity of a capitalistic economy is an asset that should be emphasized; and, in dealing with the Soviet Union, follow a policy blend of containment and détente, as either alone is insufficient and potentially dangerous.

The Real War basically is a well-organized and easy-to-read book. The various chapters are arranged in a logical sequence. The organization contributes to the flow of the narration. Each chapter begins with a quotation or two that capture the essential lesson of that particular chapter. For example, Chapter 6 begins with the following statement of Napoleon Bonaparte: "China? There lies a sleeping giant. Let him sleep! For when he wakes he will move the world." Chapter 6 goes on to concern itself with the vast potential of China.

Nixon's thesis is clearly and forcefully stated. Nevertheless, its impact is blunted, to some extent, by what appears to be unnecessary partisanship. This is particularly true in the chapter that deals with the Vietnam War, but it also appears in other sections of the book. For example, Nixon describes his 1972 presidential opponent not as Mr. McGovern, but, rather, as "the peace-at-any-price candidate." The media receives its share of condemnation. Referring to *The New York Times* handling of the Pentagon Papers, Nixon remarks, ". . . I considered this one of the grossest acts of journalistic irresponsibility I had encountered in a quarter century of public life." Of the disillusionment concerning Vietnam, he says, "Egged on by the media and often by conscience-stricken 'dissenters' who had been responsible for policy errors in the first place, American public opinion was poisoned.'' At another point he suggests that if America loses World War III it will be largely ''because of the attention, the celebrity, and the legitimacy given to the 'trendies'—those overglamorized dilettantes who posture in the latest idea, mount the fashionable protests, and are slobbered over by the news media, whose creation they essentially are.'' This kind of mudslinging detracts from the force of Nixon's statement.

Steven P. Floman

THE RETURN OF EVA PERÓN

Author: V. S. Naipaul (1932–   )
Publisher: Alfred A. Knopf (New York). 228 pp. $10.00
Type of work: Essays
Time: Early 1970's
Locale: Trinidad, Argentina, and Zaire

A collection of essays examining Third World nations and the figures holding sway over them

In his essay "Conrad's Darkness," V. S. Naipaul states that the novelist's purpose is "to awaken the sense of true wonder" through examination of and meditation upon the world around him. He claims that the novel today has lost its sense of conviction, becoming instead a format for the author's private experimentation. The writer's life rather than his work becomes mythic. Naipaul is not, of course, the first to voice this complaint; his statement links him to the tradition of authors who have raged against this very personal form of literature. In fact, Joseph Conrad, Naipaul's literary master, is quoted in the essay as describing the modern English novel not "as an achievement of active life by which the author will produce certain definite effects upon the emotions of his reader, but simply as an instinctive, often unreasoned, outpouring of his own emotions." Naipaul allies himself with Conrad, an expatriate like himself who chose English as his literary language and dedicated his career to observing, meditating upon, and finally recording the mysteries of the world.

Naipaul's collection of essays, *The Return of Eva Perón,* stands as a testament to his conviction that the writer must get outside himself, must deal with the world rather than merely his own emotional state. Born in Trinidad of Indian parents, Naipaul has an obsession with and a desire to make sense of the Third World that are understandable. With the exception of "Conrad's Darkness," the essays contained in this collection recount Naipaul's observations of these underdeveloped nations. There are his reconstruction of the events surrounding a savage sequence of murders in Trinidad, his investigation into the life and afterlife of Eva Perón, and his examination of the rise of a satanic messiah in the Congo. These essays serve a dual purpose: they inform Naipaul's Anglo-American audience of the corruption and chaos rampant in these underdeveloped nations, and they become an intermediary step in the author's own creative process. From these observations grew novels. Ahmed, the black power leader in *Guerrillas,* is clearly an amalgam of the people and attitudes documented in "Michael X and the Black Power Killings in Trinidad." *Bend in the River* derives from

Naipaul's journey up the Congo River to reexamine Conrad's Stanley Falls, now Kisangani, which he describes in "A New King for the Congo: Mobutu and the Nihilism of Africa."

"The Killings of Michael X," a work of investigative journalism, traces the career of Michael de Freitas, born in Trinidad and known at different times, in accordance with black extremist fashions in the United States, as "Michael X" and "Abdul Malik." Jumping on the black power bandwagon of the 1960's, Malik became a self-proclaimed celebrity among London's radical chic, convincing those in search of a cause that he was the greatest black leader on earth. It was a two-way sham: the press wanted a hot story and Malik wanted to provide one. He raised thousands of pounds for nonexistent black foundations and, just as London began to doubt, fled to Trinidad, calling a select group of Black Panthers to join him in founding a commune there.

While Naipaul's attitude toward the black power movement in general is never defined, he sees its presence in Trinidad as a hateful corruption that obviates the real problems: "Malik's career proves how much of Black Power—away from its United States source—is jargon, how much a sentimental hoax. In a place like Trinidad, racial redemption is as irrelevant for the Negro as for everybody else. It obscures the problems of a small independent country with a lopsided economy, the problems of a fully 'consumer' society that is yet technologically untrained and without the intellectual means to comprehend deficiency."

Second in command at the commune is Hakim Jamal, an American whose line is black publishing and education. He raises money for a nonexistent black Montessori school and a black publishing house that publishes nothing. Together Malik and Jamal run the commune and write the biography of Michael X, based more on fantasy than reality and using a rhetoric of violence borrowed from the Panther movement in the United States. The biography becomes more real to Malik than the actual facts of his life: he transforms into the character and murders three members of the commune as an enactment of threats made by the character Michael, not the person. Malik thereby becomes the myth he and Jamal created.

In what can only be referred to as a "literary murder," Gail Benson, a white woman living on the commune, is chopped at ruthlessly by a hired killer and buried while still alive. Benson provides a suitable climax for the biography. Steve Yeates, a dissident American, is drowned five days later. Joseph Skerritt, another doubter, one month later is pushed into a pre-dug grave and killed by a shower of boulders. Malik is convicted of murder and hanged in the Royal Jail in Port of Spain in May 1975.

Like "Michael X," "A New King for the Congo" chronicles the career of a black revolutionary. Seizing control of Zaire in 1965, General Mobutu sets out systematically to eliminate all trace of Belgian imperialism, a goal that proves, according to Naipaul, both counterproductive and unrealistic. Mobutu's traditional military garb is abandoned in favor of a safari-type leisure suit designed to be antithetical to the European suit and tie. The local lingala, a bastardization of French, English, and tribal dialect, is declared the state language. Businesses are nationalized, turned over to Africans who often lack managerial experience. Even the art becomes self-consciously African: "art that no longer serves a religious or magical purpose, attempts an alien representationalism and becomes mannered and meaningless, suggesting a double mimicry: African art imitating itself, imitating African-inspired Western art."

Mobutu, not unlike his counterpart in Trinidad, believed that the facts of history, like the events of one's life, could be altered through literature. He had history books rewritten, giving the Belgian occupation little more than a footnote. Yet, typical of Mobutu's simplistic view of the world, Zaire's problems were blamed entirely on that "brief" period of foreign occupation. For an understanding of history he substituted a glorification of Africa with himself as divine sovereign, thus becoming not a ruler but a cult figure. He even went so far as to have his mother enshrined as an African Madonna. This bogus vision of the world is ultimately paralyzing: "The cult of the king already swamps the intellectual advance of a people who have barely emerged. The intellectual confusions of authenticity, that now give such an illusion of power, close up the world again and point to a future greater despair."

Naipaul's fascination with Mobutu is in keeping with his general interest in the Third World, yet this journey into Zaire is of special significance in that the author retraces Conrad's imaginary journey up to the Congo into the Heart of Darkness. The journey is Naipaul's attempt to come to terms with this writer whose influence on his own work has been profound. Conrad "discovers" Kurtz, an ivory trader who had transfixed a tribe of natives. Naipaul discovers Mobutu: the structure is similar yet the colors have been inverted. Instead of a white who trades in white commodities, he finds a black who trades in the commodity of black nationalism.

If Mobutu became a messiah in Zaire, Eva Perón was accorded sainthood in Argentina. There was no need for Eva to record the events of her life; it was done for her innumerable times but, unfortunately, with little more accuracy than Jamal had given Malik's. The facts of her life have become so obscured by the legend that no one can be sure when or where she was born. Yet her crusade to help the poor and her unwillingness to accept a society based on inequality canonized her in the minds of the Argentinians. Like Mobutu, her solutions were simple, tangible, and immediate. If there are poor people, they should be given more money. And, quite literally, she passed out money to the poor. What is significant here is not the facts of Eva's life, but the Argentinians' spontaneous and universal urge to see her immortalized. The thousands who filed past her corpse, embalmed at a cost of over $100,000, paid homage to her simple doctrine of love for the poor and hate for the rich.

Eva was the inspiration, yet it was her husband Juan Perón's task to fulfill her promise of equality. It was one thing to identify the problem, to name trade unions and redistribute colonial landholdings, but to reorganize and restructure society effectively was impossible. In the thirty years following his takeover and up to his death in 1974, Argentina experienced economic disaster: inflation soared wildly leaving the peso almost worthless, and torture and murder became commonplace. Even Argentina's rich soil was unable to produce as it had in the past. It is not enough merely to locate the enemy.

Simple doctrines, simple solutions: these are themes that connect this collection of essays. Mobutu, Michael X, and Eva Perón were all leaders with facile answers. It is their naively logical vision that seems to have propelled each one of them into a position of power or influence. Naipaul depicts a world peopled with gullible followers in search of visionary leaders. Naipaul himself is a man with a vision, yet his, like Conrad's, encompasses the complexities of reality; he offers no simple solutions. At a time in which reality is continually obscured and history rewritten, Naipaul's works are a constant reminder of the real world, replete with paradoxes, inconsistencies, and imperfections.

Elizabeth Lubin

RITES OF PASSAGE

Author: William Golding (1911–   )
Publisher: Farrar, Straus and Giroux (New York). 278 pp. $10.95
Type of work: Novel
Time: The Napoleonic era
Locale: At sea between England and the Antipodes

A young man en route from England to Australia is initiated into the complexities and cruelties of life

Principal characters:
EDMUND TALBOT, a young man of the upper class
THE REV. ROBERT JAMES COLLEY, an Anglican minister
CAPTAIN ANDERSON, captain of the vessel and an avowed hater of clergymen
MR. CUMBERSHUM, an officer
MR. DEVEREL, an officer
MR. SUMMERS, an officer
BILLY ROGERS, a member of the crew
ZENOBIA BROCKLEBANK, a passenger of shady reputation
MR. BROCKLEBANK, her "father"
MR. PRETTIMAN, a rationalist

Rites of Passage is a marked change from other Golding works, a novel of 18th-century characters presented in a familiar 18th-century form: the journal. Edmund Talbot is a complacent young man of upperclass origins who is on his way from England to Australia to participate in the colonial government there. His journal is intended for the entertainment of his godfather, whose generosity has obtained him this post. Talbot is a novice at sea life, alternating in his journal's first entries between attempts to master the sailors' language and bouts of *mal de mer.* He also introduces a strange company of passengers: Mr. Prettiman, a contentious rationalist; the Rev. Mr. Colley, a buffoonish minister; Mr. Brocklebank, a boor; and Brocklebank's painted companion, Zenobia.

For many days Talbot's attentions are occupied with observation of his fellow passengers and pursuit of Zenobia, the only attractive woman on board. But there are suggestions of trouble. The ship's officers hint that "this is not a happy ship," reacting with incredulity to Talbot's praise of their devotion. Captain Anderson is taciturn at best, given to explosions of violent temper. From the beginning Talbot's treatment of him is impolitic. He neglects to read the Standing Orders, the captain's set of rules for passengers, and breaks the most important rule by speaking to the captain on deck without permission. Anderson's high-handed manner prods Talbot into subtle rebellion, and when Anderson's pathological hatred of clergymen leads him to forbid services, Talbot aggravates the situation by insisting that services be held in the passengers' saloon.

Unable to retaliate against the influential Talbot, the captain becomes increasingly unpleasant in his treatment of Colley. Colley's peculiar appearance and obsequious behavior have made him an object of ridicule from the beginning, but Captain Anderson's treatment reduces him to a laughingstock. When Colley repeats Talbot's mistake of speaking to the captain without permission, he is roared at to go and read the Standing Orders. When Colley returns to apologize, Anderson deliberately knocks him down and sends him scurrying below decks.

Colley's story has so far been told by Talbot alone, and because of Talbot's absence at a crucial moment the reader is denied an important scene. Seizing the opportunity of a "sailor's entertainment" above decks, Talbot makes his assignation with Zenobia in his cabin. It is soon evident that he has missed something important, but he is unable to ask what has happened without admitting that he was not present. Talbot tries in vain to piece together Mr. Deverel's "How he does hate a parson!" and Mr. Prettiman's indignation over "a display of monstrous and savage superstition!" But the "entertainment" is not yet over. The next day, Talbot and the other passengers watch in amazement as Colley proceeds in full ecclesiastical garb to the fo'castle where the crew have their quarters. The passengers are in as much suspense as the reader, since they can see nothing but hear continual roars of laughter and applause. Colley finally emerges dressed only in a common seaman's shirt, blind drunk.

After several days Lieutenant Summers tells Talbot that Colley has not moved nor spoken since the day he came back from the fo'castle. He has lain on his bed face downward, apparently willing himself to die. Summers impresses on Talbot his particular responsibility toward the man and convinces Talbot that it is his duty to intercede with the captain on Colley's behalf. Talbot's mention of his journal has a strong effect on Anderson, who is obviously worried about his culpability in the matter. But before any progress has been made, Colley is found dead.

On one of his visits to Colley's cabin just before the man's death, Talbot had noticed a sheaf of papers. Colley's letters to his sister, which Talbot transcribes for his godfather, tell the other side of the story. Through Colley's manuscript the reader now sees the pathos instead of the ridiculousness of his history. The pathos lies in his total failures of perception. Colley has no idea that he is despised, having an unshakable faith in the dignity of his bearing and station in life. While Talbot is sometimes wrong in his judgments, they are at least based on rational observation. Colley, however, simply idealizes everything around him. He interprets Talbot's avoidance of him as the shyness of a soul in crisis, and Talbot's ramblings in search of a spot to meet with Zenobia are pitied as evidence of spiritual restlessness. If Talbot is idealized as the epitome of a noble gentleman, the sailors are Colley's natural men, children of God, even gods themselves. One in particular, a handsome sailor named Billy Rogers, is Colley's hero.

Through Colley's account the reader learns what happened at the "entertainment" Talbot missed. It was a crossing-the-line ceremony at the equator, when the "god of the sea" comes aboard and presides over ceremonies in which monsters and demons cavort and those who are crossing for the first time are dunked. This ceremony is cruelly designed to humiliate Colley, who is dragged from his bed and "called to judgment" before the god Neptune. Dunked repeatedly and smeared with filth, Colley is rescued only by Summers' firing of Prettiman's gun to restore order. Colley escapes, but the next day insists upon going forward to convert the wrongdoers. His last entry is written in an ecstasy of forgiveness and love, "a great love of all things, the sea, the ship, the sky, the gentlemen and the people . . ."

The denouement is already known: final humiliation and death. But what humiliation was severe enough to kill him? An inquiry is held, with Talbot, Summers, and Captain Anderson presiding. In spite of Colley's own assertion that "what a man does defiles him, not what is done by others," Talbot is convinced that Colley's humiliation was a mass sexual attack in the fo'castle. The important witness here is Billy Rogers, the young sailor Colley so much admired. Talbot accuses him of sexual "beastliness," demanding the names of the men who attacked the minister. Billy appears to be trapped, but after a long pause asks with perfect self-possession, "Shall I begin with the officers, sir?" Even Talbot agrees that the proceedings must be stopped, for Billy has it in his power to smear the reputation of every officer on board.

Ironically, the final clue to the puzzle of Colley's behavior comes from the obtuse Mr. Prettiman. Prettiman and his fiancée Miss Granham announce themselves shocked by Colley's behavior as a minister, since Billy Rogers has informed Prettiman that Mr. Colley chewed tobacco. Prettiman repeats Rogers's exact words, that "he'd knowed most things in his time but he had never thought to get a chew off a parson." Talbot accepts this at face value, but later in the privacy of his cabin he finally realizes the truth. Colley's infatuation with his "young hero" Billy Rogers, some odd phrases from Summers ("You know what a beast he made of himself?") and Prettiman's story all come together at last. It was Colley who was guilty of sexual "beastliness" toward a compliant and jeering Billy Rogers. A less complacent and more thoughtful Talbot concludes, "With lack of sleep and too much understanding I grow a little crazy, I think, like all men at sea who live too close to each other and too close thereby to all that is monstrous under the sun and moon."

Rites of Passage itself is a voyage into the monstrous. The story begins in England at the end of an "age of reason," but the nearer the ship draws to the equator, the more topsy-turvy the world becomes. The crossing-the-line ceremony serves as a brilliant focus for the savagery Golding seeks to demonstrate. When ships crossed the equator, monsters roamed and a law of misrule prevailed. In *Rites of Passage* it is the occasion for a frenzy of atavistic hatred toward Colley, the frenzy that is Golding's special province: "nothing, *nothing* that men can do to each other can be compared with that snarling, lustful, storming appetite. . . ."

Golding's construction of the novel cleverly draws the reader into the popular dislike of Colley. The reader is set up to despise him through Talbot's account and is prevented from pitying him too early by Talbot's ignorance of his crossing-the-line humiliation. When Summers reproves Talbot for thoughtlessness, the reader feels culpable. Although Colley is persecuted, however, his ultimate downfall is brought about by the vice within himself. For Golding such vice is the major fact of human existence. Toward the end of the book, Mr. Deverel takes Talbot aside and explains the mystery of Captain Anderson's hatred of the clergy: Anderson is the bastard son of a lord who palmed off his pregnant mistress to a clergyman. Through the interest of his real father Anderson was able to rise in the service, but after the old man's death he had no more hopes of such patronage. The explanation is exceptionally weak; as Talbot exclaims, "It would surely be more reasonable in him to detest a lord!" It is possible that Golding meant it to be weak, because in the last analysis there is no satisfactory explanation for human evil. Virtue fails, and vice triumphs. "True indeed," says Talbot, "and how should it be not?"

Lisa Halttunen

THE SCAPEGOAT

Author: Mary Lee Settle
Publisher: Random House (New York). 278 pp. $11.95
Type of work: Novel
Time: 3:00 P.M., June 7—8:00 A.M., June 8, 1912
Locale: Lacey Creek, West Virginia

The strong characters of determined women influence the outcome of a West Virginia mine strike

> *Principal characters:*
> LILY LACEY, the eighteen-year-old daughter of a West Virginia mine owner, home for the summer from Vassar
> MOTHER JONES, a historical figure of the late 19th–early 20th century, famous for her part in organizing the first locals of the United Mine Workers and known as the "Miner's Angel"

On June 7, 1912, at Lacey Creek, a West Virginia mine community, most of the miners, a combined work force of hillbillies and immigrant Italians, are on strike. A few are still working for small landowners, like Beverly Lacey, but they are under pressure to quit and join the others who already belong to the United Mine Workers. Mr. Lacey himself is under pressure from the Eastern investors who want to buy him out and have begun hiring local roughnecks and thugs to protect scabs and end the strike forcibly.

Working the mines, the Laceys, in one generation, earned their place among the respectable gentry of the region, but by 1912 they have given up all but one mine and are living well by reputation only. Beverly Lacey, dying of tuberculosis, can hardly concentrate on the demands of the strikers. His wife and two of their three daughters are pained by the crimp the strike has put in the social season. The third daughter, Lily, a self-proclaimed socialist, is the only one who acknowledges the historical relevance of the moment. She wants to be involved but, at eighteen, she is more interested in heroics than in workers' demands. A true bluestocking, Lily ardently advocates a dozen causes at a time. Her favorite one is Eduardo Pagano, an Italian mine worker whom she tutors on her vacations from Vassar. Her hope to set Eduardo free through education is approved by Mr. Roundtree, an Englishman who manages a mine for the Imperial Mining Company. Roundtree is in love with Lily and shares her dreams of giving Eduardo, a naturally brilliant boy, a more promising future than the mine pit.

The striking workers, evicted from company housing, are living in a makeshift tent community on Jake Catlett's land. Catlett is a member of the United Mine Workers, and the small strip of Union-owned land he lives on is the only safe place for the miners on strike. When Mother Jones arrives in town to organize a local of the union, she knows from the start that only the real threat of violence will inspire the miners to act. Jake is against violence and vetoes Mother Jones's plan to set up a picket line to keep out the strikebreakers.

The guards are itching for action, eager to do more than just protect the scabs. They are under the command of Dan Neill, an unstable local boy who loves Lily Lacey. The scabs are a motley crew of foreigners who do not speak English. They do not even know that they will be used as strikebreakers. Dan Neill has isolated them in a boardinghouse to prevent them from learning why they have been hired.

Lily Lacey, meanwhile, is enchanted with the tensions and excitement the strike has brought. This is her chance to prove herself as more than just a spoiled member of the privileged class. Her attempts to get involved with the miners are rebuffed, and her own family barely tolerates her preaching against "bloated capitalists." Lily begs Eduardo Pagano to take her into an empty mine shaft so that she can share something of the workers' experience. Eduardo refuses with scorn, but she is more determined than ever and that night goes down in the mines alone. When she comes out of the blackness of the pit, visibly shaken and covered with coal dust, she runs into Dan Neill. He misinterprets her disarray and presumes that she has been raped by Eduardo Pagano.

It is long past midnight. The strikers are going over their demands to form a union, and Mother Jones proposes a prayer meeting at the mines attended by all the women of the tent community. She knows that the scabs are being sent to the mines against their will and believes that a prayer meeting might just work to get them to come over to the strikers' side.

Her plan almost succeeds, but no one has taken into account the guards, who have been drinking and bragging about how to end the strike their own way. However, without a picket, the strikers have not given them an opportunity to defend the mines or protect the scabs. When Dan Neill spreads word of the alleged "rape," he triggers all of their pent-up anger and frustration.

In retaliation, the guards invade the miners' tents looking for Eduardo Pagano. Eduardo's mother manages to guide him to safety, leaving behind, to block the guards in their pursuit, an innocent cousin who just arrived from Italy. He is chased and shot down by the guards as a scapegoat. Eduardo has already escaped, accompanied as far as Richmond by Lily, playing the heroine and accomplice. Neither of them knows what has just happened, and they dream only of the unexplored world of promise that awaits them somewhere else.

Although *The Scapegoat* is a novel of a single day with each chapter covering not more than a few hours, the actual narrative, as told from several points of view, ranges from the distant past to fifteen years into the future. These constant shifts in perspective and jumps in time constitute a collage rather than a linear plot with a beginning, middle, and end. The author, Mary Lee Settle, wants to show how events are not seen clearly by the people involved because they are often blinded by personal obsessions and limitations.

The Scapegoat also tells how strong women thrive at a time when they are not allowed to be active citizens much less socialists and U.M.W. organizers. The author presents the figure of Lily Lacey with sympathetic irony, showing her to be an extremely naive and presumptuous young woman but also a character of integrity and promise. Introducing into fiction a historical personage like Mother Jones usually creates awkward situations within a novel, but Mary Lee Settle describes a persuasive character who is entirely credible. Recreating Mother Jones, the author explores the options of a woman so dedicated that she sacrifices her own nature to her political commitment. Eduardo Pagano's mother is a third strong woman. Her power is rooted in the mysteries of Roman Catholicism, but, since the author believes that mystery and coincidence can determine history, Mrs. Pagano has a key role in realizing the outcome of the strike.

Of the many voices narrating *The Scapegoat*, those of the women are the most compelling. The men, like Beverly Lacey who is drained by mortal illness and Jake Catlett who is torn between the old world and the new, are not developed much beyond their typical functions as the impotent landowner and the slow, but wise, worker. The greatest problem with *The Scapegoat* is that the dividing line between the authorial voice and the voice of fictional characters is not always defined clearly enough, and the changing point of view can be confusing. Descriptions of future events that have no bearing or shed no light on the past seem self-conscious and without distinct purpose.

In *The Scapegoat*, Mary Lee Settle has succeeded in portraying with lucid realism and human detail an important phase of American history. Where historians describe the actions of men, Settle rediscovers the crucial involvement of resilient women.

Julie V. Iovine

THE SEARCH FOR SOLUTIONS

Author: Horace Freeland Judson
Publisher: Holt, Rinehart & Winston (New York). 211 pp. $16.95
Type of work: Essays

An introduction to the method of scientific inquiry combined with a presentation of current scientific knowledge and a series of interviews with contemporary scientists.

Science is fun. It has all the delights that accompany the effort to solve a problem. First one must be fully immersed in the problem, understand what is known about it, identify with it, and comprehend the limits within which one is working. Next, one must set it aside and mull it over in the subconscious levels of the mind. And then, perhaps on the fringes of sleep, perhaps in the middle of a conversation, the "aha," that glorious feeling of solution, will emerge.

Judson likens contemporary science to art in prior epochs. The search for solution is the same. He shows art works from centuries past that illustrate hydrodynamics—turbulent flow that is still not fully understood by modern science. Unlike artists, however, scientists cannot stop with description, or even with the finding of a solution. Two steps remain: to publish the results and to convince the scientific community. Science must go from the private to the public to be effective.

Nature is patterned. Upon the patterns of nature, humankind in ten thousand years has superimposed its own patterns. Science is a process of recognizing and understanding patterns. The patterns of nature are built from very few themes. Bubbles and rocks break up at 120° angles. The honeycomblike hexagonal arrays that result pack together in the closest of fits. In three-dimensional geometry the simplest pattern is the tetrahedron or pyramid shape, with angles of 109° 26′ 16″. It also packs closely and is extremely important in modern biology. The spiral is another of nature's forms: the spiral of Archimedes with equal distances and Descartes' equiangular spiral.

Dmitri Mendeleev's creation of the periodic table in chemistry in 1869 is an outstanding example of perceiving and then imposing pattern. His table formed the basis for correcting errors in what was previously believed and for predicting the discovery of missing elements.

Change, systematic change, is another aspect of nature that scientists seek to understand. A pervasive puzzle that appears again and again is "the scale effect." Length is linear, surface is square, and volume is cubic. So when a tree doubles in height, its surface increases four times, and its volume eight times. For this reason, Galileo concluded in 1638, a tree cannot grow more than 300 feet high. His method was a "thought experiment." The surface-to-volume ratio sets upper and lower limits to the size of living things. Insects cannot grow much larger than the smallest mouse because they transport oxygen into their bodies by tubes on the surface of their skin.

Length, area, and volume are changeable elements, or *parameters,* in a problem. A parameter is a variable that scientists must hold constant except when deliberately varying it.

Chance has an important place in science. The prepared mind will notice the unexpected and perceive its significance. Error often plays a role in discovery. Max Delbrück has called this "the principle of limited sloppiness." A scientist must be careful enough to trust his or her observations but sloppy enough that the unexpected sometimes happens. The discovery of immunology, X rays, and penicillin all relied, in part, on chance factors.

Chance is also inherent to the processes of the universe. There are some things that will never be known. These fall into two categories: classical ignorance and quantum ignorance. The first refers to interactions that are so complex that they are forever incalculable. Scientists use probabilities to predict outcomes in this area. The second refers to the Heisenberg, or uncertainty, principle. At the subatomic level of events there is an irreducible minimum of uncertainty. One cannot simultaneously determine position and momentum of a particle nor can it be determined when a given radioactive atom will decay.

A mid-20th-century scientific idea that has had revolutionary impact is "feedback." The phenomenon occurs in many nonliving processes and "at every point and every moment in the processes of life and thought." During the 18th-century industrial revolution, governors were added to machines to enable them to self-regulate energy flow. In 1920, George Mead applied feedback to the learning of speech. In 1940, Norbert Weiner applied it to computer development. These were all precursors to cybernetics, or information theory.

In biology many systems form feedback loops. Predator and prey wax and wane in numbers depending upon the population of the other. Hormones regulate physiological systems. RNA regulates protein synthesis in the cell. Other examples can be found on the developmental and social psychological levels. Science itself is also dependent upon feedback for formulation and reformulation of theory.

Models are an essential element in the process of science. They are radical abstractions that reduce the real problems to manageable form by excluding irrelevant aspects. Models fuse the creativity of play with the seriousness of work, a fusion that is very effective.

Model-building occurs on three levels. The first is to predict the behavior of an object, as with a model airplane. The second is to predict the behavior of an elaborate system, as with a model of a weather system. The third is to build theory. For example, Linus Pauling's model of the structure of proteins, the alpha helix, was a theory. It accounted for known facts and predicted new facts that would be found.

Models or theories are persuasive because they predict the unexpected. Pauling's model of the alpha helix predicted certain spacing of the amino acids. Max Perutz measured that spacing and found it to be right. Newton's theory of gravitation explained Edmund Halley's calculations of his comet even though the comet had formed no part of the original theorizing. Einstein's theory of relativity accounted for an irreducible disagreement between observation and Newtonian calculation. It is this power—strong prediction—that makes theory convincing.

Theory and data are inseparable aspects of the process of science. Data, or evidence, and its unreliability has been discussed at length in relation to courtroom proceedings. Evidence is just as suspect in the proceedings of science. A single piece of evidence may reflect a significant finding, an artifact, observer error, or observer faking. For this reason, some scientists assert the primacy of theory over evidence. They throw out data when developing their theory because often the data are wrong.

On the other hand, hypothesis can be an enemy as well as a friend. A scientist looking to confirm an hypothesis may affect the outcome of an experiment; these are known as "observer effects." Observer effects are minimized by strictly adhering to the rule of random assignment of subjects. Random assignment eliminates the unconscious choice of bigger, smarter, or prettier to one condition and not to the other. Data are sometimes affected simply by virtue of the experimental set-up; these are called "experimenter effects." For instance, in doing drug effectiveness studies all subjects must be given pills or injections although only some subjects receive the actual drugs. Otherwise the expectation of improvement causes improvement even if the drug is ineffective. Likewise, experimenters must not know which subjects received the actual drug or they look harder for improvement. Proper testing of drugs uses a "total blind" procedure.

The back and forth movement between evidence and theory is constant. Evidence accumulates, a theory is developed, other scientists collect more evidence, and the theory is refined or refuted, leading to more evidence, more theory. There is also a back and forth movement among scientists and laboratories. Judson calls this the "shuttle effect." Fakery and incorrect observation get sifted out in the process.

Judson ends his book by mentioning the eight problems still in search of solutions: the origin of the universe, the origin of the solar system, the origin of life, the basis of natural selection, development and differentiation, aging and death, neurobiology, and how humans think. He is urging science on.

The Search for Solutions is an array of beautiful color pictures, large-type text, and small-type figure captions. In addition there are boxed interviews with famous scientists, accompanied by their photographs, at the end of most chapters. Judson's stated purpose is to explain the method of science, which is poorly described by historians and philosophers as a linear and methodical process. Science is an exciting process; it is "what scientists of all kinds *actually do*." So, in order to explain the scientific method he presents many examples of science in action. These moments from the history of science are interesting in and of themselves, but the organizing principle does not work. It is often unclear why a particular example is in one place rather than another. To further the appreciation of what scientists do, there are the interviews. These also are interesting in themselves, but their placement does not follow logically from the text. It is unfortunate that Judson's format does not allow him to describe modern and historical developments in the physical, biological, and chemical sciences in a more systematic way.

Reading the book is somewhat like reading a textbook. There are all the glossy pictures, some of which add beauty and clarity to the prose and some of which are irrelevant. There is also lots of white space, perhaps to convince the reader that there is not that much to read.

It is unfortunate that he refers to the scientist as "he" and to humankind as "man" and that he disregards his own caution about the social sciences to use economics as an example of science in action. Nevertheless, Judson's writing style is easy, and what he writes about the method of scientific inquiry is clear and interesting. His knowledge and appreciation of science shine through.

Michele Hoffnung

THE SECOND COMING

Author: Walker Percy
Publisher: Farrar, Straus and Giroux (New York). 360 pp. $12.95
Type of work: Novel
Time: The present
Locale: Linwood, North Carolina

A man and a woman find a sense of purpose in a world fraught with frivolity and hypocrisy

> *Principal characters:*
> WILL BARRETT, a retired lawyer living in Linwood, North Carolina
> MARION PEABODY BARRETT, Will's deceased multi-millionaire wife
> LESLIE BARRETT, their daughter
> ALLISON HUGER, an insane asylum escapee
> KITTY HUGER, Allison's mother and Will's former sweetheart
> DR. DUK, Allison's psychiatrist
> JACK CURL, a minister who manages the Barretts' nursing home
> JASON CUPP, Leslie's fiancé
> LEWIS PECKHAM, the golf pro of the Linwood Country Club
> VANCE BATTLE, Will's doctor and golf partner
> REVEREND WEATHERBEE, a retired minister living at the Barretts' nursing home

When Will Barrett was a young boy, his father took him quail hunting in Georgia. There in the densely overgrown swamp-forest, his father shot and killed a quail, reloaded his double-barreled English Greener, and, aiming at a second quail, he missed, wounding Will instead. Again he reloaded the Greener and this time shot himself, leaving one cartridge untouched in the shotgun.

Will eventually became a Wall Street attorney and married Marion Peabody, a New England heiress. He retired at a young age to Linwood, North Carolina, where he and his wife would have the time and money to devote themselves to what they loved. For Marion that meant food and philanthropy; for Will that meant golf. Marion's money built the St. Mark's Nursing Home while Marion ate, steadily gaining weight until a cyst, impossible to locate within her copious layers of fatty tissue, caused her untimely death. Will was left with Marion's $60,000,000 estate, a nursing home, and a daughter, Leslie, a born-again Christian soon to be married to Jason Cupp, also a born-again Christian.

Will has what most people in Linwood consider an ideal life: plenty of money and plenty of time to enjoy it. Yet to Will his life seems frightfully incomplete. He has developed a slice in his golf game. He periodically falls face down, often on the golf course in a bunker or on a fairway, thinking about the cartridge left in his father's Greener.

At the same moment that Will is lying stretched out on the fairway, Allison Huger is sitting stone-faced on a park bench in Linwood. She has just escaped from Valleyhead, a local sanatorium, after undergoing thirty-one sessions of shock therapy. Several days earlier, just prior to her thirty-first shock treatment, Allie's parents came to Valleyhead to discuss her future with the psychiatrist, Dr. Duk. Allie had unexpectedly inherited a farm adjacent to the Linwood golf course and an island off the coast of Georgia, where Arab investors were already drawing up plans for a 144-hole golf complex. The Hugers and Dr. Duk agree that at least part of the inheritance should go toward finding a comfortable yet permanent home for Allie but that the bulk of the property should be managed by a trustee since Allie would probably never be competent to manage it herself.

Left momentarily alone in Duk's foyer, Allie steals $450 from her father's jacket, which she finds there. Returning to her room, she writes an elaborate plan for her escape in a notebook that she carries, hidden in her robe, to her next shock treatment. Patients are never watched carefully after treatment since they are too dazed to act independently. It is the perfect opportunity for escape. When Allie regains consciousness, she discovers the notebook in her pocket and carries out the plan, which leads her from the sanatorium to a dry goods store and finally to her park bench.

Sitting in the center of Linwood wearing newly purchased clothing and carrying a new back pack and sleeping bag, Allie wonders who she is, where she is, and how long she has been locked away. The next phase of her plan is to find the farm she has inherited and stake her claim. The farmhouse, she discovers, burned down years ago, but the greenhouse built to the side of a mountain is still standing. Upon inspection, Allie decides it will make as good a home as any.

Several days later Will is out golfing and slices a new ball into the woods. It hits the greenhouse, breaking a window pane and arousing Allie from a nap. While searching for his ball, Will finds Allie. In their brief exchange both realize that they share a unique brand of insanity. Will is the first to understand Allie's odd speech patterns and Allie, in turn, understands Will's strange disorder.

On his next round of golf, several days later, Will returns to the greenhouse, this time looking for more than a golf ball. He finds Allie struggling to move an enormous Grand Crown stove from the cellar of the burned farmhouse up to her greenhouse. Will suggests she use a block-and-tackle and offers to lend her equipment from a garage he owns in town. Allie accepts his offer, the first help she has accepted in years. By using pulleys, she moves the stove to the greenhouse where she is able to clean its many beautifully wrought parts and restore it to working condition. Having completed this task, Allie decides that her true calling in life is that of a hoister. She feels as long as she has her block-and-tackle she can lift anything.

While Allie is hoisting, Will is lunching with an odd assortment of guests. Leslie's future in-laws have come to discuss the rehearsal dinner even though Leslie and Jason refuse to have a rehearsal; Jack Curl, an Episcopal minister, is there asking Will for funds to build a faith-and-love community; Lewis Peckham, Linwood's golf pro, is also present, suggesting Beethoven and bourbon to cure Will's slice. To complicate matters further, Kitty Huger, his old flame, has shown up with her husband requesting that Will act as guardian to their insane daughter.

Unable to face lunch with these guests, Will retreats to his bedroom to find the Greener with the single cartridge. He realizes that his father's suicide had been a waste: it had proved nothing, asked no questions, found no answers. Will devises a plan that both asks a question and demands a yes-or-no answer. True, the plan could result in his death, but at least he would die with a clearer vision than his father had.

Will plans to lose himself within the maze of caves beneath the golf course and wait for a sign from God. A sign would prove God's existence; no sign would prove either that God does not exist or that he does not care. Will finds a comfortable chamber beneath the ground and waits patiently for over a week, drinking water but eating nothing. The experiment, however, is complicated by an abscessed tooth. Will is prepared to starve, but not with a throbbing toothache. Weak from hunger, he struggles desperately to retrace his path within the cave, becomes hopelessly lost, and crashes through a nest of bats, landing, miraculously, in Allie's greenhouse, which is heated in winter by air currents from the caves.

Allie hoists the unconscious Will onto her planting table where she bathes him and dresses his wounds. Pressing her naked body against his, she restores his warmth. Will, now Allie's legal guardian, awakens in the arms of his spiritual guardian. Perhaps the toothache was his answer after all.

Leaving the greenhouse late that night, Will experiences a series of seizures that leave him unconscious again, and he is taken to Duke University Hospital. Upon regaining consciousness, he is told he has an imbalance in his PH level. Hourly injections of hydrogen ions will correct this, and his sanity will be restored. He is moved to the nursing home where the medical staff can administer his ions.

The ions perform as predicted, leaving Will content to watch *Hollywood Squares* with the rest of the patients. One morning, however, his equilibrium is disturbed by a visit from Kitty, who alleges that he has violated her defenseless daughter. She vows to take Allie someplace where she will be safe from lecherous men like him. Just as Will is settling back to watch the *Morning Movie* he remembers that his PH level has not been checked in over twelve hours and that Allie needs his help.

With the bravura of a melodrama hero, Will races to the greenhouse, proposes to Allie, and carries her away to a Holiday Inn where they will be safe from Dr. Duk and Kitty. While Allie sleeps, Will takes his father's Greener and heaves it off a cliff. That one cartridge had never been fired but it might as well have been, because for years, Will realizes, he had been a walking dead man. He decides to give away the $60,000,000, money left him by a dead woman, and open a new law practice. Before returning to the greenhouse, Will stops at the nursing home where he recruits a retired gardener, a cabin builder, and a developer to help Allie manage her property. And finally, he asks the slightly senile Reverend Weatherbee to marry him and Allie.

As its title implies, *The Second Coming* is a novel about rebirth. In finding each other, Allie and Will find a purpose in life. Allie's awakening comes literally from Will's golf ball but figuratively from her learning to help another person. She becomes a hoister, hoisting stoves, but more often, fallen mortals. Her greenhouse, warmed by the stove and the steady air currents of the cave, becomes a church free of institutional hypocrisy, a place where both plants and people can thrive. Will's rebirth also comes from learning to help another. Despite his running a lavish non-profit nursing home, he never actually helps another person until he becomes a guardian to Allie. At the end of the novel, like a true guardian angel, Will gathers unto him the unwanted elderly, giving their lives renewed meaning.

Satisfaction, in Walker Percy's world, does not come from feats of philanthropy, nor from playing good golf; it comes from acting productively, from demonstrating life in a world full of death, from choosing a greenhouse over a Greener. Will Barrett shows that, as his name indicates, he will indeed bear and be fruitful.

Elizabeth Lubin

SHOW PEOPLE

Author: Kenneth Tynan
Publisher: Simon & Schuster (New York). 317 pp. $11.95
Type of work: Essays
Time: 1902–1978
Locale: England and the United States

Portraits of five show business greats including Ralph Richardson, Tom Stoppard, Johnny Carson, Mel Brooks, and Louise Brooks, that reveal their personal and professional lives as well as five different facets of the entertainment world

Kenneth Tynan introduces *Show People* profiles by saying that each of the five people that are profiled works in show business and that all are people he admires enormously. In addition, each is one of the very few giants in his or her field.

Sir Ralph Richardson is a great classical actor of the English theater. He, Sir John Gielgud, and Sir Lawrence Olivier form the "formidable trio" of English actors. Sir Ralph is the oldest, lacks the "obvious good looks" of the other two, and ripened as an actor a little later. Unlike Gielgud and Olivier, he has not established himself in the "Big Four" tragic Shakespearean roles but rather has played a full range of classical roles, most notably that of Falstaff. He has been cast as the Common Man instead of the tragic or poetic hero.

Born in 1902 in Cheltenham, Ralph, at seventeen, was an office boy in a Brighton insurance company. He had little education or taste for his job. When his paternal grandmother died leaving him five hundred pounds, he left his job and joined a semiprofessional acting troupe. By 1921 he had achieved professional status. He did not become a star until 1944 when, at forty, his lack of physical glamour no longer mattered so much. In 1947 he was knighted along with Olivier. He is portrayed, in 1977, as a man of enormous wit and talent.

Tom Stoppard was born in 1937 in Zlin, Czechoslovakia. When the Nazis invaded his homeland two years later, his family moved to Singapore. In 1942 he moved with his mother and brother to India. His father died in a Japanese air raid in 1946. An emigrant, Stoppard is "more English than the English," writing his adopted language magnificently.

In 1974, Stoppard espoused a desire to keep social relevance out of his plays, "to have the courage of his lack of convictions." Convictions, he found, were too confining. But by 1977 his political commitment is quite apparent. In his play *Every Good Boy Deserves Favour* he attacks the Soviet use of brainwashing to silence political dissenters. He also flew to Prague to visit Vaclav Havel, a playwright who has been imprisoned for his active support of Charter 77, a document urging the Czech government to respect human rights, especially free speech. Stoppard recognizes Havel as his "mirror image—a Czech artist who has undergone pressures that Stoppard escaped when his parents took him into exile." Tynan develops this theme throughout the profile.

Stoppard began his writing career in local journalism after leaving school at seventeen. His first play, in 1960, was *The Gamblers;* his first big London success was *Rosencrantz and Guildenstern Are Dead;* his masterpiece, *Jumpers.* Stoppard is well read, rational in his play construction, and, now, highly politicized.

Johnny Carson has avoided appearing on stage and in film, shuns public gatherings, and yet comes to life for ninety minutes nearly every night in front of close to 14,000,000 viewers on the "Tonight Show." He is very private, he smokes heavily, and he is brilliant at what he does.

Every night he does the monologue, "the *salto mortale*—circus parlance for an aerial somersault performed on the tightrope . . . and he does it without a net." He chats with his guests without notes or prepared questions. Performers line up to appear with him, get paid bottom dollar, and are on the line in the "hot seat" next to Carson. Fellow comedians love working with him, others sometimes freeze when they meet on the air "for the first time, . . . host, interrogator, and judge." Carson plays a wide variety of comic characters himself, writes much of his own material, and is hilariously spontaneous on the air.

Carson was born in 1925 in Corning, Iowa. At twelve he bought a junior magician's kit and worked hard to master basic skills. He stuck with it through high school, the navy, and college, always moonlighting as a magician. After college graduation, he held a traditional set of jobs before his television success. Carson is not world famous; what he does is not transportable. But he does it better than anyone. He entertains more viewers, sells the most products, and avoids issues that are the most controversial.

Mel Brooks is a "short little Hebrew" comedian from New York. One of the best comic filmmakers in the business, Brooks' approach is to "set off atom bombs of laughter." Brooks is a master at comic improvisation. He and Carl Reiner used to convulse their friends with impromptu dialogues. Then, in the early 1950's, Reiner bought a tape recorder to preserve some of their routines, and from this came the Two-Thousand-Year-Old Man who stars on four albums.

Brooks was born in 1926 to a very poor Jewish immigrant family.

His father died when Brooks was two, and the loss was great. Brooks'
memories are of poverty, depression, and thoughts of suicide. His
routines reflect all of these, as well as a fear of death.

His show business career began in the Catskills at sixteen when he
met a young sax player named Sid Caesar and was given the opportunity to fill in for a sick stand-up comic. In 1947, Caesar hired Brooks to
write for him, which Brooks did on and off for twelve years. In 1960,
Brooks and Reiner made their first record. In 1962 his first film, a three
and a half minute cartoon entitled *The Critic,* opened and won two
Academy Awards. Brooks wrote, produced, directed, and starred in
his latest film, *High Anxiety.*

Louise Brooks was a silent movie queen; she made twenty-four films
in the years 1925 through 1938. Her two masterpieces are *Pandora's
Box* and *The Diary of a Lost Girl.* She was born in 1906 in Cherryvale,
Kansas. Her mother instilled in her a love of liberty and encouraged
her to dance. By fifteen, Louise Brooks was an unparalleled beauty.

Hers is a typical story of stardom: wild parties, wild drinking, wild
sex. Brooks was a beauty used by men; an actress accused of not
acting; a star dropped because of her independence. Her allure is still
apparent at 72 when Tynan, an ardent fan, travels to Rochester, New
York, to screen six of her films at the International Museum of Photography and to visit her. She flirts with him as she shares her life story.

Show People is good entertainment. Kenneth Tynan uses his years
of notes, reviews by himself and others, conversations, interviews,
and scripts to bring each of the five personalities to life, revealing
strengths, weaknesses, idiosyncrasies, motivating forces. He reveals
but he does not judge, thus opening and expanding the reader's mind.

The breadth of the book is remarkable. Tynan knowledgeably explores five different areas of show business from the classical theater
to silent movies. He appreciates each as an art form at the same time
probing its social meaning. The essays are not parallel in construction.
Each is shaped by the person and the art form. The emotional range of
the essays is also broad, from the humor of Mel Brooks' profile, to the
poignancy of Louise Brooks.'

Michele Hoffnung

SIDE EFFECTS

Author: Woody Allen (1935–   )
Publisher: Random House (New York). 149 pp. $8.95
Type of work: Short stories
Time: Ancient times to the present
Locale: New York City

A collection of sixteen stories that examine a variety of subjects, including the efforts of New York men to find sexual and intellectual fulfillment, Socrates' death, time travel, and a joke by Abraham Lincoln

The characters and situations of the sixteen stories presented in *Side Effects* provide the opportunity for Woody Allen to deliver an unending stream of humorous lines along with his observations on sex, politics, food, intellectuals, and his central preoccupations, love, and death. "Fabrizio's: Criticism and Response" is Allen's satire of "one of the more thought-provoking journals" and the critics who find hidden meanings where none exist. Fabian Plotnick, a restaurant critic, reviews Fabrizio's Villa Nova Restaurant. According to Plotnick, "the linguine . . . has a pervasive Marxist quality to it . . . all life was represented here in this antipasto, with the black olives an unbearable reminder of mortality." Plotnick's article elicits responses from readers who themselves further interpret the food at Fabrizio's.

In the outrageous story "The Kugelmass Episode," Sidney Kugelmass is a professor dissatisfied with his marriage. When his analyst fails to help him he turns to Persky, a magician from Brooklyn. Persky has invented a box that can transport one into the pages of the novel of his choice. Kugelmass chooses *Madame Bovary*. All goes well for Kugelmass, and he enchants Emma Bovary. Then Persky reverses his magic, returning Kugelmass and Emma to New York for a weekend, where Persky's machine breaks down. Kugelmass is forced to spend a full week with Emma in New York. She gets bored watching television, meets a "sensitive" Off Broadway producer and asks Kugelmass for money to enroll in the Neighborhood Playhouse. Kugelmass is in despair, hating Madame Bovary, before Persky finally repairs his box, returning Emma to the novel. When he tries Persky's machine again it explodes. Persky is killed, and Kugelmass is transported into Remedial Spanish where "a large and hairy irregular verb—raced after him on its spindly legs."

Dr. Ossip Parkis, a surgeon from New York, is the central character of "The Lunatic's Tale." He spends years searching for the perfect woman. Several marriages, nights at singles bars, and newspaper ads all yield flawed women. Finally, Parkis meets Olive Chomsky. Olive is charming, brilliant, and humorous. Unfortunately, the lines around her eyes reminded Parkis of his Aunt Rifka. Tiffany Schmeederer, on the other hand, is "an empty little yo-yo" with a body that "comes along every few million years and usually heralds an ice age or the destruction of the world by fire." Parkis is torn between the two women. He enjoys life with Olive, but is sexually satisfied only with Tiffany. Parkis's solution is to switch the two women's brains. Parkis marries the brilliant Olive, now in Tiffany's body. However, he becomes dissatisfied with his perfect woman, developing "instead a crush on Billie Jean Zapruder, an airline stewardess whose boyish, flat figure and Alabama twang caused my heart to do flip-flops." Parkis then becomes a lunatic.

Insanity is also the lot of Willard Pogrebin, who attempts to shoot the President of the United States. In the Army, Willard was secretly given LSD. At the Veterans' Hospital he was treated with electric shock. Later he took peyote and cocaine at a Black Mass in California. To repair his ravaged mind, Willard became a follower of the Reverend Chow Bok Ding. The hero of "Nefarious Times We Live In" then attempted to restore his emotional stability through PET—Perlmutter's Ego Therapy. Perlmutter turns out to be a Nazi who holds his charges in place with Dobermans. Willard finally moves to San Francisco, where he is kidnapped, drugged, tickled by experts, and forced to listen to country and western music. Willard "was then brought into a room where President Gerald Ford shook my hand and asked me if I would follow him around the country and take a shot at him now and then, being careful to miss. He said it would give him a chance to act bravely and could serve as a distraction from genuine issues, which he felt unequipped to deal with."

The humor of Woody Allen characters also lies in the composite of strange mannerisms and activities they embody. Sandor Needleman, a philosopher, fights with Dwight D. Eisenhower, then president of Columbia University, over "whether the class bell signaled the end of a period or the beginning of another." He proves "that sentence structure is innate but that whining is acquired." At various times Needleman has been a Communist, a Nazi, an opponent of nuclear testing, and lover of a particular brand of tuna fish. He dies after being "tapped" on the head by a wrecking ball. "His last, enigmatic words were, 'No thanks, I already own a penguin.' "

Woody Allen tells us in "My Apology" that he admires Socrates for having the courage to die for his principles. Allen wants to emulate that bravery and give his own life "authentic meaning." Yet in the end he turns out to be "a cringing vermin," afraid to die. At the last moment, Allen-Socrates is pardoned by the Athenian Senate and is honored instead of killed. Also saved at the last moment is Cloquet, accused of killing Brisseau in "The Condemned." Just before his execution the real murderer confesses. In both cases the saved men are reduced to silliness. "Cloquet sank to his knees and kissed the floor of his cell . . . Three days later, he was back in jail for showing up at the Louvre in bikini underwear, with a fake nose and glasses." Allen-Socrates tells the parable of the cave after his pardon, concluding by having the man who sees the world in all its clarity open a meat market, marry a dancer, "and die of a cerebral hemorrhage at forty-two."

"The Shallowest Man" is the story of Lenny Mendel. For years he plays poker once a week with a group of men that includes Meyer Iskowitz. One day Iskowitz does not show up for the game; it turns out that he is in the hospital dying of cancer. Mendel is afraid of death and does not want to visit poor Iskowitz, who is without any family. Finally, to preserve his reputation with his poker friends, Mendel visits the hospital. When the nurse, Miss Hill, comes into the room, Lenny falls in love with her. Now Mendel returns every day to visit Iskowitz. Mendel's attention toward Iskowitz wins him the admiration of the other poker players, but his plans are set back when he learns that Miss Hill is engaged. At the same time Mendel "dared not make a move for Miss Hill, finding himself in the awkward position of not wanting her ever to dream that he was there so frequently for any reason other than to see Meyer Iskowitz." Iskowitz, too, is unaware of Mendel's true motive. He tells Mendel that he loves him and has never been closer to another human being and then dies contented. Miss Hill and her fiancé break up, and Mendel dates her.

Woody Allen's characters in *Side Effects* become comic through their exaggerated qualities. For many of the heroes—Sidney Kugelmass, Ossip Parkis, and Lenny Mendel—an all-consuming desire for the perfect woman leads them to actions they would otherwise consider insane. Intellectuals such as Sandor Needleman and Fabian Plotnick do not lose touch with reality. Rather they see concrete things—food, clothes, travel—in terms of their bizarre philosophies. Alongside the bizarre is a common urge for success and self-preservation on the part of the characters. Sandor Needleman protests nuclear tests by sitting on a test site. Yet, "when it became apparent the test would proceed as planned, Needleman was heard to mutter, 'Uh-oh,' and made a run for it." The appeal of the characters and the source of their humor lie in the normality and reality of their concerns. The joy of reading *Side Effects* comes from the insights it gives each reader into his own problems and desires, to see the ridiculous side of his own life.

Richard Lachmann

SMILE PLEASE

Author: Jean Rhys (1890–1979)
Publisher: Harper & Row (New York). 151 pp. $10.95
Type of work: Autobiography
Time: Late 19th century to 1979
Locale: Dominica, West Indies; England and Continental Europe

An unfinished autobiographical account of segments of Rhys's life given as a series of vignettes, written at the end of her life

Jean Rhys, angered by what others had written about her, wanted to set the record straight in *Smile Please.* To do so, late in her eighties, and in poor health, she did not attempt a continuous narrative, but chose instead to do a series of vignettes. The book is divided into two sections: "Smile Please," which concerns her childhood in Dominica and in which she was moving from the vignettes toward a continuous narrative, and "It Began to Grow Cold," which consists "of material that does not claim to be finished. . . ." It includes the period from her first journey to England to her last quiet years in Devonshire.

The first section of her unfinished autobiography provides a glimpse of Rhys as a small girl in the beautiful but divided world of Dominica. The lush beauty of the island is contrasted with the dark superstitions of the natives. Her father, a hard-working doctor, was an imprudent manager, and early in Rhys's life one of their lovely estates had to be sold. Her two brothers were sent to school in England, and her older sister went to live with relatives in Nassau. Jean, left at home with a sister seven years her junior, found her "loneliness was very sudden." It seems, however, that loneliness was to be her lifetime companion.

Jean Rhys loved reading the few books the family had, but her nurse, Meta, who "didn't like her much," Rhys said, did not approve. Meta was surely less than an ideal nurse, by any standards, if Rhys's memory can be trusted. On walks with Jean, Meta walked so fast that the child had to run to keep up. She terrified Rhys with tales of zombies, werewolves, centipedes, and the like. Meta eventually left, or was sent away, but the damage was already done, according to Rhys: Meta had introduced her to a world of fear and distrust.

Her grandmother and two aunts lived at Geneva during Rhys's childhood, and she visited there often. Then came a big family quarrel, and she stopped going. Rhys went back later, but the house had burned down.

The next chapter opens with the question: "How old was I when I smashed the fair doll's face?" Two dolls had arrived from England; one fair and one dark. As Rhys gazed in admiration at the dark doll her younger sister snatched it away, and in spite of Rhys's protests, she was told she must let her little sister have it. She walked into the garden, and in the shadow of a mango tree, took up a large stone and smashed the fair doll's fair face. Later she vividly remembered the guilt that was half triumph.

Rhys began quite early to catalog the numerous people who "didn't like" her. It almost seems that with each entry she divided herself further from the rest of the world. It is apparent that Rhys found it easy and natural to withdraw into herself from what was, to her, essentially a hostile world. She seemed to allow her own inner life to substitute for the "real world," and throughout her life she returned to it for extended periods. It is, very probably, this inner life that was the core and catalyst of her writing, the one aspect that kept her, in her eyes, from being a failure.

In another vignette she recalled a riot by the natives in Dominica. Their anger was directed against the editor of a local newspaper who wrote an article attacking the power of the Catholic clergy. Rhys had attended for a short time the Catholic school, even though she was brought up as a Protestant. There she went through a period of not only wanting to become a Catholic, but also to become a nun. The student body was predominantly black, and it was here that Rhys learned "They hate us. We are hated. Not possible. Yes it is possible and it is so."

When she was twelve, Jean Rhys was taken to Castries to be a bridesmaid at her uncle's wedding. And, even though an Englishman, Mr. Kennaway, stared at her with a look that said "Not a pretty little girl," she received some dresses that she liked, her "stockings no longer drooped," and she no longer thought of herself as an outcast.

In another chapter Rhys explained that she became very good at "blotting things out," particularly sexual experiences. "Gradually this withdrawal became curiosity, fascination." She enjoyed going to the new Carnegie library, sitting in a rocking chair on the veranda, plunging into the "real" world of books, and forgetting everything else. She liked books about prostitution, and remembered one, *The Sands of Pleasure,* by Filson Young. She said, "It must have been well written, otherwise I would never have remembered it so perfectly to this day."

In the final chapter of the first section, Rhys went to England with her aunt. In the cabin of the ship, she saw that her favorite brooch had been crushed, and she put it away. "Already my childhood, the West Indies, my father and mother had been left behind; I was forgetting them. They were the past." This "blotting" ability anticipates what is to follow in the second section of the book, "It Began to Grow Cold."

Jean Rhys described her first impressions of England—its tunnels and trains, its boardinghouses where one must make an appointment to take a bath. Rhys, from the tropics, always hated the thought of "coldness," and in England she experienced coldness on more than one level. There she went to the Perse School for girls, but left after one term to go to the Royal Academy of Dramatic Arts, hoping to become an actress. There, a man in the group asked Rhys to marry him. "Having a proposal made me feel as if I had passed an examination."

Her father died in Dominica, and her mother summoned her home, since there was no money to pay her way at the academy. Deciding "they don't want me back," Rhys took a job in a musical comedy called *Our Miss Gibbs*. She experienced the ups and downs of a stage career and described how her love for books completely left her at that time. She also learned to hate landladies. It was during this period that she had her "first real affair with a man," an affair that lasted eighteen months. Pondering the end of her love affair, she wondered why that of her friend had ended with an elaborate marriage and hers had not.

In another chapter Rhys recalled an abortion and her contemplated suicide. She had an abortion without guilt, received money from her former lover through his solicitors with some anger, decided that she would never be able to get another job, and considered drinking a bottle of gin and jumping out of the window. Then a gift-laden, three-foot high Christmas tree was also delivered from her former lover. She was saved from the jump by an acquaintance who pointed out that her room was not far enough above the ground. Rhys lugged the tree off to a children's hospital, and then her memory became muddled.

Her friend helped her find new quarters, a room in Fulham, where "World's End" was the sign on all the buses. On her first walk in the new place, she bought some pens and blank exercise books, returned to her room, and wrote herself out of her love affair. She then put the exercise books in a suitcase, not looking at them for seven years. Nevertheless, they became the beginning.

Not happy in Fulham, Rhys moved back to Bloomsbury. She became part of a new "nightclub" and met a man who proposed, but it came to nothing. She found work in a canteen for soldiers, but in 1917 the canteen was amalgamated with another, and she was again, "positionless." Befriended by a Belgian refugee and his wife, she met at one of their so-called "nursery teas" Jean Lenglet, a rather silent young man who became her first husband. He proposed later, at another party, asking her to come to Paris. It was what she had been waiting for, and she agreed.

She received no encouragement from her friends except Camille, who explained that everyone else was jealous. It was 1919 before she was able to book passage to Paris. She then wrote to the former lover who had continued his financial support, and with great pleasure told him it would no longer be needed. He warned her against the marriage, but she boarded the boat, vowing that she would never go back to England.

In Paris, neither of them had money, but they were happy at first. They had a child, but he died in infancy. In the next vignette, Rhys finished her first novel, *Quartet*. While in London to sell the novel she met Leslie Tilden Smith, with whom she had an affair. Back in Paris, she wrote the first half of *After Leaving Mr. MacKenzie*, and was divorced by Jean Lenglet. She returned to London, married Leslie Smith, and wrote the second half of *Mr. MacKenzie*. Her earlier notebooks became the foundation for *Voyage in the Dark*. After completing *Good Morning, Midnight*, Rhys did not write for some time. Leslie died, she met his cousin, Max, and they were married.

In one section of *Smile Please,* she took part in an imaginary trial, while Max, husband number three, spent six months in jail for misappropriation. The book ends after Max's death. Rhys lived out her days walking up and down the passage in their little cottage, afraid of spiders, mice, and the people in the village. Meta's eerie early instruction was, indeed, long-lasting.

If, as it now seems, Jean Rhys's novels are being plucked out of obscurity to receive feminist approval, Rhys herself would undoubtedly be surprised. She had faith in her novels because so much of her life was in them, but feminist leanings were never a part of her life.

Smile Please has a foreword by Diana Athill, a chronology of the life of Jean Rhys, a bibliography of her works, and a center section of photographs of Rhys, Rhys's family, and a few family dwellings. Athill's foreword goes to great lengths to give Jean Rhys favorable treatment. She is aware, of course, that *Smile Please* is not a finished literary work, yet she struggles overmuch to apologize for its shortcomings.

The writing in *Smile Please* is choppy, fragmented, unemotional; the style is pedestrian. Many segments end with a formula statement of no great importance. Overall, the reader senses in the Jean Rhys of *Smile Please* an overwhelming and unappealing self-interest. Unless one is a devotee of her novels, the reaction to all the introspective self-consciousness, the drab mental meanderings, is likely to be: "So what?"

To Jean Rhys's fans, the autobiographical glimpses of unrelated portions of her life might well be of interest. To others, her unfinished autobiography, *Smile Please,* might rather be a frustrating experience.

Alice C. Parker

SMILEY'S PEOPLE

Author: John Le Carré
Publisher: Alfred A. Knopf (New York). 374 pp. $10.95
Type of work: Novel
Time: The present
Locale: London, Paris, Hamburg, Berne, and Berlin

British counterintelligence expert George Smiley comes out of retirement to undertake a freelance investigation that leads him to the long awaited confrontation with his adversary, the Soviet agent called Karla

Principal characters:
GEORGE SMILEY, retired head of the British Secret Service, known as the Circus
OLIVER LACON, second in command to the new chief of the Circus, Saul Enderby
TOBY ESTERHASE, retired head of the Lamplighters, surveillance arm of the Circus
CONNIE SACHS, retired head of the Circus Soviet research section, known as "Mother Russia"
PETER GUILLAM, Smiley's protégé and close friend, now head of the Paris office of the Circus
GRIGORIEV, highly placed Soviet official in Berne, Switzerland
KARLA, head of Moscow Centre, Soviet counterpart to the Circus, and George Smiley's long-time enemy

George Smiley, the intrepid Cold War warrior of author John Le Carré's fertile imagination, returns to the precincts of murder, mystery, and Cold War tensions in Le Carré's newest work, *Smiley's People*. Devotees of Le Carré's specialized approach to the genre will recognize that *Smiley's People* picks up a number of threads from its predecessor, *Tinker, Tailor, Soldier, Spy*. Most of the regulars appear, although some of them in new guises or new jobs: Saul Enderby now has Smiley's job as head of the British secret service, the Circus. Oliver Lacon has become Enderby's second in command and heir apparent; Connie Sachs, nicknamed "Mother Russia," earthy and omniscient about Soviet affairs, appears close to death. Toby Esterhase, former head of the Lamplighters, is out and discredited. Smiley's protégé, Peter Guillam, is working in Paris, and finally, the Circus itself is recovering from the latest organizational upheavals imposed by a nervous government. The Circus is being run by an "interministerial steering committee" known as the "Wise Men." George Smiley himself, the quintessential Cold War warrior, is languishing in enforced retirement, literally a spy without portfolio.

This is the new world of international espionage, a world controlled by bureaucrats and more concerned with clean hands than blown covers or safe networks. Old warriors like George Smiley cannot work within such a system. Outdated, outmoded, and outfoxed, Smiley has retired to his home in Bywater Street to lick his wounds and to ponder the loss of love and honor in an absurd world that was never too reliable. His usefulness terminated by the Circus, Smiley has left behind some unfinished business. Over his entire career and much of his personal life as well, hangs the shadow of Smiley's opposite number and nemesis, the enigmatic Karla of Moscow Centre. In *Smiley's People*, George Smiley has a rendezvous with destiny, a rendezvous that takes him to the geographical edge of freedom, the Berlin Wall. However, Smiley still has a trick or two left, and Le Carré gives the reader Smiley at his best: Smiley outside the system, Smiley seeking help from his people, Smiley closing in on Karla. There is no glamour, only suffering; no victories, only lesser defeats.

The plot begins with events outside of Smiley's control or knowledge. There has been a murder, a particularly brutal murder of Vladimir Miller, a Russian émigré, former top spy for the British, and powerful link to the dissident émigré groups flourishing in Paris and London. Vladimir was once Smiley's agent; Smiley was his "vicar," known by the work name of "Max." As Smiley tells Oliver Lacon, "For three long years, Vladimir was the best source we ever had on Soviet capabilities and intentions—and at the height of the cold war." But, like his mentor, Vladimir had fallen on hard times. His undiminished concern with Soviet networks in the West made him an embarrassment in the enlightened era of détente. For Vladimir, like Smiley, there is no place in the new Circus. Vladimir's murder comes as an unpleasant surprise to Lacon and the top echelon of the Circus. It is necessary to dispose of the ugly episode quickly and quietly. In a middle-of-the-night meeting at a safe house in London, Lacon appeals to Smiley's discretion and loyalty.

Lacon wants Smiley to work outside the system, outside the Circus, to tidy up the loose ends of Vladimir's life and presumably of the old man's meddling, which led to his death. Smiley learns at this meeting that the day before he died Vladimir had called the Circus asking to speak to "Max." His tone was both urgent and pleading. "Tell Max it concerns the Sandman. Tell him I have two proofs and can bring them with me." "Sandman" was Vladimir's code name for Karla.

Among the several old contacts Smiley visits along the way to pick up clues are two former Circus colleagues, Toby Esterhase and Connie Sachs. Toby now calls himself Signor Benati and runs a less than reputable art gallery. He, too, was upended in the Circus reorganization, but his contacts among the Lamplighters, the operatives who trailed suspects and monitored electronic surveillance, are still strong.

Toby has simply gone underground.

Toby originally worked with Smiley in moving Vladimir from Moscow to the safety of Paris and then to London. Smiley's hunch that Vladimir may have contacted Toby first proves correct. Toby reluctantly and angrily spills a story of demands from Vladimir to travel to Germany and arrange an exchange of documents, an enterprise designed to reveal Soviet information important in Vladimir's view, but more likely just another of Vladimir's anti-Soviet obsessions as Toby sees it, who sent him packing.

After his visit with Toby, Smiley calls on Connie Sachs, the former resident Soviet expert at the Circus. While Smiley may be able to argue that his visit to Toby Esterhase had "fallen within the crude lines of Lacon's brief," there is no question but that his next visit "led for better or worse to the forbidden province of his secret brief." Smiley finds Connie living out her sodden life in illness and near-senility in the countryside as proprietor of a dog kennel. He has come to "Con," as he calls her, for "her own mountainous memory"—the long forgotten details about old cases and old agents that only she remembers. It is from these visits with two of his people that Smiley begins slowly and steadily to unravel a complicated many-layered secret that will lead him to Karla.

In Germany, Smiley finds Otto Leipzig dead and through tangible clues begins to glean facts about Karla's role in Vladimir's murder. Otto was working a Soviet attaché named Kirov. Smiley's conclusion is that Otto got too close to Kirov's real work and Karla's hoods dispatched him in their usual coldly efficient fashion, exactly as they had Otto's best friend—Vladimir. From another of Otto's friends Smiley learns of Kirov's mission: "To make a legend for a girl."

Believing that there is a link from the Russian agent Kirov to Karla to Vladimir's murder, Smiley travels to Paris to put some of the pieces together with the help of his protégé and long-time friend, Peter Guillam. Peter, who once headed the Scalphunters, the Circus's agent recruiters, has been reassigned to the Paris network. Smiley has Peter arrange a meeting with Saul Enderby, head of all Circus operations. The meeting, held in Enderby's private safe house in London, results in Smiley's receiving Circus approval for the final pursuit of Karla. But Enderby wants Karla alive, for interrogation.

Smiley and Guillam move on to Switzerland to follow a lead on a highly placed Soviet official named Grigoriev. Toby Esterhase has moved to Berne ahead of Smiley and checked out Grigoriev's home and habits. Smiley moves into a safe house established long ago by Toby. He and Guillam begin their quiet tracking of the Russian, a man who has undisputable links to Karla. Through a series of events—all orchestrated by Toby's Lamplighters—Smiley learns that Grigoriev receives from Moscow each month an unusually large amount of money, which he deposits into a bank. Married to a harridan who controls his every move, Grigoriev is an official with an impeccable reputation and a mistress. Aware of the Russian's vulnerability, Toby convinces Smiley that Grigoriev can be turned.

When Toby and his cohorts trap Grigoriev and bring him before Smiley, Toby's postulate is borne out. Grigoriev tells them the whole history of his posting in Berne and Karla's role in it. It has been Grigoriev's job to protect Karla's daughter, a mentally disturbed young woman in need of specialized care. The "legend" is the cover story that got her safely out of Moscow, where she was branded a misfit and a criminal, and brought her to an institution in Berne. Grigoriev pays her bills with the money Karla sends him, visits her in the role of her "uncle," and reports on her progress to Karla. Karla, for his part, has revealed a very human side of himself that may be his ruin in Moscow Centre. But even Grigoriev does not know these facts. It is Smiley, with his long history of studying Karla and digging into Karla's background, who fits all the pieces together at last. Karla has made a legend for his own daughter, using Moscow Centre funds. He is compromised, and now Smiley can at long last offer him a way out.

The conclusion of *Smiley's People* is a rapidly paced, tension-filled sequence of events that has Smiley sending a letter to Karla via Grigoriev. Delivery to Karla is the last price Grigoriev must pay before Smiley will allow him to defect.

At the Berlin Wall Smiley, Guillam, and Toby wait and watch. In the ferocious cold of the night, a figure begins the long walk across the bridge from East to West.

> From beyond the rampart, Smiley heard light footsteps and the vibration of an iron fence. He caught the smell of an American cigarette as the icy wind wafted it ahead of the smoker. He realized he had no real name to address his enemy: only a code-name, and a woman's at that. Even his military rank was a mystery. And still Smiley hung back, like a man refusing to go on stage.
>
> And suddenly, there he stood, like a man slipping into a crowded hall unnoticed. One little man, hatless, with a satchel. He took a step forward and in the halo Smiley saw his face, aged, weary, and travelled.

At last, face to face, Smiley's quest is ended.

John Le Carré has long set the standard for the espionage novel. In such works as *The Spy Who Came in From the Cold; Tinker, Tailor, Soldier, Spy; The Honourable Schoolboy,* and now, *Smiley's People,* Le Carré has evolved a world in which spying for one's country is a tough, often thankless, always dirty occupation. Le Carré's spies teeter on the seesaw of international give and take where loyalties are frequently up for grabs—in this world the heart may be as significant a yardstick as the head.

Smiley's People, like Le Carré's other novels, has a complex, at times enigmatic, plot. Characters and events come and go with disarming rapidity. The reader has to observe clues and revelations while Smiley's steady, ponderous logic pervades over all. *Smiley's People* appears to be Le Carré's swan song to his much put-upon hero, George Smiley. If so, such an event is much to be lamented by Le Carré fans. For George Smiley has emerged as the most human—and humane—spy of Cold War literature. The novel *Smiley's People* is a taut, carefully crafted denouement to George Smiley's quests for his "black Grail," Karla, for his own professional vindication, and for his fragile peace of mind. Readers can only hope that in his act of setting George Smiley gently aside, Le Carré has a new hero waiting in the wings. A fitting epitaph for George Smiley (when he does officially depart literary life) may be borrowed from Joseph Conrad: "He was one of us."

Ilona Fucci

A SOLDIER'S EMBRACE

Author: Nadine Gordimer (1923–   )
Publisher: Viking Press (New York). 144 pp. $8.95
Type of work: Short stories
Time: The present
Locale: South Africa

Tales of love and politics in racially divided South Africa

Principal characters:
> CHIPANDE, the black revolutionary leader in "A Soldier's Embrace"
> MAXINE, the misunderstood family outcast in "Siblings"
> DR. FRANZ-JOSEF VON LEINSDORF, the white geologist who takes a black lover in "Town and Country Lovers"
> PAULUS EYSENDYCK; THEBEDI, the white boy and black girl who become lovers in "Town and Country Lovers," part two
> RUTHIE HARDER, the mad one in "A Mad One"
> ANITA GONZALES, the aging, alcoholic whore in "The Need for Something Sweet"
> THE CHIEF, leader and modern-day Judas of a small village that is burned down in "An Oral History"

"A Soldier's Embrace," the opening story of the collection by the same name, begins in South Africa the day a cease-fire is signed. Caught in the buoyant, joyful crowd composed of both the colonial army and the black freedom fighters, a young white woman is jostled and pushed through the street. Her path is suddenly blocked by two soldiers, enemies just hours before, now locked in clumsy embrace. One is white and the other is black. The woman wraps an arm over each man's shoulder, kisses both on the cheek, and thus becomes a part of the embrace, a part of the celebration. For an instant, race and emotion are fused, joined through the shared relief of being alive after a long and bitter struggle. Through this riveting incident, in this first story, Nadine Gordimer immediately defines her turf—racially torn South Africa—and proceeds, through the next eleven stories, to illuminate the contrasting lives of the people who populate it. In this first story, the embrace is eventually dissolved and the wife returns home to her husband. He is a liberal lawyer, a sympathizer with the revolution, and has done much through his profession to ensure its success. Now that his hopes have been realized, he yearns for a consulate position within the new administration, or even a post in the university. Chipande, his old friend, who emerged from the revolution as a leader, is vague and speaks only in generalities. While his wife ponders the incident in the street, the lawyer frets over his future. Everything is suddenly different now; many of his white friends have already departed. Unable to rekindle the old camaraderie he once shared with the new black leadership, he does—over Chipande's belated and emotional entreaties—the only thing he can do. Taking his wife, he leaves the country and the way of life he worked so long to champion.

"A Lion on the Freeway" continues the disenfranchisement theme, describing the late-night, haunting sound of lions groaning in the zoo. Although born and raised in captivity, there is something in the lions that cries for release on hot summer nights, a peculiar noise that is carried on a breeze over the freeways and into the beds of terrified listeners. The tragedy and irony of the lions' imprisonment in a land where they are supposedly kings is, of course, intended as a parallel and a warning to their human counterparts.

"Siblings" chronicles a teenager's fascination with, and education by, a cousin's self-destruction. Maxine, long an outcast and gladly forgotten member of the family, wanders aimlessly through life, creating scenes, getting arrested, and eating prodigious quantities of doughnuts. When a young cousin takes, at the urging of his own family, a renewed interest in her, presenting her with a dress for her birthday, she is overcome with joy. She tries the dress on in front of him, baring her nakedness along with the scars she has accumulated over a desperate life; baring for him too his first sight of unclothed womanhood in all its stages of change and deterioration. When she has gone, he watches her from the window, knowing somehow that he has seen all women, but will never see this particular one again.

"Time Did" also deals with the changes women undergo, but focuses instead on the changes they go through, over time, with men. In bed with a lover of many years, an unnamed woman listens as her man describes intimate relationships he is having with two other women. She hears him say: "I am between two girls at the moment," and realizes how long it has taken for him to be able to say such a thing to her. She knows, without dramatics, that something has happened to him; the time has finally arrived when things can happen to him without happening to her. She sees that she represents, finally, the thing he most fears: "that final softening of flesh that is coming to you as a man one day, your death as a lover of women."

"A Hunting Accident," in which a gun is accidentally discharged, harmlessly, concerns itself with the consequences of violence and human error, emphasizing along the way how thin the line can be between a harmless incident and disaster. "For Dear Life," as subtle a pro-life story as can be found anywhere, is told from within the womb, as well as through the eyes of an expectant mother. Past incarnations, hopes, and failures are recalled, future ones envisioned.

Speaking to herself, to her unborn child, a woman says: "No one will know who you are; not even you. Only we, who are forgetting each other, will know who you never were."

In "Town and Country Lovers," parts one and two, Nadine Gordimer returns to the central theme of her collection, the consequences of interracial relationships. In the first part, a lonely geologist falls in love with and takes into his home a poor black girl. Their relationship blossoms slowly and naturally, but is embarrassingly and irrevocably torn by the intrusion of authority. The two are tried for violating the Immorality Act and, although acquitted for lack of evidence, are publicly humiliated. The geologist observes in the end that, "Even in my own country it's difficult for a person from a higher class to marry one from a lower class." In the second part of this story, a similar situation arises when two childhood friends, black and white, grow up and consummate their relationship, ending with the girl, Thebedi, becoming pregnant. Although she is already married, the obviously white condition of the baby is ignored until her lover takes matters into his own hands and kills the infant. He is acquitted of the crime, naturally, and Thebedi, talking to reporters afterwards, says: "It was a thing of our childhood, we don't see each other anymore."

A cross-section of complicated and sometimes bizarre lives runs through "A Mad One," while "You Name It" tells of a married mistress living with the secret of her third child's parentage. In "The Termitary," children watch in fascination as men with seemingly mysterious powers search out a queen termite from the basement of a rotting house. The next to last story, "The Need for Something Sweet," tells of an impossible relationship between a naive young man and an older, disillusioned, and alcoholic, woman. "You don't realize it will all happen to you," she warns. The young man understands only later, when he himself has become older and embittered and remembers her name. In the last story of the collection, "An Oral History," the fall of a chief and his village—a fall brought about by his own betrayal—to the convulsions of his country's hatred, represents the final capitulation of old values to new.

The skill of Nadine Gordimer, her subtle and not-so-subtle stitching of romance and politics, is apparent in all of the stories in this collection. Still, the effects of this curious blending are cumulative. Taken together, they represent an eloquent and powerful balance of passions. Although the setting itself, South Africa, is unique, the characters are universal. They see, think, and feel the things all people do; and through them the reader is able to experience a land and its customs personally. In this land, her land, passion may abound. Still, it is a passion that is ever looking over its shoulder; looking to see what the winds of politics, prejudice, and the inflexible rules of a harsh society might bring. There is fear here as well: fear of race, fear of age, fear of death, and fear of self. There is also hope, although it proves throughout to be a fleeting thing. Gordimer, a realist, might wish she could believe in some ultimate "triumph of the soul," but she has seen too much, too close up, to truly believe this possible. Glimpses of what might be are tantalizingly offered, as in the opening scene in "A Soldier's Embrace," when, for a moment at least, humanity hugs itself as one, or, as in "Siblings," when, stripped of her clothes and humility, Maxine rises above herself to represent her gender. However, these glimpses are fleeting. More enduring, and, perhaps more effective, are the warnings: the groans of the caged lions at night, the grim denial of urgings in "Town and Country Lovers," and the chilling, "this will happen to you," predictions of Anita Gonzales in "The Need for Something Sweet."

A Soldier's Embrace is a penetrating and, at times, ruthless exploration into the human condition. In lesser hands, such a delicate balance between love and politics might never have been achieved. Gordimer's ability to tell moving, readable stories about a land and people she understands makes her work impressive. Her ability to charge and sustain such material with the constantly shifting insights of love, hate, hope, and despair makes it remarkable.

David Alvarez

SOLO

Author: Jack Higgins
Publisher: Stein and Day (New York). 183 pp. $11.95
Type of work: Novel
Time: 1972
Locale: London; Belfast, Northern Ireland; Hydra, Greece

A famous concert pianist, who doubles as an international assassin, is pursued by a British army officer, the father of a girl the pianist has accidentally killed while making a getaway

Principal characters:
JOHN MIKALI, a world-famous concert pianist and hired killer
COLONEL ASA MORGAN, a career army officer who seeks revenge for his daughter's death
DR. KATHERINE RILEY, an American psychologist and an expert on the terrorist killer mentality
JEAN PAUL DEVILLE, a French criminal lawyer who is a Russian secret agent
HARRY BAKER, Detective Chief Superintendent of the Special Branch of the Metropolitan Police at Scotland Yard
LIESELOTT HOFFMANN, a sympathizer of a German terrorist group, the Baader-Meinhof gang
LIAM O'HAGEN, an Irish Republican Army (IRA) commander

A hooded man with a Cretan accent enters the home of Maxwell Joseph Cohen, a British clothing manufacturer, on the evening of July 21, 1972. He forces the frightened maid to take him to Cohen, and at the door of Cohen's study, he shoots the prominent Jewish businessman in the head. Pursued by police through London, the escaping killer runs down and kills a fourteen-year-old girl who is riding her bicycle. Five minutes later, he ditches the car and crosses a park to Albert Hall, where he plays Rachmaninov's *Concerto No. 2 in C minor* to a packed house.

The man who shot Max Cohen is John Mikali, a world-renowned concert pianist who is also an international hit man. Born in San Francisco to a Greek seaman and the daughter of an American schoolteacher, Mikali's musical genius is evident at an early age. Orphaned at age six, he is brought up by his American maternal grandmother, his Greek paternal grandfather, and a Cretan nurse named Katina Pavlo. His career as an assassin begins just before his eighteenth birthday when Katina Pavlo is struck and killed by a truck. Young Mikali avenges her death by pushing the truck down a concrete ramp, crushing the driver.

Within twenty-four hours of his first killing, Mikali joins the French Foreign Legion, where he demonstrates his courage under fire and becomes a practiced and efficient killer. After his discharge, he discovers that his beloved grandfather, Dmitri Mikali, a left-wing university professor, has been tortured and murdered by members of the Greek military. Although admittedly apolitical, he hunts down and assassinates the officers responsible for Dmitri Mikali's death. This exploit brings him into contact with Jean Paul Deville, an eminent French criminal lawyer, who is also a Russian secret agent. Under Deville's direction, Mikali begins to assassinate government officials and prominent businessmen throughout the world, coordinating his "hits" with his concert schedule.

Until that day in 1972, no one has been able to identify the assassin. Yet, by accidentally killing a fourteen-year-old girl, Mikali unleashes her father, Colonel Asa Morgan. Morgan, a cold, brutal paratroop commander—"the original soldier monk," as a British intelligence officer describes him—vows revenge. The British intelligence service proves unable to restrain him as he attempts to find his daughter's killer.

Morgan begins by consulting Dr. Katherine Riley, an international expert on the terrorist mentality. The Cretan lover, as Mikali is known to police around the world, had seduced a Baader-Meinhof sympathizer named Lieselott Hoffmann on the night that the East German Minister of Finance was shot. Riley has been allowed to visit Lieselott in prison, and Morgan approaches the psychologist to gain access to and information from Lieselott.

In the meantime, Mikali initiates a relationship with Riley, in part because "She's company," as he tells Deville, and in part because he wants to make sure Morgan will not discover him. Mikali is as skillful a lover as he is a pianist and a killer, and Riley finds herself increasingly attracted to him. Yet, she is also fascinated by the relentless, destructive Asa Morgan, whom she fears and despises but from whom she cannot break away. Unaware that Mikali is the killer whose life Morgan wants, Riley becomes the instrument through which each man pursues the destruction of the other.

When Lieselott fails to produce the information he wants, Morgan turns his attention to the weapon used against Max Cohen. His search takes him to Belfast and to Liam O'Hagen, an IRA commander. O'Hagen in turn sends Morgan to Brendan Tully, the leader of a rival faction, who directs Morgan to a pair of underworld figures in London. Tully murders O'Hagen, and O'Hagen's deputy, a young man of eighteen, avenges his leader's death.

Morgan pursues the two underworld figures for several days, burning down their illicit liquor business and killing one of their men in his pursuit of information about the gun that was used to kill Cohen. However, Morgan learns only that a man with a hooded mask and a Cretan accent purchased the weapon, and after the encounter with the weapons dealers, Riley, who had joined him briefly, leaves in anger. The next morning, he visits the spot where the fleeing killer dumped the getaway vehicle. There, in what seems to be merely a coincidence, he notices a poster announcing John Mikali's concert at Albert Hall at 8:00 p.m. Returning to his flat, Morgan reads through *Who's Who* and back issues of the newspaper, discovering that Mikali had served in the French Foreign Legion and that the dates and locations of his concerts coincided with every assassination.

Convinced that Mikali is his daughter's killer, Morgan departs for Greece immediately. He has already learned from Riley that Mikali is vacationing on the island of Hydra before a series of concerts in Albert Hall. Morgan evades the British police who have been pursuing him and bribes a fisherman to take him to Hydra. There he poses as a journalist seeking to interview Mikali. Yet Mikali is prepared for Morgan's appearance. On a cliff at the edge of the island, Mikali shoots his pursuer. A bullet strikes Morgan, who falls backward into the sea.

Morgan is not dead, however. He is rescued by an old fisherman, whose wife treats Morgan's wound. The bullet has passed through his upper left arm. Meanwhile, Katherine Riley arrives at Hydra to visit Mikali. Meeting her on the day of his encounter with Mikali, Morgan exposes Mikali's other identity. Although stunned by his revelation, Riley remains physically attracted to Mikali, and she is torn between her loyalty to him and her growing concern for the ravaged British army officer. She contacts Harry Baker of the Special Branch of Scotland Yard, who provides Morgan with a new passport to return to England and promises to watch him.

Upon his arrival in London, Morgan is confined by police to his London flat. With the assistance of an old friend, he escapes, reaching Albert Hall in time for Mikali's concert. During the concert, Mikali notices Morgan coming through the exit door. He plays a dramatic finale, greets his admirers, then retires to an empty reception room to face his relentless pursuer. Katherine Riley arrives first, but Asa Morgan steps into the doorway minutes later. The two men draw their guns, but Mikali hesitates. Morgan fires killing the pianist instantly. Katherine Riley, witness to the final confrontation, disappears into the darkness of the same park from which Mikali had emerged after killing Morgan's daughter two weeks earlier.

The novel focuses entirely upon the two main characters—Mikali and Morgan. The two men are very similar. Both are able soldiers who operate best under extreme stress. Dedicated to lives of violence and danger, they are calculating in their dealings with others and incapable of establishing long-term relationships with the opposite sex. Finally, both men seek revenge for the deaths of those once close to them, even though they realize that taking the life of the murderer will not bring the person back to life. The theme of revenge provides the link between the male characters—not only Mikali and Morgan, but also O'Hagen's young deputy and the London weapons dealers. It also provides the structure around which Higgins builds his story.

Solo is a gripping novel, in large part due to the intensity of its main characters. The novel is compact, and its rapid pace allows the reader to sense the relentlessness of Morgan's pursuit of Mikali. By focusing entirely upon the male principal characters, however, Higgins loses track of his supporting characters, notably Dr. Katherine Riley. While Mikali and Morgan are well developed and psychologically convincing, Riley is not. Her relationship with the two men reveals much about their personalities, and she serves as the means through which they discover each other. Yet very little of her own personality emerges in the novel. Similarly, Deville, Mikali's "boss," appears to be somewhat inconsistent. Mikali is, as a British official admits, a nonpolitical killer. His "hits" range from Greek generals to Jewish businessmen to Communist officials. However, Deville, who works as an agent of a Russian spy organization in bitter rivalry with the notorious KGB, is responsible for giving Mikali these mystifying assignments.

Despite these flaws, *Solo* is a well written and tightly constructed work. The main characters are fascinating personalities, and the reader will find few dull moments as the story unfolds.

Arlyn Miller

THE SPIKE

Author: Arnaud de Borchgrave and Robert Moss
Publisher: Crown Publishers (New York). 374 pp. $12.95
Type of work: Novel
Time: 1967 to the early 1980's
Locale: Various locations including Washington, D.C.; New York; the
U.S.S.R.; Vietnam; Paris

*A young reporter uncovers a Soviet plot to undermine the United States
government through covert manipulation of the news media and infiltration by
Soviet agents*

> *Principal characters:*
> ROBERT HOCKNEY, an ambitious American journalist
> MICHEL RENARD, a French journalist
> VIKTOR BARISOV, a KGB agent
> LEN ROURKE, editor of the *New York World*
> PHIL KREPS, a former CIA agent
> PERRY CUMMINGS, Hockney's childhood friend and a secret
>   agent for the KGB
> NICK FLOWER, former head of CIA counterintelligence
> MILORAD YANKOVICH, national security adviser to the Presi-
>   dent of the United States
> SENATOR SEAMUS O'REILLY, one of the few politicians who
>   recognize the Soviets' plan for world domination
> JULIA CUMMINGS, his aide and an old friend of Hockney's

When the story opens in May 1967, Robert Hockney is a Berkeley
student with leftist sympathies. Hockney's ambition, as he tells a
friend, is to be "The greatest reporter in America." Only a few weeks
later he manages to publish, in the radical newspaper *Barricades,* an
article exposing CIA recruiting activities on campus. Thanks to the
article's success, *Barricades* sends Hockney to Europe to probe for
CIA involvement in European politics. But Hockney's additional purpose is to get himself hired by the prestigious *New York World.*

Having information that the chief of the French Agence Mondiale
d'Informations, Jacques Bonpierre, may have CIA connections, Hockney makes an appointment for an interview. At the agency he also
meets a staff member named Michel Renard, who hates Bonpierre for
"spiking," or refusing to publish, many of his stories. Renard believes
that Bonpierre is controlled by the CIA and, having his own personal
score to settle, agrees to help Hockney.

Renard's motivations are more complicated than Hockney realizes,
since Renard is in the process of being wooed by a Soviet intelligence
agent, Viktor Barisov. In attempting to enlist Renard, Barisov is helping to implement Plan Azev, a blueprint for achieving Soviet domina-

tion of the West by 1985, an end to be achieved by a quiet program of subversion from within. A major objective is to discourage a peaceful settlement of the Vietnam War, since eventual defeat would foster domestic upheaval in the United States and discourage military intervention abroad. Control of foreign news reportage is a vital element in the plan. Renard already believes that France's safety is best assured by an understanding with the Soviets, and through pressure from both Barisov and his own wife Renard is drawn into the Soviet camp.

Hockney, knowing nothing of Renard's involvement with the Soviets, writes an article exposing Bonpierre. The article's success brings him back to the United States in triumph and precipitates Bonpierre's suicide. Hockney is now a hot item, and the *New York World* not only hires him but offers him his choice of assignments. Hockney unhesitatingly chooses Vietnam, where he hopes to write about the "political sickness" of U.S. involvement.

In Vietnam, Hockney renews his friendship with Michel Renard, who was transferred from Paris after Bonpierre's death. Hockney relies on his friend's superior knowledge of the country to help him discover the "true story" of the war. Through a Vietnamese girl named Lani, Hockney also visits Can Lai, supposedly the scene of a massacre by a CIA pacification team. Although convinced of Lani's sincerity, Hockney is disturbed by the Vietnam CIA chief's equally sincere denial of any activities in Can Lai. Hockney does not check into the story any further. A seed of doubt has been planted in his mind, but he lets the story drop.

In the summer of 1969, Hockney returns to New York, once more in triumph. Told he can "write his own ticket," he requests a special assignment in Washington to investigate activities in the intelligence community. He goes to Perry Cummings, who holds a responsible position in the Pentagon but who has in the past shown liberal sympathies. Perry sends him to Phil Kreps, a former CIA agent who has been threatening to expose CIA activities.

Through Kreps and other contacts at the Institute for Progressive Reform, Hockney is able to write a series of very damaging articles on the CIA, playing an instrumental role in the formation of the Select Senate Committee on Intelligence. He also becomes friendly with the new CIA director, Bill Crawford. Hockney uses a tip from Crawford to accuse former CIA counterintelligence chief Nick Flower of operating an illegal mail intercept program. Upon the printing of Hockney's article, Flower is immediately fired.

Hockney requests an interview with Flower, and the former counterintelligence chief informs Hockney that he has been systematically duped by all of the men he considered his best news sources. Perry

Cummings is a Soviet agent who sends vital military information to the Soviets; Phil Kreps has connections with both the Cubans and the KGB; the *World*'s editor, Rourke, is being blackmailed through threats to expose his former involvement with the CIA; and the Institute for Progressive Reform is merely a front for a massive Soviet espionage ring. Hockney is incredulous but disturbed, particularly after a conversation with Perry Cummings in which Cummings sounds distinctly nervous. Fearing that his entire journalistic career may have been built on a series of lies, Hockney decides he must investigate all the important news sources of his career.

Describing vaguely to his editor a very big story he would like to pursue, Hockney obtains a year off at half salary. His first stop is Amsterdam, where Phil Kreps is now working. Hockney finds several suspicious connections in Kreps's work. A visit to Michel Renard in Paris confirms his worst suspicions there too, as Renard admits his connection with the Soviets. The different threads come together with the kidnapping of German businessman Franz-Josef Faber by the revolutionary organization STAR. Hockney had earlier seen a detailed dossier on Faber in the files of Kreps's Institute. It is now clear to Hockney that an international conspiracy is at work, and he resolves to expose it.

Returning to New York, Hockney places the story before his editor, Rourke, but Rourke's reluctance to pursue it forces Hockney to resign. He spends the years of the Carter administration barely scraping by as a free-lance writer, but after President Billy Connor's election he makes a comeback with an article detailing the radical backgrounds of several key members of Connor's administration, many of whom were connected with the Institute for Progressive Reform. On the suggestion of his old friend Julia, Hockney tells his story to Senator Seamus O'Reilly, who has long been convinced that the United States is gradually forfeiting world power to the Soviets. Both agree that what is needed above all is a defector from the Soviet Union, someone who can tell the story of Plan Azev first hand.

They find their man in Viktor Barisov, who has fallen into disfavor and may soon be a candidate for a labor camp. Through the aid of Hockney and the British intelligence service, Barisov defects and becomes the key witness in a series of public hearings concerning Soviet penetration of the United States government. Before a disbelieving audience, Barisov recounts the details of Plan Azev, its subversion of the media and its latest objective of depriving the West of access to fuel and cheap raw materials, particularly in the Middle East. The real bombshell is dropped when Barisov begins naming Soviet agents: the names include many of President Connor's chief advisers, and the vice-president himself is named as an unwitting collaborator under the influence of Perry Cummings.

Simultaneously with Barisov's revelations, it is discovered that the Soviets have begun an invasion of North Yemen. In spite of dire predictions from his national security adviser, Milorad Yankovich, President Connor's stance has been to ignore the situation. With the complete embarrassment of his administration by Barisov, however, Connor is forced to take a different tack. He must deal with Senator O'Reilly, who demands the firing of all agents named by Barisov, replacement of the vice-president by O'Reilly himself, and Connor's support for O'Reilly's nomination to the presidency in the next election. Hockney marries Julia and becomes the new Washington bureau chief for the *New York World*.

The Spike is a gripping modern spy novel. The characters are not particularly compelling as individuals, since the author's interest clearly lies in the mechanics of global intelligence operations, but this detracts little from the force of the book. As far as their work is concerned, de Borchgrave's and Moss's journalists and intelligence agents are quite realistic. Viktor Barisov is not a fanatical Communist but an ambitious man seeking power in the most effective way open to him; when that fails and his life may be in danger, he readily switches his allegiance to the Americans. Hockney is often torn between presenting the "real story," as he experienced it, and modifying it into a form he knows will sell.

The book is an interesting study of the difficulties encountered in seeking out the truth in politics. As Hockney discovers, it is as important to know why someone is giving you information as it is to know the substance of the information itself. His attempts to break through the web of lies that has been spun around him make for a fascinating story.

Lisa Halttunen

STILL LIFE WITH WOODPECKER

Author: Tom Robbins
Publisher: Bantam Books (New York). 277 pp. $12.95
Type of work: Novel
Time: The last quarter of the 20th century
Locale: Seattle, Washington; Hawaii; Algeria

A love story that takes place inside a pack of Camel cigarettes between an outlaw and a princess, both redheads

Principal characters:
>BERNARD MICKEY WRANGLE (alias the Woodpecker), outlaw and protester against the confining rules of society
>PRINCESS LEIGH-CHERI FURSTENBERG BARCALONA, lover of Bernard Mickey Wrangle
>KING MAX FURSTENBERG BARCALONA, exiled monarch of a small European country living on a CIA stipend with his family in Seattle
>QUEEN TILLI FURSTENBERG BARCALONA, wife of King Max, mother of the Princess
>GULIETTA, long-time personal servant to the Furstenberg Barcalona family
>A'BEN FIZEL, Algerian Prince betrothed to Princess Leigh-Cheri
>CHUCK, a bumbling CIA operative assigned as chauffeur and handyman to the Furstenberg Barcalona family

Still Life With Woodpecker begins in Seattle, Washington, home of Princess Leigh-Cheri Furstenberg Barcalona. Princess Leigh-Cheri's parents, King Max and Queen Tilli, have been in exile since she was very young. As a result, she grew up in Seattle as a normal American girl except for the blue blood in her jeans. This blue blood, plus the realization that she was a real princess, kept her constantly in the midst of activities and causes.

After dropping out of college, Princess Leigh-Cheri is morose until she reads about the Geo-Therapy Care Fest to be held on the island of Maui in Hawaii. Her favorite activist, Ralph Nader, is to speak at the three-day festival dedicated to the discussion of the future of the world. Heartened by their daughter's improved emotional state, King Max and Queen Tilli agree to Leigh-Cheri's attendance at the Care Fest. It is decided that Gulietta will accompany her as chaperone.

On the flight to Hawaii, the Princess meets Bernard Mickey Wrangle. Coincidentally, both are on their way to attend the Geo-Therapy Care Fest although with different intentions. Bernard intends to bomb the proceedings with five sticks of dynamite. Bernard is an outlaw—not a common criminal, but an outlaw. The Woodpecker is rather taken with the Princess's beauty and further attracted to her red hair. His own flaming locks are dyed black as a disguise. Arriving at Maui and having a penchant for tequila, Bernard ingests a bit and by mistake bombs the hotel where the Care Fest is to be held one day early.

Even drunk, the Woodpecker is the "master of a blast," and no one is hurt. Unknown to Bernard, however, Gulietta witnesses his blast. The next day at the beach she points out the "boom-boom" man (she speaks no English) to Princess Leigh-Cheri, who decides to place Bernard under citizen's arrest. The Woodpecker, sought by law enforcement agencies for many years, is not about to go quietly.

After several drinks, the Princess and Bernard are getting to know each other, but the party breaks up because the Princess is to be interviewed by *People* magazine. Still not having turned Bernard in to the authorities, she leaves for her interview. The next day at the Care Fest activities, as she is standing under the tropical sun, she is met by Bernard, who is carrying a shade parasol.

After pressing the parasol, on which is written his address, into Princess Leigh-Cheri's hands, Bernard disappears. The next day, Princess Leigh-Cheri shows up at the sloop *High Jinks* where he is staying and is startled to find that Bernard is a redhead like herself, for he has removed the black dye from his hair in anticipation of her visit.

Surprised and upset, Princess Leigh-Cheri hurries off to the second half of the Care Fest, which is turning into a shouting match between the speakers and the audience. Because of the explosion and subsequent two-day delay, the schedule is shortened. The panel on birth control is combined with the panel on child care. Princess Leigh-Cheri is beginning to question her causes and their usefulness although she does not know it. She is also beginning to fall in love with the Woodpecker, which she does not realize either.

Back in Seattle, King Max and Queen Tilli are making arrangements for A'ben Fizel to become Princess Leigh-Cheri's fiancé upon her return. Chuck reports to the CIA that King Max is planning a revolution to regain his kingdom using planes and rockets, after overhearing and misinterpreting a phone conversation about a basketball game between the Seattle Supersonics and the Houston Rockets to be played in Seattle's Kingdome.

Meanwhile, Princess Leigh-Cheri has gone back to the sloop *High Jinks* after hearing that the police have arrested someone for the bombing of the hotel. Bernard is still on the boat. Apparently, he has placed two of the three remaining sticks of dynamite in the back of a rented Toyota belonging to two travelers.

After a lengthy discussion about outlaws, poets, and the problems of princesses, Bernard and the Princess make love. Bernard returns to

Seattle to court the Princess. However, he is not a courtier but an outlaw, and following disastrous attempts at presenting himself to the King and Queen he finally gives up and retires to the nearest bar. But Chuck is tailing him, and Bernard is soon arrested in a slightly intoxicated state by the FBI.

Bernard eventually pleads guilty and is sentenced to a prison term with eligibility for parole in twenty months. The only things in Bernard's cell are a cot with a foam rubber mattress, a chamber pot, a 40-watt bulb, a pack of Camels with no matches, and a small window. The Princess has decided that she would go through the jail experience with Bernard in her own attic. Gulietta is to be her jailer.

Princess Leigh-Cheri has nothing in her attic room to keep her company except a pack of Camels and the realization that Bernard is going through the same experience. The Princess becomes adept at tossing the pack into the air and catching it in her teeth, behind her back, with her eyes closed. Then one day she begins reading the printing on the pack of cigarettes and is amazed at how much information is contained on a pack of Camels.

It is in July that Princess Leigh-Cheri begins to "rotate on the lunar wheel," becoming a participant in lunar ception. It is also in July that Gulietta, running out of the cocaine supplied by the drug-smuggling friend of Bernard's and owner of the *High Jinks,* asks King Max and Queen Tilli for a salary and back pay. The back pay alone amounts to a small fortune, and Gulietta goes on strike against all except the Princess. Gulietta's strike wears on as does Leigh-Cheri's self-imposed exile. She begins to notice more and more interesting facts about the pack of Camels, things such as the pyramids, minarets, temples, camels, and the word "choice." Beyond its importance on the Camel cigarette pack, "choice" is the one word that encompasses all of Bernard's outlaw philosophy.

After intensive research into the meaning of a pack of Camel cigarettes she becomes deeply involved in pyramid power and the last group of space travelers, the Red Beards. The Red Beards are credited with giving earth beings the pyramid and its secret powers. The Princess feels that she has discovered something important. She also realizes that she can get in to see Bernard disguised as his lawyer. Before she can visit Bernard, she receives a note from him telling her how wrong it is to create a movement around her internment. Apparently, much to Leigh-Cheri's surprise, her cause has become known nationally, and other women are imitating her. Bernard is very displeased, the note is harsh, and the Princess is deeply hurt.

While Leigh-Cheri is locked in her attic, a real revolution is taking place in her home country. The revolutionaries have decided that they want a ruler of the old line in power. King Max is considered too old guard and Princess Leigh-Cheri a little "daffy," so Gulietta, who has been revealed as King Max's half-sister, is to be the next queen.

Princess Leigh-Cheri has agreed to marry A'ben Fizel if he will build her, in his country, a perfect pyramid. The wedding is to take place when the pyramid is completed. The Princess enjoys A'ben Fizel but still loves the Woodpecker and is apprehensive about the completion of the pyramid. On the night before her wedding, news reaches Leigh-Cheri that Bernard has been shot in Algiers. She goes to the pyramid for solace, and deep inside the pyramid she encounters a young gentleman with a red beard. Bernard has had his passport stolen, and the man who has been shot was an imposter. The Princess falls tearfully into Bernard's arms just in time for two of A'ben Fizel's eunuchs to see them.

A'ben Fizel is not pleased and seals off the pyramid with the Princess and Bernard inside, announcing that his intended bride has been kidnapped and killed and that the pyramid is to be forever closed. Bernard and Leigh-Cheri are entombed with nothing except a wedding cake, champagne, and the dynamite Bernard had brought to blow off the tip of the pyramid as a wedding present to Leigh-Cheri.

After spending many days inside the pyramid, both are getting rather desperate. While Bernard is sleeping, the Princess makes a bomb out of the dynamite and places it by the door. When Bernard regains consciousness, he and Leigh-Cheri are in an Arab clinic. Neither is seriously hurt, but both have lost their hearing. It is arranged that upon their release they will vacation with Queen Gulietta before returning to Seattle. Back in Seattle with their new hearing aids, they both believe they can hear the chipmunk at the center of the earth running the little wheel. It is running smoothly. They have found a way to make love stay.

Still Life with Woodpecker is a sensitive, sometimes funny but always irreverent look at human nature. Robbins's stream-of-consciousness style coupled with his philosophical wanderings create vivid images. He has the ability to make the obvious and near obvious elusive through philosophical discussions. Robbins looks at age-old problems in a kaleidoscopic light with interesting results. He will not and does not solve any of these problems, but it is pleasant to see traditional values examined in this way.

R.A. Parker II

THE STORIES OF RAY BRADBURY

Author: Ray Bradbury
Publisher: Alfred A. Knopf (New York). 884 pp. $17.95
Type of work: Short stories
Time: The present; the 21st century
Locale: Green Town and Mellin Town, Illinois; Mars; Mexico

*A collection of 100 stories about Martians, dinosaurs, vampires, other odd-
ities, and small-town Midwesterners, dealing with mankind's often thoughtless
and sometimes devastating effect on the universe*

Bradbury's stories can be grouped conveniently according to subject
matter. He introduces vampires with human problems, dinosaurs, and
Martian cities peopled with ingenious creatures. He describes characters in eerie situations: a wife replaced by a marionette; a brother
cleverly trapped and executed in an electronic casket; a computerized
house standing alone amidst atomic devastation, still purring effi-
ciently; a child and a man each experiencing the depths of fear for the
first time. In all of Bradbury's stories, his meticulous attention to detail
and his extensive creativity are evident.

In several of these stories, Bradbury introduces an extended family
of sophisticated and sensitive vampires who live contentedly in Mellin
Town, Illinois. In "Homecoming," fourteen-year-old Timothy is despondent because he is different from others in his family; he is not a
vampire, but merely a human. As relatives begin to gather from all
parts of the globe to celebrate Allhallow Eve, Timothy anticipates the
needs of his relatives by polishing coffins, gathering spiders and toad-
stools, and performing other tasks in an effort to "belong." But the
relatives shun him. He asks his sister Cecy, who can move from creature to creature invading their bodies and inhabiting their minds, to
help him. Cecy enters Timothy's body, and for a moment he is transformed; he cavorts above the relatives on new-found wings, and he
gulps down a glass of ruby blood with relish. The relatives welcome
him as one of them, but then Cecy tires of her game and leaves him,
sick and different once again. Timothy's mother tries to comfort him
by telling him he is loved, but Timothy cries desolately.

In "Uncle Einar," another of Bradbury's vampire stories, an unfortunate accident brings Uncle Einar to Mellin Town, Illinois. Uncle
Einar, a vampire with magnificent sea green wings, was flying home to
Europe after drinking too much wine when he hit a high tension wire
and was knocked to the ground. A young woman, Brunilla Wexley,
discovered him the next morning. Brunilla, an ugly girl, was proud to
know a man with such magnificent wings. Uncle Einar found beauty

behind Brunilla's ugly exterior, and they were married. Their life together was placid, but Uncle Einar chafed under the knowledge that he could never fly again. His night vision had been destroyed in the accident, and flying by day was too dangerous because of his conspicuous green wings. Then one blustery March day, his children asked him to accompany them to a kite flying contest. Uncle Einar was inspired! He tied a tail of rags to his belt and gripped the end of a string of twine in his teeth and soared away. He could now fly by day.

"The Traveler" and "The April Witch" each provide additional views of Cecy, who is able to transport herself magically through time and space to enter any living being. In "The Traveler" Cecy, whose body lies in her bed while she travels, feels she must prove her ability to contribute to the family. She begins a mysterious trip. Meanwhile, Uncle John, a disreputable relative who once tried to expose the family as vampires in order to collect the bounty, arrives desperately seeking Cecy. He is going insane because he hears holy church bells ringing in his head. He needs Cecy's help to drive the bells from his mind. After a frantic search for Cecy, looking into the eyes of every bird, toad, fish, and squirrel, Uncle John finally succumbs to his fear. He kills himself, and Cecy returns. She has been living inside Uncle John all the time, creating fear and guilt. She announces, "Tell Father what I've done. Maybe now he'll think I'm worthy."

"The April Witch" shows Cecy responding to a very human desire —the need to fall in love. One fresh April morning Cecy enters an unsuspecting Ann Leary. Instantly, Ann, who is a sensible and independent woman, can sense Cecy within her as a strange impulse to speak and act against her natural inclinations. Ann meets Tom, a persistent beau whom she has adamantly refused to encourage. Cecy, in Ann, flirts with Tom, delighting in the sensations of love she is feeling. Ann is horrified, and Tom is confused. The struggle between Ann and Cecy continues into evening, with Ann fighting the alien thoughts spoken involuntarily from her lips. Cecy forces Ann to give Tom her Mellin Town address, then, exhausted, she leaves Ann's body. She has enjoyed the brief sensation of love and longs to experience it first-hand, but she knows she would forfeit her magical powers if she ever loved a mortal.

Ray Bradbury's dinosaur stories raise several provocative questions concerning man's effect on his environment and his ability to understand the other inhabitants of his planet. In "A Sound of Thunder," set in 2055 A.D., Mr. Eckels, seeking the ultimate challenge, pays to travel 60,000,000 years backward in time to hunt the most ferocious prey, tyrannosaurus rex. Time Safari Inc. constructed a special pathway that floats suspended above the jungle floor. This protects the tiniest insects and plants from being inadvertently trampled by the hunters. The men believe that significant danger exists for the present if a single thing would be altered 60,000,000 years in the past. "A little error here would multiply in sixty million years." Eckels is emphatically warned by his guide not to step off the pathway. Nevertheless, at the moment he faces the charging tyrannosaurus rex, Eckels stumbles off the path in his blind rush toward safety. Eckels and his guide return to the year 2055, but it has altered drastically: ignorance and brutality have replaced refinement and civilization. Eckels is horrified to discover the remnants of a butterfly crushed on the bottom of his boot. He is responsible for the tiny error that has changed Time. His guide shoots him.

In "The Fog Horn," Johnny and McDunn work together manning a lighthouse located on a remote point in the North Sea. Suddenly a huge dinosaur as big as a destroyer emerges from the deep and swims slowly toward the lighthouse bellowing in eerie response to the foghorn's mournful call. McDunn explains that the same monster appeared a year earlier. It was as if it were looking for someone gone 10,000,000 years ago. The dinosaur charges the lighthouse, which collapses, trapping the men under the rubble. All night Johnny and McDunn listen to the dinosaur's anguished bellows. In the morning, the dinosaur is gone. Johnny feels the depths of its sorrows.

Bradbury's Martian stories approach the question of space exploration from an interesting perspective. In "Mars is Heaven," the third expedition from Earth lands on Mars. The men are surprised to discover a small town that resembles the Earth towns where they grew up. They advance several theories to explain this: perhaps an unknown rocket left Earth years earlier to escape its problems; perhaps parallel development within the universe can occur. The Earthmen are welcomed by the town's inhabitants and are joyously shocked to discover their own dead relatives living here comfortably. The men abandon caution and delight in their unexpected reunions. Only the captain speculates nervously: perhaps the Martians, in order to protect themselves from unwanted invasion, have used telepathy and hypnosis to play on his crew's wants and desires. In the morning, all the men from Earth's third expedition are dead. As they carry the coffins for burial, the relatives' faces shift, slip, and shimmer in the Martian light.

In "The Earth Men," another expedition lands on Mars and the captain and crew seek a hero's welcome from the inhabitants. Instead of provoking astonishment and excitement because of their long trip, they meet with annoyance or indifference. They are piqued by this reaction. Sent to Mr. Xxx, a psychologist, they try to understand the Martians' attitude. He takes them to a room where they are greeted with wild cheering and applause. The crew relaxes to bask in this hero's welcome until the captain realizes that they have entered an insane asylum! The Martians believe that their talk of space travel is nothing more than delusions. Mr. Xxx allows the captain the opportunity to prove his sanity, so the captain takes him to his spaceship. Mr. Xxx marvels at the strength of the captain's sensual hallucination and the power of his hypnotic suggestion. Mr Xxx can *see* the ship. He kills the captain as the only cure for his insanity. The rocket hallucination does not disappear. Mr. Xxx concludes that now he is insane also, so he shoots himself.

Ray Bradbury's collection of short stories is provocative and entertaining science fiction at its finest. The depth and scope of his imagination are incredible as he provides his readers with three modes of travel: "small town explorer, space traveler, and wanderer with Count Dracula's American cousins." His genius as a writer stems from his ability to absorb the sensations of living and transform them into bizarre, sensitive, macabre, or simply strange tales, which always carry a gentle admonition or ironic warning to Man. In his introduction to this collection, Bradbury says, "My stories have led me through my life. They shout, I follow. They run up and bite me on the leg—I respond by writing down everything that goes on during the bite. When I finish, the idea lets go, and runs off." Because of the pleasure he provides his readers, one can only hope that Ray Bradbury will continue to be bitten for many years to come.

Marilynn Malin Hufcut

THE THIRD WAVE

Author: Alvin Toffler
Publisher: William Morrow Co. (New York). 544 pp. $14.95
Type of work: Social science

An analysis of the attributes of an emerging new civilization, based on the premise that historic changes occur in observable cycles or waves

As headlines grow increasingly grim, prognostications for the future become bleaker and more devoid of hope for the resilience of modern civilization. For futurologists as well as many others who speak or write of the future on the basis of their hunches, guesses, or pseudo-empirical study, it is no longer a matter of how but whether civilization will survive the coming debacle. The Apocalypse is said to be just around the corner, and those who hear the thundering hoofbeats of the Four Horsemen are compelled to issue warnings of the relentlessness of their approach in ever more strident tones. The new millennium is rushing in; its frightening roar has drowned the voice of reason. *The Third Wave* strives to raise that voice with resounding clarity above the din of global panic.

The voice in which Alvin Toffler writes is calm, rational, and reassuringly optimistic. He begins his book by delineating the imminent "super-struggle," the clash between those who have a vested interest in preserving the old order and those whose vision or common sense tells them to yield to the coming of the new. Toffler firmly establishes his theoretical premise: the new civilization is already emerging and the choices are clear—an enlightened approach is necessary to avoid total annihilation.

Toffler calls the new civilization the Third Wave. The analogy to a rising tide suggests the inevitability of change. This Third Wave, writes Toffler, will collide with the Second Wave and carry all before it. The Second Wave is industrialism, or civilization as it exists today, and its coming swept away an agricultural way of life (the First Wave) and changed the face of the world forever. The Third Wave will achieve the same all-encompassing change over a shorter and more intensified period of time.

The Second Wave, that is the Industrial Revolution, radically altered the lifestyle of the world's population in the 1700's. According to Toffler, the Second Wave drove an invisible wedge between producers and consumers, thus creating the need for a market system of exchange, which in turn gave birth to existing social systems. The factory became the model for social institutions and reformed today's social personality in ways that proved to be most expedient for the maintenance of this system. The hidden code of Second Wave civilization can be summarized as Standardization, Specialization, Synchronization, Concentration, Maximization, and Centralization. All social institutions, from the factory to schools to the nuclear family, fostered and reinforced the principles of this code. Human metabolism was geared to the machine, and humans developed into extensions of the machine age.

The architecture of all civilizations, Toffler hypothesizes, is made up of components that he calls the biosphere, the techno-sphere, the socio-sphere, the info-sphere, and the power-sphere. Revolutionary changes are occurring in all of these spheres at once, for they are all intermeshed in a complex web that is the matrix of a fundamental world-view.

During the Second Wave, the fundamental world-view that prevailed made industrialism, or what Toffler calls "indust-reality," the social imperative for every nation. Regardless of whether a nation was capitalist or socialist, industrialism made the market paramount in the organization of the economy. This meant that the economy of the civilized world was founded on a market system whereby the producing element made goods or services for the consuming element.

Imperialist nations exploited nonindustrial or First Wave nations for their natural resources and their manpower, while proclaiming their world-view as the only true one. Within industrial societies, lip-service was paid to democracy or socialism while political power was wielded by the centralized control of a few elites. The split between producers and consumers, vital to this system, gave rise to sex-role differentiation, the "massification" of the media, and the "monolithic consciousness" that hammered out standardized human beings who were needed to operate the machines of the industrial age.

Not only is this system outmoded, writes Toffler, it is teetering on the verge of a catastrophe that threatens destruction on a global scale. The moment has come to reconstruct society. Our civilization has reached a revolutionary turning point, the completion of the entire historical process of market-building. "The step-by-step creation of this essentially sociocultural and psychological structure for exchange . . ." Toffler states, "can be likened to the building of the Egyptian pyramids, the Roman aqueducts . . . The heroic age of market-building is over . . . marketization will no longer be the central project of the civilization . . . The Third Wave will therefore produce history's first 'transmarket' civilization . . . a civilization able to move onto a new agenda—precisely because the market has already been laid in place."

This "new agenda," as Toffler sees it, must take the form of the construction of a decent democratic society based on the recognition of the three key principles of Third Wave governments: minority power, semi-direct democracy (a blend of professional representation and self-representation), and a decision division among the various levels of society. These three principles are an outgrowth of every individual's need for community, structure, and meaning. Third Wave civilization will be built on a diverse energy base rather than nonrenewable sources such as petroleum; a diverse technological base incorporating breakthroughs in biology, genetics, electronics, materials science, space and undersea exploration; a "de-massified media," that is a flow of information from many sources at once; and an "electronic environment" made up of computers plus computer chips implanted in an "intelligent" material environment. In fact, Toffler views the development of the computer as the single most liberating technological force since the invention of the wheel. Computers will help effectuate a feasible shift of work back into the home, or the "electronic cottage," a shift that promises to revitalize the family as a cohesive force of the Third Wave civilization.

It is in describing this new civilization that Toffler becomes most rhapsodic:

> Instead of a society synchronized to the tempo of the assembly line, a Third Wave society will move to flexible rhythms and schedules. Instead of the mass society's extreme standardization of behavior, ideas, language, and life-styles, Third Wave society will be built on segmentation and diversity. Instead of a society that concentrates population, energy flows, and other features of life, Third Wave society will disperse and de-concentrate. Instead of opting for maximum scale on the 'bigger is better' principle, Third Wave society will understand the meaning of 'appropriate scale.' Instead of a highly centralized society, Third Wave society will recognize the value of much decentralized decision-making.

Furthermore, Toffler believes society is now moving in a direction opposite to the world of highly centralized bureaucracy as depicted in Orwell's *1984* and Huxley's *Brave New World*. He proposes the idea of an emerging "practopia—neither the best nor the worst of all possible worlds, but one that is both practical and preferable to the one we had . . . One can glimpse in it a civilization that makes allowances for individual difference, and embraces (rather than suppresses) racial, regional, religious, and subcultural variety. . . ."

According to Toffler, it is an immediate imperative that this peaceful transition to a Third Wave society is achieved. He says there is only one option open at this juncture in history—society must be willing to re-shape itself and its social institutions in order to deal with the new realities on the horizon. Not a "new man" but a new social personality must be forged to accomplish these goals, a personality derived from those traits that are to be rewarded by the economic system of the Third Wave—self-reliance, versatility, adaptability, and the willingness of the individual to ''prosume'' or make things for his or her own use. The Third Wave will need men and women who are capable of thinking for themselves and who can utilize appropriate technology in a balanced world of self-reliant yet interdependent individuals. The scope of these changes is global. The battle for these changes is the ''super-struggle.'' It is this super-struggle that is the future's single most determining factor. The temper of the future depends on the outcome of the conflict between those who would blindly preserve the old order of Second Wave industrialism and those who are working to facilitate the transition to the Third Wave civilization.

''By launching a vast process of social learning,'' writes Toffler, ''we can head off the totalitarian thrust. We can prepare millions for the dislocations and dangerous crises that lie ahead.'' The transition to 21st-century democracy will not happen suddenly, he believes, in a spasm, but must be constructed on many levels at once by many different people committed to the need for a political overhaul. It is *The Third Wave,* Toffler seems to believe, that will become their manifesto.

Alvin Toffler's plea for worldwide enlightenment is impassioned but redundant. Like a battering wave, he drives home his theories with merciless repetition. At times, this technique stirs the reader to almost immediate action, but overall it irritates and insults or drums incessantly. The problems and solutions as he presents them seem overwhelming, leaving the reader with the feeling of helplessly drowning in the Third Wave. However, Toffler's insights are remarkable, and his analysis is both exhaustive and lucid, sometimes making the issues crystallize in a way that no other futurologist has been able to accomplish in a single book. *The Third Wave* is provocative and sane reading —there is no shrillness to his arguments. The book does not take up where *Future Shock* left off. It takes the speculation of that work and carves out a sharp profile of the face of the future as seen by Alvin Toffler.

A. S. Maulucci

THIRTY SECONDS

Author: Michael J. Arlen
Publisher: Farrar, Straus and Giroux (New York). 221 pp. $9.95
Type of work: Current affairs
Time: Spring and Summer 1979
Locale: New York City and its environs

The story of the development of a thirty-second television commercial for long-distance telephone calls

> *Principal personages:*
> STEVE HORN, director of television commercials
> JERRY PFIFFNER, head of the creative group that devised the commercial
> GASTON BRAUN, Pfiffner's assistant
> PHIL SHYPOSH, American Telephone Company's vice-president for advertising
> HOWIE LAZARUS, editor of commercial films

Phil Shyposh, in charge of advertising for American Telephone, needed a strategy for increasing the volume, and hence the profitability, of long-distance phone calls. He turned to the N.W. Ayer advertising agency, where Jerry Pfiffner envisioned a series of television commercials that would convince people that long-distance telephoning can be casual and enjoyable. Pfiffner and his colleagues worked for months before settling on the theme "Reach out and touch someone."

Thirty Seconds focuses on the making of one of the series of "Reach out" commercials. The thirty-second commercial is titled "Tap Dancing." Rather than presenting a single, coherent narrative extolling the advertised product, "Tap Dancing" is a vignette commercial. The writers at N.W. Ayer wrote a series of five situations, each consisting of two or three scenes, presenting people making long-distance phone calls. The scenes, combined with a cheerful musical theme instead of a spoken narrative, were designed to convey the enjoyment and closeness that could come with a long-distance call to a friend or relative.

Once the basic script of the commercial had been written, Jerry Pfiffner hired Steve Horn to film the scenes that would make up "Tap Dancing." There are four hundred directors in New York who produce film for advertisements. Steve Horn is known as one of the best "with the emotional things." Horn is a perfectionist, paying attention to every detail of each scene he films, scenes that last for only a few seconds. Casting is critical to the look of the commercial. Together with Pfiffner and Gaston Braun, Horn looks at dozens of candidates for each of the roles in "Tap Dancing." One situation will depict two young women, one black and one white, doing yoga headstands in different cities, talking with each other on the telephone. Each of the actresses who tries out is asked to demonstrate an ability to talk on the phone while doing a headstand, and their performances are videotaped. The videotapes are viewed to determine the television presence of the women, their looks and naturalness before the camera. Actors build careers in commercials, cultivating an image. For example, a six-year-old boy named Kenny is in heavy demand because his two front teeth had been extracted and his permanent teeth have not come in yet. Actors and actresses are aware that they have New York, or California, or Midwestern looks, appearances that are appropriate for certain commercials but not others.

Steve Horn is as concerned with the setting of each scene as with the actors who play in those scenes. Horn and his assistants have frequent conferences, always at tables with fruit, cheese, and Perrier in the center, to discuss the merits of various locations for each vignette. Horn never films in a studio, believing that accurate locations must be used if the commercial is to have the appearance of reality. Horn has available a selection of homes that he can rent for a day of filming. He is careful to be sure that the rooms in which the black and the white yoga woman are filmed are different and that their styles are appropriate to the characters.

The two settings Steve Horn finds hardest to produce are a rodeo and an army barracks. Several assistants are put to work traveling to locales in the New York area to report to Horn on their possible use in various commercials. A ranch in southern New Jersey that is used for rodeos is chosen to film one three-second sequence. The rodeo is authentic, yet Horn wants bulls with highly visible horns in the background. Horn, who has lived his entire life in New York City, is certain that a convincing rodeo needs bulls as well as horses. He is less sure about what an army barracks should look like. In one scene a recruit, having just received his army crewcut, is telephoning his father, a barber who is seen laughing on the phone while sitting in his barber chair. None of the advertising people knows where a recruit would make a telephone call. An investigator finds that the men at West Point and Annapolis, the preferred locations for filming, do not have phones by their beds. Finally, it is decided to shoot the scene in the post exchange (PX) store at a nearby army base.

Once Steve Horn has finished shooting the film for "Tap Dancing," ten thousand feet of processed film are turned over to Howie Lazarus. It is his job to edit this film down to forty-five feet to be used in the commercial. Lazarus' job, however, goes beyond choosing the best cut out of the dozens that Steve Horn had done for each vignette. He cuts within scenes, focuses shots, and trims frames to direct attention to a face or an arm. The goal of Lazarus' editing is to produce cuts that are "crisp and tight."

During the final stages of production the commercial is passed from one specialized production house to another. After the editing, David Lucas arranges the music he wrote for the "Reach out and touch someone" theme to fit the thirty-second advertisement. Lucas, like the others involved in the project, is a leader in his field. He lists the qualities necessary for commercial songwriting. "You need sincerity, and you need the research capacity of the mind, and . . . conciseness . . . conciseness is the essence of the craft—and then you have to make it all lovely."

The final work is done by Joe Delgado. He adjusts the colors, removing excess red, adding yellow or blue. Transitions from one scene to another are made by moving the image a few degrees to the north or east in each frame. The finished film is taken to American Telephone's enormous headquarters in suburban New Jersey. Senior executives gather around a television set to watch as the commercial opens with an older man, an actor, standing backstage talking on a telephone. The view cuts to a living room, with a young girl tap dancing on a bare floor. Her parents hold the phone to the floor. The camera cuts back to the elderly actor who begins to tap dance to the same "Reach out and touch someone" tune as the young girl. As the song continues, the scene switches to the crewcut army recruit, his father back home in the barber chair; to the white woman doing a yoga headstand while talking on the phone to the black woman doing the same; and to a man talking on the phone after having won a rodeo event to a woman having won a horse race. The final scenes reveal a winning hockey player in a locker room, his son at home in the same uniform, grinning a toothless grin, and, finally, the hockey player also grinning a toothless smile as champagne is poured over his head. The commercial closes with the Bell Telephone logo.

The premiere of "Tap Dancing" takes place on July 27, 1979, at 11:49 P.M. Johnny Carson interrupts his chat with Roscoe Tanner, the tennis player, for a series of commercials. When Carson and Tanner return to the screen, Jerry Pfiffner receives a telephone call of congratulations from Gaston Braun. After discussing regretfully the lack of color in the rodeo scene, the two men wish each other a good night. Jerry's wife tries to assure her husband that no one will notice the off colors, especially in thirty seconds. Jerry replies, "In thirty seconds, everybody notices *everything*."

Thirty Seconds is a comprehensive chronicle of the process of making a commercial for television. The intricate work of producing twelve separate scenes, each coherent, each telling its own story, is well presented by Michael Arlen. The reader senses the skill of the various writers, composers, directors, actors, editors, and technicians involved with "Tap Dancing." Anyone who reads this book will watch television commercials in a new way. Rather than allowing the commercial to act as a whole, creating a mood and delivering a message, the viewer will dissect each advertisement for the many aural and visual details that go together to make the whole. *Thirty Seconds* is, thus, television criticism in the best sense, forcing the reader to view television in a new way.

Michael Arlen goes beyond an analysis of a commercial and its technical production to examine the people involved in the business of television advertising. All the people presented in *Thirty Seconds* are driven by the desire to produce a successful commercial and by the fear that their careers can be set back, perhaps irrevocably, by a failure. The effort to ensure success leads those involved to lavish on each thirty-second spot a degree of care that almost no other artwork receives. "Tap Dancing" is written, directed, edited, polished, criticized, and analyzed by dozens of people at each of the offices involved in the production. Few films or television shows receive the same concentration on each second.

Some of the people who work in advertising see themselves as artists. They measure their success, not only in business terms, but in comparison with other directors, actors, composers, editors, and writers. The effort to be more than successful, to be an artist even while making a commercial for soda pop, or automobiles, or long-distance telephone calls, endears the Steve Horns and David Lucases of the advertising business to the reader. *Thirty Seconds* conveys admiration for the skill of those who make commercials.

Richard Lachmann

TITO
The Story from Inside

Author: Milovan Djilas (1911–)
Publisher: Harcourt Brace Jovanovich (New York). 185 pp. $9.95
Type of work: Biography
Time: 20th century
Locale: Yugoslavia

> *An account of the career of Josip Tito, who led Yugoslavian resistance first to the Nazis and then to the Soviet Union, written by a close personal associate*

Principal personages:
JOSIP BROZ TITO; ruler of Yugoslavia from 1945 until his death in 1980
MILOVAN DJILAS, a prominent member of the generation who came to power under Tito following World War II; vice-president of Yugoslavia

At the time of his death in May 1980, Tito was the last surviving prominent head of state to hold power since World War II, as well as the architect and sole leader of the first (and only) East European government to defy successfully the Soviet Union. A Croatian machinist and later trade union functionary, he became prominent in the Yugoslavian Communist Party in the 1930's and in the Resistance during World War II. Sketchily educated, autocratic, given to pomp and a succession of young wives, Tito held unshared power in a country that, alone among East European satellites, resisted the bloody purges of postwar non-Communist or factionalist Communist officials. Although Yugoslavia under Tito enjoyed a degree of commerce with the West and relative freedom unparalleled among socialist states, it has never been permitted freedom of expression or self-determination as exists in the West. Nevertheless, Yugoslavia's unique characteristics bear conspicuous testimony to the man who successfully managed to withdraw his government from Stalin's circle without provoking the expected Soviet invasion.

Milovan Djilas has published twelve books in the years since his denunciation and first imprisonment, in 1956, by the Yugoslav authorities. His study *The New Class* documents the rise of a new repressive class, the official bureaucracy, in the socialist sphere and made a great impression upon its publication in the West in 1957. *Conversations with Stalin* is valuable for being the only authenticated first-hand account of Stalin the statesman to come from a fellow Communist. Most recently Djilas has written of Yugoslavia and his own experience with the Communist Party during the war and after, and he discusses Tito at length in his memoir *Wartime* (1977). In *Tito,* Djilas has attempted an analytical study that contains elements of biography and autobiography, but that endeavors to draw a portrait of the man, his motivations and nature, and the influence he has had on Yugoslavia during his thirty-five years of rule.

A compelling portrait of Josip Tito emerges. Hearty and outgoing, yet insecure among party "intellectuals" and educated officers who had been to universities, Tito played to his strengths, cultivating a greater degree of closeness to the common populace than other Communist leaders and maintaining an essential mistrust of all but the most fundamental political theory. He was above all a pragmatist, able to use theory but in no way bound to it. "Tito may not have been able to invent ideas, but he certainly knew how to use them, adapt them, and adjust them. He was able instinctively to extract from this or that ideological assumption exactly as much as was necessary to implement or promote his own goal or policy."

Djilas emphasizes that purity of ideology is impossible in a leader, and asserts that Tito's deviation from pure Communist doctrine "affirms more than it refutes his steady and unflagging adherence to Marxism and socialism." That a party pragmatist whose only real education in Marxist thought was in Moscow's Communist Party schools in the 1930's (light on theory, heavy on tactics) should somehow be truer to Marxism than the party ideologues in Moscow is an unusual assertion, especially in light of Tito's continued encouragement of the "cult of personality" that Moscow repudiated in the years after Stalin. Djilas is rather vague in substantiating his claim. One element is certainly the fact that Yugoslavia did not engage in show trials and large-scale persecutions on trumped-up treason charges, as did the Soviet Union in the 1930's and the other Eastern satellites in 1948–1953. As Djilas notes, a man who kept out of politics was guaranteed to be free from political persecution, and even a party member who got caught in a struggle for power would not be sentenced to twenty years or put to death. Yet this is ascribable only to the fact that Tito personally drew the line at such slaughter and never, in the end, found it politically necessary. In postwar Yugoslavia's most dangerous hour, as it faced the possibility in the early 1950's of intervention by the Soviet Union, Tito authorized steps taken against internal Soviet supporters that stopped just short of life sentences and executions, but that included torture and forced "re-education." Since Tito betrayed socialist ideals in so many other respects, lavishing wealth and villas upon himself like royalty and ensuring his uncontested supremacy for life in Yugoslav politics, it is difficult to see how his refusal to engage in mass murder can constitute a greater fidelity to socialism than that of the Soviet Union. Djilas seems to attribute much to the fact that Tito, unlike Stalin, was not a psychopath.

What is unique, if hardly indicative of true socialist spirit, in Tito's regime was the stability of his base of support. Djilas asserts that "If it were possible to reduce Tito to one single feature, then that feature would be partisanship, the Party." Tito relied upon the middle ranks of the party as "the skeleton and nervous system of power." He ensured that orderly hierarchies and lines of promotion existed and made no attempt to bully or disenfranchise the middle levels, even while keeping the upper ranks, including the Politburo, restricted to roles of capable administrators and advisers—never governors. His relationship with the people was benignly autocratic; he would make personal appearances at festivals and villages and delighted in visiting orphanages and dispensing large donations in cash (from state treasuries) as though from personal largesse. To the people he was "the Old Man," and the simplicity and directness of his dealings in all political matters were most clearly appropriate here, for despite the fact that Tito's personal aggrandizement in matters of power and wealth were open knowledge in Yugoslavia, no one seemed to mind; it was regarded as his due. Relations with the populace never suffered. As Tito grew older, "the link between the leader and the people grew ever more tenuous and abstract, ever more joyful, innocent, bright."

For Djilas, the personal will of the leader cannot, any more than ideological purity, prevail at all times in the face of circumstance and shifting political situations. Even the most autocratic leader, even Stalin at the height of his power, cannot see his policies imposed without distortion upon the pliant face of the country he rules. "A social system rises from the interplay of spontaneous energies generated at the bottom and organizational structures at the top. Political skill is to initiate the interplay between the spontaneous and the structured."

In other words, political pragmatism as Tito practiced it remains the best way to implement one's policies, *even if* (rather than *except when*) adapting the pragmatic approach means subordinating, seemingly or in fact, for the moment or indefinitely, the high resolve of one's ideals to the demands of expediency. Djilas's views on politics have been deeply influenced by what he saw in Tito, enough so that in attempting to criticize Tito, he is uncertain of the unfamiliar ground on which he must now stand. Except in faulting Tito on the most obvious points, such as his self-indulgence, Djilas is hesitant as to how far he can validly criticize the man, despite the profound dissatisfaction with Tito's regime that can be sensed throughout the book. Tito was weak on theory, but he manifestly did not suffer for it, and after all, pure ideology cannot be implemented. If Tito did allow the establishment of a vile concentration camp during his struggle with the Yugoslav Stalinists, Djilas must acknowledge that "In retrospect, and with all the self-criticism of which I am capable, I must admit that we could not have avoided a concentration camp for the Cominformists." If Tito enriched himself, he did so openly and allowed his top aides the same, which helped to establish a visible incentive for party stability and ensured the restoration of estates and preservation of furniture and paintings otherwise threatened under a leftist regime.

In the end, Tito appointed no successor, even made sure that no single successor was possible. This was done, Djilas asserts, mainly to prevent anyone from rivaling his eminence and competing with him in posterity, but it assured that the government following Tito would have a shared leadership and that the autocracy that Tito enjoyed through his lifetime would not continue beyond him. Even at the last, then, the unadmirable traits of Tito can be seen to have achieved a certain good, and Djilas, noting that "I can hardly render a final judgment on Tito. I cannot be impartial," remains uncertain.

The book has a disorganized, opaque quality ascribable in part to Djilas's evident haste in its composition (it was written during and immediately after Tito's final illness, and rushed into print) and in part to the abstract and synthetic mode of examination it undertakes, to which Djilas is not accustomed. The result is a valuable document, but one flawed in execution and frustrating to read, rife with verbosity, occasional vagueness, and sentences that simply cannot be understood.

Although divided into numbered chapters, the book has no readily evident organization, save that it begins in a highly abstract manner and becomes more historical, more anecdotal, as it proceeds. The earliest sections, written in a manner Djilas clearly finds uncongenial, are by far the poorest and may well put off the unwarned reader. Uneasy with drawing abstract conclusions from his wealth of variegated and contradictory experience, Djilas will make an observation only to qualify it at once:

> Tito's personal role as commander in these clashes was insignificant, perhaps negligible. But it was he who imposed a sense of danger, who established a momentum, who forced the tide to turn.

Djilas sometimes substantiates statements with elaboration that is actually paraphrase:

> Of course, words and ideas are not immutable and do not live or retain a lasting sense independent of the social and spiritual climate. That is particularly true of the language of politics, as George Orwell knew.

The word "social" means "political" in socialist discourse, so the second sentence of the above is redundant of the first sentence.

It must be noted that Djilas's publishers may be partially responsible for the distractingly bad writing. Never published in his own language, Djilas's manuscript was evidently translated without editing. As a result, what could have been an invaluable study made from a perspective no other author possesses is flawed.

Gregory Feeley

THY NEIGHBOR'S WIFE

Author: Gay Talese
Publisher: Doubleday and Company (Garden City, N.Y.). 568 pp. $14.95
Type of work: Sociology
Time: The present
Locale: Chicago, New York City, Southern California, and Washington, D.C.

A survey of the American sexual revolution and its effects on popular sexual attitudes in the postwar era

Principal personages:
    HUGH M. HEFNER, founder of Playboy Enterprises
    JOHN WILLIAMSON, founder of the Sandstone Retreat
    JOHN and JUDITH BULLARO, members of the Sandstone Retreat
    AL GOLDSTEIN, editor of *Screw* Magazine
    WILLIAM HAMLING, California publisher
    ANTHONY COMSTOCK, Victorian decency crusader
    CHARLES KEATING, leader of Citizens for Decent Literature
    GAY TALESE, author and reporter

Stalking the secret sources of America's sexual revolution, Gay Talese devoted nine years of research and personal experience to the writing of *Thy Neighbor's Wife*. Utilizing the journalistic techniques that characterized his earlier works, Talese embraces within his narrative the entire postwar period, with occasional forays into the more distant past, to summon up a montage of the lustful dreams and guilt-filled nightmares of some of the men and women who symbolize the profound transformation of American attitudes over the past 35 years.

As Talese shows, the mobilization of America for the enormous effort of World War II laid the groundwork for the sexual revolution that would burst over the country after the war. Women on the homefront, taking the jobs of men at offices and factories, eagerly exchanged the traditional passive roles of wife and mother for a measure of independence undreamed of by their mothers and grandmothers. In the theaters of war, hundreds of thousands of GI's were exposed to new cultures and to wartime attitudes toward sex, and not a few of them brought these new ideas back with them, sometimes along with European pornographic magazines and photographs that were all but unknown in the United States. The young men and women returning from jobs or combat in the early postwar years represented a generation that, confronted with the strict attitudes toward sex and conformity of the era of Dwight D. Eisenhower and Joseph McCarthy, began to rebel against the norm.

The indefatigable decency crusades of the 19th century had succeeded in driving the American market in erotic literature and photographs completely underground. A few nudist magazines and folios of "artistic" photographs, hidden under the counters of certain newsstands in certain cities, could still be purchased, but only at the risk of arrest and public humiliation. Before World War II, the attempts of a few magazines like *Esquire* and *Modern Man* to present a more forthright attitude toward sexual material were continually dashed by the efforts of the self-appointed public defenders of morality. But after the war, the soaring subscription figures of a daring new magazine named *Playboy* were a clear indication that the days of under-the-counter porn were over. The publisher of that new magazine, a young Chicagoan named Hugh M. Hefner, had sensed the secret dreams of the new American male, and he had begun to build an empire.

Beginning with an initial investment of only $600 in 1953, Hefner sought to cater to an urban male readership that had never before been tapped. Unwilling to submit to the humiliating guilt of pulp pornography and uninterested in the blood and guts style of *Argosy, True Adventure,* or the *Police Gazette,* hundreds of thousands of young American men found a seductive mirror for their own fantasies in the glossy pages of *Playboy.* Its symbol the jaunty caricature of a lustful rabbit, Hefner's magazine concentrated on the presentation of wholesome, perky "playmates," with a liberal sprinkling of quality fiction and informative articles. By the mid-1950's, Hefner had achieved astounding success, but not content to restrict the fearlessly liberated ethos of the magazine to its pages alone, Hefner himself began an ostentatious personal expression of the fantasy that his magazine had created. Working from the comfort of a huge circular bed in the master bedroom of the "Playboy mansion" in Chicago, dressed in pajamas with the alluring models and bunnies of his empire always nearby, Hefner became a nationally known character in his own right. He became the personal embodiment of the modern playboy, reveling in the guiltless pleasure of recreational sex.

By the 1960's even the traditionally sacrosanct institution of marriage was undergoing serious challenges. In southern California, the sudden proliferation of encounter groups and "open marriage" questioned the practicability of monogamy in a modern society and unleashed a Pandora's box of painful experiences. Taking John and Judith Bullaro as a couple typical of this movement, Talese follows the twisted path that led them into the group experiment that would later become known as the Sandstone Retreat. The magnetic influence of the group's leader, John Williamson, and the intense interpersonal tensions created by the voluntary dissolution of the traditional marriage bonds combine in Talese's narrative to lend a nightmarish quality to the sexual wanderings of the Sandstone group.

Talese draws an interesting parallel between the tribulations of the members of the Sandstone Retreat and the experiences of the Oneida Community in upstate New York in the 19th century and provides a striking portrait of the founder of that community, John Humphrey Noyes. In an age of unflinching Victorian morality, Noyes' magnetic personality attracted a strange collection of faithful followers who pledged solemnly to share everything, including beliefs and bodies. Records were strictly kept to prevent any undue attachments between members, and all children were raised in common. After the strong protests of the neighboring townspeople resulted in the arrest of Noyes, however, the community was forced to abandon its unorthodox ideals and return to the world of monogamy. The legacy of such sexual experiments lived on and flourished in the 1960's, but by then the leaders, like John Williamson, were neither hounded nor jailed. Instead, their activities were carefully documented and they were quoted at length in the pages of national magazines.

In the field of publishing, the continued liberalization of sexual standards was due in large measure to the inability of the legal system to define what was technically obscene, and it led to the publication of a flood of previously banned works such as *Fanny Hill* and gave rise to dozens of men's magazines hoping to cash in on the awesome success of *Playboy*. In this atmosphere, a unique publication named *Screw* magazine was born. Flamboyantly flouting the traditional limits of obscenity and good taste, *Screw*'s publisher, Al Goldstein, traveled tirelessly around the country as a self-appointed protector of the growing number of consumers of erotic films, massage parlors, and sex boutiques. Personally visiting the neon-lit islands of once-forbidden sexual delights, Goldstein published his evaluations, providing his readers with a reliable defense against sexual swindlers.

But the rising tide of sexual permissiveness was not without its sworn enemies, and prominent among them was Charles H. Keating, who founded in the 1950's a private organization called Citizens for Decent Literature. Keating's crusades followed firmly in the footsteps of antismut campaigns at the end of the 19th century that led to a federal law setting down punishments for the manufacture or distribution of obscene material. Keating's task in the 1960's was to ensure that the law was enforced and that the legal definition of "obscene" was given its widest possible interpretation.

With the election of Richard Nixon as president in 1968, and his subsequent appointment of a conservative majority in the Supreme Court, the legal balance began to shift away from the earlier liberal decisions that had made "redeeming social value" the sole criterion for the question of obscenity. Nixon himself was committed to attacking the problem of smut in America, and he appointed a special Presidential Commission on Obscenity and Pornography to study the problem and compile a report that would serve as the basis for future legislation. The members of the commission, including Charles Keating, toured the country taking interviews, visiting topless bars, and poring over endless examples of hard-core pornography. They were intent on isolating the social virus that caused pornography, but the official findings of the commission shocked and horrified even some of its members. Instead of roundly condemning pornography as grim evidence of moral decline, the commission's majority report stated that not only had it been unable to establish a link between the viewing of pornographic materials and the increase in sexual crimes, but it found that pornography sometimes provided a relatively harmless release for the sexual tensions of those who chose to utilize it. Charles Keating and the other conservative members of the commission issued a blistering minority report, but the damage had been done; the original Nixonian intention of destroying the pornography trade had backfired.

Among the books and magazines published in the wake of the commission's report was an "illustrated" edition of the report, which included a bizarre collection of pornographic images. The decision of the Supreme Court to uphold the conviction of its publisher, William Hamling, on charges of obscenity, became a landmark case.

By the early 1970's, the sexual world created by the fantasy makers of the 1950's was beginning to undergo profound transformations. Rising alongside the growing awareness of male sexuality, the feminist movement opened up a new spectrum of sexual expression. At the traditionally male domain of Playboy Enterprises, Hefner's daughter began to make her way up the corporate ladder.

Thy Neighbor's Wife describes, in a clearly written journalistic narrative, the milestones in the post-World War II sexual revolution. At the conclusion of the book, Talese recounts the stages of his own sexual odyssey during the period of research for the book. His unemotional recitation of experiences at the Sandstone Retreat, as manager of a New York massage parlor, and as the pampered guest of the Playboy Empire hints at profound personal changes. However impassioned his intellectual feelings about the sexual revolution, though, Talese leaves his personal feelings ill-defined. Having wandered into the secret no man's land of sexual experimentation, he, like America itself, seems unable any longer to establish a moral boundary.

Neil Asher Silberman

THE TRANSIT OF VENUS

Author: Shirley Hazzard (1931–   )
Publisher: Viking Press (New York). 337 pp. $11.95
Type of work: Novel
Time: The present and recent past
Locale: England and the United States

The story of two orphaned Australian sisters reared in England as they grow into womanhood and of the men who love them

> Principal characters:
> CAROLINE BELL, an orphaned Australian trying to succeed in London
> GRACE BELL, her sister
> TED TICE, an American astronomer working in England
> PAUL IVORY, a British playwright
> DORA, the British woman who raises Caroline and Grace
> TERTIA DRAGE, married to Paul Ivory
> CHRISTIAN THRALE, married to Grace Bell
> ADAM VAIL, an American industrialist

The Transit of Venus tells the story of the mundane experience of one ordinary woman, Caroline Bell, during the extraordinary period after World War II until the present. Caroline, called Caro, and her sister, Grace, are Australians who were orphaned at an early age when their parents died in the wreck of an Australian ferry. Caroline and Grace were taken under the care of an Englishwoman named Dora who had no children of her own.

The novel is divided into four major sections; the thirty-seven chapters are untitled. The first section, entitled "The Old World," contains a series of meetings and departures, colored by the shadows of the Korean War and destruction. "Contacts," the second section, chronicles the developments through which the characters become conscious of the past and begin to order their lives in relation to it. The third section, "The New World," offers the prospect of a new beginning to the characters but is brought to a close with the sense of despair and destruction. This despair and destruction also characterizes the fourth section, "The Culmination," as well as the contemporary society it describes.

The Transit of Venus opens with a raging, violent storm. The storm is not only described but reported upon in the first sentence of the novel. "By nightfall the headlines would be reporting devastation." This sets the tone for the novel and at the same time it focuses the reader's attention on the unreality of language. Indeed the reference to "headlines" at the head of the chapter declares the novel's intentional creation of several levels of meaning in which the language of the author seeks to combine elements from other modes of representation, such as reporting, poetry, and painting. This linguistic self-consciousness becomes obvious in the unique style of writing that characterizes the introductory paragraphs. The language is employed in such a manner that the reader becomes aware of style as much as events and descriptions. Slowly, this stylized poetic language gives way to a more narrative form. What makes the stylistic aspect of the novel so unusual is the way in which it serves to capture and set off the central characters, functioning almost as the setting for a jewel or the frame for a picture. In this case, however, the frame is too large for the picture, and the ornate language of the novel only serves to highlight the drab and ordinary character of its central figure, Caroline Bell.

The novel begins at the country home of Professor Sefton Thrale and his wife, Charmian. The first character to arrive is an American astronomer, Ted Tice, who has come to work with the eminent but ailing astronomer Professor Thrale. It is in the Thrale home that Ted first meets Grace Bell. Grace is engaged to the professor's son, Christian Thrale, a government official. The first chapter ends with a short declarative sentence, "And the lights went up by themselves, as on a stage," which, like the first sentence of the chapter, serves to remind the reader that these are not real events at the same time that the novel's plot begins to weave its spell.

The second chapter is characterized by a dominant narrative tone, the events reported by an omnipresent detached observer. The descriptions of place and character appear to be as repressed by the conventions of society as are the actions of those characters. There does, however, appear to be a hidden explanation for this blank tone. The first section of the novel concerns the difficulty of rational existence in a world that appears to have lost its own claims to rationality. Just as the novel begins with an eruption of nature, the entire section is colored by the echoes of the recent world war. The Korean War is casually mentioned in the second paragraph of the novel, and by the fourth chapter it is revealed that "Mars in truth had covered Venus." Thus the transit of Venus can be read to mean the movement of a modern Venus, Caroline Bell, in a world dominated by the violence and disruptions of Mars. Caroline's identification with Venus is not mere speculation. Her last name is Bell, which clearly indicates "belle," and later in the novel her benefactor, Dora, is described as being obsessed with the Venus de Milo. What is perhaps more interesting is that Caroline is not actually beautiful. She may be graceful and able to attract a series of interesting men, but she is clearly portrayed as a common Australian woman struggling to maintain her existence in a country where she is not completely acclimated. The novel's interest is the way it describes the movement of ordinary people in extraordinary times.

Ted Tice is the first man in the novel with whom Caroline becomes romantically involved, but their relationship is told with such propriety that at times it is difficult to know exactly what has happened. The novel has no difficulty describing scenes or characters, yet appears especially strained in representing moments of social intercourse. For instance, in a pause in conversation between Ted and Caroline, the author comments, "A silence can easily fall between those who do not consider themselves a topic." Moments later Caroline exclaims, "They are cutting down the very color . . . The green we only knew about from books." Although the constantly self-reflexive language of this novel is interesting and although the uncomfortable tone of the language may represent the characters more than it does their author, at times the reader grows impatient at characters who "blush for the universe."

Caro's relationship with Ted Tice continues throughout the novel, but they are not finally united until the last pages. During the novel Caro has a relationship with Paul Ivory, a married playwright who is perhaps the one great love of her live. But Ivory is married to Tertia Drage, and they have a small child. Caro later meets an American industrialist, Adam Vail, whose wife has committed suicide. They marry and move to New York. While married to Vail, Caro meets a South American poet, Ramon Tregear, whose poetry she translates. Finally, at the end of the novel she once again meets Ted Tice, who is married to a woman named Margaret. They realize their love, but Caro decides she must leave him. Ted, however, finds her at the airport, her flight delayed by a strike. He tells her he has told his wife of their love and will be following her to Rome the same night. At the end of the novel they sit in the waiting room of an airport and observe a sign, "Passengers in Transit" while Caro remembers other departures and farewells. They end their existence within the book as they began it, completing the orbit of their life together within the fictional universe of the novel.

The Transit of Venus is admirable for trying to create new modes of discourse suited to modern experience. The constant reference to poetry and painting in the novel serves to highlight the way in which reality is influenced by the method of its representation. Thus, history becomes a fiction that nonetheless must be lived through, and fiction tries to orient experience in terms of reality. In this respect *The Transit of Venus* is very much a novel of manners, yet it is radically different from similar novels of that genre of the 19th century. For as society changes, the language that is used to describe it must also change. If *The Transit of Venus* is not completely successful in its overall effort, it is all the more interesting for having attempted so ambitious an undertaking.

John Carlin

THE TWYBORN AFFAIR

Author: Patrick White (1912–   )
Publisher: Viking Press (New York). 432 pp. $14.95
Type of work: Novel
Time: 1912–1940
Locale: France, Australia, and England

A grim and uncompromising account of a tormented homosexual's stoical efforts to reconcile his nature with a hostile and finally sordid world

Principal characters:
> EDDIE/EUDOXIA/EADITH, a young Australian, who appears sometimes as a woman
> EADIE TWYBORN, Eddie's socially prominent, unhappy mother
> JOAN GOLSON, an inquisitive friend of Eadie's

The Twyborn Affair follows the life of Eddie Twyborn, born "with a woman's mind" into a good Australian family, as he wanders in various guises through the different levels of English society in a fitful quest for solace from the stigma of his homosexuality and, more generally, his grim perception of all human nature and of life itself.

The story, which ranges across two continents and three decades, opens on the French Riviera where Curly and Joan Golson, a vulgar Australian couple who have inherited a fortune, are spending the summer of 1912 in indolent leisure. During a motor ride through the countryside, Joan spies a small cottage where a genteel couple, a young woman and dignified elderly man, are walking among the overgrown shrubbery in their yard. Although she catches no more than a glimpse of them, Joan becomes fascinated by the two and returns to her hotel wondering about their relationship and hoping to meet them.

The story then shifts to the point of view of the young woman, who is writing in her diary, into which the reader is allowed a glimpse in alternating scenes. The woman, Eudoxia, had indeed noticed Joan Golson and moreover recognized her from a past life, although she does not pause to explain what their earlier acquaintance was. Upset by the Golsons' presence, which she feels threatens the precarious happiness she has found, she accepts the assurances of her lover that she faces no real danger. He, an elderly Greek named Angelos, is the center of her present life, although they both feel, without admitting it, that she will someday leave him. Eudoxia and Angelos, purportedly married for the sake of appearances, live in a quiet, peaceful life in their cottage, and she resolves to avoid any encounter with Joan Golson in the nearby village resort.

Joan, however, remains infatuated, wondering about the mysterious couple and particularly the alluring young woman. Her complacent husband offers no objection, and Joan takes a second ride the following afternoon, approaching the cottage on foot in the gathering dusk to catch a glimpse of the couple, who are visible through the window as they play a string duet together. Protected by the near-darkness, Joan approaches the front gate to gaze rapturously at the performance, and when the woman rises afterward to close the shutters, she returns home intent on effecting a meeting.

Eudoxia had in fact noticed Joan and is deeply upset at the woman's unwelcome attentions. Writing in her diary, she notes that Joan was a tiresome friend of "Eadie," someone Eudoxia knew as a child. The reader gets the vague impression that Eadie was Eudoxia's mother. More specific details remain inaccessible, however, as Eudoxia does not of course give full accounts of her past when writing down her day's events and impressions.

In her resort hotel, Joan Golson pursues her petty pleasures while wondering about the mysterious Eudoxia and making a resolution, never acted upon, to write a letter to "poor old Eadie Twyborn" and tell her about the summer's activities. She reflects how Eadie had never got over some unspecified disaster that befell her. In a burst of good fortune, Joan encounters Eudoxia one afternoon as the younger woman has fallen on the sidewalk, injuring herself slightly, and insists on taking her up to her room. Eudoxia allows herself to be cared for, and the complacent Curly drives her home afterward. Although Joan senses something familiar about Eudoxia, she does not recognize her, and the two later meet for lunch. Eudoxia extends an invitation for the Golsons to visit.

Joan is rapturous with anticipation, but the social visit is a disaster. The cranky Angelos is rude and inhospitable, probably because Eudoxia, acting out of some embarrassed timidity, had not told him of the invitation, and the Golsons retreat, mortified. When Joan returns a few days later, the couple has abruptly departed, leaving only an indignant landlady who leads Joan through the house, vengefully pointing out every evidence of the couple's seemingly sordid personal life.

Eudoxia and Angelos frantically flee the village, riding an over-crowded train to a foreign city where they settle in a shabby pension and where the ailing Angelos dies that night. Eudoxia is left to fare as best she can. Book I ends when Joan, looking toward returning to Australia, writes to Eadie, describing at length her encounter with Eudoxia but saying nothing that might lead Eadie to recognize her child.

Book II opens in 1920 on a liner en route to Australia, aboard which Eddie Twyborn, recently discharged from the army, where he was decorated for valor in World War I, is returning home for the first time in years. Eligible and attractive, he fends off advances from repellent young women and friendly homosexuals, remaining aloof and deeply unhappy. One debutante tells another how Eddie had caused a scandal in Australian society years earlier by fleeing the night before his wedding to a nice young woman. Meanwhile, Eddie keeps to himself, tossing unhappily in his bunk in a scene in which it is revealed that Eddie and Eudoxia are one.

Eddie returns to his parents' estates, where his father, a preoccupied judge, and his mother, an alcoholic, have lived alone since the disappearance of their only child. Although they do not know of his homosexuality or partiality for women's guise, their efforts to get along amiably lead only to mutual discomfort and misunderstanding. Eddie avoids a social gathering at which the returned Joan Golson would be present and decides finally to try to make a life for himself working as a ranch hand on an outback sheep station, a reasonably acceptable pursuit in which well-to-do Australian young men occasionally indulged.

In the longest section of the book, Eddie adapts himself to living among uneducated and laboring ranch hands, working for a prosperous ranch owner, Greg Lushington, who is closer in social class to Eddie than his co-workers are. He develops an attraction for his immediate boss, a taciturn man, but is careful not to show it. During Greg's absence, his adventuresome wife seduces Eddie, not realizing that he is one of the homosexuals she deplores. Angered by his betrayal of his likable employer with Mrs. Lushington, Eddie begins to loathe the woman. Meanwhile his boss, who considered Eddie a friend, realizes Eddie's homosexuality and rapes him in a barn. A few days later, grief-stricken and remorseful, he visits Eddie's room, urging him to reciprocate. Eddie, realizing that his relationships with all three people are essentially ruined, departs once more, bringing Book II to a close.

The final section takes place in fashionable London in the late 1930's, where Eddie, now the middle-aged "Mrs. Trist," runs a fashionable brothel with the aid of a well-connected friend, a peer named Gravenor who has fallen in love with her. The two pursue their hopeless unconsummated love affair, Eddie strongly drawn to Gravenor but unwilling to do anything that would reveal his real nature to his deceived suitor. With the outbreak of World War II, Gravenor departs on a secret mission, possibly never to return, and Eddie abruptly discovers his mother, now widowed, living alone in London. He meets her and is recognized, in a touching scene. He finally is persuaded to accompany her back to Australia, where they will live out their lives together as two quiet spinsters. The day Eddie comes to pick up his mother and make final arrangements, he dresses as his male self without telling her, presumably to get a new passport. On his way over he is killed by a German bomb. Eadie Twyborn remains waiting at her hotel, anticipating the arrival of a son about whose death—because, of course, he had long since destroyed all his identification—she will never know. With this cruel irony, the novel ends.

It is difficult to describe how dispiriting and oppressive *The Twyborn Affair* is. In its style, even more than in plot, it is grisly and repellent, dwelling upon details of decay, purulence, and fulsomeness in the material world. This is clearly intended as an extended metaphor of man's spiritual condition, but it is presented with such relentlessness that it seems out of proportion with any reasonable view of humanity: "By now she knew the narrow streets by heart. She knew the abridged biographies of the girls who worked for the pharmacist, every fly which crawled on the chicken livers and rabbits at the poulterer's, the almost petrified heap of excrement (human, she suspected) on the paving at the south-west corner of St. Saveur." This is the perception by an heiress of a resort town on the Riviera. When the circumstances are more common, the author is able to reach heights of perversity where few readers may care to follow.

Patrick White retains in this book the forcefulness and austerity that has made him famous, but in his last few works the stoicism and stark splendor that characterized *Voss* and *The Tree of Man* have given way to a ripeness, a preoccupation with the decaying and the ignoble presented so forcefully as to constitute a fatal aesthetic miscalculation. White seems convinced that there is something fundamentally wrong with human nature and that no idealization of things can be true to art. But his misogyny and seeming fondness for toying with both reader and characters is numbing and finally unconvincing. The fact that most of his characters, like Gravenor, are pathetically deluded, parallels the way in which White deceives and tantalizes the reader. Like the washed-up dog carcass that spoils the beachside picnic in *The Eye of the Storm,* these details are intended as metaphors for the larger human condition, but speak less about life than about the author's desolate view of it.

Gregory Feeley

UNFINISHED BUSINESS

Author: Maggie Scarf
Publisher: Doubleday and Company (Garden City, N.Y.). 581 pp. $14.95
Type of work: Social science
Time: 1975–1979
Locale: United States

A study of the depression that is prevalent among women at all stages of life, including psychiatric theory and treatment, as well as illuminating case studies

> *Principal personages:*
> ANNE MUNSON, 17, high school student, hospitalized for saline abortion
> DEBRA THIERRY, 19, depressed by her boyfriend's departure for college
> MARIE SIROTTA, 28, student and housewife in a disastrous marriage
> SANDY GELLER, 27, R.N., divorced mother of a young daughter, troubled by her own promiscuity
> KATH BARRIE, 28, first-year medical student, obsessed with a dead-end relationship
> JUDITH KARLIN, 34, professor and manic-depressive
> LAURIE MICHAELSON, 32, mother of two young children
> DIANA PHARR DAHLGREN, 48, housewife, mother of four and alcoholic
> DORIS WALSH NORDLAND, 52, wife in a marital crisis
> MARGARET GARVEY, 65, hospitalized for depression

Women suffer from depression two to six times more frequently than men. In fact, depression among women has reached such proportions that Maggie Scarf tells the reader that what began as a book about women and depression, ended up being a book about women. She found depressed women at all stages of life. The depressive themes appeared in different forms at different life stages but often were a result of "unfinished business" at some earlier stage. Almost always, the themes had to do with relationships, intimacy, and loss.

The book is organized developmentally. For each decade of life from the teenage years through the sixties, interesting and typical women who are used as case histories of depression are introduced. The specifics of their lives serve to teach about the lives of women in general, while the specifics of their symptoms, diagnoses, and treatments are used by Scarf to describe the theory and treatment of depression in general.

"In the Teens" separation from one's parents, the first love attachments of life, is the major developmental task. As with most developmental tasks, this involves pain and suffering, since it involves loss.

Ideally, separation from parents is achieved by the process of internalization, making parents a part of oneself. Separation requires inner tools that should have developed during the first twleve years of life. The growth of self-reliance and self-confidence starts slowly, early in life. Otherwise, separation becomes an unmanageable task.

Anne Munson, experiencing difficulty in separating from her family, chose a distant boarding school in order to achieve independence. However, physical distance did not bring psychological separation. Once in the hospital for an abortion, she refused to leave. She wanted to retreat to childhood, to have the hospital staff care for her.

Debra Thierry had been sent off to horseback-riding camp, against her will, at age thirteen. Before that time she had been overprotected. As a result of that crucial summer Debra felt unwanted, abandoned, unlovable. She had extreme difficulty with any separation. A serious crisis resulted from the return of her boyfriend to college. Debra was sure he would never return in spite of objective evidence of his regard for her.

Scarf believes that it is a biological given that women are more vulnerable to depression than are men. Women are bound up in relationships and loss of relationships hurls them into depression. The first, perhaps prototypic, loss is the loss of parents.

"In the Twenties" the developmental task is to establish new love bonds, ones that facilitate the transition from child to adult. Having internalized one's parents, one goes on to develop chums and to experiment with different types of friendships.

For Marie Sirotta this was impossible. Her restrictive family, her intense involvement with her father, and her rejection of her mother, made it impossible for her to separate and move on. She married a man just like her father, got placed in a life role just like her mother, and was trapped. Her marriage and her divorce sustained her depression. She returned home to work things out again.

Sandy Geller married her husband when neither had developed sufficiently as an individual. They formed a mutually dependent emotional bond and then each stood in the way of the other's continuing need to develop. Hurled into the lonely world of adults, young women often cling, undeveloped, to a man. On separating from her husband Sandy was needy but fearful of men. She lived promiscuously, getting physically close to many men, emotionally close to none. Troubled by this, she sought help.

"In the Thirties" men are typically working out their life plan. The tasks of the twenties, exploration and then commitment in work and love, usually go hand-in-hand for men since being successful in work makes a man attractive as a life partner. For women integrating these life tasks is more difficult. Some women commit to work during their twenties, then give it up for love and family in their thirties. Others commit to love and raise families in their twenties and seek careers in their thirties. Fewer women do both at once. The case studies in this section reflect the conflictual nature of being both a successful person and a successful woman—a conflict that does not exist for men.

Kath Barrie was thrown into depression by the loss of a love relationship that was deadlocked. Philip could not commit himself until he was successful as an artist. Kath, easily successful as a medical student, needed a commitment.

Judith Karlin was subject to mood swings. She had suffered from three manic-depressive episodes and was sustained on lithium carbonate; hers was the only depressive disorder that had been demonstrated to be partially biochemical in origin. Her work went well, she got too excited, acted manic, and messed things up, then fell into depression. She believed that since her standards of success were male, she asserted her femininity by spoiling her success.

Laurie Michaelson believed her depression was postpartum in nature. Incidence of depression does increase during the first three postpartum months. Scarf discusses the possible contribution of female hormones and concludes that at times there may be "a biological induced tilt" but correctly points to emotional and environmental factors as primary causes for depression. Laurie's depression came eight months after delivery. She emerged from nursing to notice the crisis in her marriage. Parenthood had complicated her marriage; this breakdown left her feeling worthless.

"In the Forties" Diana, successful wife and mother, had attempted suicide. She was hospitalized and in the context of medical and psychiatric attention instantly regained health. What would happen when she returned to the routine lack of attention from her family? Here a woman was facing several more decades of life dependent upon the family she had nurtured for her self-worth. This is a bleak view of womanhood.

"In the Fifties" women face societal assumptions of menopausal depression. Scarf is clear here—there is no such thing. Women are misdiagnosed and mistreated under that label. It is a time of life when one takes stock, which may be depressing to women because of their lives, not their hormones.

Doris Nordlund attempted suicide in the face of aging, an incompatible marriage, and her husband's affair. Her depression stemmed from the inadequate choices she made for the past fifty years. She got treatment in the form of drugs and therapy, and changed her life circumstances.

"In the Sixties" one's emotional resources are shrinking. Loved ones die. Despair often results. One looks back with regret and forward with hopelessness. Such was the problem of Margaret Garvey. She was treated effectively with electroconvulsive therapy, which often is the treatment of choice for aging patients because of the increased risks of drugs. Margaret's interest in life was reawakened.

The book ends with updates on all of the principal characters. Everyone has done well. Women's lives are depressing, but treatment for depression works. There is no mention of changing life expectations for women.

This is a valuable book. It makes intelligible the staggering statistics on women and depression, while providing thorough information on treatment options, including side effects and risks. It also places this scientific information in the context of ordinary lives. At a time when therapy is a regularly purchased item, this book can well serve as a consumer guide.

In doing all this, Scarf paints the bleakest of pictures of women's lives and never fully explores the reasons underlying women's vulnerability to depression. How can separation and individuation be facilitated for daughters so that they will not have lives adrift due to "unfinished business?" Scarf implicates the earliest of love bonds, that between mother and child, but never questions the division of labor that leaves mothers solely responsible for infant care. Perhaps the psychological patterns and needs, the conflicts of womanhood, begin there.

The book is well written, easy and interesting reading for even the psychologically unsophisticated. Scarf treats the individual women she introduces with great respect.

Michele Hoffnung

UNFINISHED TALES

Author: J. R. R. Tolkien (1892–1973)
Publisher: Houghton Mifflin (Boston). 472 pp. $15.00
Type of work: Short stories
Time: Three mythical periods: The First Age, The Second Age, The Third Age
Locale: The mythical world Middle-earth; the mythical island Númenor

A collection of fragments, notes, early drafts, and revised versions that formed the basis of the trilogy The Lord of the Rings, *with further notes and commentary by the author's son*

> *Principal characters:*
> ALDARION, the Mariner King of Númenor
> BRENDIS, wife of Aldarion
> TUOR, legendary hero of The First Age
> ULMO, Lord of the Waters
> MORGOTH, the spirit of Evil
> TÚRIN, doomed hero, heir of the Lord of Dor-lómin
> MORWEN, mother of Túrin
> NIENOR, sister of Túrin
> THINGOL, Elf-lord, King of Doriath
> ORCS, men of evil
> DWARFS, ELVES, HOBBITS, mythical creatures possessing powers of magic

It was nearly four decades ago that J. R. R. Tolkien, a professor of English language and literature at Oxford University, published his trilogy, *The Lord of the Rings*. It followed by some fifteen years the appearance of a single volume, *The Hobbit,* which would serve as an introduction to the epic romance.

The subject of the epic was the usual; the quest for that which is supernatural. In Tolkien's trilogy, the object was a ring that would impart such powers that, in the possession of one of evil, it could lead to infinite corruption.

The four books, taken singly or together, are a remarkable achievement. Admittedly, they owe a large debt to the Norse sagas and to German mythology. Much of what is remembered from the Ring of the Nibelungs turns up in only slightly altered fashion in Tolkien's writings. Yet, the author has not only imagined, but explored and—quite literally—mapped a whole new world, that of Middle-earth, as well as the Island of Númenor. He has created hundreds of characters and invented a new vocabulary for them. He has detailed scores of episodes, all designed to carry out his often exciting plot. Tolkien's scope is clearly enormous.

His influence is also great. From its earliest appearance, *The Lord of the Rings* has been hailed as a classic; within another ten years, it had become the focus of a cult. And since his death in 1973, interest in Tolkien's works has continued to grow. As a result, his son, Christopher Tolkien, also an Oxford professor, has edited and adapted for publication a number of his manuscripts. The first volume of such work was *The Silmarillion; Unfinished Tales* is the second.

"Unfinished Tales" is misleading as a title. Many of the selections included are little more than fragments, sometimes descriptive, sometimes plot sketches, sometimes delineations of characters. One of the most intriguing of these is *Aldarion and Erendis,* a thirty-three page narrative. It depicts the relationship between Aldarion, the son of the king of Númenor, and his bride, Erendis, and the change in this relationship from deep love to hatred.

Aldarion's greatest joy is in sailing the sea, while Erendis cannot bear anything connected with the water. So time after time she is abandoned by her wandering husband. When he returns at last, ready to settle down, he is given his father's crown. Deliberately, he torments his wife, hoping to provoke a display of regal passion. But Erendis is as passive as ever and instead of expressing hatred or seeking revenge, submits as meekly as "a serving-woman." Infuriated by her docility, and blaming himself for her craven attitude, Aldarion declares: "I would rather have a beautiful Queen to thwart me and flout me, than freedom to rule while (Erendis) falls down deep into her own twilight. . . ." The narrative ends there, but Christopher Tolkien, using notes found among his father's papers, tries to sketch its development. That can only be conjecture, however, due to the inconsistencies in the originals.

Although it is even shorter—not quite seven pages—*A Description of the Island of Númenor,* being exactly that, succeeds as a small, complete work of prose. In it, Tolkien describes the topography of the imaginary island, the flora and the fauna, and the inhabitants, giving something of their history as well as their occupations.

The present volume opens with a short narrative, *Of Tuor And His Coming to Gondolin.* In it, a young man is captured in battle and enslaved. He escapes and sets out to summon aid for those still held. The object of his quest is Turgon, "accounted the High King of the Noldor," and an implacable foe of Morgoth, the spirit of Evil.

Tuor is helped in his search by the forces of nature: by an ever-widening stream, by swans, by eagles. He comes across a suit of magic armor; he is wrapped in the mantle of the Lord of the Waters himself. Elves and other supernatural creatures guide and protect him until he at last reaches the city of Gondolin. After passing through the seven gates that guard it, he enters.

A much longer story, and possibly the most fascinating in the entire collection, is that called *Narn I Hîn Húrin*. It relates the story of Túrin, son of the Lord of Dor-lómin, who, after the fall of the realm, is sent by his mother, Morwen, to Thingol, the King of Doriath. Thingol, the Elf-lord, adopts Túrin as his foster son, and when Morwen sends the enchanted Helm of Hador, which will protect its wearer, to Thingol, he presents Túrin with it. Túrin remains with the Elf-lord until he is provoked by one of his followers and hounds him to his death. He is then banished. After the truth of the provocation is revealed, he is pardoned, and a group is sent to find him and bring him back. But Túrin has by now become an outlaw; soon he is the leader of a band of them.

Thingol's troops continue to pursue Túrin, but he invariably evades them. He overcomes obstacles, fights, and kills. He and his fellows are near starvation and close to freezing when they capture a dwarf, Nîm, who protects them. They cannot linger with Nîm forever, though, and so, after another struggle, they set forth again. Eventually Túrin returns to his own land, only to find it devastated. His mother has disappeared; the sister he remembers is dead. There is another sister, one he has never known, but she, too, is gone. Túrin then sets out on still another quest, this time in search of his mother and sister.

He reaches the forest of Brethil, the land of the People of Haleth, and joins them in battle against the Orcs, the evil ones. Túrin is wounded, but recovers. He remains to make his home in the forest, changing his name. One day Túrin discovers a young woman unconscious in the forest; it is his sister, although he cannot recognize her. He rescues her, and she recovers, but does not know who she is.

The two fall in love and eventually are married. Then Túrin, despite his promise to Nienor, whom he knows as Níniel, never to war again except in her defense, goes off to fight Glaurung, the dragon of Morgoth. Thanks to his enchanted sword, he slays him, but is burned by his fiery breath and faints at the side of the dying monster. Níniel comes upon them; Glaurung, avenging himself, blurts out that she and Túrin are brother and sister. In horror at her sin, Níniel, now carrying Túrin's child, commits suicide. When Túrin learns the truth, he too kills himself.

To devotees of J. R. R. Tolkien, *Unfinished Tales* will be a happy discovery. Within its covers they will find more—although only a few —of the narratives that have previously delighted them. They will also find the copious and thoughtful footnotes that shed much light on Tolkien's characters. There is a complete index as well, plus maps, charts, and tables of genealogy. The commentary alone will help to clear up any confusion in the mind of the *Lord of the Rings* aficionado. It is a useful, possibly a necessary, key to the intricacies of this complicated epic.

It may, however, prove a disappointment as well. The new works, the fragments, may be below Tolkien's usual standards. While some may have gone unpublished because they were unfinished, others may have been abandoned because they lacked promise. Those may have been false starts, leading to plot developments that did not satisfy the author and so were discarded. In any event, they were not polished to the author's satisfaction. Despite scrupulous editing, they do not represent the finished writing of J. R. R. Tolkien.

Unfinished Tales is, as a result, a hybrid. It is not really a book of tales—most of those included are too fragmentary to qualify as such. Nor is it really a book by J. R. R. Tolkien. It is, essentially, a small sampling of his writing that serves as the introduction to a comprehensive appendix to *The Hobbit* and *The Lord of the Rings*. Those who are well acquainted with those books will find the commentary of Christopher Tolkien invaluable in shedding light on unexplained or contradictory aspects of them, in increasing their knowledge of Middle-earth, its language, and its legends. The reader coming to Tolkien's masterpiece for the first time, however, may find more obfuscation than illumination.

Vivian Werner

THE VERMILION BRIDGE

Author: Shelley Mydans (1916–   )
Publisher: Doubleday and Company (Garden City, N.Y.). 369 pp. $11.95
Type of work: Novel
Time: 8th century
Locale: Japan

The story of Princess Abé, who twice ruled Japan, of the powerful Fujiwara family, and the developing religious conflict between Buddhism and Shintoism

Principal characters:
  PRINCESS ABÉ, twice Empress of Japan
  YAMATO SHŌMU, Abé's father
  KŌMYŌ, Abé's mother
  YUGE NO DŌKYŌ, Buddhist priest, later Abé's lover and Chancellor of the Realm
  FUJIWARA NAKAMARO, Abé's cousin and lover who tries to usurp her power
  FUWA, Abé's half sister and lady-in-waiting
  SAISHO, lady-in-waiting and close friend of Abé
  KIBI NO MAKIBI, Abé's first teacher and adviser
  OI-ō, Emperor after Abé's abdication

Abé's story opens when her mother is safely delivered of a long-awaited son. Kōmyō, Abé's mother, is from the powerful Fujiwara family, whose members have been advisers and consorts of the royal family for generations. Four of her brothers were ministers in Shōmu's government. Kōmyō was the Emperor's favorite for her education and wit as well as for her connections. The Emperor, thrilled when his son, Moto-Ō, is born, names him heir to the throne before ever seeing him. Ten-year-old Abé too seems enthralled with the baby. But when the child, who had seemed so healthy, sickens and dies, there is talk of sorcery. Prince Nagaya-Ō, Great Minister of the Left, accused of practicing magic against the infant heir, commits suicide.

Abé is named to succeed her father and begins to take part in royal ceremonies. With the return of the embassy to China, Chinese influence in Japan begins to increase. Abé takes lessons in Buddhism and Confucianism from the returned scholar Kibi no Makibi.

At the age of fourteen Abé is given her own pavilion, where she and Saisho become close friends. It is with Saisho that she first meets Fujiwara Nakamaro, who regales the young princess with tales of the Chinese embassy and his own achievements. The mutual attraction is reported to Kōmyō, who warns her nephew away.

When a smallpox epidemic erupts, members of the court as well as the common people are stricken with the dread disease. Throughout the palace and the country, Buddhist priests recite healing sutras at

Shōmu's request. Abé, feeling very much confined by the disease, wanders about the palace and finds the Buddhist priest, Yuge no Dōkyō, praying in an alcove. Immediately attracted to one another, they become lovers. Although love notes and poems are exchanged, the young priest soon disappears. Abé hears that he has gone into retreat.

Shōmu comes to believe that Nara is no longer an auspicious place from which to govern and agrees to move the court to Kuni, where a new royal compound is built. The move to Kuni is supervised by Nakamaro. Shōmu, although a devout Buddhist, still honors the gods of Shinto. While the court is in Kuni, he has a vision of the Roshana Buddha. He longs to build an image, but is uncertain about whether the people will support the expense. Will his august ancestors be angered? He sends a priest to consult the oracle at the shrine of the god Hachiman at Usa. Only when the message comes back through his priestess that the gods are subordinate to Buddha does construction begin—and fail.

At this point Kōmyō encourages a relationship between Abé and Nakamaro. As Abé and Nakamaro become closer, his influence over her grows.

Soon a series of earthquakes shows the displeasure of the gods, and the decision is made to return the court to Nara. Here Shōmu finds a new site for his image of Buddha and again begins building the statue. This time he succeeds. Shōmu, in failing health, becomes obsessed with the Buddha. As his health continues to deteriorate he makes plans to abdicate in favor of Abé. At the age of 32, Abé becomes the Empress Kōken. But in reality it is her parents, who have become members of the Buddhist clergy, who continue to wield the power. In April 732 the great Buddha at Todai-ji Temple in Nara is dedicated with great ceremony, and Shōmu sees his dream become a reality but dies soon after.

Kōmyō, although now a Buddhist nun, continues to advise her daughter. When Nakamaro influences Abé to name his daughter-in-law's son as her heir, a plot to force her to name a new successor and then abdicate ensues. The real target of the conspiracy is Nakamaro, who is both a strong influence on the Empress and a Fujiwara. The retired Empress is with Abé when the plot is reported and tries to talk the misguided young men out of their plan. Nakamaro, discovering that the conspirators intend to kill Kōmyō and himself, takes action, and several of the suspects die under torture. For the first time Abé becomes very angry with him; she wished to exile the men involved. Nakamaro, as Household Minister and Supreme Commander, is too powerful and too important to her for her to dismiss. When Nakamaro intimates that his brother, the Great Minister of the Right, was involved in the plot, Abé demotes him and sends him into exile.

Abé, ignorant of the conditions under which the peasants live, is warned by Kibi that heavy taxation has caused a great deal of unrest among them. Temples, priests, nuns, doctors, artisans, artists, and nobles are tax exempt, which adds to the burden of the common people. Abé, refusing to listen to Kibi's advice, continues to spend lavishly on temples.

When her mother becomes ill, Abé abdicates, on Nakamaro's advice, to care for the retired Empress. The throne passes to Oi-Ō, whom Nakamaro controls. With Abé's ministrations, her mother's condition improves slightly. With Kōmyō's apparent improvement, Abé returns to her old pavilion at the palace where she discovers that Nakamara, now Grand Minister of the Right, is making preparations for war. Abé is distracted from his actions by the relapse of her mother, and returns to Kōmyō's bedside until her death. Then Abé herself sickens from the depth of her mourning, retiring completely from court life.

Conditions continue to deteriorate in the court and in the country as Nakamaro imposes huge taxes to support his war effort. He convinces Oi-Ō to appoint him prime minister, encouraging Oi-Ō and Abé to retire to Hora Palace. Abé, sunk in mourning for her mother, accepts his suggestion. Nakamaro has become the ruler of Japan.

At Hora Abé, inactive and depressed, decides to send for Yuge no Dōkyō to draw her out of her lethargy. The two resume their previous relationship. The Emperor, fearful of reproaching Abé himself, sends word of her scandalous behavior to Nakamaro at Nara. The scolding letter she receives from Nakamaro infuriates Abé. Returning to Nara, she becomes a Buddhist nun and begins once more to conduct affairs of state, leaving only ceremonial duties for Oi-Ō. Abé, finding in Dōkyō a trusted adviser in political matters, appoints him Senior Assistant High Priest.

Nakamaro, whose position is threatened by Abé's actions, attempts to reassert his influence over her. When she does not respond he goes to Oi-Ō to gain control of the imperial seal. But Abé has also sent her men to obtain the seal, and when the opposing forces clash, one of Nakamaro's sons is killed. Nakamaro's plot to make Fuwa's husband, Prince Shioyaki, emperor is discovered by Abé, who strips Nakamaro of his lands, titles, and even his name. Open rebellion follows, and Nakamaro is killed.

Oi-Ō, who is demoted and banished, dies soon after. Abé, resuming the throne, appoints Dōkyō Minister of State and Master of Buddhist Meditation. Soon the power of the Buddhist priests and nuns grows to rival that of the Department of Shinto and the Great Council of State.

Kibi, speaking for himself and others, protests the growing influence of the Buddhists. Abé, seeing no conflict between Buddhism and Shintoism, continues to rely on Dōkyō, raising him to the rank of Chancellor of the Realm and King of Buddhist law. In addition she orders the building of Saidai-ji Temple and a palace for Dōkyō. When Kibi speaks out against these expenses, Abé responds by rebuilding the Palace Shinto Hall to demonstrate her impartiality.

Fuwa, once again her half sister's attendant and confidante, realizes that her son will not become the next emperor. Turning to sorcery against Abé, she is caught in the act. Fuwa and her son are exiled to different parts of the empire.

As Abé's health begins to decline, her reliance on Dōkyō increases, and she allows him to perform some of the ceremonial duties of an Emperor of Japan. When Dōkyō claims that the power of his seal as King of Buddhist Law is equal to that of the Imperial seal, he invites the hostility of the court. His enemies plot unsuccessfully to discredit him. Abé moves to the new palace she has built at Yuge, and it is there that her story ends when she dies at the age of fifty-two. Twice sovereign of her nation, she was the last woman to have complete rule in Japan.

Shelley Mydans has skillfully woven three themes into a cohesive whole. The story of Abé's life unfolds against the backdrop of a power struggle between Buddhist and Shinto priests and the rising fortunes of the Fujiwara family, which has remained prominent to this day. The author has captured the atmosphere of 8th-century Japan, carrying the reader there with her talent for description. The characters in *The Vermilion Bridge* are carefully drawn and vibrantly alive, and the action is skillfully paced. Although the author advanced Dōkyō's appearance several years, the work is generally historically accurate. This book should appeal to the general reader as well as those especially interested in Asian history.

Patricia J. Russell

WALTER LIPPMANN AND THE AMERICAN CENTURY

Author: Ronald Steel
Publisher: Atlantic/Little Brown & Company (Boston). 669 pp. $19.95
Type of work: Biography
Time: 1889–1974
Locale: The United States and the world

A biography of the political columnist and journalist Walter Lippmann, joining his career in print, the development of his political beliefs, and his private history as a man

> *Principal personages:*
> WALTER LIPPMANN, the most powerful American editorial journalist of the 20th century
> JACOB and DAISY LIPPMANN, his parents, wealthy German-Jewish New Yorkers
> WILLIAM JAMES and GEORGE SANTAYANA, Lippmann's teachers and mentors at Harvard
> FAYE ALBERTSON, Lippmann's first wife
> HELEN BYRNE, Lippmann's second wife
> BERNARD BERENSON, American art critic, Lippmann's friend and frequent host in Italy
> FELIX FRANKFURTER, Lippmann's friend and correspondent, a law professor and Supreme Court justice
> CHARLES DE GAULLE, Lippmann's friend, and his model for an enlightened and effective world leader

From his earliest years Walter Lippmann made it his business to become acquainted with the most prominent men of his time. He traded ideas with William James and John Maynard Keynes, advised presidents from Theodore Roosevelt to Lyndon Johnson, sat down to lunch with De Gaulle and Khrushchev, and counted Felix Frankfurter and Bernard Berenson among his closest friends. When he clashed with some of these men, as he often did, they made the decisions that counted, and he had to be content with outlining his reservations from the editorial page. His power, however, lay in his ability to persuade rather than to command, and he managed to make himself into the most respected and influential American journalist of the 20th century.

Born in 1889 in New York City, the only child of a wealthy German-Jewish family, Lippmann grew up in the insular world of the Sachs School for Boys and annual European tours. Everyone he knew shared his background. He might easily have become a professional connoisseur and partygoer like his father. His proud and talented mother was also devoted to her social world and had little time for him. Lippmann's tendency as a young man to attach himself to powerful men was a sign of both his ambition and his need to seek guidance his parents could not give him.

At Harvard he briefly sought a membership in one of the prestigious clubs, the conventional mark of undergraduate success, but he knew that his background would be held against him, and he was soon distracted by other goals. His social conscience, awakened by relief work and his reading of Wells, Shaw, and the Fabians, prompted him to found the Socialist Club in 1908, pledged to consider "all schemes of social reform which aim at a radical reconstruction of society." The club became the center of political activism at Harvard. The Progressive Movement was at its height, and optimistic crusades for justice and truth were springing up all over the country. Lippmann's youthful confidence and idealism fit the mood perfectly. William James appeared at his dormitory to congratulate him on an article he had written and was charmed by Lippmann's intelligence and desire to learn. Lippmann became a frequent visitor to James's home. His philosophy professor, George Santayana, also welcomed Lippmann as an acolyte. These two men—James, the aggressive, experimental rationalist, and Santayana, the skeptical, conservative observer—presided over Lippmann's intellectual apprenticeship.

After graduation in 1910, Lippmann decided to work toward a master's degree in philosophy with Santayana but was immediately lured away by an offer to write for a new reformist weekly, the *Boston Common*. Lippmann could not resist the exciting political atmosphere of the times and so embarked on the ten-year activist career that would take him to the highest levels of government and end with disillusionment.

Following his stint with the *Common*, he spent two years working for the celebrated muckraker Lincoln Steffens, who was then writing an exposé of the New York banking interests. From there he joined the administration of the Reverend George Linn, the new socialist mayor of Schenectady. In 1913, Herbert Croly, a polemicist who was gathering a staff to produce a popular magazine of ideas devoted to a "constructive nationalism," invited Lippmann to join him. They called their journal the *New Republic*, and it was an immediate success. Lippmann's editorial pleas for reform, along with the two books of political calls-to-arms he had already published, attracted the attention of national politicians. Teddy Roosevelt called him "the most brilliant young man of his age in all the United States." When World War I came, he asked for a deferment, joining Woodrow Wilson's administration and becoming assistant to Colonel House, Wilson's chief political factotum. Lippmann was a member of the group responsible for drawing up Wilson's terms for the peace—the "Fourteen Points."

At each step in his rise to the centers of power Lippmann shed a little of his radicalism in favor of an increasing political pragmatism. Friends from his socialist years accused him of dressing like a Wall Street banker, but their comments could not tarnish his idealism. He now had a chance to put his beliefs to work. However, the results of the Paris Peace Conference shattered his faith and persuaded him never to accept a political office again.

Lippmann viewed the Versailles Treaty as a guarantee of another war in the near future. Feeling betrayed by the atmosphere of hope he had helped create, he returned to journalism. In 1922 he published his most important book, *Public Opinion,* in which he attacked the whipping up of national hatreds by propaganda and declared that modern democracies could not rely on governmental policies based on political appeal. The world was too complex; important decisions must be left to trained professionals. Concerned for the rights of minorities, he foresaw the tyrannical majorities of totalitarianism.

For the rest of his life Lippmann acted as one of the enlightened specialists he had written about. First as the editorial page editor of the New York *World,* then as a syndicated columnist for the New York *Herald Tribune,* the *Washington Post,* and *Newsweek,* he interpreted events for the reader who did not have time to sift all the facts himself. His lucid, direct style and his ability to see through to the crucial issues took him to the top of his profession. Although he was courted by presidents, generals, and congressmen, and enjoyed having access to power, he preserved his distance and never returned to the uncritical enthusiasm of his youth.

He drifted to the right on constitutional issues, accepting the judgment against Sacco and Vanzetti and opposing Franklin D. Roosevelt's court-packing scheme. The isolationist temper of the late 1930's provoked him. He saw war coming and argued that Hitler must be made to understand that Britain, France, the Soviet Union, and the United States were willing to combine against him, not because of his internal policies, but because he threatened the general peace.

It was at this time that Lippmann's unsuccessful first marriage broke up and he married Helen Byrne Armstrong, the wife of a close friend. Apparently it was the right choice. They depended on each other more and more as they grew older.

Lippmann's most prescient and influential columns dealt with the U.S.-Soviet rivalry that dominated international politics after World War II. He scoffed at the idea of a worldwide Communist conspiracy, emphasizing the importance of spheres of influence and local revolutionary movements. In Europe, where he claimed the United States had its most vital interests, he recognized the Soviet Union's need to maintain a group of buffer states. He did not pretend to be outraged by Soviet intervention in Hungary and was sympathetic to Eisenhower's refusal to risk war. On the other hand, he supported Kennedy's threatening posture in the Cuban missile crisis, since the Caribbean was so much closer to home. In a series of articles answering George Kennan's notorious and anonymous estimate of the Soviet leadership in *Foreign Affairs* magazine, Lippmann objected to his portrayal of these men as paranoid ideologues and argued that the Kremlin responded to the same national interests and concerns that had influenced Russian policy for centuries.

Lyndon Johnson tried hard to enlist Lippmann's support for his strategy in southeast Asia. In Lippmann's view Vietnam was not an area of vital interest to the United States, and a negotiated settlement was the best answer for a civil war. When Johnson ignored his counsel and sent in troops, Lippmann became aroused, declaring that the policy showed "a lamentable lack of understanding of the revolutionary upheavals of the epoch in which we live." As always, he put his readers' interests before those of men in office. Shortly before his death in the early 1970's, he wrote "the supreme question before mankind—to which I shall not live to know the answer—is how men will be able to make themselves willing and able to save themselves."

Ronald Steel's biography—the first based on Yale's collection of Lippmann's papers—skillfully balances Lippmann's public role as a journalist and his private history as an aware and thoughtful man. Lippmann's story might easily have been swallowed up in the great events in which he participated, but Steel wisely focuses his account on what his subject actually wrote and said, including his columns, interviews, and personal letters, presenting a picture of the man that is both complete and convincing. Lippmann was a writer, and Steel's book is primarily a literary biography, but it manages to include a perceptive chronicle of public policy during Lippmann's long and active maturity by concentrating on his reactions to each successive administration. The book's clean and flexible style is entirely appropriate, achieving its effect by its accumulated weight and consistency. The author's liberal politics are neither disguised nor unduly emphasized. *Walter Lippmann and the American Century* is long and exhaustive, and unlike many other biographies, it deserves to be so. It is a model of its kind.

Thomas Palmer

WAR WITHIN AND WITHOUT

Author: Anne Morrow Lindbergh (1906–   )
Publisher: Harcourt Brace Jovanovich (New York). 471 pp. $14.95
Type of work: Diaries and Letters
Time: 1939-1944
Locale: Englewood, New Jersey; Long Island, New York; Martha's Vineyard, Massachusetts; Bloomfield Hills, Michigan

The story of Anne Morrow and Charles Lindbergh's struggle against their country's involvement in a war, and the effects of this struggle on Anne Morrow Lindbergh's life as a wife, mother, and writer

> *Principal personages:*
> ANNE MORROW LINDBERGH, writer and wife of Charles Lindbergh
> CHARLES A. LINDBERGH, JR., famous aviator, husband of Anne
> ELIZABETH CUTTER MORROW, mother of Anne
> CONSTANCE MORGAN, sister of Anne
> ANTOINE DE SAINT-EXUPÉRY, French aviator and writer

In *War Within and Without: Diaries and Letters of Anne Morrow Lindbergh* the author gives her personal and emotional perspective of the years 1939-1944. After the horror of the kidnapping and murder of their son and the attendant publicity, Anne and Charles Lindbergh escaped to England, then to France. As the war heated up in Europe, Charles Lindbergh decided to return to the United States to help develop Army aviation installations.

The diary begins on April 28, 1939, as Anne and their two sons, Jon, seven years old, and Land, two years old, return home. They move into the Morrow homestead, "Next Day Hill," in Englewood, New Jersey, where they plan to stay until they can find a home of their own. The difficulties of settling in are complicated by Charles's presence in Washington much of the time and Anne's growing despondency about the war. In late June, they rent a house on Lloyd Neck, Long Island, from which Charles can commute by air to Washington, D.C. It is there that Antoine de Saint-Exupéry visits them. He has just written a beautiful, insightful preface to Anne's French edition of *Listen! the Wind,* and Anne is moved to find someone who talks to her about her craft, not just because she is her "father's daughter or Charles' wife." This is the only meeting they will have, but Anne's thoughts return to Saint-Exupéry throughout this book.

The war continues to escalate in Europe, and on September 3, 1939, when Anne hears that Britain has declared war on Germany, she finds it almost more than she can bear, for war is a personal horror to her. Charles's fear is now that the United States will join in the war and that there will be no chance for a negotiated peace. To warn the American people against an administration that Charles sees as denying them their right to decide whether or not to enter the war, Charles resigns his commission on September 15, 1939, and makes his first speech opposing the war. From this moment the Lindberghs are seen by many of their British, American, and French friends as traitors.

Anne accepts the reality of their situation and immerses herself in writing *The Wave of the Future,* a moral argument for isolationism. The book is criticized for advancing Fascist views, and Anne is consoled by a letter from W. H. Auden, who sympathizes with the problem that "everything one writes goes out helpless into the world to be turned to evil as well as good."

Through all this, however, Anne is still able to find peace and joy through her relationship with her children and with Charles. The sharpened awareness and appreciation of the world, "learning better to catch joy on the wing," is Anne's emotional support. After the birth of their daughter, Anne, in October 1940, she and Charles escape to Florida for a solitary boat trip through the Everglades, the Keys, and finally the Dry Tortugas.

They return to their anti-war activities, traveling across America and speaking out against the war. Charles, against Anne's advice, makes the claim that the Jews are one of three groups pressing the United States into war. In the backlash Charles is denounced as a Nazi and an anti-Semite.

Meanwhile, the Lindberghs have moved to "Seven Gates Farm" on Martha's Vineyard to escape the pressure of living so close to New York. Charles continues speaking against the war until December 7, 1941, when the Japanese bomb Pearl Harbor. Immediately he is ready to put all his energies into the war effort, but the Roosevelt administration permits him no war work. While denying him clearance for a job, they issue a statement that Charles Lindbergh is working on a "project" of "vital interest to the government," a statement that shocks Anne and Charles. It is only "a pretend job on paper to satisfy the talk," says Anne.

When Saint-Exupéry's new book, *Flight to Arras,* comes out, Anne deduces from its advertising that her preface, name, and praise have been removed from *Wind, Sand and Stars,* his earlier book. She feels unjustly accused of "bowing abjectly to an 'inevitable' wave of totalitarianism," of being a "coward and a defeatist."

Charles finally secures a job with Ford Motor Company, in Detroit, and after a three-month separation Anne and the children move to nearby Bloomfield Hills. In August 1942, Anne has a baby boy, Scott. After finishing *The Steep Ascent,* she finds a new form of artistic expression in sculpture classes at Cranbrook Academy of Art, while Charles tests new planes and does high altitude experiments.

In April 1944, Charles goes to the Pacific Theater as a civilian adviser and an observer of the planes he has previously tested. In July, Anne travels to San Francisco to visit her brother and his wife and await Charles's return from the Pacific. But after a month, she returns home without him. As Charles's war work with Ford is at an end, Anne and the children move to Connecticut. It is there that Charles joins them in September 1944.

These diaries and letters convey much more than a day by day account of life; they explore feelings, conflicts, and rationales. In a sense, Anne Morrow Lindbergh can serve as a model to today's "everywoman." She feels herself a divided woman, unable to be "a full-time Mother and a full-time Artist and a full-time Wife-Companion and also a 'Charming Woman' on the side!" Anne's relationship with Charles is strained during his anti-war work, for it has isolated her not only from her "class" and friends but from her family as well. Her heart is inclined toward immediate aid for Britain and France, but she understands Charles's position and stands by him. Even though the attacks on them make her bitter, she is still able to admire the strength and purity of her husband's beliefs.

Her loyalty to Charles is repaid, however, for he is eager for Anne "to share his life, his problems, his decisions. . . ." as well as to pursue her own writing career. Charles admires Anne's talent and pushes her relentlessly to develop it. The diaries suggest that most of their arguments are centered around Anne's failure to write. Charles complains that Anne is temperamental, "can't write on the flying trips, can't write at home when you're having a baby, can't write when people criticize you a little, can't write when we're moving, can't write during a war." Anne herself says plaintively, as they are settling into their fourth home in three years, "I want to go back again to being a *bad* housekeeper and a *good* writer!"

Yet the home life is meaningful to her. The children are particularly important. With them she tastes "real joy, real peace." "Scott's arms around me, Anne's yellow braids, Land in the bathtub. Jon's eyes when they are happy—a kind of secret happiness, a joy he lets me in on for an instant. Anne's face lit up with that angelic smile like day slowly breaking over her serious little face." Yet the other side of motherhood is presented as well: the author recalls the day that little Anne messed up the bathroom floor, Land and Jon broke furniture, and then dragged a dead skunk into the house in Bloomfield Hills. And, of course, underlying all is the remembrance of the loss of her first child in the tragic, notorious kidnapping.

Throughout the years covered in this diary the reader can sense a strengthening relationship between Anne and Charles. Anne stuck by her husband at great cost to herself, a fact of which Charles was well aware. Their times together, from Florida trips to simple evening walks, enabled them to share with each other and build the ties of marriage, like "those old twisted hemp ropes . . . not beautiful at all, but tough and holding."

Anne Morrow Lindbergh's diaries are open, often painfully so, as their author confesses to dreaming "of 16-year-old love" or to day-dreaming of "praise in connection with my work, or talk, or wisdom." They expose a woman still suffering the *"angoisse inguerissable,"* "[t]hat adoration of an impossible he or she." The importance to Anne of her meeting with Antoine de Saint-Exupéry, in August 1939, is a constant theme throughout her diaries and letters. Even though she never sees him again and they can no longer share ideas, he remains a constant image in her mind throughout these years. She writes every book wondering how he will receive it and reads his books seeking understanding and forgiveness for her position against the war. A haunting fact of *War Within and Without* is that the period it chronicles begins with the year in which Anne meets Saint-Exupéry and ends with the year of his death.

War Within and Without works on several levels. Most simply, it covers the events of the war as seen by an extraordinarily sensitive woman. Second, it offers insights into the life of one of America's heroes as he falls from favor because his conviction of what was best for his country ran counter to the views of the Roosevelt administration. Third, it shows the struggles of an artist to create, to write, in the face of many difficulties, not the least of which was an occasional failing of confidence. Finally, it shows a woman facing the dilemma of trying to be a good mother, a good wife, and a good writer, and seeking to take joy in all these roles. Anne Morrow Lindbergh, in her "Introduction" summarizes her book well:

> I find, in the end, I have revealed, not an annotated record of those years, but simply an intensely personal story of two individuals: a complex man and his struggle to follow what his background, his character and integrity demanded; and a complex woman of quite a different background, who must reconcile her divided loyalties in a time of stress. It is not so much history or a factual wartime record as it is simply a personal story.

Pamela Murfin

WHO'S ON FIRST

Author: William F. Buckley, Jr. (1925–   )
Publisher: Doubleday and Company (Garden City, N.Y.). 275 pp. $9.95
Type of work: Novel
Time: 1956-1957
Locale: Budapest, Paris, and Washington, D.C.

The story of the CIA's role in the race between the United States and the Soviet Union to launch the first orbiting satellite

> Principal characters:
> BLACKFORD OAKES, Yale alumnus and CIA agent
> ANTHONY TRUST, his friend and fellow agent
> RUFUS, their superior
> VIKTOR KAPITSA, a Russian rocket scientist
> TAMARA KAPITSA, his wife, also a scientist
> VADIM PLATOV, Viktor's friend, a scientist who has defected to the United States
> BORIS BOLGIN, chief of European operations for the KGB
> THEO MOLNAR, a Hungarian student rebel
> FRIEDA DARVAS, his fiancée
> ALLEN DULLES, Director of the CIA under Pres. Dwight D. Eisenhower
> DEAN ACHESON, Secretary of State under Pres. Harry S Truman

In William F. Buckley's novel *Who's On First,* Blackford Oakes, Yale '51, the ultimate elitist spy, makes his third appearance. The time is 1957, when the Soviet Union has just invaded Hungary and is threatening to launch the first orbiting satellite. "One cannot exaggerate the importance of going up first with a satellite," CIA Director Allen Dulles tells his friend and political adversary, former Secretary of State Dean Acheson. "It will affect the way we are regarded in every chancellery in the world."

It is the task of Oakes, together with his friend and fellow spy, Anthony Trust, and their mentor, the mysterious master spy Rufus, to kidnap a Russian rocket scientist and obtain enough information to help the Americans launch a satellite first. They are to kidnap the brilliant Viktor Kapitsa, a man with little love for the Soviet leadership who spent eight years in a Gulag concentration camp. To convince Viktor he should aid the Americans, Oakes and Trust work with Viktor's closest friend, Vadim Platov, a Russian scientist who has defected to the United States.

Oakes and Trust succeed in abducting Viktor and his wife Tamara from a group of Soviet scientists who are in Paris for a conference. They take the couple to a secluded farmhouse, where Vadim tries to win Viktor's confidence. In a letter to the Soviet embassy, Oakes and Trust profess to be Algerian terrorists, fighting a guerrilla war against the French in their native land. They offer to release their hostages if they are furnished with Soviet arms.

Meanwhile, complications entangle Oakes. Immediately before the abduction, he was in Hungary, at the time of the popular uprising and the subsequent Soviet invasion. He helped several rebels escape, but his closest contact, a student named Theo Molnar, was captured and hanged by the Soviets. Theo's fiancée, Frieda, and his friend, Erno, now in Paris, are convinced that it was Oakes who betrayed Molnar. At the urging of Joszef, another Hungarian refugee, who is also an undercover KGB agent, they kidnap Oakes and announce their intention to kill him in revenge for Molnar's death. Oakes's desperate efforts to convince Frieda and Erno that he was Molnar's friend and that Joszef is the traitor are successful. In the fighting that ensues, Joszef is killed.

When Oakes rejoins Trust, he learns that Viktor will reveal the secret of the Soviet rocket fuel, the one obstacle to a successful American missile launch. Viktor does not wish to defect; instead, he and Tamara will return to the Soviet Union where they have agreed to send the CIA further information occasionally. The Kapitsas will corroborate the story that they were kidnapped by Algerian terrorists. The Soviets, suspecting no plot, deliver the arms as promised, and Viktor and Tamara are released. It has been an ideal CIA operation—quick, clean, and nonviolent, a tribute to Rufus's planning and Oakes's and Trust's execution.

Unknown to them, the plot has been discovered by Oakes's old adversary, Colonel Bolgin, the head of KGB activities in Europe. Viktor and Tamara are arrested when they return to the U.S.S.R., and Viktor is tortured until he confesses. The Soviets propose a new deal, using Vadim as a conduit. Viktor will be executed, they tell his friend, unless Vadim helps them solve the problem that stymies their own missile program. They need a machine called the Van de Graaff, which increases the power of the transistor crystals used for communicating with the rocket. Vadim agrees, telling Bolgin and the KGB where to locate a Van de Graaff, which is loaded onto a ship in Portsmouth, New Hampshire.

It is not easy for Vadim to betray his adopted country. The night before the ship is to sail, Vadim tells Oakes what he has done. Oakes is caught between his loyalty to his country and his sympathy and admiration for Viktor, a generous and courageous man who has already suffered too much. He finally decides to say nothing, allowing the Soviets to acquire the Van de Graaff and saving Viktor's life.

The final decision does not rest with Oakes, however, for Vadim has also told other American officials of his actions. President Eisenhower orders the Soviet ship sunk. But Dean Acheson, talking with Dulles again, suggests urging the President to reconsider. "In my judgment, the domestic mood is dangerously flabby . . . Why not let them go ahead and wake us up by firing their blasted satellite?" Acheson's view prevails; the ship crosses the Atlantic safely, Viktor is released, and the Soviets amaze the world by launching the first orbiting satellite.

Oakes, meanwhile, has taken a leave of absence from the CIA, and has announced to Sally, his impossibly patient and beautiful girl friend, that he has done this so she will marry him. But, in a postscript set in 1969, when the United States has landed the first man on the moon and claimed ultimate victory in the space race, Oakes is back with his old employer.

Most successful spy novels fall into one of two groups. There is the kind of unpretentious entertainment offered by Ian Fleming's James Bond series, books where the hero kisses and kills with equal skill. On the other hand, with writers like Graham Greene or John Le Carré, the spy novel crosses the boundary between genre writing and serious fiction.

In *Saving the Queen,* the book in which Blackford Oakes made his first appearance, William F. Buckley offered a different kind of spy novel—a witty, literate escapade, relying on accurate details and an intricate plot. *Saving the Queen* was successful largely because of its aristocratic English setting—a milieu where wit and elegance are invaluable weapons.

Who's On First is a more ambitious book, and one that demands more of its author. The reader is told of Blackford Oakes's sense of commitment but remains unconvinced that Oakes is more than a good-looking, fast-talking Ivy Leaguer. This shallow characterization is symptomatic of the entire book. The flashback scenes depicting the Soviet invasion of Hungary and Stalin's concentration camps lack the required authenticity. These are situations where style is not enough. No one who has ever read Solzhenitsyn on the Gulag Archipelago could possibly take *Who's On First* seriously. Because of these failings, even Buckley's witty ironies about Dean Acheson and the making of American foreign policy lose their effect. There is no reason why William F. Buckley should not use a spy novel as a way of raising serious issues. If these issues are to be taken seriously, however, the author must use the vehicle successfully, but Buckley does not.

Jay Wickersham

WILL

Author: G. Gordon Liddy (1930–   )
Publisher: St. Martin's Press (New York). 374 pp. $13.95
Type of work: Autobiography
Time: 1930-1977
Locale: The United States, particularly Washington, D.C.

The story of G. Gordon Liddy's life and experiences, especially his years in Washington, D.C., where he worked on the 1972 presidential campaign of Richard Nixon, and the time he served for his part in the break-in of the Democratic National Committee headquarters

> *Principal personages:*
> G. GORDON LIDDY, lawyer, general counsel of the Committee to Re-elect the President
> SYLVESTER LIDDY, Liddy's father
> MARIA ABBATICCHIO LIDDY, Liddy's mother
> FRANCES PURCELL LIDDY, Liddy's wife
> PETER MAROULIS, Liddy's lawyer and friend
> E. HOWARD HUNT, Liddy's colleague in directing the Watergate break-in
> JOHN DEAN, counsel to the President
> EGIL KROGH, Deputy Assistant to the President
> JEB MAGRUDER, Liddy's supervisor on the Committee to Re-elect the President

Born in 1930, G. Gordon Liddy grew up in comfortable circumstances. Sylvester Liddy, his father, was a successful trademark lawyer who was knighted by the Danish government. Liddy's mother, Maria Abbaticchio Liddy, an exotic-looking woman of Italian descent, raised her son in the Roman Catholic Church and sent him to parochial schools for his early education. As a boy Liddy was sickly, but he learned about "strength and bravery" from his mother's stories of her family's exploits. Yet, when the young Liddy looked into himself, he saw only "weakness and fear." Afraid of many things (most of them quite normal), Liddy writes of himself: "I had seen the fruits of fearlessness (from family stories) and the power of the will (in Nazi Germany). I could no longer live without them. It was 1936, and I was six years old." Because of this realization at such a tender age, Liddy decided to conquer the things he feared by confronting them. To overcome his fears Liddy resolved to become steel-like: he knew, he says, that to conquer them would take years of psychic and physical pain. At age 11, Liddy decided to learn to kill without emotion in order to be ready to fight in World War II. To accomplish this he worked for a neighbor killing chickens until he "could kill like a machine."

By the time Liddy graduated from prep school in 1948, he was "transformed," no longer small, weak, and fearful. "I was five feet, nine inches tall, physically very strong. Psychologically I had gone beyond the desirable self-confidence to the excess of arrogance." Liddy attended Fordham University as had his father before him. Upon graduation in 1952, he received a commission in the U.S. Army Reserve but failed to see combat in Korea. When Liddy entered Fordham Law School in 1954, he was also on active reserve with the Army. It was during a period of reserve training that Liddy was indoctrinated in clandestine activities, experience he would find useful in later years. In 1957, the same year in which he completed law school and joined the FBI, Liddy married. He takes relish in describing how he selected Frances Purcell to be his wife: "I had chosen her to be the mother of my children because of her strength and size. She could bear half a dozen high performance children." In this regard Liddy writes: "I felt keenly an obligation to achieve my maximum genetic potential."

Liddy spent the next five years with the FBI assigned to offices in Indiana, Colorado, and Washington, D.C. During this time the first three of Liddy's six children were born. Following his resignation from the FBI in 1962, Liddy joined his father's law firm in New York City, but friction between father and son caused the younger Liddy to leave after three years.

At this point Liddy decided that politics offered him the challenge he needed. He joined the staff of the district attorney's office of Dutchess County, New York. In 1967 he decided to run for the congressional seat in New York's 28th district; Liddy wanted to get to Washington where he "could affect things on a national scale." He lost the election but because of his work in Richard Nixon's campaign, he was given a job with the Treasury Department's Organized Crime Unit as a special assistant to the secretary. While at the Treasury Department, Liddy worked on Operation Intercept, the attempt to stop the drug traffic into the United States at the Mexican border, and on the Air Marshal Program to curb the hijacking of airliners. In 1971, because of friction with a Treasury Department superior, Liddy transferred to a low-echelon job at the White House with responsibility for advising on such matters as narcotics, bombing, and firearms and for keeping an eye on the Treasury Department's performance in these areas. Actually, Liddy's first assignment in 1971 was to stop leaks of secret information to the press in the aftermath of the Pentagon Papers incident. It was at this time that Liddy first met E. Howard Hunt. Together Liddy and Hunt planned and carried out the break-in in Los Angeles of the office of the psychiatrist of anti-Vietnam War activist Daniel Ellsberg. In December 1971, Liddy "went into the closet" to begin clandestine activities for Nixon's 1972 campaign.

Liddy, whose title was general counsel for the campaign, proceeded to draw up an elaborate intelligence operation, which was repeatedly scaled down by Attorney General John N. Mitchell. It was Liddy's group—Hunt, James McCord, and several Cuban-Americans—who broke into the Democratic National Committee headquarters in the Watergate Complex on more than one occasion, and it was Liddy's group, minus Hunt and Liddy, that was arrested in the Democratic campaign offices during the early morning hours of June 17, 1972. James McCord, who went along to replace a defective device, was a direct link to the White House. Within a short period Hunt and Liddy were also arrested. Liddy was tried and convicted as a co-conspirator. Judge John Sirica sentenced Liddy to 20 years in prison, and fined him $40,000. Sirica also sentenced him to a one and a half year prison term for refusing to testify before the Watergate grand jury. During the entire period of his arrest, trial, and imprisonment, Liddy resolutely refused to give any evidence either at his own trial, to the grand jury, to the Senate committee investigating Watergate, or to the House Judiciary Committee considering the impeachment of Richard Nixon. Liddy's conduct in prison was no less resolute. Burning his flesh over an open flame was not always enough for Liddy to prove himself. Sometimes he had to take on inmates and prison officials in the battle of wills. To Liddy's credit, he did use his legal training to aid fellow prisoners. This and assorted "manly" feats earned for Liddy the respect of the other inmates.

Liddy had spent about four years in jail when, in 1977, President Carter commuted his sentence to eight years "in the interests of justice." Eligible for parole, Liddy was released in September of that year.

It is difficult to feel much sympathy for Gordon Liddy. His book does nothing to dispel the image of him as someone slightly off-center, particularly during the time of the arrests for the Watergate break-in and the subsequent trials of the principal defendants charged with that crime. *Will* is primarily Liddy's justification for his part in that event. There is the sense that, from Liddy's point of view, this book is meant to inspire. Unfortunately much of the book has a hollow ring to it.

The most important thing for Liddy throughout his life has been the toughening of his will. This has meant enduring physical as well as psychic pain, no matter how severe. It meant that his wife and children had to be ready to do the same if necessary. Perhaps Liddy would have been better off if he had been able to accept some of his early fears and had not driven himself to the extremes that he did in order to "build incredible willpower."

The account of Liddy's growing years and his early attempts at a career is fairly prosaic. Liddy was attracted to the Army, the FBI, and to politics. He boasts of the firearms he owns and of his skill with a pencil as a lethal weapon. He takes pains to describe the elaborate intelligence plan, code name GEMSTONE, that he devised for use in Nixon's 1972 presidential campaign.

But looking back over the events leading up to the Watergate break-ins (even as Liddy recounts them), it is readily apparent how inept Liddy and his co-conspirators were.

Liddy has been the last of the Watergate burglars to publish a personal account of Watergate and its aftermath. His silence was bred out of a sense of loyalty; he refused to talk until after the statutes of limitation had run out. According to Liddy, Jeb Magruder, to whom he reported for a time, perjured himself during Liddy's trial. Judge Sirica was incompetent, and the trial itself a farce. Liddy was ready to kill Howard Hunt when they were in prison together if so ordered, because of the deal Hunt had made with the grand jury. In fact, Liddy was ready to be killed himself if necessary, and he told a shocked John Dean as much after the fiasco of the break-in. For Liddy there were some straight shooters—Maurice Stans, finance chairman of the Committee to Re-elect the President; Richard Kleindienst, Mitchell's successor as attorney general; and Peter Maroulis, Liddy's lawyer and long-time friend.

In a sense it may be hard for the average person to believe that people like Liddy exist. But Watergate and its fallout demonstrated that they did exist, perhaps more of them than was thought possible. They were hangers-on of sorts, a rag-tag, inept bunch attracted by money, adventure, and power, but they could be dangerous. Fortunately, Liddy and his cohorts were uncovered before inflicting serious damage. In the final analysis, Gordon Liddy's story is laughable and lamentable.

Louis Sasso

A WOMAN'S AGE

Author: Rachel Billington
Publisher: Summit Books (New York). 469 pp. $12.95
Type of Work: Novel
Time: 1910–1975
Locale: Northumberland, England; London; Eureka Island

Four generations of women in an upper-class English family struggle with "their biology and needs for success" in changing times, but always within the world of aristocratic privilege

> *Principal characters:*
> LADY VIOLET HESKEATH NETTLEFIELD (VI), daughter of Eleanor and Tudor, wife of Nettles, mother of Violet and Tudor, active Labour Party minister and politician
> LADY ELEANOR HESKEATH FITZGERALD BLUMBERG, Vi's mother
> VIOLET NETTLEFIELD OAKLEY, daughter of Vi, mother of Ethne, successful author of children's books
> ETHNE OAKLEY, daughter of Violet
> HENRY NETTLEFIELD (NETTLES), lover of Eleanor, husband of Vi, father of Violet and Tudor, Northumberland farmer
> MAY FIG, nanny to Vi and to Araminta's and Vi's children
> MOLLY MANNERING, Vi's lifelong friend
> ARAMINTA TRIGEAR, Vi's friend from Oxford

A Woman's Age begins in Kettleside, the country house of Lord Tudor Heskeath, his young wife Eleanor, and their five-year-old daughter, Vi. It is Vi who tells her story. Her world includes the care and love of Nanny Fig, the glamour of her eccentric mother, the steadiness of her father. When Vi is five, her mother runs off with her lover, Nettles, and settles on Eureka, an island off the coast of Ireland. Vi remains with her father and Nanny, until five years later when her father is killed in World War I.

From age ten to fifteen Vi lives in Eureka with her mother and Nettles. She is tutored by Augustus, a bright young pacifist. World War I and other events of the world reach Eureka infrequently and indirectly.

Nettles is frequently in London on business and is largely responsible for arranging Vi's education. It is he who enrolls her in Shoreham Abbey School for Girls in England. There Vi learns normal upper-class behavior, becomes reacquainted with her father's family, and makes a lifelong friendship with Molly Mannering, a girl whose roots and affinities are outside of the upper class.

When Eleanor establishes a home in London, Nettles is relegated to visiting while Vi is introduced by her mother into society. One significant day she visits her paternal grandfather to introduce herself. He takes her to lunch but stops short of accepting her and taking her home. On her way home she spots Nanny Fig, whom she loves dearly, and whom she now realizes was let go without references when Vi left Kettleside for Eureka. Vi, overwhelmed by this injustice, experiences the budding of social consciousness.

In 1923, Eleanor leaves for America with Carter Fitzgerald who becomes her second husband. Again Vi feels deserted. This, plus the dullness of the London social scene that pushes women into early marriage, leads Vi to Oxford where she rejoins her friend Molly. At Oxford Vi socializes with Augustus, her former tutor, now a don, and his homosexual friends. Through one of them, Leonard, she meets Araminta, who becomes a friend for life, and Howard Shakespeare, who will be her first husband.

Vi's marriage to Howard does not last long. The first year of separation Vi spends with Araminta, her husband Leonard, and their twins. She is also reunited with Molly, who has fallen in love with George Briggsworthy, a devout Catholic, who is separated from his wife. Through Molly and George, Vi is introduced to Father Wilson who has a growing spiritual influence on her.

Vi has her first affair, after her passionless marriage, with a member of Parliament. It is a significant affair because its inception causes Vi to reflect on the importance of lovemaking. The place of passion is a theme that runs throughout the book. The affair is also important because it ends when Vi disagrees strongly with his Labour politics, the beginning of her political evolution.

Eleanor marries Moses Blumberg, a New York psychiatrist. The major effect of her mother's remarriage on Vi is that her allowance is cut off. Vi divides the London house into flats, renting one to Augustus, one to a cousin, and living in the third. Thus, she supports herself.

Nettles turns up at Vi's door one Sunday afternoon in 1933. As she is on her way to visit Molly and George for the holiday, Nettles joins her. They fall in love, become lovers, and eventually become engaged. Everyone is dismayed: he is 50, she 23. He had been almost a father to her, and he had previously been in love with her mother. Amidst the difficulties of disapproving friends, Vi visits Araminta who now has three baby daughters. Her friend is struggling, with Nanny's help and in Leonard's absence, to keep food on the table, care for her babies, and paint.

Early in 1936, Vi's and Nettles' daughter Violet is born. Araminta comes to Kettleside to assist; she too is expecting very soon. Araminta's first son is like a twin brother to Violet. The mothers tend the babies together with Nanny's aid. Araminta remains to make her home at Kettleside and Vi quickly becomes pregnant again. The second child is a son, named Tudor.

In 1937, Vi takes a trip to London to attend Molly's and George's wedding. Molly was injured in the Spanish Civil War, and George's first wife is now dead. Eleanor turns up in London, on the run from Blumberg. She is introduced to George's mother, Mrs. Briggsworthy, and the two form an outlandish friendship and move together to Eureka.

Toward the end of 1939, Vi finds herself bored with motherhood. Since the war is having an impact on her life, Vi becomes active in Women's Voluntary Service. She is good, she is needed, and so she leaves her family to work in London. During the New Year holidays when Vi cannot get away, she calls home and Araminta hints that Nettles is having an affair. When he comes to London to see her, he is killed by a bomb. Only later does Vi discover that he was dying of cancer. She also finds out that he had slept with an acquaintance of theirs, just as Vi has slept with Leonard. Need and affection, not deep love, are responsible.

Vi goes to Kettleside with Nettles' body to bury him and to recover from his death. Araminta has another set of twins. Vi realizes that like her mother Eleanor she cannot be satisfied solely with the role of mother and wife. Unfortunately, her mother has ended up with nothing. Vi heads back to London to turn her attention to politics.

Here Violet takes up the story. She too is growing up in an eccentric household. Her father is dead, her mother is an occasional visitor. She lives in her mother's home with Araminta and her many children. At the age of 10, her mother picks her up from school one day, takes her to London, then to Eureka, and finally enrolls her in Shoreham Abbey. Violet likes school and prepares for Oxford. Her mother has become a successful Labour Party candidate, despite her aristocratic background.

Violet, unlike her mother, reflects the spirit of the 1950's. She marries Mike, a civil servant, gives up the university, has a baby, and devotes herself to being a full-time mother and wife. She refuses Kettleside and Nanny. The baby, Ethne, is to be swamped with love.

But two years later Violet is unfulfilled. She makes the most of an opportunity to write children's books, and is successful. She resolves not to have another baby. A passionate affair with a cousin ends in an accidental pregnancy. Ethne is a child of the 1960's, raised with few restrictions, wild about the Beatles, searching for meaning. She falls in love with a California boy, runs off with him to Eureka and gives birth to their son.

Vi becomes a peeress, converts to Catholicism, and travels to India at the age of 70 to study birth control. She becomes ill and dies there after refusing to displace on a departing flight a woman trying to get to her dying husband's bedside. At the end of her life, she feels spiritually happy although she is reluctant to give up her place on earth.

This is a book about women. It is about women's lack of control over their own lives, the struggle between biology and the need for success. It is also a book about social class. Women of the Heskeath line—Eleanor, Vi, Violet, and Ethne—have independent wealth, the privilege of fine education, and social standing, as well as intelligence and talent. Other women close to them, like Molly, Araminta, and Nanny Fig, have few of these privileges. The same women's struggles are different for them.

Vi and Araminta are age mates. Araminta is beautiful, social, and talented as a painter. Vi is less sure of herself and less clear about her talents when they first meet. Araminta becomes an earth mother. She has eight children, fifteen grandchildren, and three great-grandchildren at her deathbed. She is rich in love and affection. But this is only possible because she has been fully supported by Vi. Vi becomes an active politician. She dies alone in far-off India. Her life is possible only because Araminta has raised her children. Each is grateful to, and perhaps jealous of, the other.

It is also a book about values. As Vi says, her life is in constant struggle between humanitarian and spiritual values. She reflects on marriage and divorce, contraception and abortion, family and individual needs, passion and love. The characters, especially Vi, are interesting and complex. The privilege of her class is hard to appreciate. And the remoteness, to those who do not seek it out, from the real world, war, and poverty, is hard to imagine.

Perhaps the novel's finest feature is its network of rich and complex mother/daughter relationships. They are not sentimentally portrayed. Daughters start out seeming nothing like their mothers; they mature, and the similarities and differences emerge as each faces, in turn, the conflicts that are an inevitable part of being a woman. Through Eleanor, Vi, and Violet the readers see the impact of social changes on women's choices. The role of wife and mother is not enough for any of them. Eleanor does nothing constructive. Vi ventures into the political arena alone. Violet is successful and yet maintains her marriage. Ethne refuses to marry, although she has a mate and a son, and her future is unknown. Perhaps it will be less conflict ridden since she rejects the wife/mother role at the outset.

Michele Hoffnung

CUMULATIVE AUTHOR INDEX
1954–1981

(Figures within parentheses indicate years; other figures indicate page numbers.)

I

CUMULATIVE AUTHOR INDEX—1954–1981

CUMULATIVE AUTHOR INDEX—1954–1981

CUMULATIVE AUTHOR INDEX—1954–1981

v

CUMULATIVE AUTHOR INDEX—1954–1981

CUMULATIVE AUTHOR INDEX—1954–1981

CUMULATIVE AUTHOR INDEX—1954–1981

CUMULATIVE AUTHOR INDEX—1954–1981

CUMULATIVE AUTHOR INDEX—1954–1981

CUMULATIVE AUTHOR INDEX—1954–1981

CUMULATIVE AUTHOR INDEX—1954–1981

CUMULATIVE AUTHOR INDEX—1954–1981

CUMULATIVE AUTHOR INDEX—1954–1981

XIX

CUMULATIVE AUTHOR INDEX—1954–1981

CUMULATIVE AUTHOR INDEX—1954–1981

CUMULATIVE AUTHOR INDEX—1954–1981

XXIII

CUMULATIVE AUTHOR INDEX—1954–1981

CUMULATIVE AUTHOR INDEX—1954–1981

CUMULATIVE AUTHOR INDEX—1954–1981

CUMULATIVE AUTHOR INDEX—1954–1981

XXVII

CUMULATIVE AUTHOR INDEX—1954-1981

CUMULATIVE AUTHOR INDEX—1954–1981

CUMULATIVE AUTHOR INDEX—1954–1981

CUMULATIVE AUTHOR INDEX—1954–1981

CUMULATIVE AUTHOR INDEX—1954–1981